Hampshire
County Council

Please return/renew this item
by the last date shown.
Books may also be renewed by
phone or the Internet.

Hampshire County Council
Library & Information Service

11/05   **http://libcat.hants.gov.uk**

BRITISH
MUSIC
HALL

BRITISH MUSIC HALL

AN ILLUSTRATED HISTORY

RICHARD
ANTHONY BAKER

Foreword by Roy Hudd OBE

SUTTON PUBLISHING

First published in the United Kingdom in 2005 by
Sutton Publishing Limited · Phoenix Mill
Thrupp · Stroud · Gloucestershire · GL5 2BU

British Library Cataloguing in Publication Data
A catalogue record for this book is available from the British Library.

ISBN 0 7509 3685 1

Typeset in 11/14pt Garamond 3.
Typesetting and origination by
Sutton Publishing Limited.
Printed and bound in England by
J.H. Haynes & Co. Ltd, Sparkford.

*Dedicated to the memory of
my parents and my brother*

✠ PROGRAMME. ✠

MONDAY, MAY 8th, 1899, and Every Evening

1 Overture.
2 The Sisters Crossley. Duettists & Dancers
3 Mr. Reuben Hill. Character Vocalist
4 Mr. Geo. D'Albert. Vocalist
5 Miss Lucy Weston. Serio & Dancer
6 La Tostta. Mandoline Soloist
7 Mr. Dan Crawley. Comedian
8 Letta & Minni. In a refined Speciality Act
9 Mr. Walter Lawley. Tenor Vocalist
10 Miss Lily Lena. Serio & Dancer
11 The Poluskis. Eccentric Comedians
12 Bella & Bijou. Sketch Artistes
13 Mr. Tom Leamore. Comedian.
14 Lucretia. Speciality Dancer
15 Brown, Newland & Le Clerq. Sketch Artistes
16 Mr. Harry Randall. Comedian
17 Miss Bessie Wentworth. Comedienne & Dancer
18 Mr. Will Evans. Eccentric Comedian
19 Miss Elaine Ravensberg. Burlesque Artiste
20 Mr. Dan Leno. Comedian
21 Mr. Geo. Layton. In a new and dramatic Song, entitled, "Beaconsfield," Or "Peace with Honour."
22 Miss Alice Lloyd. Comedienne & Dancer
23 Mr. Eugene Stratton In a melody new and original Nigger Romance entitled "My Little Octoroon." Written and composed by Leslie Stuart Special Scenery by W. T. Hemsley.
24 Miss Billie Barlow. Comedienne
25 Mr. Chas. Mildare. Whistler
26 Miss Harriett Vernon. Burlesque Artiste
27 The Zanettos. Jugglers

This Programme is subject to alteration.

Manager ... ... Mr. FRANK GLENISTER
Musical Director ... ... Mr. W. TAYLOR

NOTICE.— The Management will feel obliged to any persons who will point out any item in the Programme which they may consider objectionable.

CONTENTS

ACKNOWLEDGEMENTS

I owe a deep debt of gratitude to Tony Barker (for allowing me to base my notes on Fred Barnes, Kate Carney, Harry Champion, G.H. Chirgwin, Leo Dryden, T.E. Dunville, Gus Elen, Marie Kendall, Malcolm Scott, Eugene Stratton and Vesta Victoria on his biographies in *Music Hall* magazine); to Norma Adams, Marita Staite and Frank Tabrar (for help in connection with Joe Tabrar); Luanne Beaton and Ian Munro (with Alice Lloyd); Peter Burgess (Talbot O'Farrell and Dick Henderson); Sue and the late Don Castling (Harry Castling); Richard Coleman-Wood and Brian Cowen (Kate Carney); Will Fyffe junior (Will Fyffe); Michael Hankins (George Arthurs); the late Philip Hindin (Coram and Wee Georgie Wood); Mary Logan (Alec Hurley); Michael Parker (G.H. Elliott); Patricia Farmer and Cicely Lindquist (Felix McGlennon); Annie Shead and the late Iris Terry (Vesta Victoria); Jan Potterveld (Harry Champion); Roy Hudd OBE (for a splendid foreword); Ryan Edwards (for technical help); my diligent editors, Christopher Feeney and Hilary Walford; Caroline Gibb (for invaluable genealogical assistance); Terry Lomas, Eddie Trigg and Max Tyler, of the British Music Hall Society (for membership details, contact Howard Lee, Thurston Lodge, Thurston Park, Whitstable, Kent CT5 1RE); Richard Mangan, of the Mander and Mitchenson Theatre Collection; the Frank Matcham Society (for supplying the photographs of Frank Matcham and the Opera House, Blackpool); (for membership details, contact Doug Oldfield, 42 Ecclesbourne Drive, Buxton, Derbyshire SK17 9BW); Patrick Newley; Michael Pointon; my far-sighted agent, Robert Smith; the City of Westminster Archives Centre for permission to publish the cartoon of Zaeo; Lynn Tait for permission to publish her picture of Southend Hippodrome; David Higham Associates, the literary executors of Louis MacNeice, for permission to republish 'Death of an Actress'; the staff of the British Library, the British Newspaper Library, the Bodleian Music Library, the Family Records Centre, the London Metropolitan Archive and the London Library; and the staff of many cemeteries across London. Uncredited illustrations are from the author's collection.

BEAUTIFUL NELL

SUNG BY The Great VANCE

WRITTEN BY STACEY LEE ESQ.

COMPOSED BY R. COOTE.

"BEAUTIFUL GIRL WITH BEAUTIFUL EYES,
BRIGHT AS THE MORNING AND BLUE AS THE SKIES,
BEAUTIFUL TEETH AND HAIR AS WELL
BEAUTIFUL, BEAUTIFUL, BEAUTIFUL NELL."

ENT. STA. HALL

Pr 3/-

LONDON.

FOREWORD

by Roy Hudd OBE

Oh no! Not *another* book about music hall. As a lifelong enthusiast of, performer in and trumpeter of music hall, I see them all – from erudite fact-filled weighty tomes to naive, 'good old days' whitewashed fantasies. In my capacity as President of The British Music Hall Society I get asked to write more forewords than jokes these days. I have to own up: in most cases a cursory whip through the book is enough to make me shout, 'we've heard it all before!' or, 'how can anyone make sure an exciting period of popular entertainment so dull?' I don't write too many forewords, I assure you.

But this one did spark more interest than most when I saw it was written by Richard Anthony Baker. Richard is a regular contributor to The British Music Hall Society's magazine *The Call Boy* as well as to *The Stage* and BBC Radio. He and I tend to think along the same lines when it comes to our favourite subject, so, of courst, I read on.

I wasn't disappointed. The book is a great read, whether you are into music hall or not. It is the sort of book that I, with my grasshopper mind, like best. It is like an evening in a good music hall: no matter what time you arrive, or, in this case, what page you turn to, you always find something entertaining, fascinating or moving.

It, quite rightly, gives you all the bare bones of music hall history, but, thank heaven, it avoids being a dull, chronological list of the facts and figures and highs and lows of a long-dead industry. The story jumps about. Just a mention of a venue, a song or a performer sends the author into wherever he fancies. My kind of bloke.

Richard regales us with salty gossipy tales, highly perceptive pen pictures of so many great (and not so great) performers and colourful stories of much neglected provincial halls – and the fruity characters who built and ran the places.

Another largely ignored, but important part of Richard's story is Australian music hall. Their performers were coming over here long before Rolf Harris and Kylie.

My own favourite stories are those about some of *the* most important people of all: the songwriters – those ill-used observers of everyday life who had the wit, expertise and God-given gift of putting into words and music the hopes, fears and philosophies of the people who made up the music-hall audience. And boy – could they write tunes; after no more than a couple of hearings their great choruses stay in the mind like the Lord's Prayer. But just look at the pathetic few bob so many of these hugely important cogs in the music-hall engine left in their wills. It is sad proof of how little they were appreciated. When you read of the fortunes amassed by today's over-hyped and legally protected writers – well there ain't no justice.

As a performer I just caught the end of music hall's successor, variety. When I joined, it was the time of half-empty theatres and desperate attempts to pull in the punters. Top of the bill were either unknown 'kings of rock an' roll' or naughty, immobile ladies (with nowt on) in shows like *The Nine O'Clock Nudes* and *This Is The Show*. It was a sad end to a glorious period. It had to end, of course, and if you want the perfect explanation as to what finished it, turn to the final page. There, the last of the red-nosed comics, Jimmy Wheeler, gives his own brilliant summing-up of the whole business.

This volume isn't just 'another book about music hall'. It is a funny, gorgeous, riotous gallop through our entertainment heritage. There is no one alive today who can tell us, first hand, just what that golden period was really like, but, if it was anything like the broad-stroked picture Richard paints, how I wish I'd been there.

Roy Hudd OBE
President, The British Music Hall Society
Suffolk, 2005

CHAPTER 1

IN THE BEGINNING

Victorian Britain does not deserve its reputation for prudery. The idea that the nineteenth-century middle class was so offended by nakedness that piano legs were covered up is a ludicrous legend. The truth, albeit concealed, was that pornography was rife, as was prostitution, especially child prostitution. More than 50,000 prostitutes operated in London in the middle of the century. As for the protection of children, the age of consent stood at 12 until 1871 and was then raised only to 13. In the first fifty years of Victoria's reign, nearly a quarter of the prostitutes in York were aged 18 or under.

In addition, life expectancy in Victorian Britain was horrifically low. Between 1838 and 1854, men had to expect not to live beyond the age of 40. For women, the figure was 42. Epidemics of cholera and typhoid killed thousands. More routinely, 7,000 people died of measles every year. No wonder. Public hygiene was disgusting. Human excrement and slaughter-house refuse were routinely pumped into the Thames, causing such a stench that Disraeli walked about the Palace of Westminster with a handkerchief clutched to his nose. Brighton flushed its sewage onto local beaches until 1874. Torquay was four years behind.

Food was deliberately adulterated. A report issued in 1863 indicated that one-fifth of all meat came from diseased cattle. Overcrowding helped disease spread fast and London was the most densely populated city in the world. The number of families living in one room was put at 150,000. When education was made compulsory in 1870, the full extent of the debility of children became apparent. Vast numbers of them were found to be suffering from defective eyesight and hearing, awful dental problems and a widespread lack of personal cleanliness. Barely thirty years later, only two out of every five men volunteering for the Boer War were deemed fit for military service.

Work was both hard and hard to come by. A medical officer at the London Hospital reckoned that the worst paid and most industrious people he saw were seamstresses. They could work from 3 a.m. until 10 p.m. and earn between only 3 shillings (15p) and 4 shillings (20p) a week. When the social researcher Charles Booth conducted his extensive survey of life in London at the end of the nineteenth century, he found that close to one-third of all Londoners were living on or close to the poverty line.

Life for the working classes, then, was wretched. Entertainment provided the only escape from grim reality. In the early years of the nineteenth century, customers at inns staged their own entertainment. When tavern owners began employing professional entertainers, local unpaid amateurs continued to perform. These places were known as free-and-easies. Many future stars began their careers there, but, as early as the first year of Victoria's reign, some saw only a pernicious influence:

The epidemic of vocal music has more particularly spread its contagious and devastating influence amongst the youth of the Metropolis, the London apprentice boys. These young gentlemen generally give vent to their passion and display their vocal abilities in the spacious room appropriated to that purpose of some tavern or public house and these meetings are most aptly denominated Free and Easies: free as air they are for the advancement of drunkenness and profligacy and easy enough of access to all classes of society with little regard to appearances or character.[1]

More even-handedly, the Scottish comedian W.F. Frame neatly summarised the role of the free-and-easy:

There was no charge of admission to a free-and-easy, at which refreshments were supplied at the usual rates. Anyone who was bold enough could make an appearance at such a concert, his friends doing the needful by handing his or her name to the chairman, who, like the pianist, was paid at the rate of 5s [25p] a night. The chairman[2] was frequently a good vocalist himself and, if necessary, would sing a song. A free-and-easy was a happy, go-as-you-please sort of entertainment and a capital preparatory school for budding amateurs.[3]

Another early and important influence was the song-and-supper room. In London, three predominated. An advertisement in *The Era*[4] in 1851 described the Coal Hole, which stood in Fountain Court, just off the Strand, as 'the oldest and most popular of the singing establishments'. It was home to (among others) John Rhodes, a bass singer and the Coal Hole's landlord; J.A. Cave, the first singer to introduce the banjo into Britain; and Joe Wells, who, according to the writer Edmund Yates, was 'a dreadful old creature . . . who used to sing the most disgusting ditties'. From 1853, Renton Nicholson (1809–61) staged mock trials run by his Judge and Jury Society at the Cyder Cellars and, from 1858, at the Coal Hole. The tavern lost its licence in 1862 and was later closed and demolished so that the Strand could be widened.

The second was Evans's Supper Rooms at King Street in Covent Garden, probably the most important of the three. Filling the basement of a family hotel, the Grand, in the late eighteenth century, it was converted into its new role by W.C. (William Carpenter) Evans. Its heyday came after a former actor, John 'Paddy' Green, became Chairman and Conductor of Music in 1842. He undertook further conversions two years later and succeeded Evans as proprietor the year after that. Evans's most popular entertainer was the character singer Sam Cowell. In fact, by 1851, he had become so popular that he grew lax about the times of his performances. One night, in response to cries of 'Cowell' from the audience, Paddy Green told them:

Gentlemen, I have done my best to introduce many good and deserving singers to your notice, but you won't have them. You insist on having Cowell and none but Cowell. You have pampered him to such an extent that he has got too big for his clothes and now presumes upon the position you have given him. Cowell comes when he likes, goes when he likes and does what he likes – and you encourage him. In fact, he is your God. But, by God, he shan't be mine.[5]

Cowell arrived shortly afterwards and made his own speech, telling Green he was no longer a schoolboy and should not be treated like one, but he was taken aback when the audience started hissing him. He never appeared at Evans's again.

The patrons of Evans's included Dickens and Thackeray. On the menu were mutton chops, devilled kidneys and baked potatoes, served by the so-called Calculating Waiter, a man named Skinner, who became something of a character:

> Standing guard at the exit, he used his powers to the full on nervous youths waiting in the queue to state what they had had for supper:
> What have you had, sir? – Chop.
> One chop, two and six. – Potatoes.
> Potatoes, three and nine. Any bread? – No bread.
> No bread, four and two. – One tankard of stout.
> One tankard of stout, five and ten. Cheese? – No cheese.
> No cheese, six and four. Sixpence for the waiter, sir. Thank you, seven and four – eight shillings. Thank you, sir! Next, please.[6]

At one stage, diners were entertained by songs then considered risqué (or, to quote the critic Clement Scott, 'songs of unadulterated indecency and filth'). This ended when all such ribaldry was replaced by glees and madrigals sung by groups of young choirboys. In 1879, however, the saucy songs of the comedian Arthur Roberts caused Evans's to lose its licence, only to have it reinstated the following year.

The Cyder Cellars (or Cider Cellars), which stood next to the stage door of the Adelphi Theatre in Covent Garden, was the third of the halls' famous precursors. Dating from the late 1820s, they were opened by W.C. Evans, who acted as Chairman three times a week, Charles Sloman presiding on three other nights. Thackeray chronicled the Cyder Cellars' regulars: country tradesmen and farmers, young apprentices, rakish medical students, university 'bucks'; guardsmen and members of the House of Lords. Thackeray himself was a regular, going twice in October 1848 to hear W.G. Ross sing at two in the morning. As with Evans's Supper Rooms, however, a marked change of entertainment policy was introduced in 1853. *The Era* reported that 'instead of ribald songs, coarse allusions and a specious immorality, glees, madrigals and choruses form the staple attractions'. All the same, 'Baron' Renton Nicholson's dubious Judge and Jury trials continued here: in 1859, the *Liverpool Daily Post* described him as an 'obscene and foul fellow, who . . . solaces decrepit debauchees and precipitates unthinking young men into ruin'. Nicholson was an extraordinary character. In and out of prison, he scraped a living at various times as a pawnbroker, a jeweller, a newspaper editor, a cigar shop owner and a wine merchant, but it was the mock trials he presented that earned him the notoriety he deserved. In seemingly endless sentences, Edmund Yates painted a vivid picture of them:

> [The courts were] presided over by Nicholson himself as the Lord Chief Justice in full wig and gown, the case being argued out by persons dressed as, and, in some instances, giving also imitations of, leading barristers and the witnesses being actors of more or less versatility and mimetic ability. The whole affair was written and arranged by Nicholson, who deported himself on the bench with the most solemn gravity, the contrast between which and his invariable speech on taking his seat – 'Usher! Get me a cigar and a little brandy and water' – was the signal for the first laugh. The entertainment was undoubtedly clever, but was so full of grossness and indecency, expressed and implied, as to render it wholly disgusting.[7]

It was an all-male affair. Women appearing in the trials were, in fact, men dressed up and, according to the writer, J. Ewing Ritchie, 'everything was done that the most liquorish (drunken) imagination could suggest or that could pander most effectually to the lowest propensities of depraved humanity': 'I dare not even attempt to give a faint outline of the proceedings. After the defence came the summing-up, which men about town told you was a model of wit, but in which wit bore but a small proportion to the obscenity.'[8] The trials were often satirical send-ups of real contemporary cases, such as the murder in Washington in 1859 by a New York City Congressman, Daniel Sickles, of the American attorney for Columbia, Philip Barton Key, who had been having an affair with Sickles's wife. The American public viewed the killing as a crime passionnel and Sickles was acquitted. Even so, Nicholson's treatment of the case seemed particularly tasteless:

> The Lord Chief Baron Nicholson has the honour to announce the recent extraordinary trial at Washington as it would have been conducted, had the tragedy and the crime which led to it been committed in this country. The Judge particularly invites the presence of his American friends now in London and, to them and to his usual patrons, he promises a treat in the shape of forensic eloquence unrivalled in the history of proceedings in British law courts.[9]

Nicholson had friends in high places and his juries often included members of both Houses of Parliament. In contrast to the Liverpool newspaper, the *Dictionary of National Biography*, a very sober publication in Victorian times, found him worthy of inclusion: 'The trials were humorous and gave occasion for much real eloquence, brilliant repartee, fluent satire and not unfrequently [*sic*] for indecent witticism.'

In spite of Nicholson's notoriety, he was overshadowed by W.G. Ross, who built his reputation on one song, 'The Ballad of Sam Hall' (*c.* 1840), which recounted the thoughts of a chimney sweep the night before his execution for murder:

> My name it is Sam Hall.
> I rob both great and small,
> But they makes me pay for all.
> Damn their eyes.

With each succeeding chorus, the word 'damn' was replaced with a stronger expletive. The theatre writer W.J. MacQueen-Pope was greatly moved by it:

> It was a piece of stark realism and Ross brought great dramatic art to his rendering of it. He entered and did not start to sing right away. He was restless, his eyes darting about him, but not seeing what they looked at . . . Ross gave a performance of high tragedy, excusing nothing of the squalor of the crime, making no attempt to whitewash the character, just expressing the scattered thoughts of the bestial criminal, who could already feel the noose round his neck, but who lacked the finer feelings to make any fervent appeal for sympathy or even to speculate on what went beyond. As a piece of characterisation of its kind, it is doubtful if it was ever excelled. Certainly it was never forgotten by any individuals who saw Ross do it.[10]

When Ross sang it at the Cyder Cellars, people were turned away at the doors every night. His picture, priced one shilling (5p), could not be printed fast enough to keep pace with demand.

There was increasing demand, too, for this whole new form of entertainment. It needed its own name. The term 'music hall' emerged. It was used first, as far as one can tell, when a singing room attached to the Grapes Tavern at Southwark in south London was renamed a music hall at the end of 1847. The idea was probably to make a gathering for sing-songs sound rather more upmarket, more like a concert hall, perhaps. This *folie de grandeur* continued when the owners of chains of music halls chose, as part of a theatre's name, Hippodrome, formerly an open-air course for horse and chariot racing in ancient Greece and Rome, and Alhambra, the palace of the Moorish kings of the Spanish city of Granada. Later still, cinemas followed the same tradition. An odeon, for instance, was a theatre for musical contests in ancient Greece and Rome.

London's first purpose-built music hall was the Canterbury, situated in what is now Westminster Bridge Road. When the manager and entrepreneur, Charles Morton, took it over in 1849, it had a room in which free-and-easies were staged. Morton improved and refurbished the room and, in 1851, obtained a music licence. Once this licence was in place, the amateur element of music hall melted away. Morton set to work putting up a new building. A graphic impression was given of the area before the Canterbury was built: 'The Lower-marsh or, as it is termed, the New-cut, was an avenue of miserable hovels and, redolent of soul-sickening scents arising from miasmatic mud, small cottages of the most contracted dimensions, flanked by ditches, which were crossed by means of wooden planks, gave an air of semi-rurality to the scene.'[11]

The first Canterbury Hall, which opened in 1852, would not have been a success had Morton not signed up Sam Cowell. In fact, Cowell proved such an attraction that, only two years after building his first hall, Morton began work on the second. More land was bought behind the houses in Lower Marsh and the last of the skittle sheds and hovels in Whiskey Place were cleared away. Built around the old hall and incorporating part of it, the second Canterbury was finally completed in 1855, the last touches being made three years later with the addition of an ante-room, a supper room and a grand staircase. To top it all, an art gallery was opened in an annex. Wags called it the Royal Academy over the Water. Morton, who was keen to prove that the Canterbury was no longer a mere tap-room, discovered a copyright loop-hole which allowed him to present

The Canterbury, London's first purpose-built music hall. *(Richard Anthony Baker)*

selections from Verdi's *Il Trovatore* and Donizetti's *Lucrezia Borgia* and *Lucia di Lammermoor*. Indeed, he was the first to introduce the music of Gounod's *Faust* to an English audience.

J. Ewing Ritchie described a visit to the Canterbury:

A well-lighted entrance attached to a public-house indicates that we have reached our destination. We proceed up a few stairs, along a passage, lined with handsome engravings, to a bar, where we pay sixpence [2.5p], if we take a seat in the body of the hall, and ninepence [about 4p] if we do the nobby[12] and ascend into the balcony. We make our way leisurely along the floor of the building, which is really a very handsome hall, well lighted, and capable of holding fifteen-hundred persons; the balcony extends round the room in the form of a horseshoe. At the opposite end to which we enter is the platform, on which is placed a grand piano and a harmonium, on which the performers play in the intervals when the professional singers have left the stage. The Chairman sits just beneath them. It is dull work to him; but there he must sit every night, smoking cigars and drinking, from seven till twelve o'clock . . . The room is crowded and almost every gentleman present has a pipe or a cigar in his mouth. The majority present are respectable mechanics or small tradesmen with their wives and daughters and sweethearts . . . Now and then, you see a midshipman or a few fast clerks and warehousemen, who confidentially inform each other that there is 'no end of talent here' . . . Everyone is smoking and everyone has a glass before him; but the class that come here are economical and chiefly confine themselves to pipes and porter. The presence of the ladies has also a beneficial effect; I see no indication of intoxication and certainly none of the songs are obscene.[13]

At the end of 1870, Morton's interest came to an end when the hall was assigned to Edwin Villers, who razed it to the ground six years later and built the third Canterbury on the site. This was reconstructed to the designs of the greatest of all British theatre architects, Frank Matcham, in 1890.

Largely as a result of opening the Canterbury, Charles Morton became known as the Father of the Halls. Although he spent his entire working life as either a licensed victualler or the owner or manager of music halls, he was teetotal, attributing his longevity to 'a love of work and temperance of habit'. His greatest indulgence was a cup of cocoa and a biscuit.

He started seeing plays when he was still a youngster. Before he was 13, he went to the Pavilion in Whitechapel, which specialised in melodramas, particularly nautical dramas. Although he started work early in life, he continued going to the theatre as often as he could. At Drury Lane, he was captivated by the tragedian William MacReady; and, when the Swedish singer Jenny Lind was in Britain, he was always in the audience.

Morton first worked as a waiter at a tavern. As with many inns at the time, it operated as a bookmaker's too. Morton studied form and, if the horses he recommended came home first, he usually received a large tip. He watched the harmonic evenings staged at his own place of work and visited others on his nights off. At the age of 21, he took his first pub, the St George's Tavern in Pimlico, and ran a free-and-easy there. From Pimlico, he moved to the Crown in Pentonville and, after five years in the business, took over the India House Tavern in Leadenhall Street, concentrating on improving its catering.

Morton also patronised the supper rooms and, when he was at Evans's one night, he decided to run a completely new form of enterprise at the Canterbury Arms in Lambeth, which, until then, had been known only for its occasional sing-songs. When Morton moved there in 1849, it consisted of no more than a parlour and four skittle alleys. Morton began refurbishing it and introduced concerts for men only on Mondays and Saturdays and, later on, a ladies' night, also on Saturdays. Over the next two years, he assembled a company of above-average quality: with his brother, Robert, as Chairman, he introduced Billy Williamson, an untrained tenor, Tommy Keats, who specialised in drunken ballads, and Walter Ramsey, who gave satirical recitations.

During the 1860s, Morton grew tired of merely owning a music hall in Lambeth, moved into the West End and converted the Boar and Castle Inn in Oxford Street into the Oxford music hall. He leased the Canterbury to the showman, William Holland, who became known as the People's Caterer. Holland was the greatest of all Victorian showmen. A rotund figure with a frock coat and an impressive moustache, he ran theatres and halls all over London. He was instrumental in building the career of George Leybourne, put the tightrope walker Blondin under a year's contract, toured the provinces with a giantess, Marion ('eight feet two inches [249cm] and still growing'), and inaugurated wildly successful shows and contests at the North Woolwich pleasure gardens. His first, a baby show in 1869, attracted 20,000 people on its first day alone.

Charles Morton, the Father of the Halls.
(Richard Anthony Baker)

As for the Canterbury, it was converted into a cinema in 1921 by three brothers, Phil, Syd and Mick Hyams, the sons of a Russian immigrant. They went on to build most of London's so-called super-cinemas, including the 4,000-seat State Cinema, Kilburn, and the 3,000-seat Trocadero at the Elephant and Castle. The Canterbury was hit by enemy bombs in 1942 and what remained was demolished in 1955.

Many ventures followed for Morton. He, too, ran the North Woolwich Gardens and he staged operatic selections at the Philharmonic in Islington. An American tour in 1874 left him

SAM COWELL (Samuel Houghton Cowell)
Born London 5 April 1820
Married Emilie Marguerite Ebsworth, 5 November 1842
    (d. 13 January 1899)
  One son, Joseph (30 October 1843–5 February 1847)
  Two daughters, both actresses, Sidney (1846–
    5 November 1925), who married George Giddons
    (actor) (marriage dissolved) and Florence (1852–26
    March 1926), who married (1) John Parselle (actor)
    (1820–17 February 1885), (2) A.B. Tapping (actor)
    (1851–31 December 1928)
Died Blandford, Dorset, 11 March 1864

with severe losses and, the following year, he was declared bankrupt, a stark contrast from his pioneering days at the Canterbury, when he was able to pay Sam Cowell between £60 and £80 a week to sing twice a night.

Cowell, a short and unprepossessing man, was the son of an actor, Joseph Leathley Cowell. He spent his early years in the United States. While his father was working there, Sam attended a military academy near Philadelphia, making his stage debut at the age of 9 at a benefit for his father in Boston.

His acting career started in earnest in 1840 at the Edinburgh Adelphi, which was managed by his uncle. By the late 1840s, he had decided to concentrate entirely on character singing, a move which propelled him to the top of his profession.

In 1857, Cowell began his first tour of England, criss-crossing the country, staging a concert nearly every night and setting himself an exhausting schedule. The tour finished at the end of the year. Further similar tours took place in 1858 and 1859.

Cowell's success led to overwork and heavy drinking and, by the time he embarked on a tour of America and Canada during 1860 and 1861, he was an alcoholic and heavily in debt. Throughout the trip, his wife kept a diary, which she bequeathed to her granddaughter, Sydney Fairbrother.[14] In it, she recorded events that played an important part in the period immediately preceding the American Civil War. Her entry for 6 November 1860 read: 'What a day this is . . . in the States! It decides the Presidency for the next four years and, in the present agitated state of North and South, the usual excitement is redoubled. The chances are greatly in favour of Abraham Lincoln . . . If so, there is a great fear of disunion between North and South.'[15] And on 15 April 1861, she noted: 'The Civil War is on us at last. The tremendous agony of suspense endured by the citizens here [New York] has been succeeded by gloom and disappointment.'[16] On a personal level, the diary is a tragic account of her husband's self-destruction.

Sam, his wife and elder daughter, Sidney (*sic*), left Liverpool aboard the *Asia* on 29 October 1859 and arrived in New York on 13 November. (He had planned to be in America for forty-four weeks, but stayed for two years.) Even by today's standards, their schedule was gruelling.

After two months in New York, the family travelled north, visiting Boston, Massachusetts, Providence, Rhode Island, Worcester and Springfield, Massachusetts, and New Haven, Connecticut, where Mrs Cowell noted: 'What an audience! I never heard more genuine shouts and screams of laughter.' Towards the end of February 1860, the family returned to New York. The major part of the tour then began. The Cowells travelled to Philadelphia and Pittsburgh, where the first signs of Sam's drinking problems materialised. After two nights of 'conviviality', he promised to touch no more spirits until July, but, the follow-ing night, he could not get through his first song without brandy. Mrs Cowell noted: 'Sudden abstemiousness has made him very ill before, so he must become so (please God) by degrees.'

'Lord Lovel'

(a parody)
(*c.* 1842)
originally a ballad, possibly fifteenth century

(The instruction in *120 Comic Songs Sung by Sam Cowell*, published by Davidson, Peter's Hill, St Paul's, London, is that the song should be sung Mock Pathetic.)

> Lord Lovel, he stood at the castle gate,
> Combing his milk white steed,
> When up came Lady Nancy Bell
> To wish her lover good speed, speed, speed,
> To wish her lover good speed.
>
> 'Oh, where are you going, Lord Lovel?' she said.
> 'Oh, where are you going?' said she.
> 'I'm going, my Lady Nancy Bell,
> Foreign countries to see-ee-ee,
> Foreign countries to see.'

Subsequent verses tell that, after a year, Lord Lovel was missing Lady Nancy. He rode back to London only to discover that she had died and her body recently buried. He ordered the coffin to be opened; he kissed the corpse's lips; and then died himself. His body was buried near hers. A red rose bush was planted on top of her grave and a brier on top of his. They grew as high as the church steeple, where they tied themselves into a lover's knot.

In 1859, Cowell's agent, Morrison Kyle, a Glasgow music publisher, brought an action at the County Court, Bath, to recover £50 from a Bath rector, who had agreed to let Cowell have the Lecture Hall, Bath, for two nights, but had then changed his mind. Counsel for the defendants said 'Lord Lovel' was one of the most blasphemous things he had ever had to deal with. He read out part of it, but was greeted only by laughter. The rector said an old parishioner had given him a programme, in which some lines in the lyrics had been underlined. He understood that Cowell sang in 'low places' in London. At the end of the hearing, which lasted five and a half hours, the jury found in favour of Cowell.

Sam Cowell, music hall's first star, with his wife, Emilie.
(*British Music Hall Society*)

At the start of May, the party travelled to Montgomery, Louisiana; to Atlanta; and then back to Nashville, by which time financial problems and homesickness were beginning to take their toll: 'Oh, England, that we three were once more on thy hospitable shores and had said farewell forever to this upstart country'; then back to Louisville, where Sam was very ill: 'He is so weak that he can hardly stand and [he has] wasted away, almost to a skeleton'; by steamer, they continued to Cincinnatti, where Mrs Cowell described Sam as 'feeble as an infant . . . merely skin and bone . . . He said "This is our last chance, Em. If this is a failure, I shall go crazy indeed."' Fortunately, his appearance was a success, especially after he had sung 'Lord Lovel': 'How the people roared with laughter! They applauded and they shouted, while I, listening, heard my dear boy's voice all tremulous and faint, I knew by his tone how exhausted he was.' Nine days later, Mrs Cowell recorded that Sam's condition was worsening. A doctor was called and told Sam that he must rest. Back in New York in June 1860, however, Sam was eating so well that he celebrated by drinking most of a pint of sherry.

At the beginning of July, Sam left for Canada, where he was later joined by Mrs Cowell and Sidney. Before they departed, Sam played Hamilton, Ontario, from where he wrote to them: 'My reception last night could not have been better had I have been in the Music Hall, Edinburgh, and the whole business stunning. $95 in the house too, and the prospects are good for tonight. Thank God!! Before beginning, I had half a dime.'[17]

Before he headed for Quebec, a woman invalid attended one of his concerts on doctor's orders: '"Take a dose of Sam Cowell!" [and your] health will be benefited by a hearty laugh.' Back in New York, Sam was so ill that Mrs Cowell believed he was close to death. Only a few weeks later, however, he went out on 'a heavy spree' which brought on an attack of the DTs.

Returning to London, Cowell made his first public appearance at Weston's in August 1861. He was given an uproarious reception. He was contracted to the Canterbury, so was not allowed to sing at Weston's, but he thanked the audience for the way in which they had greeted him. In a short speech, he told them that he had made a great deal of money during parts of the tour, but had lost a very great deal during others. In fact, he was almost destitute.

Three months after his death in 1864, a concert, at which Sims Reeves was the main attraction, was arranged to raise money for his widow and children.

CHAPTER 2

FIRST GENERATION

Music hall was beginning to organise itself and, when Cowell returned from America, he found many entertainers well established in the affections of music-hall admirers. One was Frederick Robson, who, in his short life, was regarded as one of the most exciting actors and comic singers of his day. At the age of 9, the highly respected drama critic James Agate asked his father who had been the greatest actor he had ever seen. Agate's father, who had seen Macready and Irving, replied without hesitation: 'Little Robson', a reference to Robson's height; even in adult life, Robson stood less than 5 feet tall (152cm), his large head out of proportion to the rest of his body.

When he was still a boy, Robson was taken by his mother to see plays in London and to hear Charles Sloman sing. He was immediately stage-struck. Back home, he saved his money to buy a toy theatre. At 15 he was apprenticed to a copper-plate engraver and printer, but, after four years, he started his own business only to abandon it when he was 21 to try his hand at acting. After an unsuccessful debut at a theatre in Catherine Street, he joined a company at the Bower Saloon in Lambeth, playing character parts. (This theatre, which had been licensed since 1837, became a warehouse for Price's candles forty years later.) Robson also added J.A. Cave's 'The Country Fair' to his own growing repertoire of songs. He sang it for the first time at the Grecian Theatre in February 1847. It became the song most associated with him, together with 'Vilikens and his Dinah', probably a street ballad, which he revived for a production of *The Wandering Minstrel* in 1853:

> FREDERICK ROBSON (Thomas Robson Brownbill)
> **Born** Margate, Kent, 22 February 1821
> **Married** Rosetta Frances May, Lambeth, south London, 21 September 1842 (d. 31 July 1899, aged 77)
> One son, Frederick Henry
> One daughter, Frances
> **Died** London, 12 August 1864

> It is of a rich merchant I am going to tell,
> Who had for a daughter an unkimmon nice girl.
> Her name it was Dinah, just 16 years old
> With a werry large fortune in silver and gold.
> Sing-in Too-ral-li, too-ral-li, too-ral-li, da.

Robson's reputation as a comic singer spread across north London where he was employed at free-and-easies for a guinea (£1.05) a night plus refreshments. He could have made his name as a music-hall artiste in song and supper rooms, like his contemporary Sam Cowell, but he chose the stage instead. After a period in Dublin, he returned to London, where he became one of the mainstays at the Olympic just off the Strand. Among his most popular roles was that of a street musician, Jem Baggs, in *The Wandering Minstrel*. By the early 1860s, however, Robson had developed a drink problem. He became unreliable, occasionally lost his memory and grew to hate the stage:

> He was morbidly timid and nervous, he could never realise the great position he had attained and was ever haunted by a fear that his fall would be as sudden as his rise; success had a delirious effect on him and to deaden his stage fright, which he could never overcome, he resorted to stimulants – with the usual result. Robson had been famous scarcely seven years when his powers began to fail and his terror of facing the audience became so great that, while waiting for his cue, he would gnaw his arms until they bled and cry out piteously 'I dare not go on, I dare not!' until the prompter had at times to thrust him before the footlights.[1]

Robson died of heart and liver failure.

During the course of the 1850s, Harry Clifton,[2] the son of a carpenter, established himself as both singer and songwriter. His songs fell into three categories: comic, Irish and so-called motto songs, those whose stories had a moral. According to *The Era*, Clifton's songs were 'equally popular and acceptable in the drawing-room of the rich as in the cottages of the poor'.[3]

His most durable song was '(Pretty) Polly Perkins of Paddington Green' (1863), a tale of un-requited love. In the lyric, marriage was proposed, but Polly Perkins chose instead the 'bow-legged conductor of a twopenny bus':

> (She was as) Beautiful as a butterfly
> And as proud as a queen,
> Was pretty little Polly Perkins
> Of Paddington Green.

HARRY CLIFTON (Henry Robert Clifton)
Born Hoddesdon, Hertfordshire, 1832 (baptised 20 May)
Married, but separated
Died Shepherd's Bush, London, 15 July 1872
Left approximately £6,000 to one of his company, Frances Edwards

---

In July 1863, a review of Clifton said the song was 'creating . . . a sensation in London'.[4] It certainly earned a great deal of money for its publishers, Hopwood and Crew, enough for them to present Clifton with a diamond ring, which he described from then on as his Pretty Polly Perkins ring.

In 1864, he wrote 'A Dark Girl Dress'd in Blue' ('I lost my heart and senses, too, thru' a dark girl dressed in blue') and, the following year, he produced his most successful song of all, a motto song called 'Paddle Your Own Canoe'. (Canoeing was then very much in fashion.)

Clifton was credited with having written both words and music. The composer was, in fact, Charles Coote, who later became the managing director of Hopwood and Crew. On occasions, Clifton plagiarised the melodies of other songs. He set another of his motto songs, 'Work, Boys, Work and Be Contented', to the music of the marching song of the American Civil War,

'Tramp, Tramp, Tramp, the Boys are Marching'.

Clifton's popularity stretched nation-wide. He began a tour of Britain and Ireland in April 1865 that continued well into 1867. He played a different town or city nearly every night. He started in Preston, played Burnley the following night, Rochdale the night after that, Bury after that, and so on.

On his death, *The Era* paid tribute: 'The popularity which his songs attained is best denoted by the fact that even now they are whistled by every street-boy, played by every barrel organ and sung in every town and hamlet in the United Kingdom. The kindly nature of the man was breathed throughout his verses. His motto appears to have been "Help one another, boys."'[5]

Harry Sydney (*c.* 1826–1870) was a favourite entertainer of both Dickens and Thackeray. He wrote most of his own material, which included comic, sentimental, topical and political songs. He appeared at Evans's, where his annual song about the Boat Race was always an event, especially with the rival crews. He was also to be seen at Weston's in Holborn and the Colosseum in Regent's Park, becoming resident singer at the Lansdowne music hall on Islington Green, run by Sam Collins, in 1862. *The Era* maintained

Harry Clifton, singer of so-called motto songs. *(Richard Anthony Baker)*

that his political songs were without rival: 'although Conservative in his views, politicians and public men of every shade of opinion were freely and generally good-naturedly criticised in these effusions.'[6]

Thomas Hudson (*c.* 1791–1844) was one of music hall's earliest writers. An educated man, he began life as a grocer, but eventually devoted himself to both writing and singing comic songs. He appeared frequently at the Cyder Cellars. Every year between 1818 and 1831, he published collections of his works, including 'The Spider and the Fly' (1830), which was popular for many years, and a song about scandal-mongering, 'I Never Says Nothing to Nobody' (1825):

The newly-married couple so happy
Seem both the quintessence of love.
He calls her before every sappy (?)
My darling, my duck and my dove.
In private, there's nothing but strife,
Quarrelling, fighting o'er-flow body;
In short, quite a cat-and-dog life,
But I never says nothing to nobody.

'Barney Brallaghan's Courtship' (c. 1830) is typical of the charm and innocence of his songs. It is a serenade to Brallaghan's sweetheart, Judy Callaghan, listing the reasons he thinks she should marry him:

I've got an old tom cat.
Thro' one eye he's staring.
I've got a Sunday hat
Little the worse for wearing.
I've got some gooseberry wine.
The trees had got no riper on.
I've got a fiddle fine,
Which only wants a piper on.
Only say you'll have Mr Brallaghan.
Don't say 'nay', charming Judy Callaghan.

In spite of his popularity, Hudson earned very little. On his death, he was all but penniless. A benefit concert held in a room at the back of the Princess's Theatre in Oxford Street,[7] as well as substantial help from the Duke of Cambridge, the Lord Mayor of London, MPs and other music-hall entertainers, prevented his family from starving.

Robert Glindon (c. 1799–1866) appeared at many of the early places of entertainment operating in London in the 1840s, such as the Coal Hole, the Cyder Cellars, Dr Johnson's Concert Room, which opened in Bolt Court, Fleet Street, in about 1835 and closed in 1863, as well as at the Grecian Theatre and the Vauxhall Gardens.[8] By day, he painted scenery at Drury Lane and created part of London by Night, a huge diorama, an early form of moving pictures, which created a sensation at the opening of the Colosseum Theatre in Regent's Park in the mid-1820s. By night, he sang comic songs, mostly studies in domestic humour. He sang some written by Thomas Hudson, including 'Jack Robinson', but also wrote some himself, including his best-known song, 'The Literary Dustman' (1845). Thirty of Glindon's songs were published in a small book that same year. One, 'Yankee Wonders', mocks the Americans for exaggerating things:

There's a woman as large as a tree.
I can't say in what State they found her.
But, set off in a trot from her knee,
It will take you a week to get round her.
There's a man cheats a cock of its crowing
And he does it so shrill and so prime
That the sun was observed to be glowing
Full two hours before its right time.

John Labern (*c.* 1815–1881) wrote songs at one time considered obscene. Two collections, *Labern's Comic Song Book* and *Labern's Original Comic Song Book*, were issued by a publisher of pornography, John Duncombe, of Holborn Hill. As a singer, Labern appeared at the Vauxhall Gardens and the Cyder Cellars. As a writer, he produced songs for several of music hall's early entertainers, including W.G. Ross, J.W. Sharp and Sam Cowell.

Sharp's *Vauxhall Comic Song Book*, an early book of music-hall lyrics, includes 'The Opening Night', written in commemoration of the opening of the Cyder Cellars in September 1847:

> Behold, how snug we've made the Cellars.
> So, buyers may you nightly prove,
> You'll find us nightingalish fellers
> And music ever on the move.

Labern's style eventually went out of favour. By 1873, he was running a shop near Tottenham Court Road selling newspapers and snuff.

After a lacklustre start to his career, J.H. Stead found the song that was to make his name and his fortune: 'The Perfect Cure' (1861). He sang it in the garb of a French curate: a long black coat, a large white neckcloth, gaiters and a large-rimmed low black hat. Most remarkable, however, was the strange jumping dance he performed at the end of each chorus. During each performance, it was calculated that he made as many as 500 jumps, all accomplished without him bending his knees. He merely jumped stiff-legged from his toes.

The song was a sensation. People flocked to the Royal music hall to see this phenomenon. Although Stead found one other successful song, 'That Blessed Baby', it could never equal 'The Perfect Cure' and, although he earned a lot of money

J.H. STEAD (James Hurst Stead)
Born 1827 (?)
Married
Died Camden Town, north London, 24 January 1886
Left £3,135

J.H. Stead sang a song with a peculiar dance and left a fortune. (*Richard Anthony Baker*)

while it was popular, the word went round that he had lost a great deal when a private bank, in which he had invested, collapsed.

So, when he was taken ill in 1885 (at first with a chest complaint, but later with mental problems), his friends rallied round to raise money for him and his family. Hundreds of pounds were collected in the months before Stead died in a slum in central London. After he died, it soon became obvious that, in spite of the squalor in which he chose to live, he was a comparatively wealthy man. The music-hall press was indignant and all the money that was raised was returned to the donors.

The career of one of music hall's earliest female singers, Mrs F.R. Phillips, reached its peak in the mid-1870s. She was associated with many songs, including 'No Irish Need Apply', a song alluding to what Irishmen believed was a ban on them working at the Great Exhibition of 1851. Mrs Phillips wrote the lyrics to the melody of a Thomas Hudson song, 'The Spider and the Fly':

> At Balaclava,[9] Inkerman[10] and through the Russian War,
> Did not the Irish bravely fight, as they've oft done before?
> And, since that time in India, they made the rebels fly,
> Our generals never hinted then 'No Irish Need Apply'.
> If you want a second Wellington, I say it's all my eye.
> You'll never get one while you write 'No Irish Need Apply.'

Mrs Phillips was particularly popular at the Middlesex:

This lady has been long before the public and she is, without question, one of that public's greatest favourites. Strange to say, she has achieved her position without the aid of a good voice . . . But then, to use a common phrase, 'it's the style that does it'; and, indeed, Mrs Phillips has a style peculiarly her own and her songs are invariably so well written and are given with such expression that she never fails to take her audience by storm.[11]

> Mrs F.R. PHILLIPS (Mary Ann Dunn)
> **Born** 1829 (?)
> **Married** Frederick Powys Royle, a professor
>   of music, Rotherham, south Yorkshire,
>   18 July 1853 (d. 1884)
>   Daughter, Kate, married Joseph Long
> **Died** Lambeth, south London,
>   10 December 1899

Mrs Phillips, known towards the end of her life as Ma Phillips, gave her farewell concert at the South London Palace in 1887.

> Mrs CAULFIELD (Louisa Mat(t)ley)
> **Born** 1821 (?)
> **Married** John Caulfield (d. 1865)
>   One son, John (d. 1879), who married
>   Constance Loseby (1850–1906)
>   One daughter, Lennox Grey
> **Died** Lambeth, London, 11 September
>   1870

Mrs Caulfield was one of the first female entertainers to appear at Evans's and the newly opened Canterbury Hall. Her husband, John, who had worked as an actor at the Haymarket theatre, was the hall's Chairman. Mrs Caulfield specialised in female versions of the popular comic songs of the day. She had two particular successes, one of which was a nonsense song, 'Keemo Kimo' ('Dolly – Won't You Try Me, Oh?') (1840):

Keemo, Kimo: Where? Oh, there! My high, low!
Then in came Dolly singing;
Sometimes medley winkum lingum up-cat
Sing song, Dolly – won't you try me oh!

Her other big success was 'As they Marched through the Town' ('The Captain with his whiskers') (1869). In common with her husband and their two children, Mrs Caulfield also appeared at the Haymarket.

Sam Collins, originally a chimney sweep, became one of the halls' most popular singers in the 1840s. Wearing a brimless top hat, a dress coat, knee breeches, worsted stockings and brogues, he made his way from one hall to another, his clothes tied up in a bundle and a shillelagh on his shoulder. He specialised in Irish songs: his first great success was 'The Rocky Road to Dublin', written by Harry Clifton.

Sam Collins was one of Charles Morton's first stars at the Canterbury. He was successful enough to be able to buy a pub, the Rose of Normandy in Marylebone High Street, in 1858 and rebuild the adjacent music hall to accommodate an audience of 800. Three years later, he took over the Lansdowne Arms is Islington, which he converted into a music hall, seating a thousand people. Named Sam Collins' Music Hall, it opened in November 1863, eighteen months before his death. His widow ran it after his death. It remained Collins' for nearly a century and, during that time, many people claim to have seen ghosts here. Marie Lloyd swore that she saw an old Irishman appear in her dressing-room, grin affably and walk through the wall. It was at Collins' that Sir Norman Wisdom made his professional debut in December 1945. After being badly damaged by fire in 1958, Collins' was demolished, although much of its façade survives as part of an elegant bookshop.

SAM COLLINS (Samuel Collins Thomas
 Vagg)
Born London 1827 (?)
Married Anna ——
Died London, 25 May 1865
Left under £4,000

Sam Collins lent his name to a famous London hall.
(Richard Anthony Baker)

CHAPTER 3

PIONEERS

Sam Cowell and others of his period always appeared on stage looking down-at-heel. A new trend emerged with the arrival of Alfred Vance or the Great Vance, as he came to be called. Vance, followed by G.H. MacDermott, George Leybourne and Arthur Lloyd, chose to play the fop, the swell, the dandy, the modish man about town. Appearing in a well-cut jacket, Vance dropped silk handkerchiefs all over the stage, suggesting, as one writer put it, 'a reckless demeanour that breathed opulence'.

ALFRED VANCE (Alfred Peck Stevens)
Born 1839
Married Susan Tingey, 26 December 1869 (separated 1875)
Died south-west London, 26 December 1888
Left £39

In his early twenties, Vance set up a black-faced act with his brother. In 1861, Messrs Alfred and E. Vance advertised themselves as 'the excelsior black gems . . . the refined versatile impersonators of Negro life'.[1] After a change of partner, Vance was on his own, appearing that Christmas as the clown in *Jack, the Giant-Killer* at the Theatre Royal, Newcastle.

During 1862, he called a halt to black-faced impersonations and began appearing as the smart young man of his day. Having perfected his act in the provinces, he made his London music-hall debut in 1864. A reviewer at the London Pavilion noted: 'Mr Vance is one of the prominent draws here at present . . . His comicality is of an easy and spontaneous character. Altogether, there is a freshness and geniality in Mr Vance's efforts worthy of every acknowledgement.'[2]

One of his best-known songs was 'Walking in the Zoo' (1869). Others included a motto song, 'Act on the Square, Boys' (1866), in other words, 'act openly or honestly'; 'Clicquot' (1867), extolling champagne; 'The Chickaleary Cove' (1870), roughly translated as 'the artful fellow' ('chickaleary' was probably a hybrid of 'cheeky' and 'leery'); and 'Dolly Varden' (1872), the 'very impersonation of good humour and blooming beauty' in Dickens's *Barnaby Rudge*. Vance was sometimes criticised for the nonsense of his songs. At other times, he tended towards the risqué, but he and his choruses became so popular that, in Liverpool, for example, graffiti based on his song 'Come to Your Martha, Come, Come, Come' (1868) were scrawled on walls. (The central character in the song was Martha Gunn, who, for more than seventy years, was in charge of bathing machines in Brighton.) One who could not understand Vance's popularity was Mr E.,[3] an occasional correspondent in *The Performer* in the 1930s: 'His voice was loud enough and fairly distinct, but rather spoiled by a nasal accent.'[4] Nevertheless, Vance became a personal favourite of the Prince of Wales, later Edward VII, who presented him with a handsome jewelled stick. After it was stolen from him, the thief returned it with a note saying that Vance was not 'the sort of chap I'd rob'.

During the mid-1870s, Vance toured England and Wales extensively, but his long absences from London undermined his reputation there:

> When he returned to the London halls, other singers had established themselves and new audiences sprang up – facts which were decidedly hostile to him, but which he had to face. With the increase of music halls, too, came a flood of additional comic singers; so that, of late years, competition has been twenty times more acute than when poor Vance commenced his professional career. To his honour, however, be it said, he occupied a good position to the bitter end.[5]

The Great Vance. The Versatile! The Inimitable! *(Richard Anthony Baker)*

During the late 1880s, Vance appeared to slow down. Some of his vigour disappeared; even his singing, Mr E. would have been distressed to hear, deteriorated. Towards the end of his life, he appeared at the Harp music hall in Ramsgate. He shared the bill with the singer-songwriter, F.V. St Clair, who said that he saw more champagne flow that week than he had ever seen. Glass after glass was handed up to Vance, most of it going to the rest of the company backstage.

On Boxing Day, 1888, Vance was appearing at the Sun music hall nearly opposite the Knightsbridge Barracks, when, halfway through his third song, he stopped at the line, 'For the rest of my natural life', rapidly left the stage and collapsed. His head was bathed, medical assistance was sought, a cab was called and he was taken to hospital. By the time he arrived, he had died, apparently of a heart attack. He was 49.

His funeral was, to say the least, controversial. A clergyman from Bedfordshire asked to take the service as he wanted to make a personal statement. He told the mourners that, when he was young, he fell into bad company, began drinking heavily and neglected his studies. He met Vance one night at the bar of the Oxford:

> I'm afraid I was in a rather uproarious state and using language which I should not. Anyway, I felt a tug at my coat. I turned and found a man, evidently a stage professional. He compelled

me to go aside with him, saying, as he did so, 'My dear lad, evidently you're with people who are no good to you. Pull yourself together, you young fool, and come out with me.' He made me go to a little brougham, took me to his lodgings, pulled me round and sobered me. Indeed, he was earnest and so kind and cheery that he made me feel ashamed. I told him who I was and how my parents were paying and praying for me to study to serve my God. 'You shall do it yet, my lad,' said my mysterious awakener and helper . . . Week after week, night after night, he took me about with him around the music halls – to do his turn and then home to his place. He never left me till he had set me on my feet again and had seen me pull round (and) resume my studies.[6]

One of Vance's obituarists wrote:

At his most triumphant period, [he] was constantly being snapped at by cavillers, who endeavoured to show that he had won his position by a fluke. He bore no ill-will to those who had ceremoniously criticised him and did many a good turn for persons who, in their time, had acted anything but generously to him Like a plucky warrior, he stuck to his post and died working in the thick of the fight.[7]

G.H. MacDermott modelled himself on Vance. In turn, actor, playwright, music-hall star and theatre proprietor, he began his working life selling the *Islington Gazette*. Then he joined the Navy, serving nine years in all. Amateur shows on board ship made him think he could earn his living in the professional theatre and, when he left the Navy, he started work at a theatre in Dover, where two performances were staged nightly, one for a military audience, the other, civilian. Accustomed to hard work in the Navy, it was nothing to MacDermott to play as many as seven different parts in a week.

GILBERT HASTINGS MACDERMOTT (Michael
　Farrell)
Born Islington, north London, 20 August 1845
Married (1) —
(2) Annie Milburn
　Three sons, Edward (b. 1884); Gilbert
　(b. 1886); James (b. 1887)
　Daughter Annie Louise Mary (1889–1980)
　(professionally known as Ouida
　MacDermott) who married (1) Sydney
　Wood (b. 1 April 1885), brother of Marie
　Lloyd, July 1909, (2) J. Chapman
　(professionally known as Jay Laurier), 23
　December 1912
Died Lambeth, London, 8 May 1901
Left £13,594

Moving to London, MacDermott appeared at the Oriental Theatre in Poplar, a theatre that survived until 1964, and then, in 1870, at the Grecian Theatre, where he augmented a small salary by writing plays for an extra £5 each, sometimes using the pseudonym Gilbert Hastings. In 1872, his dramatisation of Dickens's *The Mystery of Edwin Drood* received particularly good notices.

In 1873, Henry Pettitt, who was also involved with the Grecian, wrote a song that encouraged MacDermott to start a new career as a music-hall singer. On Christmas Eve 1873, MacDermott opened in a pantomime at the Oriental, called *Harlequin Aladdin or The Wizard, The Ring and The Scamp*. It is unclear whether Pettitt had any part in the show, but, by the spring of 1874, MacDermott was appearing at halls billed as the original Scamp, singing Pettitt's song 'The Scamp':

If ever there was a damned scamp,
I flatter myself I am he;
From Brigham to Odger,
There isn't a dodger
Who can hold a candle to me!

In all, four 'scamps' are named in the song: Cain, who killed his brother, Abel; the American Mormon leader, Brigham Young; Arthur Orton, the Tichborne claimant;[8] and George Odger, an un-educated shoemaker, who became a prominent trade unionist. One night, when MacDermott was singing the song at the London Pavilion, Odger's son, who was in the audience, protested loudly about his father being denounced as a scamp. A court case ensued; the magistrates ruled in favour of the son; and, from then on, MacDermott had to change the lyric.

Even so, the song caused a scandal. One London paper described it as: 'A glorification of vice of the meanest order . . . its distinguishing feature is the self-satisfied relish with which the singer bursts out, after the enumeration of his disgraceful action, into a chorus apropos of accursed rascality. The song is one which could only exert an evil influence.'[9]

G.H. MacDermott changed the image of music hall with his 'War Song'. *(Richard Anthony Baker)*

But the song established MacDermott as a star. At the end of July 1875, he sailed for New York and worked in America until the following spring. In 1876, he had a new hit, 'Hildebrandt Montrose', which poked fun at the aesthete movement five years before Gilbert and Sullivan's *Patience* – with two more to follow in 1877, 'Dear Old Pals' and 'MacDermott's War Song'. Despite his experience, a new song or a new venue set MacDermott's nerves on edge:

When I sing at a new place, I am so nervous that I drink off a pint of champagne the moment before I go on just to get Dutch courage. The glare and the glamour of the singer's life are very often fatal. He has little to do and is surrounded by many friends. Probably I have wasted thousands in horse-racing and betting. It is the excitement of the moment that does it. An actor has his parts to study and he has also a social status. That is what we have not. I say we have more temptations to excess than almost any other people – either drink or betting.[10]

The 'War Song' made the greatest impact on music hall that audiences had so far witnessed. Russia, which was on the point of invading Turkey, was threatening Britain's naval supremacy in the Mediterranean. Each night at the London Pavilion, MacDermott whipped up such strong patriotic feelings that army recruitment officers were dotted among the audience watching out for the most fervid young nationalists:

> We don't want to fight but, by Jingo, if we do,
> We've got the ships, we've got the men, we've got the money too
> We've fought the Bear before and while we're Britons true
> The Russians shall not have Constantinople.

MacDermott's salary rose from £6 to £25 a week and, for two years, the song was all the rage:

> G.W. Hunt wrote the song and sent it to me, saying 'Dear Mac, I am afraid you'll find this song too strong to sing. If so, throw it away, but 'them's my sentiments'. They were my sentiments too. I am not an ardent politician. But that was a moment when national sentiment – patriotism – was touched. The song embodied the spirit of the moment and found an echo in everybody's bosom. For my own part, I swear I never sang that song without feeling every word of it. How it went! I let 'em have it every time and they returned the chorus as earnestly.[11]

When Hunt first sent MacDermott the song, MacDermott tried it out, decided he did not like it and did indeed throw it away. Later, however, the chorus kept coming back to him; so much so that, when he returned home in the early hours of the following morning, he and his wife spent an hour searching for the screwed-up piece of paper. When he found it, he went through the song again, changed his mind and paid Hunt £5 for it.

G.W. HUNT (George William Hunt)
Born *c.* 1838
Married
  Two sons, Arthur and William
  One daughter, Laura
Died Brentwood, Essex, 1 March 1904
Left £502

MacDermott began the song upstage, making his way down to the footlights with a series of dramatic little hops, each hop underlining the determination of the lyric. Then, he made a threatening gesture to accompany the line 'The Russians shall not have Constantinople'. It was that line which echoed the public attitude exactly. MacDermott sang the song night after night to thunderous applause.

It marked an important juncture in the history of the halls since visitors to London, who would never previously have dreamed of visiting such infamous places, crowded into the Pavilion to hear MacDermott. MPs, even, it was said, Lord Beaconsfield (formerly Benjamin Disraeli), made their way from the Commons to cheer MacDermott. Music hall, which until then had been despised in Parliament, suddenly acquired a welcome political perspective. The lyrics were quoted by statesmen; they were shouted in the street; they even alarmed the Russians.

There were stories that MacDermott was subsidised by the Conservatives, but he told the songwriter Richard Morton that he would never sing a song until he was convinced that it was absolutely suitable for him. 'I cannot afford to risk a failure,' he said.

The song was later parodied by Henry Pettitt. It provided the Drury Lane pantomime favourite, Herbert Campbell, with his first big success:

I don't want to fight, I'll be slaughtered if I do.
I'll change my togs [clothes],
I'll sell my kit and pop [pawn] my rifle too.
I don't like the war. I ain't a 'Briton true'.
And I'll let the Russians have Constantinople.

The success of MacDermott's 'War Song' had an unfortunate repercussion on its writer. He was known from then on as Jingo Hunt, but, over the years, the word 'jingo' acquired a pejorative sense: its definition changed from 'patriotic' to 'nationalistic'. Hunt eventually defended himself:

The Solicitor General in one of his most important speeches made the following remarks: 'When an opponent in politics calls you "a Jingo", ask the man what he means. A factious opposition show their poverty of invention by seizing upon a word used in a popular song to hurl at those who do not choose to agree with them.' I certainly never imagined, when I introduced the word 'jingo' in the 'War Song' that so much would be made of so little. However, a man who loves his country and desires that it should retain its foremost position among nations will – thanks to the Liberals – be henceforth known as a Jingo.[12]

After the 'War Song', G.H. MacDermott enjoyed just one more success, a Fred Gilbert song, 'Charlie Dilke upset the milk' (1885). During that year, a distinguished politician, Sir Charles Wentworth Dilke, was named in a divorce case. At that time, divorce had been possible, other than by a private Act of Parliament, for less than thirty years; Dilke was considered a possible future Prime Minister; and the woman at the centre of the scandal was Virginia Crawford, the sister-in-law of Sir Charles's younger brother, Ashton. The allegations against Dilke were severe: prosecuting counsel accused him of 'coarse, brutal adultery more befitting a beast than a man'. Dilke was charged with 'having done with an English lady what any man of proper feeling would shrink from doing with a prostitute in a French brothel'.

Every day, the papers salivated over each detail of the case. Gilbert did little to improve an already delicate situation by writing this song for MacDermott:

Master Dilke upset the milk
Taking it home to Chelsea.
The papers say that Charlie's gay
Rather a wilful wag.
This noble representative
Of everything good in Chelsea.
Has let the cat, the naughty cat
Right out of the Gladstone bag.

Audiences loved the song and its fame spread far and wide. It was translated into every language imaginable: one scholar even framed it in Latin hendecasyllables, but it brought MacDermott further allegations of impropriety. He had his own ideas about how to control questionable material:

What I should like to see is a music hall censor, who should license our songs, just as there is a censor who licenses a play . . . At present, we have many censors and the music hall is always

In the early days of song publishing, there were so many loopholes in copyright legislation that it was almost incomprehensible. G.W. Hunt was sucked into the maelstrom by a comic singer, Harry Wall, who had given up his career to manage that of his wife, Annie Adams. He took to his new role with rather too much enthusiasm: he was once fined for hitting a man who had hissed at her, but that was nothing compared to the problems he created by exploiting the confusion over copyright.

He began his campaign while Annie was on a tour of America between 1871 and 1873. In court, he contended that the sheet music of the Hunt song, 'When the Band Begins to Play', was being sold illegally by publishers in New York. American lawyers argued that the song was in the public domain, having been 'daily dispensed to hungry music urchins by street hand-organs in the City of London over 100 years previously'. Needless to say, this angered Hunt, who said that they might as well have contended that it was 'popular with shoeblacks prior to the construction of Noah's Ark'. He insisted he had written the song in 1870 and added: 'My songs have been republished in the United States under anybody's name but mine for the past twelve years.' Wall secured an American copyright for the song, but lost his case.

Back in Britain, Wall caused anxiety and panic among music-hall proprietors, publishers and artistes alike. He formed an organisation he called the Copyright and Performing Right Protection Office, demanding fees from theatre owners when they allowed the performance of a song, whose copyright, Wall alleged, was being breached. There was no doubt that Wall represented some publishers, possibly only minor ones, but no one in the business knew which. One of his critics suggested his organisation would be better called the Society for the Suppression of Permitting Music to be Performed in Public.

Wall had some success in extracting money from frightened proprietors, but he eventually overstepped himself. By 1888, he was regularly visiting theatres and music halls suggesting that each proprietor subscribe 10 guineas (£10.50) a year to his Copyright Protection Association, as it was now called, or 'take their chance' against being sued for breach of copyright. A complaint was made to the Law Society about the way the Association was run and, in August 1888, Wall was sentenced to three months' imprisonment for practising as a solicitor.

looked at through green spectacles and as an article without the official stamp of decency. Then, the public winks and thinks there's something naughty . . . We are confined by all manner of regulations imposed by our managers. Your songs are read to see if they are safe. If there's a risky line, out it goes. If you afterwards introduce a line on the stage, you are liable to instant dismissal . . . My song about Sir Charles Dilke . . . is fair comment for the newspapers; he is fair capital for me. But read the song and you will not find a word of offensive personality in it. It is merely a skit on a scandal . . . Even in my political songs I never make a personal attack . . . I never gag and never patter, merely singing my songs just as they are published.[13]

Hunt was the first man to earn his living by selling songs to entertainers, a career he pursued (at first, without serious competition) for more than thirty years. He began writing songs at the age of 19. After spending some time in South Africa, he returned to Britain in about 1860, settling in Islington. In November 1860, the Philharmonic Hall opened in Islington High Street. (It was subsequently the Islington Empire, was converted into a cinema in 1932, was closed in 1962 and later demolished.) Hunt went there soon after the opening to see two singers popular at the time, Tom MacLagan and Fred French. With the United States on the brink of civil war, he wrote a powerful song about slavery, '(Poor Old) Uncle Sam', which earned enormous acclaim for MacLagan.

Besides MacLagan, Hunt wrote for every major singer of his day. Arthur Lloyd achieved his fame with Hunt's 'The German Band' (1865):

G.W. Hunt, music hall's first songwriter.
(*Richard Anthony Baker*)

> I loved her and she might have been
> The happiest in the land.
> But she fancied a foreigner
> Who played the flageolet
> In the middle of a German band.

Lloyd was the son of a comic actor. In 1856, he joined the company at the Theatre Royal in Plymouth, but, after two seasons there, he returned home to work with his father in a show, which was staged at various venues throughout Scotland.

Lloyd made his music-hall debut at the Whitebait in Glasgow at a salary of £4 a week. (Years later, he appeared there at £60 a week.) For several years, he toured Britain enjoying increasing popularity and eventually making his first London appearance in 1862 at the Philharmonic, Sun and Marylebone music halls.

In 1863, Lloyd wrote an enormous success, 'The Song of (Many) Songs', the sheet music of which sold by the thousand. Four years later, he sang 'Not for Joe', the idea of which came to him from hearing a bus conductor repeatedly tell his passengers 'Not for me. Not for Joe'. Lloyd used to say that, by the time he had left the bus, he had the chorus and melody

Arthur Lloyd, the Royal Comique.
(*Richard Anthony Baker*)

ARTHUR LLOYD (Arthur Rice Lloyd)
Born Edinburgh, 14 May 1839
Married Catherine Olivia King (professionally known as Katty King), Kennington, south London, 31 July 1871 (d. London, 2 May 1891)
Six children: (1) Annie (b. Clapham, south London, 1873; married Joseph Henry Murray; d. Edinburgh 7 June 1923); (2) Harry Robert (b. Clapham 1874; d. London, 1948; married first Margaret Leah Russell (also known as Lily Day) and secondly Catherine Maud Kennett (d. Farnborough, Kent, 1965) in 1904 (dissolved 1925)); (3) Dulcie (b. *c.* 1875); (4) Katherine (b. Dublin, 1876); (5) Lilian (b. Dublin, 1877); (6) Arthur (b. *c.* 1879)
Died Edinburgh, 20 July 1904

complete. It became the first comic song to sell 100,000 copies of sheet music.

In 1876, Lloyd was credited with writing the MacDermott hit 'Hildebrandt Montrose':

'Au revoir, ta ta!' you'll hear him say
To the Marchioness Clerkenwell while bidding her good day.
'I'll strike with you a feather. I'll stab you with a rose,
For the darling of the ladies is Hildebrandt Montrose.'

The truth emerged some years later. Lloyd wrote the melody, but it was originally intended for a song he sang himself, 'Promenade Elastique'. MacDermott had brought back the lyric (albeit an Americanised version) from a visit to New York, where it was all the rage, written and sung by Ned Harrigan (1845–1911), one-half of a double act, Harrigan and Hart. The first two lines of the chorus ran: 'Ta-ta, ta-ta, my baby dear, I'll meet you in the park when the weather it is clear.' English audiences were not then ready for references to 'my baby', so MacDermott persuaded Lloyd to anglicise the lyric for him.[14]

After the success of 'The German Band', Hunt received a letter from an unknown singer working in the North and the Midlands, asking for a similar song. Hunt replied: 'When you, sir, are another Arthur Lloyd, I will write you another German Band.' The singer was George Leybourne. Through talent and hard work, Leybourne came to challenge Lloyd's position and, over the next few years, Hunt wrote practically all of Leybourne's greatest successes.

George Leybourne, the Lion
Comique. (Richard Anthony Baker)

GEORGE LEYBOURNE
Born Gateshead, Tyne and Wear,
17 March 1842
Married Annie Fisher
One son, one daughter,
Florence Isabella
Died Islington, north London,
15 September 1884

Leybourne and Hunt had an eccentric method of working. Hunt often went to Leybourne's house in the morning. He remained downstairs, playing some of his tunes on the harmonium, while Leybourne stayed in bed upstairs, shouting out from time to time when he heard something that pleased him. Hunt said: 'An appointment would be made. Leybourne would invariably be horizontal. To save time, I would resort to the harmonium. By the time he was down, he would know the melody. He had a fine ear for melody and, of the fifty-odd songs he had of mine, all were sung and he never made a failure.'[15] The two greatest songs of Leybourne, dubbed the Lion Comique, are still heard today: 'Champagne Charlie' (1866) and '(The Daring Young Man on) the Flying Trapeze' (1867).

Leybourne began his working life as an engineer, but, after seeing Arthur Lloyd perform, he found a new ambition. Lloyd said Leybourne had told him: 'After I had listened to you one night, I went home to Newcastle and told my father that I had made up my mind to be a comic singer. The old man replied "You! A comic singer! And where, I should like to know, do you get your comicality from? It can't possibly be me and certainly it is not from your mother."'[16] Using the name Joe Saunders, Leybourne made one of his earliest music-hall appearances in the early 1860s at the Lord Nelson in Stepney, east London, where he earned 12 shillings (60p) a week.

During 1865, while working at Collins', Leybourne met the pianist there, Alfred Lee, who started writing songs for him. These provided the breakthrough Leybourne needed. The first was 'Champagne Charlie', for which Leybourne wrote the words:

> Champagne Charlie is my name,
> Champagne Charlie is my name
> Good for any game at night, my boys
> Good for any game at night, my boys,
> Champagne Charlie is my name,
> Champagne Charlie is my name
> Good for any game at night, my boys,
> Who'll come and join me in a spree?

Leybourne was a tall and handsome man with a commanding stage presence. His voice was untrained, but an intuitive sense of drama helped him convey a song superbly. 'Champagne Charlie' established him. By June 1867, Leybourne and Lee produced 'The Flying Trapeze', based on the exploits of the French trapeze artist, Leotard, who caused a sensation at the Alhambra in 1861 when he performed his act over the audience without a net. He returned to London from his native France several times before dying of smallpox in 1870 at the age of 28:

> He'd fly through the air with the greatest of ease,
> A daring young man on the flying trapeze.
> His movements were graceful. All girls he could please
> And my love he purloined away.

It was when William Holland took over the Canterbury that Leybourne secured his place at the top of his profession. Holland paid him £30 a week and gave him a carriage drawn by four white horses so that he could ride about town to advertise himself. (The comedian Harry Liston mocked the ritual by riding about in a carriage drawn by four white donkeys.) In time, Leybourne's salary reached £120 a week.

Offstage, he began to live the life of the man-about-town he portrayed on stage. He drank champagne by the tankard and, like so many music-hall folk, he was generous to a fault. Fair-weather friends borrowed his money and drank his wine; at the same time, he helped poorer people, paying their doctors' bills.

Towards the end of his life, as work became scarcer and his fair-weather friends disappeared, he suffered deep fits of depression. The music-hall proprietor Oswald Stoll used to recall that, when, while still in his teens, he booked Leybourne to appear at the Parthenon in Liverpool, there was no sign of him when the programme started. Stoll went round to his lodgings and found him huddled in a chair. 'Come along, Mr Leybourne, your friends are waiting for you,' he said. 'Friends!' replied Leybourne. 'I have no friends. My curse upon the men who called themselves my friends.'

Stoll managed to persuade Leybourne to go to the theatre. There, Leybourne collapsed in the wings, but, when the band started playing his music, he jumped up and strode onto the stage. Full of his old charm, he sang five songs and was wildly applauded. Once back in the wings, he again collapsed.

One of his last songs was Joseph Tabrar's 'Ting, Ting, That's How the Bell Goes' (1883), a song about a waitress working in a tea shop, which has a bell on each table. The man who had glorified champagne ended up singing about tea.

He died penniless: 'I don't say it is wrong for a man to drink champagne; but, if to drink it, his wife and children are to be robbed, then I think we had better be without it.'[17]

In 1944, *Champagne Charlie*, a feature film about Leybourne and Vance, was released, starring Tommy Trinder and Stanley Holloway. It is fun to watch, but bears little similarity to the truth.

CHAPTER 4

TROIKA

A year after Leybourne's death, music hall's three greatest entertainers emerged: Marie Lloyd, Dan Leno and Little Tich. Marie, who could load an apparently innocent song with silent innuendo, delighted audiences across Britain. At home, however, she endured a largely unhappy private life. Dan, the star of a long run of spectacular Drury Lane pantomimes, saw his career ended by a series of nervous breakdowns. The diminutive Tich became famous across Europe for dancing in boots nearly as long as he was tall. Towards the end of his career, the stunt crippled him.

Audiences loved Marie Lloyd not only for how she entertained them, but equally for what she was: a big-hearted woman who laughed in the face of adversity. A star by the age of 20, she stayed at the top of the bill until her premature death thirty-two years later. She sang a wide range of character songs that changed as she matured from pert young woman to plump middle-aged matron. She also sang saucy songs, made saucier by a wink, a naughty look, a flick of her dress. Generous to the point of self-deprivation, she was unlucky in love, the victim of two husbands who beat her.

Born Matilda Wood, Marie was the daughter of an artificial flower maker, who also worked as a barman at the Eagle music hall in the evening. After leaving school, she had a number of jobs, but set her sights on becoming an entertainer after her mother's sister, a dancer, known on the halls as Louise Patti, had returned from a trip to the Continent. At her local parish church, Marie formed a troupe called the Fairy Bell Minstrels, which included her younger sister, Alice, and staged a show in which she recited a temperance song, 'Throw down the Bottle and Never Drink Again'.

Probably at the suggestion of her father, Marie made her music-hall debut early in 1885. Still called Matilda Wood, she sang 'The Good Old Times', a song owned, in fact, by another entertainer, Jessie Acton. Within a week, she was earning 5 shillings (25p) a turn at three other halls. Marie briefly changed her name to Bella Delmeyer (or

MARIE LLOYD (Matilda Alice Victoria Wood)
Born Hoxton, London, 12 February 1870
Married (1) Percy Courtenay, 12 November 1887 (divorced 1904)
  One daughter, Myria Matilda Victoria (professionally known as Marie Lloyd junior; b. 19 May 1888; d. 26/7 December 1967)
(2) Alec Hurley, 27 October 1906 (registered at birth 24 March 1871 in Whitechapel, east London, as Alexander Early; d. 6 December 1913)
(3) Bernard Dillon, 21 February 1914 (separated 1920; d. 6 May 1940)
Died Golders Green, London, 7 October 1922
Left £7,334

Marie Lloyd, the Queen of Comedy. (Richard Anthony Baker)

Yours Always
Marie Lloyd

Delmere or Delmare) and sang Nellie Power's song 'The Boy in the Gallery', before being signed up by the agent George Ware, who had written the song and who dreamed up her new name, Marie Lloyd:

> The boy I love is up in the gallery.
> The boy I love is looking now at me.
> There he is. Can't you see?
> Waving his handkerchief
> As merry as a robin that sings on a tree.

Over the next three years, Marie appeared at larger and better halls in the London area, her big break coming in 1890 when George le Brunn and a schoolmaster, W.T. Lytton, wrote her first big success, 'Wink the Other Eye'.

In the autumn of 1890, Marie made the first of five trips to America, appearing at Koster and Bial's music hall in New York and attracting welcoming notices. The following year, she was booked for her first pantomime, *Humpty Dumpty* at Drury Lane, also starring Tich and Leno. Within a matter of months, her weekly earnings had shot from £10 to £100 (by today's standards, £6,000).

In 1892, Marie set off on her first extended tour of provincial halls with a number of new songs, one of them eventually becoming one of her most durable, 'Oh! Mr Porter', written by George and Thomas le Brunn.

> Oh, Mr Porter, what shall I do?
> I want to go to Birmingham and they're taking me on to Crewe.
> Send me back to London as quickly as you can
> Oh, Mr Porter, what a silly girl I am!

At the end of 1892, Marie was back at the Lane with *Little Bo-Peep, Little Red Riding Hood and Hop of My Thumb* and in 1893 with *Robinson Crusoe*. In one scene in *Robinson Crusoe*, Marie had to kneel at the bedside and say her prayers. One night, Little Tich, who was standing in the wings, thought he would replace sentiment with hilarity. He shouted at Marie: 'Look under the bed.' She did and then, not finding the expected chamber pot, searched the stage for it. The audience was in hysterics, but Augustus Harris, who ran the Lane, was incandescent with rage. He even considered sacking Marie, but relented. Even so, it was the last time that either Marie or Little Tich appeared at Drury Lane.

Marie made her second trip to New York in 1894, but it was not as happy as the first. She was harassed by the manager of the Imperial Theatre, where she appeared, and was then sued by her previous American employers, Koster and Bial. After a visit to South Africa and another to America, Marie appeared in her only musical comedy in 1898, *The ABC Girl*, in which she played a waitress. It toured for eight weeks, but quietly died before reaching the West End. More successful was a new Harrington/le Brunn song, 'Everything in the Garden's Lovely' (1898).

After a disastrous marriage to a violent man-about-town, Percy Courtenay (they were together for seven years and had a daughter, Marie's only child), Marie had a new man in her life, Alec Hurley, a singer who eschewed all the raucousness of the music hall. (In a later generation, Bud Flanagan of the Crazy Gang modelled his quiet singing style on Hurley.) Marie and Alec toured Australia together in 1901 and married in 1906. He was different from Courtenay: modest and mild-mannered, but, needless to say, professionally forever in Marie's shadow, something that eventually resulted in them growing apart. Marie met her third husband at her daughter's wedding: Bernard Dillon, a successful 20-year-old jockey. She was flattered by the attention he paid her and, less than three months after Hurley's death in London in 1913, she and Dillon married in Oregon. He turned out to be even more violent than Courtenay.

Before all that, in 1907, Marie undertook her most extensive transatlantic tour to date, but this time she ran into criticism, a rare experience for her. The showbiz paper *Variety* found that it was enjoying her younger sister, Alice, better.

When Marie travelled to America with Dillon in 1913, there was further trouble. Immigration officials agreed to admit her, but insisted that Dillon return to Britain. Marie refused to let him go and lodged an appeal. As a result, she spent the first night of her visit as an undesirable immigrant on the infamous Ellis Island. She won her appeal, but, for the duration of her tour, she and Dillon were ordered to live apart. On her return to Britain, Marie made it clear she never intended to appear in America again. In fact, her fifth American tour was her last foreign trip anywhere. Within two months, the world was at war.

Marie was determined to be as charitable in wartime as she was in peacetime. Before 1914, the music-hall world knew her as a woman who never turned away someone in trouble. She bought boots for poor children and often handed her weekly earnings to a local orphanage. During the First World War, she staged shows and arranged dinners for troops and gave most of her earnings in the provinces to the wounded. Her private philosophy was summed up in the song, 'A Little of what you Fancy Does you Good' (1915), written by George Arthurs and Fred W. Leigh.

The passing of the years did not treat Marie well. Her health started to suffer and, after years of punishingly hard work and cruelty at the hands of two husbands, she succumbed to a nervous breakdown. She fought back, but, from then on, did much less work, even though there were further hit songs, the first, 'Don't Dilly Dally' (1919), written by Charles Collins and Fred W. Leigh:

> My old man said 'Follow the van.
> Don't dilly-dally on the way.'
> Off went the cart with the home packed in it.
> I walked behind with my old cock linnet.
> But I dillied and dallied,
> Dallied and dillied,
> Lost my way and don't know where to roam.
> I stopped on the way to have the old half quartern
> And I can't find my way home.

The second acknowledged Dillon's maltreatment of her, 'It's (I'm) a bit of a ruin that Cromwell knocked about a bit' (1920), written by Harry Bedford and Terry Sullivan:

It's (I'm) a bit of a ruin that Cromwell knocked about a bit,
One that Oliver Cromwell knocked about a bit.
In the gay old days, there used to be some doings.
No wonder that the poor old Abbey went to ruins.
Those who've studied history sing and shout of it.
And you can bet your life there isn't a doubt of it.
Outside the Oliver Cromwell last Saturday night,
I was one of the ruins that Cromwell knocked about a bit.

Ill health dogged Marie's last few years. At the Edmonton Empire one night in October 1922, she collapsed as the curtain fell. Three days later, after several hours in a coma, she died in the arms of her sister, Rosie, with tears on her cheeks.

Her death stunned the nation and, at her funeral, at least 50,000 people lined the route. T.S. Eliot wrote: 'No other comedian succeeded so well in giving expression to the life of [an] audience – in raising it to a kind of art.'[1]

The Marie Lloyd mystery: *Marie Lloyd's Blue Book* was reviewed in *The Era* in August 1896, but a copy has never been seen.

Dan Leno vied with Marie as the most accomplished and most popular entertainer in music hall. A small, wiry man, he looked permanently worried. As Marie once famously commented: 'Ever seen his eyes? The saddest eyes in the whole world. That's why we all laughed at Danny. Because if we hadn't laughed, we should have cried ourselves sick.'[2] And yet, Leno's comedy ensured him the starring role in no fewer than sixteen consecutive Drury Lane pantomimes. Like Marie, his life came to a tragic and early end.

Dan Leno was born in a tiny slum, the site now covered by St Pancras station in London. His parents were itinerant entertainers, who called themselves 'Mr and Mrs Johnny Wilde, singing and acting duettists'. Dan's father, an alcoholic, died when Dan was only 4. Dan's mother remarried. Her second husband was another alcoholic itinerant performer, whose stage name was Leno. Before long, Dan was part of the family act. He made his professional debut at the age of 4 at the Cosmotheca music hall in Paddington, which flourished under Joe Cave during the 1860s. He was billed then as 'Little George, the Infant Wonder,

DAN LENO (George Wild Galvin)
Born London, 20 December 1860
Married Sarah Reynolds (professionally known as Lydia Reynolds), Hulme, Greater Manchester, 15 December 1883 (she married secondly Charles Best, a comedian, in Brixton, south London, 26 June 1907)
Two daughters, four sons: Georgina Louisa (b. 2 October 1884; married Sydney Reginald Lubbock 1903)
John William (b. 16 April 1888)
Ernest George (b. 26 May 1889; married Marjorie Bowyer, daughter of Frederick Bowyer, July 1911)
Sidney Paul (b. 31 July 1891; became Dan Leno junior)
Herbert Dan (b. 3 May 1893)
and May Lilian (b. 10 October 1895)
Died London 31 October 1904
Left £10,945

Contortionist and Posturer'. Dressed in his mother's black stockings, he did a short dance his older brother, Jack, had taught him. By the time Dan was 6, he and Jack were a dancing double act, the Great Little Lenos, sometimes appearing at music halls, sometimes busking outside pubs. When Dan was 8, he made his debut as a solo performer as the Great Little Leno at the Britannia, Hoxton.[3]

During his teens, he turned to clog-dancing, winning the title Champion Clog Dancer of the World at the Princess's music hall in Leeds. Clog-dancing never caught on in southern England and Dan dropped it from his act after a while.

An illustration of the itinerant life of such performers as Dan, his mother and stepfather was given by a man who came to be a close friend, Arthur Stevens. Early in 1875, the Leno family had played four small halls in Leicester: Paul's; the Rainbow and Dove; the Antelope; and the Barley Mow. They then played Sutton-in-Ashfield for a week. It was while they were walking the twenty miles through Nottinghamshire to Newark to fulfil a further week's engagement at the new White Hart in Carter-gate that Stevens met them for the first time. At the lodging-house where they had stayed the previous night, they had had to forfeit breakfast as they could not afford it. Stevens treated them to bread and cheese at an inn in the village of Kelham:

> During the week, he [Dan] stayed at Newark, I was a frequent visitor to the new White Hart and saw the lad give several performances. He sang and danced with exceptional ability for one so young and, during his show, a variegated rat ran round him, perched upon his shoulder or found a resting-place in the outside pocket of his costume. The Australian or variegated rat was then quite a novelty in this country and hence it added an extra effort to what was in itself a very smart and attractive turn. The landlord was delighted with the lad and prophesied that he would go a long way if he had a fair chance.[4]

As an adult, Dan made his first appearance in London in October 1885 at the Foresters in the Mile End, a hall which lasted until 1960. He sang two songs, 'Going to Buy Milk for the Twins' and 'When Rafferty Raffled his Watch'. For nearly twenty years, Dan played the halls in the guise of a wide range of comic characters: the railway guard, the detective, the County Councillor, the holiday-maker and many more. As time went by, his songs grew shorter. They were merely the quickest way of getting to his patter, in which he lovingly satirised whichever character he was playing. The unseen 'Mrs Kelly' was a favourite, which he recounted somewhat camply: 'You know, Mrs Kelly, of course. Mrs Kelly. Mrs Kelly. You know Mrs Kelly. Good life a-mighty! Don't look so simple. She's a cousin of Mrs Niplett's and her husband keeps the little what-not shop at the – Oh! You must know Mrs Kelly!'

Dan appeared in his first pantomime as Dame Durden in *Jack and the Beanstalk* at the Royal Surrey Theatre in 1886/7. The run of Drury Lane pantomimes began in 1888. He was teamed with Herbert Campbell, who, with a big round face, a loud voice and weighing more than 20 stone, was the perfect foil.

Leno achieved such fame that he once shared a matinée performance with the great classical actor Sir Henry Irving, who sought advice on the running order from the music-hall writer H. Chance Newton:

> 'I suppose' [Irving] added, 'being, I may say, the chief star in this variety bill, I ought to follow Mr Leno.'

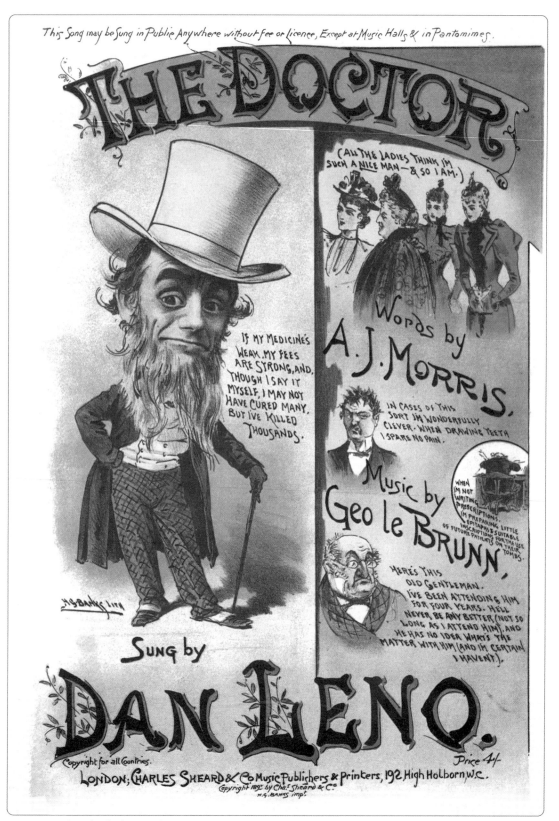

Dan Leno, the Chief of Comedians. *(Richard Anthony Baker)*

'I hope you will do nothing of the kind, Irving,' I replied. 'Dan Leno is not only the greatest comedian and greatest comic dancer in the music halls, he is also a tremendous favourite in pantomime and at every theatre wherever he appears. If you follow him, even with a lighter kind of recitation than you usually give at charity matinées, you'll have the hardest job an actor ever had.'

'It was because I knew that you knew Leno that I sent for you,' said Irving, 'and asked for your advice. Of course, I shall take that advice.' Irving not only kept his promise to me and preceded dear, droll little Dan at that matinée, he also waited in the wings and saw Dan's turn. Irving laughed until he cried at Leno's business.[5]

Dan made his one and only American appearance in 1897, a four-week engagement at Hammerstein's Olympia music hall in New York. It was a mistake to announce him as the Funniest Man on Earth and reviewers gave differing accounts of his first night: 'It was absurd to presume that a London concert-hall singer could throw a New York audience into paroxysms of laughter. The jokes and the humour of the English vaudeville stage are, as a rule, so terribly out of date that the importation of them to this country is apt to be a failure.'[6]

Another New York paper was more generous: 'When the New York public gets to know Dan Leno well and Dan Leno gets to know the New York public well, there is no doubt about it: he'll be nearly as big a favourite here as he is on his native heath.'[7]

Dan was relieved to get back to London. In 1898, he had two new ventures to try, *Dan Leno's Comic Journal*, a weekly paper, which he edited and which ran for nearly two years, and a musical comedy, *Orlando Dando*, which toured for six weeks, earning him £125 a week. (He starred in two further musical comedies, George R. Sims's *In Gay Piccadilly*, which toured during 1899, and Herbert Darnley's *Mr Wix of Wickham*, which toured in 1902.)

Dan was now at the height of his powers. Having left his impoverished childhood far behind him, he and his wife lived in a large detached house set in 3 acres in Brixton, south London. He was earning huge sums, although he lost a lot in a management enterprise with Herbert Campbell; a leading comic singer and pantomime favourite, Harry Randall; and another comic, Fred Williams. They were involved with five theatres, a 700-seater near Clapham Junction, which they renamed the Grand Hall, Clapham; a larger hall nearby; the Croydon Empire; the Granville at Walham Green, which was designed by Frank Matcham; and the Palace at Camberwell. The owners of chains of halls, which by now were doing big business, ruined the venture by inserting a clause in the contracts of all entertainers they employed, barring them from appearing at theatres owned by Dan and his partners. It was a move that cost the four men thousands of pounds.

In the first months of the new century, Dan grew progressively unstable. A drink problem, which he had inherited from his father, turned chronic; he became increasingly deaf; and nervous problems beset him. During 1901 and 1902, his condition fluctuated but, in 1903, he spent several months in a nursing home in Camberwell, south London. Although he was judged well enough to return home at the end of August, the Drury Lane management took the precaution of hiring Harry Randall for its forthcoming pantomime, *Humpty Dumpty*, in case Dan had to withdraw. In the event, Dan was well enough to appear and roles were reshuffled so that Randall could be accommodated too. However, there were terrifying scenes backstage with Dan repeatedly locking himself in his dressing-room. It turned out to be his last pantomime – and that of Herbert Campbell, too. Both men died in 1904.

The actor/manager Sir Seymour Hicks theorised on the cause of Dan's death:

Leno was killed by his friends. He paid the penalty of genius by becoming a continual show. His busy brain worked all day as well as all night and the tiny willing frame, at last no longer able to support the labour that an extraordinary intellect imposed on it, burnt itself out and the world was poorer by a thousand peels of laughter.[8]

As with Marie, thousands of people followed Dan's funeral route. A few days later, Max Beerbohm summed up his appeal:

Dan Leno's was not one of those personalities which dominate us by awe, subjugating us against our will. He was of that other finer kind: the lovable kind. He had, in a higher degree than any actor I have ever seen, the indefinable quality of being sympathetic. I defy anyone not to have loved Dan Leno at first sight. The moment he capered on with that air of wild determination, squirming in every limb with some deep grievance that must be outpoured, all hearts were his.[9]

Little Tich's Big Boot dance was famous throughout Europe. Standing only 4ft 6in (137cm) high, he performed a highly individual routine in shoes that were just half that length, managing at one point to stand on tiptoe. In time, he came to hate the act. It became excruciatingly painful and, in fact, for the last thirteen years of his life, he refused to do it at all. He also resented his shortness, telling his third wife that he would have forfeited all his fame for a more natural height.

A lack of stature was not the only odd thing about Little Tich. When he was born Harry Relph in 1867, his father, a Kent publican, was 77, his mother, 32; and Harry, their sixteenth child, had, in all, ten fingers in addition to his thumbs. He spent his first seven years in the village of Cudham, where his father kept the Blacksmith's Arms. His local nickname was Young Tichborne. As a boy, he was quite stout and the people of Cudham jokingly compared him with Arthur Orton, an obese butcher who gained national notoriety for falsely claiming to be Roger Tichborne, the missing heir to a large estate in Hampshire.[10]

When his father was 84, the family moved to Gravesend, where Harry started going to pubs at which entertainment was staged. At the age of 12, he made his debut at a free-and-easy doing a 'funny dance' and then graduated to the Rosherville pleasure gardens,[11] where he joined a troupe of black-faced minstrels on stage and played a penny whistle. He worked next at Barnard's music hall in Chatham, billed as Young Tichborne and earning 35 shillings (£1.75) a week. After that, from the age of 12 to when he was 17, he worked in black face all over Britain, often walking from one town to the next.

LITTLE TICH (Harry Relph)
Born Cudham, Kent, 21 July 1867
Married (1) Laurie Brooks, Illinois, 20 January 1889
   Son, Paul (b. 7 November 1889)
   (2) Julia Recio, London, 31 March 1904 (d. 7 January 1926)
   (3) Winifred Latimer (aka Ivey Latimer), 10 April 1926 (d. 17 December 1973)
   Daughter, Mary Winifred (b. 23 February 1918; d. 4 May 2000)
Died Hendon, north London, 10 February 1928

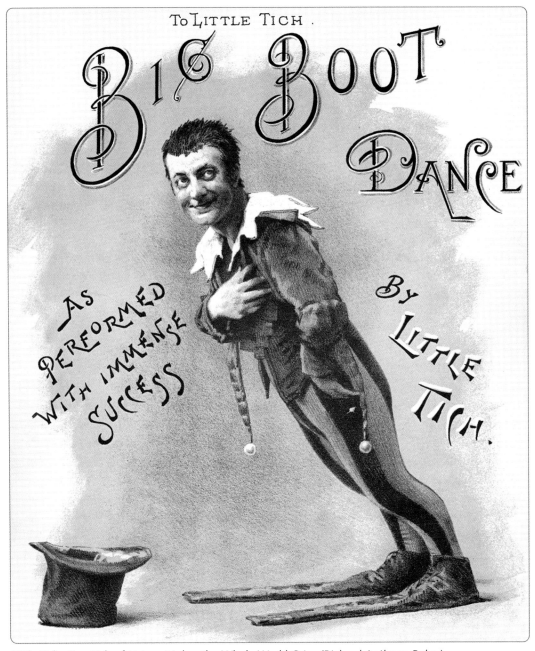

To LITTLE TICH.

BIG BOOT DANCE

AS PERFORMED WITH IMMENSE SUCCESS

BY LITTLE TICH.

Little Tich: One Tich of Nature Makes the Whole World Grin. *(Richard Anthony Baker)*

Realising then that he was not going to grow any taller than 4ft 6in, he continued billing himself as Young Tichborne, adding further epithets, the Pocket Mackney (after the black-faced comedian, E.W. Mackney), Little Black Storm or the Picco Soloist. All that changed in 1884 when he switched to the snappier Little Tich (or Titch) and made his London debut at two halls, the Marylebone and the Foresters. A reviewer called him 'a nigger[12] impersonator with . . . an original vein of drollery': 'The peculiar configuration of Little Tich's legs has something to do with the comicality of his dancing . . . In the expression of his face, there is a world of humour, while his absurd business in a big boot dance [was] attractive.'[13]

Although he was soon appearing at four halls, London audiences did not take to him immediately. He had to go to America before he was fully appreciated at home. He set off early in 1887 with his boots, his piccolo and a cello he had learned to play. The Chicago State Opera Company put him under a two-year contract and advised him to stop blacking up because, as the manager said, audiences would see he was not really black. In April 1889, he came back to London to appear at the Empire at £12 a week. After another trip to America, he was in Britain again in the autumn of that year – and this time, he clicked. Within six months, he was at the top of his profession. In 1889/90, he played Bantam, a page to the Baron in *Babes in the Wood* at the Princes Theatre, Manchester. During 1890, he consolidated his role as a star in London. By the time he arrived at the Theatre Royal, Drury Lane, on Boxing Day to appear in *Humpty Dumpty* alongside Marie and Dan, he was a big name. But he did not enjoy pantomime that much: he felt it was too crowded a business for a comic to be able to establish himself and, in any case, he thought he could earn more away from panto. At the Lane, he was being paid £80 a week. He thought he was worth £100.

In 1895, Little Tich formed his own company to produce musical plays. They all failed and Little Tich vowed never to appear in a play in London again, although he broke his promise in both 1900 and 1902.

Little Tich was clever enough to realise that comic dancing was an international art. Comedy without words (as the comics of silent movies later discovered) travels the world. In the early 1890s, Little Tich conquered Austria, Belgium, Germany, Holland, Hungary and Spain. He enjoyed his biggest overseas success in Paris, although, oddly enough, he did not appear there for the first time until later in the decade. At first, he divided his time between London and mainland Europe. Soon after the start of his European career, he developed a dance which became almost as popular as the Big Boot dance: the Serpentine dance, a dance with a skirt and scarf, which parodied the American dancer Loie Fuller,[14] who, in fact, suggested the burlesque to him. Little Tich called himself Miss Turpentine. To this routine was added a third dance, a fandango, in which he wore a large wig, fixed with a comb, and a spangled tutu.

From 1897, Little Tich was a star of Paris. He became a friend of Toulouse-Lautrec, who is said to have made some drawings of him, although, if he did, none survives. In 1910, the French government made him an Officier d'Académie. Yet, strange to say, he chose not to work in Paris between 1907 and 1923. Except for a week in Brussels, he ignored mainland Europe between 1907 and 1914. The truth was that, although he was not part of the British music-hall circle, as Marie Lloyd and Dan Leno were, he enjoyed working in Britain more. When he returned to Paris in 1923, it was only because work was harder to find in Britain and because, by then, he was new to a younger generation of French theatregoers.

The shape of his act (a song, some patter, a dance in character) had barely changed since 1890, although each year he added new songs and new characters to his act, jettisoning old ones along the way. Among the most characteristic of his songs was 'I'm an Inspector' (1895), written by Harry Wright and Fred Eplett:

A most determined man am I, a man of brain and muscle.
I'm never hasty, no, not me. I'm never in a bustle.
Cool and calm, I always keep with firm determination.
My word is law whene'er I speak to my men in the station.

[Spoken] When I'm in a temper, I think nothing of picking up a constable in each hand, giving them a good shaking and throwing them in the corner like pieces of tissue paper.

The police inspector was one of dozens of characters Little Tich played over the years. There were also the gas inspector, the dentist, the toreador, the zoo keeper, the waiter, the steeplejack, the gamekeeper and the best man, all of whom he committed to wax during a recording career which lasted from 1911 to 1917. Many of his songs were written by Alf Ellerton and Will Mayne, although he wrote some himself: words, music and orchestral arrangements.

When he decided to give up the Big Boot dance, some audiences reacted badly. At the Nottingham Empire, he was jeered and he never returned to the city. On a tour of Australia in 1926/7, pennies were thrown onto the stage at Adelaide: he abandoned the trip. A photographer, Jack Cato, saw Little Tich receive a hostile reception in Melbourne:

There was a rough hooligan element in the house and his type of humour was new to them and his characters unknown. They were disappointed and they threw pennies to him. As he continued, more and more pennies came at him until he stood in a ring of them. It was a tragedy; they broke his heart. He had come on to the stage cocky, perky and full of beans; he left it a shrunken old man, bewildered and heartbroken. Poor, tiny, sensitive little man, he never recovered his self-esteem.[15]

And so, during the 1920s, Little Tich's career began to fail. In 1921/2, his earnings were £9,750 (by today's standards £195,000). By 1925/6, they had fallen to £2,200 (£66,000).

During a two-week engagement at the Alhambra in 1927, he introduced a new number, 'The Charlady at the House of Commons'. Wearing a frock and apron, he carried a bucket and mop, which featured in some of his comic business. On the first Wednesday, however, he was hit on the back of his head by the mop. He appeared unaffected by the accident, but, on the following Sunday, he suffered a stroke and never spoke again. He lay paralysed for three months before he died. In a tribute, the writer J.B. Priestley wrote:

He had only to say 'I went in' and his tiny legs went hurtling across the stage and we saw him bursting through an invisible door. If he said he would show us what he thought about some obstreperous fellow, his dumb show would almost explode into wild careering round the stage, punching and kicking away, defying men of any weight to come near him. The clever eyes would give us a wink or at least a twinkle, asking us to join him as a sophisticated performer, pretending for our amusement to be an indignant jockey or [an] outraged lady in court dress. He would suddenly take us behind the scenes with him, doing it with a single remark . . . He would drop a hat and be unable to pick it up, because he kicked it out of reach every time and then mutter, half in despair, 'Comic business with chapeau.' Little Tich was a really great comedian, a star of the first magnitude.[16]

CHAPTER 5

DENS OF ANTIQUITY

Throughout her career, Marie Lloyd was unfairly blamed for being risqué. Men with a new, dirty joke to tell would say: Have you heard Marie's latest? It might be the early morning milkman shouting 'You got up early, Marie' and Marie shouting back 'No, 'Urley got up me.' Whatever the gag, Marie would never have been allowed to tell it on stage. And yet her blue reputation dogged her from the start of her career to the end.

It was so much so that when the newly formed London County Council set up a Theatre and Music Halls Committee in 1889 to regulate the halls, it took a hard line against Marie and many other entertainers too. Its attitude is easily understood. The Committee was weighed down with puritans. The vice-chairman was George Russell, who led a powerful pressure group, the National Vigilance Association, which had been formed four years previously 'for the enforcement and improvement of the laws for the repression of criminal vice and public immorality'. Its members included a prominent Methodist, John McDougall, who became popularly known as MuckDougall, and Frederick Charrington, who had renounced a £1 million fortune from his family, Charrington, the brewers, to campaign in favour of temperance.

The Association championed some useful causes. In common with the social reformer Josephine Butler, it wanted an end to what was then known as the white slave trade, the luring of thousands of young women into sex slavery. The campaign was difficult to wage, as people resolutely refused to believe that there could possibly be such a callous business. But, in 1880, the Prime Minister, William Gladstone, who had a particular interest in the rehabilitation of fallen women, announced a government grant of £100 for each woman who was repatriated after being trafficked abroad. In addition, warnings were issued to women not to respond to advertisements promising theatrical work in foreign countries.

But, in its campaign against the music hall, in particular the lyrics of certain songs, the Association merely made itself look foolish. Behind the campaign was a fear by the middle-class Establishment that music hall was growing too powerful. This new form of entertainment, created by the working classes for the working classes, might somehow free them from their position at the foot of the social scale. Anarchy would prevail. The workers must be kept in their place.

Outside Lusby's music hall in the Mile End Road in the East End of London, Frederick Charrington was making an individual contribution to the campaign by handing out leaflets headed 'This Way to The Pit of Hell': 'You can go to the theatre or music hall and there your eyes can gaze upon the indecent dance and there you can hear the filthy song, but, unless you are born again, you can never see the glories of Heaven and you will never hear the song of the redeemed.'[1]

Lusby's owners, George Adney Payne and Charles Crowder, took High Court action against Charrington and an order was granted restraining him. He then began distributing a pamphlet which quoted the evidence of a young woman:

> I am nearly 21 years of age. I remember being taken to the hall one night in 1880. A young man took me. I had drink given me at the bar of the public house. I had more than was good for me. The young man then took me away and seduced me. After that, I attended the hall habitually . . . I used to go there for the purpose of prostitution . . . The men at the hall door never objected to my going into it and I never saw other prostitutes objected to.[2]

Crowder then tried to get Charrington imprisoned, but a judge merely ordered a halt to the distribution of the leaflet on the understanding that offensive references to Lusby's would be removed.

Other members of the Theatres and Music Halls Committee included George Lidgett, whose sister, Mary, was prominent in the National Vigilance Association, and Captain Edmund Verney, who was also sympathetic to the Association's principles and who, satisfyingly, was later sentenced to a year's imprisonment for helping to procure a teenage girl for an immoral purpose.

The puritans' finest hour came in 1894. It was an open secret that the promenade behind the circle of the Empire in Leicester Square was the haunt of prostitutes of both sexes. In the 1890s, prostitutes were a natural part of the street scene in the West End. Those of the highest class (courtesans, in fact) were to be found at the Empire. Far from being outraged by their presence, the theatre historian W.J. MacQueen-Pope deemed them part of the entertainment:

The Empire, Leicester Square, home of the wicked promenade. *(British Music Hall Society)*

Here, you could walk up and down, glance at the stage or sit at a table and have your drink and watch the most amazing procession of glorified Vice pass by. The women of the Empire promenade have no counterpart today. It may be a good thing. It surely is. But the sights of London are the poorer for it. These women were astounding in their professional magnificence. With the slow but dignified gait of caged tigresses, they promenaded up and down or sat at tables to be entertained by men. They drank with you, they laughed and talked with you, but they seldom accosted you and never importuned. You knew what they were there for and they knew that you knew.[3]

A campaign to oppose the renewal of the Empire's licence was led by the editor of the National Vigilance Association's magazine, *Vigilance Record*. She was the Mary Whitehouse of her day, a woman bearing a name that was as appropriate to the cause as that of Mrs Whitehouse: Laura Ormiston Chant.

Mrs Chant acknowledged that many people saw her as an 'imperious, sour-visaged, unhappy, wretched, miserable Puritan, who wanted to make London unspeakably dull'. She was, according to the writer Compton MacKenzie, a subject of public ridicule: 'In Kensington High Street, hoarse-voiced hawkers of penny toys used to inflate a little balloon figure of Mrs Ormiston Chant which finally collapsed on their trays with a faint squeak: "'Ere you are! One penny! Mrs Chant collapses in 'orror at the sight of the living pictures [*tableaux vivants*]!"'[4]

Undeterred by being caricatured by *Punch* as Prowlina Pry, Mrs Ormiston Chant explained her views at a meeting of the Playgoers' Club: 'The music hall supplies a class of entertainment to suit people who, out of sheer tiredness of brain or want of a superior education, could hardly appreciate a play. . . . The music hall caters for people who have a small proportion of brains.'[5]

The Empire's manager, George Edwardes, argued that the theatre's closure would result in 700 people losing their jobs. London County Council, however, ordered it to be shut temporarily so that canvas screens could be put up between the promenade and the auditorium. The night after the Empire reopened, the future Prime Minister, Winston Churchill, then a cadet at Sandhurst, was in the audience, together with a number of university graduates and other young men from Sandhurst. They were all opposed to the screens. Churchill wrote:

The entire crowd, numbering some two or three hundred people, became excited and infuriated. They rushed upon these flimsy barricades and tore them to pieces. The authorities were powerless . . . In these somewhat unvirginal surroundings, I now made my maiden speech. Mounting on the debris and indeed partially emerging from it, I addressed the tumultuous crowd . . . I . . . appealed directly to sentiment and even passion, finishing up by saying 'You have seen us tear these barricades down tonight. See that you pull down those who are responsible for them at the coming election.'[6]

Eventually, on a technical issue, it was ruled that the Council had exceeded its jurisdiction and the promenade remained until 1916 when the theatre was no longer a music hall.

Throughout the music-hall world, Mrs Chant was a laughing-stock. The Canadian comedian R.G. Knowles had a joke about her: 'Mrs Chant went to heaven. She knocked at the door. "Who's there?" asked St Peter. "Mrs Chant" went the reply. So, Peter put the catch on the door and shouted "Angels! Put on your pyjamas!"'[7]

Mrs Ormiston Chant, aka Prowlina Pry. *(Richard Anthony Baker)*

Before the end of the 1890s, Mrs Chant appeared to mellow, although only slightly: 'People who toil all day in ugly places and other sordid conditions need to have somewhere to go in the evening where brightness, colour and music can help them to forget the greyness of life for a while . . . and there is no reason why the supply for the demand should come from contaminated instead of pure sources.'[8]

W.T. STEAD (William Thomas Stead)
Born Embleton, Northumberland, 5 July 1849
Married Emma Lucy Wilson in Tynemouth, Northumberland,
    10 June 1873
Six children: William (b. 1874; married Lottie Royce
    (d. 1907)); Henry (b. Darlington 1875; married Jeannie
    Maclelland, 1902 (d. on ship Marama 1923)); Alfred
    (b. Darlington 1877; married Elaine Kitterage Bowles, 1901
    (d. Dresden, Germany, 1933)); Emma Wilson
    (b. 1879, d. 1966); John Edward (b. Wimbledon, south-
    west London, 1883; married; d. Greenwich 1949); Pearl
    (b. 1889; married John Gilliland (d. 1973))
Died off Newfoundland, 15 April 1912
Left £24,654

Alongside Mrs Chant stood W.T. Stead, one of music hall's most virulent opponents. He denounced theatre in general as Editor of the *Pall Mall Gazette*, a post he took up in 1883.

In 1885, Josephine Butler and Catherine Booth, the wife of William Booth, the founder of the Salvation Army, persuaded Stead to publish a series of articles on child prostitution. Their intention was to help push through Parliament the Criminal Law Amendment Bill, which, after years of obstruction and opposition, would increase the age of consent from 13 to 16. The articles, which were a sell-out, found wickedness in the theatre: 'It is said that, at a certain notorious theatre, no girl ever kept her virtue more than three months . . . Some theatrical managers are rightly or wrongly accused of insisting upon a claim to ruin actresses whom they allow to appear on their boards.'[9]

The Salvation Army, capitalising on the public mood, launched a so-called national purity campaign; 4,000 people signed a petition supporting the bill; and, at a public meeting, the National Vigilance Association was formed. On the committee were, among others, Stead and the Booths' son, Bramwell.

Stead and Booth, over-zealous in their efforts to prove it was easy to buy a young girl for prostitution or slavery, arranged to acquire a girl themselves, albeit with the knowledge of her mother. The stunt backfired on them and they appeared at the Old Bailey charged with abduction. Booth was acquitted, but Stead was sent to prison for three months.

In 1890, Stead began his *Review of Reviews*. When he went to the London Pavilion in 1906, it was his first experience of a music hall. He found it 'drivel for the dregs'.

Those who came to gloat over indecency were pretty considerably sold, but the audience, unintelligent and vulgar though it was, seemed to be thrilled for a moment by the beauty of the spectacle. Even in such mortals who grin over coarse allusions to 'Little Mary', who revel in scantily veiled allusions to adultery and who treat the personation of a hiccoughing drunken husband as a masterpiece of humour – even they, far down though they be in the scale of animated beings, are capable of responding to something higher.[10]

W.T. Stead deplored the halls years before he visited one. *(Richard Anthony Baker)*

In 1912, Stead, en route for a peace congress in New York, was one of the 1,500 people who lost their lives on the *Titanic*. At the impact of the collision, he was smoking a cigar in the first-class lounge and was last seen helping women and children to escape. He would have found absolutely no consolation in the publication of at least 150 maudlin songs about the disaster, including one by Britain's own topical tunesmith, F.V. St Clair, 'The Ship that will Never Return'. St Clair worked quickly. The song was performed for the first time the night after the tragedy.

Marie Lloyd suffered her first real trouble with the do-gooders in 1896. She had a new song, 'Johnny Jones', written by le Brunn and Lytton. Like many music-hall songs, it had a chorus that could follow and relate to any number of stories outlined in its verses. In this case, the chorus ran:

'What's that for, eh? Oh! Tell me, Ma.
If you won't tell me, I'll ask Pa'
But Ma said 'Oh, it's nothing – shut your row!'
Well, I've asked Johnny Jones, see! So I know now.

The first verse was innocent enough – all about a boy who pulls Marie's hair and thumbs his nose at her. The second was a little more daring. That involved Marie finding her sister sitting in the dark with her boyfriend and being told to go out and play. The third verse veered towards the lewd. It told of Marie's father taking her to London, where they see a number of women 'with yellow hair', one of whom winks at her father. And the fourth verse? Well, really! Mother is making sets of pretty clothes – too large for a doll, but too small for Marie. So, this is a song about prostitution and pregnancy.[11]

A group called the Social Purity Branch of the British Women's Temperance Association did not like it and, as a result, opposed the renewal of the licences of the Oxford and the London Pavilion, where Marie was appearing. Both licences were, in fact, granted, but the Theatres and Music Halls Committee expressed the view that 'greater care ought to be exercised in the selection of songs'. Marie's riposte was a song called 'You Can't Stop a Girl from Thinking', written by le Brunn, John P. Harrington and Joseph Tabrar.

George Leybourne also acquired a reputation for vulgarity. Two songs were considered particularly risqué: 'If Ever I Cease to Love' (1870), written by Leybourne himself, and 'They All Do It' (1876), written by John Read and sung by both MacDermott and Leybourne. *The Era* had some advice for Leybourne: 'We appeal to him to avoid the course into which of late we have found him drifting. We allude to the "gagging" of his songs with double entendre. He can talk very funnily without descending into this.'[12]

It can only have been the 'gagging', which was not included in the published songsheet, that *The Era* found distasteful, since the lyric itself seemed innocuous:

May cows lay eggs, may fowls yield milk,
May the elephant turn a dove.
May Bobbies refuse to eat cold meat,
If ever I cease to love.

In 'They All Do It', there was possibly a case to answer. Its second verse and chorus ran:

For hours three or four, lovers spooning at the door
On any moonlight evening may be seen,
Though, if they have a lark, they have it in the dark
And they 'do it', though they say 'they didn't mean.'
When creeping down the stairs, comes the old man unawares
And kissing catches the couple in the act,
The mother from above says 'Don't interfere, my love.
You can't dispute this most important fact.

They all do it. They all do it.
They all do it, though oft-times they rue it.
Yet they all do it. They all do it.
And so it will continue to the end of the world.'

Leybourne was also rebuked for the so-called inanity of some of his songs in a review of the bill at the London Pavilion in 1874: 'Whilst . . . George Leybourne . . . chanted in toneless voice a drinking dirge concerning the merits of some sparkling wine, we caught ourselves wondering how any audience – no matter how degraded – could stand this uninteresting drivel.'[13]

The allegations of smuttiness continued too: 'If George Leybourne doesn't moderate his patter in connection with his song, 'I Say, Cabby' and his visit to the "Academy of Arts", he will get himself disliked and will probably cause some music hall proprietor to receive a wigging at the next meeting of the licensing magistrates.'[14]

In 'I Say, Cabby', written by Joseph Tabrar, Leybourne sang of his intention 'to court every girl that I can'. Some patter is printed: 'I tell every girl I meet "My heart is thine alone." And they all believe it. What a lot of little sillies.' The prudes would not have approved of the promiscuity underlying the song and, in fact, Leybourne was repeatedly warned about indecency.

So was Arthur Roberts, one of the most versatile performers of his generation, switching effortlessly between music hall, comic opera, musical comedy, revue and radio.

The son of a tailor's cutter in Savile Row, Roberts's life changed utterly at the age of 12 when his father died. He had to find work quickly and was employed for two years writing out the Latin names for seeds at Covent Garden market: no 'more Hell-invented, soul-destroying job [was] ever conceived by man or devil', he wrote. In his spare time, Roberts found he could sing and he began to perform duets with a schoolmaster friend of the family. He also joined a local choral society.

> ARTHUR ROBERTS
> **Born** 21/29 September 1852 (?),
>   Kentish Town, London (?)
> **Married** (1) ?
>   Daughter and son, Jack, by Amelia
>   Charlotte Gruhn 1894 and 1895
>   (Jack d. Maida Vale, London,
>   12 December 1899, aged 25)
> (2) Ada Ellen Wright, Thanet, 1922
> **Died** Westminster, London,
>   27 February 1933

One day, Roberts was approached outside his home by an old man who told him that he had heard he could sing. Roberts responded by performing Henri Clarke's song, 'The Mad Butcher', whose jaunty tune compensated for a mundane lyric:

> I'm the mad butcher . . . I'm the mad butcher!
> I'm the mad butcher . . . they say I'm insane.
> I'm the mad butcher . . . I'm the mad butcher
> Driven to this by my false Mary Jane.

As a result, the old man invited the young Roberts to work for him during the following summer on the sands at Great Yarmouth: his wage, £1 a week. After some hesitation, his mother agreed he could go. Next summer, three times every morning, he stood on a makeshift stage on the beach and sang to the holiday crowds. In the afternoon, he sang on the

Arthur Roberts, reprimanded for being near the knuckle.
(Richard Anthony Baker)

pier and in the evening at one of the local hotels.

At the end of the summer, he had to find another job to help support his family. In the late 1860s, he became a clerk, but, not long afterwards, he and six friends formed a singing troupe called the Star Comedy Company. He also found work at smoking concerts at a hotel near his home. Similar engagements followed as a result of which he decided to pay his first visit to a music hall, Turnham's, later the Metropolitan, in Edgware Road in west London, where he saw Fred Coyne. Roberts thought he could do better and decided there and then to turn professional himself.

The start of his climb to fame can be dated from his first appearance at the New Star at Bermondsey in south London in October 1875. His major breakthrough came when he was booked for the Oxford in September 1876. The song, 'If Only I Was Long Enough', written by T.S. Lonsdale and W.G. Eaton, suddenly made his name. During the whole of 1877, he appeared at halls in London, occasionally finishing the evening at Evans's. This was where he acquired his reputation for singing indecent songs. Many years later, he explained:

> In those times, artistes were allowed more licence in their songs. They had, in fact, to supply the stuff that was demanded. Otherwise, they would never be successful. They had to give the public what it wanted. We had to sing songs for saucy people in saucy times. There was no help for it . . . Just before the Middlesex Licensing Sessions were due to be held, all artists were severely warned to be careful about what they did and sang. But after the licence had been passed, I am afraid we all lapsed into our old habits again to supply the demand.[15]

Roberts appeared in three Drury Lane pantomimes: *Mother Goose* in 1880/1, *Robinson Crusoe* in 1881/2 and *Sinbad* in 1882/3. In each show, he was teamed with James Fawn. Their appearances marked the start of a long friendship and, even when they were not at Drury Lane, they frequently appeared together, usually encouraging each other to be more and more outrageous. At the Oxford, dressed as a couple of clergymen, they sang 'Goodness Gracious!', their very first duet in *Mother Goose*, although, on this occasion, they added verses that were never sung in front of children. H. Chance Newton, who had known Roberts from his amateur days, wrote:

This comical couple took to duetting in the halls . . . and therein they warbled some few numbers, which were . . . 'very near the knuckle'. Indeed, as the irrepressible Arthur will tell you . . . the pair very often got into trouble and had to be warned by the authorities . . . The . . . association was really a very happy and hilarious one, as naturally two such real humorists, so unlike in method, were able to bring down the house between them, as indeed, either of them could do separately.[16]

As a solo entertainer, Roberts's best-known song, 'I'm Living with Mother Now' (1881), also brought him trouble. Was it the reference to wickedness or kissing – or something else?

> Lend me a cab fare, Sammy.
> Now, won't you, there's a dear.
> Well, buy me a baked potato.
> I feel so awfully queer.
> Your eyes are so dreadfully wicked.
> Oh, kissing I couldn't allow.
> You might have done so a few months ago,
> But I'm living with mother now.

Roberts's panto appearances had made him well known to middle-class audiences, who would otherwise never have frequented music halls; so, he planned a clever career move. He turned legitimate and was away from the halls for practically twenty years. He gave a farewell performance at the Trocadero and was next seen in a series of productions at the Avenue and Comedy Theatres.

Roberts made his return to the Palace in 1904 in a selection of sketches. Indeed, he spent much of his time from then on in sketches at most of the leading halls in Britain. He also tried revue: C.B. Cochran's shows *London, Paris and New York* (1920); *Fun of the Fayre* (1921); and *Phi-Phi* (1922). Cochran paid Roberts a retainer of £1,000 a year, but the arrangement was ended in 1924.

In November 1924, a special matinée performance was given at the Alhambra to mark Roberts's fifty years in the theatre. James Agate reckoned there were four music-hall stars whose brilliance had never been surpassed: Dan Leno, Marie Lloyd, the doyenne of male impersonators Vesta Tilley, and Roberts. 'His songs and, above all, the blazing indiscretions of his patter offered the youth of that period a way of escape from over-insistence upon the proprieties.'[17]

Sadly, we shall never know the nature of those blazing indiscretions, as Roberts again improvised his patter with jokes and remarks that would never have been sanctioned by the authorities. There was one MP, Henry Labouchere, who believed the law should have nothing to do with what Agate referred to as the proprieties. He had spent his youth in brothels and beer-houses; he married an actress, Henrietta Hodson; and so, it might be thought that such liberality would suit him. Yet, he was the MP, who, during one drowsy late-night sitting in the Commons in 1885, ensured that homosexual conduct was criminalised, a law that brought about the downfall of Oscar Wilde and caused thousands of men to live in fear until it was abolished in 1967. Even so, Labouchere believed the London County Council should play no part in regulating the entertainment at music halls:

Bolton, the birthplace of music hall. *(Richard Anthony Baker)*

A music hall entertainment is not very intellectual. Indeed, it is wondrous that so many human beings should listen with apparent delight to the sort of songs and the sort of singers that are the lions of these establishments. The law, however, ought not to suppress entertainments because they are vulgar, nor to close places of entertainment because all those who frequent them are not pillars of virtue.[18]

None of this banter came as any surprise to those who had spent their lives working in the profession. Long before the glory years that spanned the end of the nineteenth century and the beginning of the twentieth, muck-rakers with little better to do had stirred up trouble.

As early as 1842, rival publicans at Bolton in Greater Manchester were so irritated by the success of the Star, one of the town's most popular meeting-places, that a number of them formed an association opposed to singing saloons, claiming they had a demoralising effect. (By 1853, Bolton had about ten pubs with singing rooms attached and around a dozen more, where there was often music. On some nights, as many as 4,000 people crowded in. The owner of the Star described it as the oldest music hall outside London. He was probably right. It opened for business in 1832 and had become such a success by 1840 that new premises were opened.) In 1852, the Star burnt down, leaving about fifty people without jobs. As the annual licensing sessions were about to be held, the Star's opponents seized the opportunity to campaign for the withdrawal of its licence. A Baptist minister, who had visited the Star, said there were at least 1,000 people there, most of them aged between 12 and 25. He addressed a local public meeting:

A tall, well-dressed female came onto the platform and attracted their attention by a song. I do not say that the song was immoral, but I do affirm that the gestures of the lady who sang it, together with the stimulating influence of the drink and whole scene, were calculated to excite the basest passions of the human mind . . . My heart sickened at what I heard . . . I felt that I was in the very suburbs of hell.[19]

In addition, evidence was presented from local youngsters imprisoned in Manchester and Liverpool, describing the Star as the centre of a juvenile crime ring: 'The Star Inn is the greatest evil in Bolton'; 'I should never have been here, were it not for the Star Inn.' However, people who wrote to the *Bolton Chronicle* argued that the singing saloon was generally more orderly and better run than the ordinary pub. Magistrates withdrew the licences of both the Star and another hall, the Millstone, but restored them a month later, when it emerged that no formal complaint had been made against either place.

Details about entertainment in Leeds were given eleven years later when a former secretary of the National Temperance Society, Thomas Beggs, gave evidence to a Commons Select Committee:

There are three or four casinos in Leeds which [attract] mostly factory operatives . . . I regard these casinos and concerts as very great evils . . . Very often songs are sung of an obscene and indecent character. In the leading casino in Leeds, on the night I visited it . . . there was a boy and girl, certainly not more than 13 and 14 years of age, representing some scene of *The Henpecked Husband* and the allusions were of the filthiest description . . . In most of them, songs, which, I am sorry to say, used to be popular when I was a boy and of a very indecent character are quite common.[20]

Magistrates in Sheffield ordered the city's music-hall proprietors to ensure that all skirts worn on stage should reach below the knee, while in Nottingham, it appeared that one free-and-easy could be very different from the next:

> There are grades of respectability ranging downward from the comfortable and well-tended apartment, where tradesmen, neighbours and mostly persons known to each other, hold their weekly meetings and where, at all times, the limits of law and propriety are decorously observed; to the miserable and pestiferous den, to which none but the lowest and most depraved of the population of both sexes are in the habit of resorting and where drunkenness, obscenity and ruffianism are the principal features of the night's amusement and all sense of moral degradation is lost in loathsome excesses.[21]

Ballet once formed part of the entertainment at the Alhambra music hall in Leicester Square, London, but Middlesex magistrates refused the theatre a music and dancing licence on account of indecency: the cancan had been danced there.

By and large, the Church quietly deprecated music hall, although clerics who stepped out of line were dealt with harshly. One such was Stewart Headlam, who was dismissed as curate of St Matthew's, Bethnal Green, the church where Marie Lloyd's parents were married, on account of a lecture he had given. Educated at Eton and Cambridge, Headlam, a Socialist and unorthodox Christian, put up half the bail (£1,250) Oscar Wilde needed before his third trial, even though he scarcely knew Wilde. It lost Headlam some friends; even his maid left his service. As for his views on music hall, it was these comments that brought about his downfall:

I believe that really good songs would be as popular as silly ones. 'Let me write the songs. I don't care who writes the sermons,' said someone; and there is no doubt that Mr MacDermott or George Leybourne have far more influence in London than the Bishop of the diocese . . . I have not said anything about what to many is the main evil of the music halls – that, in some cases, they are much frequented by loose women. I don't think it at all fair to blame a place for the people who go there. I also think that the large proportion of music-hall audiences are respectable working people and clerks. But that prostitutes do go there is undeniable. But I don't think that is any reason why respectable people should keep away – rather, perhaps, all the more reason why they should go; if some of the wives and sisters of the upper and

Stewart Headlam (right), a churchman who lost his job through supporting music hall. (*Richard Anthony Baker*)

middle classes would go and not let their brothers and husbands say music halls are not fit places for them, it would indeed be well.[22]

A former Bishop of London, John Jackson, wrote to Headlam: 'I do pray earnestly that you may not have to meet before the Judgment Seat those whom your encouragement first led to places where they lost the blush of shame and took the first downward step towards vice and misery.'[23] Headlam became Secretary of the Church and Stage Guild and did not receive absolution (in the form of a letter from the Archbishop of Canterbury, Dr Randall Davidson) until he was on his deathbed.

Headlam was forty years ahead of his time. A one-act play, written by the Vicar of Brixton, Revd A.J. Waldron, and entitled *Should a Woman Tell?*, was staged at the Victoria Palace in 1913. Waldron addressed his audience: 'Prejudice against music halls is being broken down. People are beginning to realise that music-hall entertainment can be clean, intellectual and refreshing. I firmly believe that, in the midst of the stress of one's labours, laughter is a necessity.'[24]

From time to time, local dignitaries demonstrated their sensitivities over music hall. In 1870, the manager of the Theatre Royal in Plymouth, John Riley Newcombe, introduced into a pantomime caricatures of the Mayor, Town Clerk and Chief of Police dancing the cancan. The stuffy local council was not amused. It approved a resolution 'expressing deep disapprobation of the exhibitions . . . representing individuals in public positions . . . in a grotesque and unbecoming manner'.

A curious personal feud occurred in the late 1870s, involving G.H. MacDermott and Birmingham's Chief of Police, Major E. Bond. MacDermott had sung a song in Birmingham, 'Running 'Em In', which Bond viewed as a satirical attack on him. Determined to have his revenge, he waited until MacDermott appeared in a pantomime, *King Koko or Pretty Prince Floribel and the Fairy Roses*, at Day's Concert Hall in 1880. James Day, one of the proprietors, was then summonsed for staging plays without a licence. Part of the prosecution case was that MacDermott, who played King Koko, had made 'suggestions . . . of a very indecent and improper character and calculated to demoralise people who attended'. The case failed and Bond was called before the local Watch Committee to explain why he had written to a newspaper complaining about 'shameful and degrading scenes' at Day's.

Scandal also surrounded one of the greatest gymnasts of the nineteenth century, Zaeo. The puritans loudly objected to posters advertising her at the Aquarium music hall in Westminster and so ensured she was a sell-out.

ZAEO (Adelaide Chilver)
Born Norwood, south London,
    1863/6/8 (?)
Married H.W. (Henry William) Wieland,[25]
    her agent (b. Germany, 1847/51(?);
    d. 9 July 1922; the agency was
    founded in 1870)
    Two children, Harry (b. 28 March
    1897), and Olga
Died central London 2 April 1906

Zaeo, an exotic name for one born in south Norwood, dreamed as a child of being a gymnast, even though, by her own admission, she was a 'stick of a girl', small-bosomed, round-shouldered, her head always drooping. Her parents died when she was still young and she was adopted by relatives. She came under the influence of H.W. Wieland, who became her agent and eventually her husband. Her training was relentless: 'I practised regularly from five to seven hours a day and I still practise unceasingly. Even one day's cessation, if I

Zaeo, the Marvel of the World. *(City of Westminster Archives Centre)*

am travelling or in any way prevented, has its effects in diminishing the ease . . . of my movements.'[26]

Zaeo made her first appearance at the Alexandra Palace in London in 1878. The *Daily Telegraph* was impressed: 'Her gyrations on the high trapeze, from which, at one time, she hangs by the nape of the neck, are all accomplished with a quick grace of motion . . . As a wire-walker, she displays a remarkable command of equilibrium.'[27]

Her audiences, however, most enjoyed seeing her thrown into the air by a catapult. Two years later, she was at the Aquarium. *The Era* reported:

She makes a start by going through her marvellous exercise on a thread of wire so thin as to be invisible to the naked eye. Her only balancing appliance is a small Japanese umbrella and, with the aid of this, she performs the journey from one side of the hall to the other and then halfway back again to show that she is thoroughly at her ease upon her slender perch, even when called upon to turn round.[28]

After that engagement, Zaeo went to mainland Europe, expecting to stay for a fortnight. Instead, she was there for ten years, appearing at many of Europe's biggest cities, including Valencia, where she was paid £200 for a single performance and immediately handed half of the money to a local Hospital for Incurables.

When she returned to the Aquarium in 1890, a poster advertising her appearance made her look near naked. The National Vigilance Association declared it 'indecent' and 'horrible' and two clergymen on the Theatres and Music Halls Committee described it as a 'most gross and wanton insult to the delicacy of London's moral feeling'. Their intervention made it certain that the Aquarium was packed out every night. The manager had hesitated at paying the salary Zaeo demanded. They agreed on sharing terms and, at the end of the first week, Zaeo was paid more than the Aquarium had ever paid anyone.

The lesbian dancer Maud Allan, wearing little but beads, caused a sensation when she came to London in 1908. The daughter of a cobbler (and not a doctor, as she claimed), Maud first wanted to be a concert pianist. In 1895, she left San Francisco to study music in Berlin. Her last words to her older brother, Theo, who was studying medicine, were: 'Be a good boy and be sure to graduate.' He did neither. Two months later, Maud was told by the Berlin police that he had murdered two women and had hidden their bodies in the local Baptist church. Reprieved three times, he was eventually hanged in San Quentin prison in 1898.

Maud studied piano under Busoni, but abandoned her plans to take up dancing instead. In 1906, she saw Max Reinhardt's production of Wilde's *Salome* and dedicated herself to staging her own production, *The Vision of Salome*, for which Marcel Remy wrote the score. In Marienbad the following year, she presented an after-dinner performance for King Edward, who was so impressed that he recommended her to Alfred Butt, the manager of the Palace Theatre in London.

> MAUD ALLAN (Ulah Maude Allan Durrant)
> **Born** Toronto, Canada, 23 April 1873
> **Died** Los Angeles, California, 7 October 1956

Maud created a sensation in London and broke box-office records at the Palace. Butt said she could name any salary she wanted. As part of the trappings of her stardom, Maud Allan statuettes were sold in Bond Street, society ladies wore her classical sandals, and jewellers copied her costume jewellery. In keeping with her status, she rented luxurious apartments overlooking Regent's Park. (They were paid for by one of her patrons, Margot Asquith, the wife of the Prime Minister, Herbert Asquith.)

Although *The Times* thought Maud's performance was 'absolutely free of an offence', provincial theatre owners were less sure: she was banned in both Bournemouth and Manchester. Walter de Frece, then managing director of the Palace, Manchester, was told that the local Watch Committee would withdraw his licence if he allowed Maud to dance there. Her manager promptly arranged an appearance at the Victoria Theatre, Salford, just outside Manchester's boundaries. People flocked to see her and she was acclaimed to the rafters.

Ten years later, *The Imperialist*, a newspaper founded by a racist Independent MP, Noel Pemberton Billing, printed a short paragraph about two private performances of Wilde's play *Salome*, in which Maud was to play the title role:

Maud Allan, the Vision of Salome. (*Richard Anthony Baker*)

The Cult of the Clitoris

To be a member of Maud Allan's private performances in Oscar
Wilde's *Salome*, one has to apply to a Miss Valetta of 9, Duke
Street, Adelphi, WC. If Scotland Yard were to seize a list of these
members, I have no doubt they would secure the names of several of
the first 47,000.[29]

Behind this curious announcement lay the extraordinary belief by the Vigilante Society,
formed by Billing, that the Germans had a Black Book containing the names of 47,000
leading British figures, who were 'sexual perverts'. *The Imperialist* contended that, more than
twenty years after the Wilde trials, Britain was a decadent nation still entranced by Wilde.

Maud and the producer, Jack Grein, decided to sue for criminal and obscene libel. The
action led to a bad-tempered trial at the Old Bailey, overseen by Acting Lord Chief Justice
Darling, who clashed repeatedly with both Billing and one of the witnesses, Wilde's former
lover Lord Alfred Douglas. In the event, Billing was acquitted, a ruling that was greeted with
cheers and wild applause in the gallery of the court and the street outside.

From that point, Maud Allan's career was in decline and, after 1921, she never danced in
London again. In 1938, she was involved in a car accident in California, although she was not
as seriously injured as she made out. In 1956, she died penniless and forgotten.

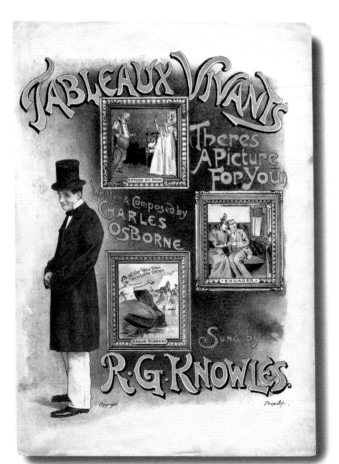

Audiences were as fickle then as
now and, when accusations of
obscenity were made, their effects
could be damaging whether
proved or not. Given the hysteria
wreaked by its opponents, it is
surprising that the halls lasted as
long as they did – and it was not
only in England that a ferocious
campaign against music hall was
conducted.

The prudes also campaigned against
tableaux vivants, static scenes of
people resembling works of art. In
Manchester in 1876, a man and five
girls were fined for a ballet scene that
was deemed indecent. *(Richard
Anthony Baker)*

CHAPTER 6

OUR FOES IN THE NORTH

Anti-music-hall hysteria reached Scotland in 1875. Glaswegian dignitaries were dismayed at the moral effects of some of the city's free-and-easies. At a meeting at the Religious Institution Rooms, evidence was given that: 'Young women, so scantily clad as to be almost naked, danced upon stages before crowds of men, sitting drinking beer and spirits and smoking cigars and pipes; whilst men sang songs both blasphemous and filthy, containing, as they did, suggestions of a coarse and indecent nature.'[1]

The head of Cunard, John Burns, who called the meeting, said:

A vast number of the young men of our city have been in the habit of visiting these saloons, where every evil influence is at work to break down their self-respect and ruin them morally and physically; and upon this point we can speak with precision, because we have the direct evidence of fathers and mothers and heads of establishments and the police themselves to prove that more young men have gone wrong by the instrumentality of singing saloons than from any other cause in the city.[2]

William Mitchell, of the local School Board, spoke of one cheap theatre, where most of the audience were children under 13:

Here, poor, ragged, barefooted boys and girls of the lowest and most neglected class, using the most filthy language and pulling one another about in the roughest possible way, nightly congregate at the charge of 1*d* [about 0.5p] . . . During some part or other of the evening, songs are sung and words are spoken and dances are danced which are either wholly or partially immoral and indecent.[3]

The Lord Provost, local magistrates and the police promised to investigate the allegations, but nothing was done: 'No prosecution is likely, though spoken of. There is really nothing wrong. It is all moonshine.'[4] By 1892, all free-and-easies had disappeared from Glasgow.

The city has a fascinating music-hall history. The Britannia, situated on the first floor of a four-storey building in Trongate, is the major surviving music-hall building in Scotland, its famous stage, stalls and gallery still virtually intact. It started out as Campbell's music hall in 1857, but had become the Britannia by 1906, when it was bought by an eccentric millionaire, Albert Pickard. Having arrived from Bradford two years previously, he set about buying flats, offices and shops until he became the second biggest landlord in the west of Scotland. It was Pickard who renamed the Britannia the Panopticon, retaining it as a music hall, but adding waxworks, sideshows, amusement arcades and a freak show.

Will Fyffe, who wrote and sang 'I Belong to Glasgow'. *(Richard Anthony Baker)*

In the music hall, amateurs were allowed to try their luck on Friday nights as the manager stood in the wings with a long hooked pole to pull them offstage should they fail. The debonair song-and-dance man, Jack Buchanan, was one who, when young, suffered this ordeal. Between 1923 and 1927, the hall operated as the Tron cinema and then became the Panopticon again until it closed in 1938. A trust, set up to restore the Britannia, is spending £4.5 million on converting it into a working museum, a monument to the entertainment and social history of Britain. It is hoped that the ground floor will be converted to a Victorian-style pub.

The Glasgow Empire, which opened as the Gaiety in 1874, was one of the best-known music halls in Britain. Standing on the corner of West Nile Street, it was originally the Choral Hall, a small theatre specialising in Shakespearean and musical plays. However, within three years, music hall was introduced. Among those who appeared at the Gaiety were Marie Lloyd, the coster comedian Gus Elen, and the last of the *lions comiques*, George Lashwood. It was such a success that on Burns Night, 1896, it closed to allow Frank Matcham to undertake an opulent conversion at a cost of £30,000. In April 1897, it reopened with Vesta Tilley topping the bill. Another major reconstruction was carried out in 1930, increasing the theatre's capacity to 2,100.

Audiences at the Glasgow Empire had a reputation for being tough on English entertainers. The top variety comedian Max Miller was once asked whether he had ever appeared there. 'No,' Miller replied, 'I'm a comic, not a missionary.' The singer Des O'Connor fainted on stage before he had even started his act. The comedian Eric Morecambe used to add that, when O'Connor came round and started to sing, the audience fainted. Another comic, Jimmy Wheeler, said he was put off by being watched by 'rows of dour Scots munching thistles'. Mike and Bernie Winters fared no better. Mike began the act by doing three minutes on his own. When Bernie joined him, someone in the audience shouted out: 'Fucking hell. There's two of them.'

The Glasgow Empire was pulled down in 1963 to make way for an office block.

The two most accomplished exponents of Scottish music hall were Will Fyffe and Harry Lauder. Fyffe was the son of a ship's carpenter, whose love of amateur theatricals made him give up his job and establish a theatre company. From the age of 7, Will was required to play an astonishingly wide range of parts, including Little Willie in the melodrama *East Lynne*, Little Eva in *Uncle Tom's Cabin*, and, later on, Polonius in *Hamlet*. His salary was 4s 11d (just under 25p) a week plus a penny for painting the scenery. In later years, he was to earn £600 a week.

While touring in revue, Fyffe wrote two songs, hoping to sell them to Harry Lauder, but Lauder rejected both. So, at the Pavilion Theatre, Glasgow, one night in 1921, Will tried them out himself: 'I belong to Glasgow' and 'I'm Ninety-Four Today', the first portraying a drunken Clydeside workman Will had seen at Glasgow's Central Station one Saturday night. As the man fumbled

---

WILL FYFFE (William Fyffe)

Born Dundee, 16 February 1885

Married (1) Lily Bolton (died when the steamer SS *Rowan* sank en route from Glasgow to Dublin, 13 October 1921)

Two daughters, Josie and Winnie

(2) Emmeline Eileen Pooley in Southwark, south London, 18 November 1922 (d. London, 1979, in her late eighties)

One son, William (b. Thanet, Kent, 1927; married Michelle Franks, August 1950)

Daughters, including Eileen (married Peter Morgan-Fletcher, Edinburgh, 9 February 1941)

Died St Andrews, Fife, 14 December 1947

in his pocket for his ticket, the crowd in the queue behind him became increasingly irritated. Eventually, an exasperated ticket inspector asked him: 'Well, where do you come from? Do you belong to Glasgow?' The reply: 'No, my good man. I do not. Right at this moment, Glasgow belongs to me.' Will liked the line and, within a short time, he had completed both the lyric and the melody of what was to become his best-known song:

> I belong to Glasgow, dear old Glasgow town.
> But what's the matter with Glasgow for it's going round and round?
> I'm only a common old working chap
> As anyone can see,
> But, when I get a couple of drinks on a Saturday,
> Glasgow belongs to me.

Fyffe interrupted the song with patter:

> Why should all these blooming millionaires have all the money? . . . Their money's tainted. Tain't yours, tain't mine . . . They condemn a poor British working man because they see him staggering down the road drunk . . . What about these people in their blooming motor cars? They go past so quick, you don't know whether they're drunk or sober.

Fyffe, a short plump man with a long nose and twinkling eyes, made his London debut in 1916 and achieved star status when he appeared at the London Palladium in 1921, the first of sixteen appearances he was to make there. At the 1937 Royal Variety Show at the Palladium, he was the highlight of the evening. When he sang 'Wi' a Hundred Pipers an' a'', a standing ovation greeted one hundred pipers of the Greys, the Camerons and the Scots Fusiliers as they marched down the aisles and onto the stage. Afterwards, Queen Elizabeth, later the Queen Mother, declared Will her favourite comedian.

James Agate seemed to prefer him to Lauder: 'The world now holds a new and unspoiled joy. This is the Scotchman as he really is, not belaudered to the sentimental skies . . . I here and now salute a great artist and comic genius.'[5]

Will Fyffe had established himself in movies by the Second World War and returned to Britain shortly before its outbreak. Hollywood tried to lure him back with offers of a long-term contract, reportedly worth £50,000 a picture, but he was adamant that he would not leave Britain in time of war. He made up for that by appearing at the Palace Theater in New York in April 1927, February and March 1928, January 1929, and he was in the last edition of Earl Carroll's *Vanities* in 1932.

Fyffe stayed at the top of the bill until 1947, when, while convalescing after an ear operation at a hotel he owned in St Andrews, Fife, he suffered a dizzy turn and fell from a window onto a wooden ramp 20 feet below, suffering fatal injuries.

Around the world, Harry Lauder promoted the image of the archetypal Scot as a man of simple pleasures, loving his wife, his hearth, his pipe and his whisky. The son of a potter who made jam jars and lemonade bottles, he was the eldest child in a hard-working, God-fearing family of eight (five boys and three girls): money was always in short supply. So, Lauder started work while still a young boy, at one time helping a local farmer feed his pigs, at another, assisting a market gardener by picking his strawberries.

HARRY LAUDER (Henry MacLennan Lauder)
Born Portobello, near Edinburgh, 4 August
1870
Married Ann Vallance, 19 June 1891
(d. 31 July 1927)
One son, John (b. 19 November 1891; d.
on active service, 28 December 1916)
Died Strathaven, Lanarkshire, 26 February
1950

After Lauder's father died at the age of 31, the family moved to Arbroath, where Lauder was engaged as a 'half-timer' at a flax works, putting in twelve hours' work every Monday, Wednesday and Friday and attending school on Tuesdays, Thursdays and Saturdays. At about this time, he joined the teetotal group, the Band of Hope, and at one meeting was persuaded to sing: his choice of material, 'I'm a Gentleman Still'. He liked the experience and quickly became engrossed in concert-hall entertainment. Not long after, a group of travellers visited Arbroath, presenting a show, part of which was a competition for amateurs. Lauder beat twelve others to win the top prize, a gold watch. Within six weeks, he entered another competition and again came top.

When he was 14, the family moved inland to Hamilton, a coal-mining town in Lanarkshire, where he was employed first as a trapper, opening and closing the gates that controlled air currents to the pits and then as a pony driver. Down the mine, he gained a reputation as a singer and appeared at another Band of Hope concert in the Hamilton district, again singing 'I'm a Gentleman Still'.

By this time, Lauder had added some patter to his act and, after appearing in another competition concert run by one of his fellow miners, he decided to give up work in the pits and become a professional singer. In 1894, he made his professional debut in the Lanarkshire village of Larkhall and then entered a contest for comic singers in Glasgow, the first time he had appeared there. He was offered more Glasgow dates and signed up for a tour of Scotland with a violinist, Mackenzie Murdoch.

In the summer of 1897, Lauder and Murdoch decided to become their own promoters and arranged a tour that lost them money. The following year, they spent much more on advertising and, from then on, their annual tours showed a good profit.

Until then, Harry Lauder had worked frequently as an Irish comedian and that was how he made his English debut in June 1898. The manager of the Argyle music hall in Birkenhead had been recommended to book him. Lauder was an instant success, running right through his repertoire of Irish songs and then returning with a medley of Scottish songs, which proved equally popular. The manager was so pleased that he persuaded him to sign a long contract, guaranteeing him a booking every six months. His salary was to start at £8 a week and rise to £15. The success of Lauder's first appearance south of the border also convinced him to sing fewer Irish songs and concentrate on being a Scottish entertainer.

In 1900, Lauder saw Dan Leno at the Glasgow Empire. At a salary of £100 a week, Leno was singing London-style songs, which were not only understood but relished by a Scottish audience. It set Lauder thinking. If Leno could earn big money singing English songs in Scotland, then he could be successful singing Scottish songs in London. In March 1900, he bought a single rail ticket to London and, after initial disappointment, eventually found work for just one night at Gatti's-in-the-Road, singing first 'Tobermory', a song of humour and gusto, then the rollicking and jolly 'Lass of Killiecrankie' and finishing with an Irish character song, 'Callig(h)an – Call Again!' The man who became his London agent, George Foster, saw him there:

Harry Lauder, Laird of the Halls. (*Richard Anthony Baker*)

The moment Harry Lauder waddled on to the stage at Gatti's that night, something happened. In a flash, I realised that a marvellous new star had dawned in the Variety firmament. I was not alone in seeing this. The entire audience realised it too. That night, Harry Lauder sang his way into instantaneous fame and fortune. During the rest of the week at Gatti's, I had every London and provincial manager down to hear him. They couldn't understand half he said or sang . . . But everyone realised that he was a genius and that nothing like him had struck London for years.[6]

Lauder was booked for the rest of the week at a salary of £3 10s (£3.50). He began appearing at other halls in London and, within five years, he was an established favourite.

One night in 1904, the stage doorkeeper at a hall he was playing handed him a fan letter, written in an obviously feminine hand and placed in a large pink envelope. The doorkeeper and Lauder discussed it for a few minutes, the doorkeeper commenting: 'I suppose you do love a lassie, sir.'

The words lodged in Lauder's mind and, the following day, he went to see the songwriter Gerald Grafton, to start work on a song with the doorkeeper's words as a title. He sang it for the first time in *Aladdin* at the Theatre Royal, Glasgow, at Christmas 1905 and it was the hit of the show:

> I love a lassie, a bonnie, bonnie lassie.
> She's as pure as the lily in the dell.
> She's as sweet as the heather,
> The bonnie bloomin' heather
> Mary, ma Scotch bluebell.

Lauder either wrote or helped to write many of his hit songs. In 1910, he repeated his success in another Glasgow pantomime, *Red Riding Hood*, with 'Roamin' in the Gloamin'', a song he had dreamed up while watching young lovers walking at sunset near his home at Dunoon in the south-west of Argyll. Three further hits were just as popular: 'Stop Yer Tickling, Jock' (1904), 'A Wee Deoch-an-Doris' (1910) and '(Keep right on to) the end of the road' (1924):

> Keep right on to the end of the road.
> Keep right on to the end.
> Tho' the way be long,
> Let your heart be strong.
> Keep right on round the bend.
> Though you're tired and weary,
> Still journey on
> Till you come to your happy abode.
> Where all you love
> You've been dreaming of
> Will be there
> At the end of the road.

In a review of Lauder at the Victoria Palace, James Agate seemed better disposed towards him than when he was reviewing Fyffe:

Here is an artist who is the living definition of a romantic actor. Lauder does more than interpret: he brings himself and his taste for living and the smack of life itself to each and all of his characters. Long before his soldier song was over, we knew all about the lad and the village carpenter had not finished his first verse before we were familiar with that she-walrus, his late-lamented.[7]

Lauder's manager used to ensure that, whenever the Great Man appeared in a new town, there was as much pomp and circumstance as he could arrange. Arriving in Brighton to play the Regent cinema during one carnival week, Harry was met at the station by Scottish pipers. Ceremonial visits were then paid to the Mayors of Brighton and Hove. They were followed by a press reception and a drive round the town to visit the carnival judges. Just before second house at the Regent, there was to be a formal welcome by Lady Chichester in the foyer, and so on. Billy Boardman, who was manager of the Hippodrome at the time, saw an opportunity of promoting his top of the bill entertainer, the comic singer Wilkie Bard:

> I had thousands of leaflets printed and distributed over Brighton to the effect that Mr Wilkie Bard would arrive at the station at 12.30, carrying his own suitcase and take a Corporation tram to the front entirely unattended. Here he would be received by the manager of the Hippodrome and a guard of honour composed of cleaners from the theatre. After a visit to the Aquarium, Mr Bard, having refused the pressing invitation to lunch with the two mayors, would take that meal at Aunt Betty's whelk stall on the Lower Parade . . . I had bumper houses at the Hippodrome . . . and, what was more, Sir Harry quite entered into the spirit of the merry jest.[8]

In 1907, Lauder made his transatlantic debut. When the offer was first made, he was not particularly interested. He was getting plenty of work in Britain and so, in the hope of deterring any further approaches from America, he asked George Foster to quote a ludicrously high figure. At the time, he was appearing in Liverpool for about £20 a week. He telegrammed his wife, Nance, asking her to go with him if, by any chance, the offer was accepted. Amazingly, it was. Nance's reply: 'See Book of Ruth Chapter One Verse Sixteen.' Lauder looked up the quotation: 'And Ruth said Entreat me not to leave thee or to return from following after thee; for whither thou goest, I will go; and where thou lodgest, I will lodge; thy people shall be my people and thy God my God.'

In the event, family commitments prevented Nance from going and so Lauder travelled to America with their 14-year-old son, John. He was billed to open at a matinée performance at the New York Theater in Times Square. Instead of the three songs he had planned to sing, he sang six. In the evening, there was so much cheering that he had to sing ten songs before he was allowed to leave the stage.

A review in *Variety* read: 'Lauder is distinct, unique and a revelation in vaudeville. His Scotch dialect is broad at times, but it is not always necessary that he be heard to be understood.'[9]

Lauder was an instant star. He returned to America in 1908 to appear at the Lincoln Square Theater for 70 minutes. Later in his career, he spent nearly a year touring America earning a total of $120,000 in the process. In all, he made twenty-five working visits to the United States. One of the most extraordinary occurred in the winter of 1911. He was due to open at a matinée show at the Manhattan Opera House, but the liner on which he was crossing the Atlantic was delayed by storms. It was clear the ship would not dock until late that evening. The matinée was cancelled and, to try to save the evening show, twenty supporting acts were lined up in place of the original five. Lauder finally appeared on stage just before 1 a.m. His audience had waited for him.

In 1916, Lauder was appearing in a revue, *Three Cheers*, at the Shaftesbury Theatre in London. The high spot of the show was his song, 'The Laddies who Fought and Won'. At the same time, his son, now Captain John Lauder, was at the battle front in France with the 8th Argyll and Sutherland Highlanders. On New Year's Day 1917, Lauder was having coffee in the lounge of a London hotel when a page boy handed him a telegram: 'CAPTAIN JOHN LAUDER KILLED IN ACTION DECEMBER 28th OFFICIAL WAR OFFICE'.

Three Cheers closed, but for only three nights to allow Lauder to return home to see Nance. On his reappearance at the Shaftesbury, while singing 'The Laddies who Fought and Won', his voice faltered for a moment, but he composed himself and finished the show.

Lauder then decided to entertain Scottish troops abroad, the Argylls, the Black Watch, the Camerons, the Gordons and the Highland Light Infantry. With a party of entertainers, he left Folkestone in June 1917, taking with him a portable piano and thousands of packets of cigarettes. That same year, he launched the Harry Lauder Million-Pound Fund for Maimed Men, Scottish Soldiers and Sailors.

When he was knighted in 1919, the first popular entertainer to receive such an accolade, it was clear that the Establishment was extending music hall an increasingly warmer welcome.

CHAPTER 7

EMPIRE BUILDING

The proprietors of music halls came from a wide background. William Paul or Old Paul, as he was generally known, was regarded as one of the most eccentric. His hall stood in Belgrave Gate, Leicester. As his own chairman, he frequently made this type of announcement:

I always do my best to entertain you with the best turns. The very best, ladies and gentlemen, that the British Empire can supply. Now tonight, I have got Arthur Roberts coming on in a few minutes. I have got him from London and I can tell you that Arthur Roberts is the best comic singer in the world and that is the reason why I want you to give him a chance. He is the best comic singer in the world, I tell you. But I have got a better one coming next week.[1]

One Christmas, Paul was ill. That week's company was summoned at noon on the closing Saturday to the bedroom of his house, where he paid them, telling each of them that he could not know whether they had earned their money, but, if they had not, he hoped it would be on their conscience.

Some female entertainers used to resent less than complimentary remarks he made from the chair. One woman stopped in the middle of a song and told the audience: 'I will not sing another line until that man is removed.' She walked off in a huff leaving Paul's son, Jim, to lead him off too.

Once, when the comic singer Charles Coborn played at Paul's, he refused to speak to him all week after Paul had prevented him from inviting the audience to join in a chorus. When a young Vesta Tilley first appeared there in male dress, Paul stopped the band and turned on her: 'What are you doing in those trousers? I engaged you as a little girl, not as a boy. Take them off at once and put on your skirts. Ladies and gentlemen, I regret this interruption, but the band will play a selection while little Tilley retires to take off her trousers and appear as we expect to see her.'[2]

Paul had an odd way of sacking a Monday-night turn he no longer wanted. On the Tuesday morning, he invited the artiste to go for a ride in his pony and trap:

Fourteen or fifteen miles out, a halt would be made for refreshments in the middle of which the impresario would make some excuse about looking after the pony, go outside and drive off, leaving his victim marooned. When at last the unwanted artist staggered into Leicester hours late, he was promptly sacked for unpunctuality. But one comedian, fully aware of the 'bumping off' process when 'taken for a ride' turned the tables on his employer. As the trap pulled up at the inn, he complained of faintness and, before getting out, implored Paul to bring him some brandy. When the proprietor emerged with the stimulant, the trap, driven by the comedian, was disappearing over the horizon, and it was Paul's turn to walk home.[3]

In spite of his odd ways, Paul was immensely kind. Every Christmas Day, he provided the old people of Leicester with a first-class dinner and, as they left, they were each given a shilling (5p). There was eccentricity even in the manner of Paul's death. He choked while eating a supper of tripe in 1882. Seven years later, his hall was destroyed by fire.

Another odd character was Alf Milner, known as Squint Milner, who ran the Old Star in Sheffield, which was bedecked with oil paintings of all descriptions. Patrons each paid threepence (just over 1p) to see eight turns and then had refreshments of the same value returned to them. The theatre was packed every night of the week. The singer-songwriter F.V. St Clair used to tell this story of Milner:

The old man once engaged a man to clear out the rats. Milner had been out in his pony chaise and, just as he returned home, the rat-catcher was going away with a bag full of rats. Milner said 'What's ta gotten there?' The man replied 'The rats, sir.' Milner opened the bag and let the whole lot go again . . . [His] explanation was that, as rats only desert a sinking ship, if all the rats were taken away from the Old Star, the place would no longer swim. It certainly was alive with the rodents. I was once dressing and I felt something on my foot, but I thought it the end of my braces. Suddenly looking down, I saw a rat as big as a cat looking up at me.[4]

There were several music-hall impresarios, among them Henry Newson-Smith, Edwin Villiers, George Adney Payne, Richard Thornton, Tom Barrasford and Walter de Frece. But two predominated: Edward Moss, described by W.J. MacQueen-Pope as a complete diplomat, perfectly polished in manners and speech, and Oswald Stoll, a teetotaller and a non-smoker, who numbered philosophy and economics among his hobbies. Both were credited with refining music hall and giving its theatres an air of luxury. Their admirers praised them for making music hall an entertainment fit for the whole family. Their detractors said they scrubbed it so clean that they killed it off.

Edward's father, James, a comedian and travelling presenter of the diorama, introduced music hall to Greenock in Inverclyde in 1873. This was the Queen's Rooms, renamed the Lorne by James Moss. Edward was educated in Glasgow and was encouraged by his father to follow in his footsteps. James gave Edward a diorama of the Franco-German War, which Edward took on tour. It was a financial success, allowing Edward to make his start as a proprietor

> HORACE EDWARD MOSS
> **Born** Manchester 12 April 1852
> **Married** (1) Ellen Alice Bramwell 19 January 1877
>   (d. 7 December 1892)
>   Five children: Ellen Martha (b. 1877); James Edward
>   (b. 1879); Dora Alice (b. 1881); Leonard
>   Bramwell (b. 1882); and Charles Somerve
>   (b. 1883)
> (2) Florence Nellie Craig in central London,
>   30 January 1904
> **Died** Gorebridge, Midlothian, 25 November 1912
> **Left** £204,805

by buying the Gaiety in Edinburgh, which he opened when he was only 25. His campaign for a purer music hall began there and for weeks the Gaiety played to houses only half full. Moss concluded that, if he could induce a top London performer to appear at the Gaiety each week, he might keep his regular audience and encourage others to go along too. That is exactly what happened. 'Respectable' people, intrigued to see a famous entertainer, soon filled his theatre up.

Moss then bought a theatre in Leith, obtained the lease of the Theatre Royal, Sunderland, and took over a run-down music hall in Newcastle. Two theatres in Glasgow were added, as was the Newcastle Empire. Moss then returned to Edinburgh determined to build the most spectacular music hall Scotland had ever seen. It was the Empire Palace, which opened to 'house full' notices in 1892. On the first night, the audience looked in awe at the lavish interior, were given a first-rate show, which opened with the band of the Argyll and Sutherland Highlanders, and, at the end, honoured the whole enterprise with tumultuous applause.

During the 1890s, Moss collaborated on a number of projects with Oswald Stoll and, as the nineteenth century moved into the twentieth, they founded Moss Empires, which, in its heyday, was to control thirty-three theatres across Britain. Moss was the chairman and Stoll the managing director, although Stoll insisted on being allowed to operate his own theatres as long as there was no clash of interests.

Stoll was born Oswald Gray, the son of an Irish engineer, who died while Stoll was still a child. His mother, Adelaide, who had been a dancer in an act called the Three Hardcastle Sisters, married John Stoll, a retired sea-captain, who owned the Parthenon music hall in Liverpool. After he died, Adelaide and Oswald continued running the theatre. It was here that he learned the rudiments of economics. Stanley Holloway used to tell a story about a match seller trying to sell his goods to Stoll. 'Why?' said Stoll. 'Well, I've only taken fourpence all day.' 'Really?' said Stoll. 'And how does that compare with the corresponding week last year?'

Vesta Tilley, whom Stoll adored, appeared at the Parthenon regularly. She used to tell a story about the hall that nicely characterises the rowdiness of some audiences. A singer who followed her on the programme there was once greeted with such a commotion that not even the band could be heard. He took a chair from the side of the stage, sat down and told the audience: 'We'll see who gets tired first.' He was eventually driven off by an old woman in the front row, who had been yelling and screaming. She took off her boot and threw it at him, hitting him in the jaw.

In 1889, Stoll bought Leveno's music hall in Cardiff, renamed it the Empire and introduced twice-nightly programmes. During the 1890s, he opened Empires at Cardiff, Swansea and Newport and, by the time he joined Moss Empires, he was the manager of eight halls.

Stoll was a hard-liner. As part of his aim to attract family audiences to the London Coliseum, Marie Lloyd and the comedian George Robey were banned, although Stoll eventually relented over Robey. He hung notices in every dressing-room banning coarseness and vulgarity; he reprimanded members of the audience for dropping cigarettes on the carpet;

OSWALD STOLL (Oswald Gray)
Born Melbourne, 20 January 1866
Married (1) Harriet Lewis in Cardiff,
    16 October 1892 (d. 1902)
(2) Millicent Shaw in central London, 25
    March 1903
    Three sons
Died Putney, south-west London,
    9 January 1942
Left £89,961

Oswald Stoll, both colleague and rival of Edward Moss. *(Richard Anthony Baker)*

and he forbade his managers to criticise him. When one manager dared to do so, Stoll told him: 'Do not ever tell me that I am wrong. If it happens again, you will be dismissed.' Some time later, the man pointed out another mistake. 'Mr Manager,' said Stoll. 'I told you once before never to dispute my orders. Kindly now go and draw three months' salary from the cashier in lieu of notice.' Stoll so exasperated the American comedienne Sophie Tucker that she turned on him declaring: 'Mr Stoll, you ought not to be in the theatre. You ought to be a bishop.'

A few months after Stoll died in 1942, Prince Littler bought his theatres and formed the new Stoll Theatres Corporation. (Littler (1901–73) was for some years the resident manager of his parents' theatre, the Royal Artillery, Woolwich. In 1927, he and his sister, Blanche, who married George Robey, began sending out companies on provincial tours of successful London shows and, in 1931, he became a theatre proprietor, buying, in the first instance, two theatres in Leicester. He once said: 'I am not in the business for fun, but only as long as the shareholders are happy.') In 1945, Littler became Chairman of Moss Empires. In 1960, he merged Stoll Theatres and Moss Empires; ATV (Associated Television), under Lew Grade (later Lord Grade), then bought Stoll Moss in 1965; and in 2001, Stoll Moss passed into the ownership of (Lord) Andrew Lloyd-Webber's Really Useful Group for £87.5 million.

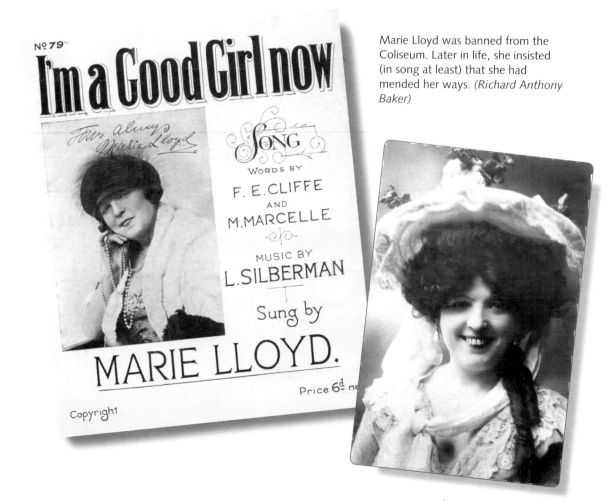

Marie Lloyd was banned from the Coliseum. Later in life, she insisted (in song at least) that she had mended her ways. *(Richard Anthony Baker)*

CHAPTER 8

MATCHLESS MATCHAM

The architect favoured by both Stoll and Moss was Frank Matcham, who virtually created the style of turn-of-the-century theatres, both legitimate and music hall: rococo and opulent, red plush and plaster cherubs, a mass of detail, grandiose and just this side of vulgar.

FRANK MATCHAM (Francis Matcham)
Born Newton Abbot, Devon, 22 November 1854
Married Hannah Maria Robinson, 9 July 1877
    (d. 13 November 1920)
   Two daughters, Evelyn (b. 1879) and Constance Amy
    (b. 1884) (Evelyn had a son, Frank Matcham Taylor,
    and a daughter, Mabel Taylor)
Died Westcliff-on-Sea, Essex, 17/18 May 1920
Left £86,390

In addition to stamping his original creativity on the theatres he built, Matcham was a master of the technical necessities: ventilation, sightlines, the storage of backdrops and so on. But he was the victim of outrageous snobbery in the architectural world. In a book about theatres and opera houses, one contemporary critic, Edwin Sachs, made this sneering comment:

There is no doubt that his plans have a certain individuality and his schemes generally serve the utilitarian purpose of the occupiers in a satisfactory manner. However, to fully illustrate such theatres in a volume dealing with theatre architecture in its best sense would be as anomalous as to include the ordinary jerry-builder's cottages in a volume on domestic architecture.[1]

It was only when two of Matcham's theatres, the London Coliseum and the Hackney Empire, were about to be reopened after restoration work in 2004 that his reputation was properly reassessed:

Matcham was emphatically not an architect's architect. No intellectual aesthete he. Matcham did theatres, scores of theatres, in late Victorian and Edwardian times. Most of his output was not high-culture venues, but variety theatres, music hall, vaudeville. His architecture was populist: highly ornamented, very colourful. Matcham was theme-building long before the cinemas of the 1920s and 1930s picked up on the idea, let alone Disney. And from the point of view of the purist architectural establishment, there is only one thing worse than slapping on the ornamentation: it's doing theme-park buildings. Being prolific didn't help either: serious architects are meant to cherry-pick the commissions, not churn them out like sausages. For years, Matcham just wasn't rated.[2]

Frank Matcham, Britain's greatest theatre architect. *(The Frank Matcham Society)*

The son of a brewery manager, Frank Matcham was educated in Torquay. At the age of about 14, he went to work at the office of a local architect and surveyor, George Soudon Bridgeman, becoming a senior assistant after a short time in London as a quantity surveyor. Then he moved to London to join the practice of one of the foremost theatre architects of his day, Jethro T. Robinson. In 1877, Matcham made the shrewdest career move of his life by marrying Robinson's daughter, Maria, and, when Robinson died a year later, Matcham took over the business, completing its unfinished work. That meant rebuilding the Elephant and Castle Theatre in New Kent Road, which had burnt down in 1878. Matcham's replacement was opened the following year, but, by 1928, it had become a cinema. He also had to negotiate modifications to the Cambridge Music Hall in Commercial Road. This theatre was destroyed by fire in 1896 and rebuilt over the two subsequent years. In 1936, it was demolished to make way for a tobacco factory.

In 1882, Matcham was asked to rebuild the Grand Theatre, Islington, followed by the Paragon in the Mile End Road. Between 1879 and 1920, Matcham was responsible for about 150 theatres, more than twice as many as his nearest rival. Few remain. These were Matcham's main music halls:

Mile End Empire (1885). William Lusby,[3] who bought a pub called the Eagle, which stood on this site, roofed in most of the gardens, so that the property could be used as a concert room. It came to be known as Lusby's Summer and Winter Palace. Lusby ran it successfully until 1878 when he sold it. A fire destroyed the hall in 1884. In its place, the Paragon, designed by Matcham, opened the following year. It was one of the largest theatres in London, covering more than an acre. It was demolished in 1937 to make way for a cinema, which opened two years later. This became the ABC in 1960 and is now the Genesis.

Alhambra, Brighton (1888). On the opening night, G.H. MacDermott was top of the bill. It became a cinema in 1910, closing in 1956. It was demolished in 1963 to make way for the Brighton Centre.

Edinburgh Empire (1892) (see Chapter 7). It closed in 1962; it is now a bingo hall.

Birmingham Empire (1894). On the site of a pub, James Day built a large music hall, Day's Crystal Palace Concert Hall, which opened in 1862. It closed in 1893 and was completely rebuilt to Matcham's specifications. The reconstruction, which took only eight months, cost £18,000. The new theatre, the Empire, which seated 2,000 people, opened in 1894 with the black-faced entertainer G.H. Chirgwin and Gus Elen on the first bill. There were further refurbishments in 1907 and 1911. During an air raid in 1941, it was damaged beyond repair. It was demolished ten years later.

Shoreditch Empire (1894). It had been a place of entertainment since 1856. After it had been rebuilt to Matcham's designs, it was known as the London Theatre of Varieties and then the London Music Hall. It was demolished in 1935.

Sheffield Empire (1895). Marie Lloyd, who was booed here, told the Sheffield audience where to stick its famous cutlery. In 1940, the Empire was badly damaged by enemy action. Nearly two years later, its stage was destroyed by fire. In 1959, the Empire was demolished to make way for shops.

Cardiff Empire (1896). Destroyed by fire in 1899. Matcham designed a new theatre, which opened in 1905. It was again rebuilt in 1915 and continued until the mid-1950s, when it became a cinema. It closed in 1961 and was demolished shortly afterwards.

Glasgow Empire (1897) (see Chapter 6). It was demolished in 1963.

Palace, Hull (1897). It was badly damaged during an air raid in 1940 and was closed for ten years. It closed permanently in 1965 and was demolished the following year.

Metropolitan, Edgware Road (1897). Containing some of Matcham's most ornate and inventive work, the Met was demolished in 1963 to make way for a motorway. In the event, the road took a different route.

Grand, Hanley (1898). An up-and-coming young impressionist, Harry Tate, was on the first bill. The Grand was converted into a cinema in 1932, but was destroyed by fire three months later.

Empire Palace, Leeds (1898). It also opened with Harry Tate on the bill. It started to falter during the 1950s. On the final night in 1961, the variety comic Nat Jackley removed his wig, adding: 'You always raise your hat when you say goodbye to an old friend.' It was demolished in 1962.

Granville, Walham Green, London (1898). It was converted into a television studio in 1955 and demolished in 1971.

Nottingham Empire (1898). It was the scene of Ken Dodd's professional debut in 1954. It was demolished in 1969.

Woolwich Empire (1899). This theatre was a particularly early music hall. It opened in 1835 and was known in its heyday as Barnard's after the family which ran it. It was rebuilt in 1899 to Matcham's designs. Towards the end of its life, it staged strip shows. It was demolished in 1960.

Newport Empire (1899). It was built on the site of a former theatre of which only the façade was retained. It was destroyed by fire in 1942.

New Cross Empire (1899). Its decor was described by the magazine *The Builder* as being of the Louis XIV period. It was closed in 1954 and demolished two years later. There is now a petrol filling station on the site.

Empire Palace, South Shields (1899). It replaced Thornton's music hall, which had become too small. During the 1930s, it was rebuilt as a cinema and was later used as a bingo club.

London Hippodrome (1900). Outside, it looks magnificent, topped by a heavy iron chariot guarded on either side by figures of Roman centurions. Inside, all was richness and elegance – and Edward Moss's demand for the means to stage water spectacles proved no problem at all. Matcham installed a vast tank holding at least 100,000 gallons of water, which could be drawn from a bourn (or stream) running under the theatre. (It was known as the Cran Bourn, hence Cranbourn Street, on one corner of which the Hippodrome stands.)

By 1909, the public appetite for circuses and water shows had dwindled and Matcham was called in to make some alterations, enlarging both the stage and the auditorium. Now, variety became the Hippodrome's mainstay, but variety on a far grander scale than most music halls could muster: scenes from operetta and ballets were part of the bill. In fact, the first presentation in England of Tchaikovsky's *Swan Lake* was seen here in 1910, choreographed by Michel Fokine. The revue *Hullo Ragtime* was the theatre's first big attraction, but fate played a cruel trick. Moss, who had been waiting for the Hippodrome's first sign of success, died just a month before *Hullo, Ragtime* opened.

The last show at the Hippodrome was staged in 1957. Then, to prepare it for the next phase of its life, a cabaret theatre, *The Talk of the Town*, the interior of the building was extensively rebuilt. According to John Earl, a noted authority on theatre history and architecture, Matcham's auditorium was utterly ravaged. *The Talk of the Town* ran for nearly twenty-five years until it was acquired by Peter Stringfellow, who turned it into a night club and discotheque. It now stands empty.

Brighton Hippodrome (1901). It was originally an ice-rink. Over the years, an amazing range of personalities appeared here, everyone from Sarah Bernhardt to the Beatles. Now a bingo hall, but some original features are still there, including fancy tiles in the doorways, depicting sea-serpents.

Hackney Empire (1901). In 2003, it underwent restoration costing about £15 million. The flavour of the original decoration was recovered; access and facilities were improved; and a new flytower and dressing-room block were built.

Palace Theatre of Varieties, Leicester[4] (1901). The opening bill featured Eugene Sandow. In the late 1940s and early 1950s, Max Miller, Benny Hill and Frankie Vaughan appeared here. Nude shows later held sway until the hall's closure in 1959. Demolished the following year.

Empire Palace, Newcastle (1903). It replaced a theatre built in 1890. The magician Chung Ling Soo topped the opening bill. It was demolished in 1963.

Shepherd's Bush Empire (1903). Every variety artiste of note appeared here until 1953 when it closed with a bill that included the variety comedian Robb Wilton. The theatre was bought by the BBC, which has staged many of its long-running television series here.

Ardwick Empire, Manchester (1904). When it closed in 1961, there were plans to convert it into a bowling alley, but, after a fire in 1964, it was demolished.

Manchester Hippodrome (1904). This theatre could stage music hall, circus and water spectaculars. For circus shows, there were a lions' den and accommodation for 100 horses. It was demolished in 1935 to make way for a cinema.

London Coliseum (1904). This was the theatre of which Stoll was most proud. He told Matcham he wanted it to surpass any other in London. Naturally, Matcham rose to the challenge and, when the theatre opened, audiences saw that no expense had been spared: the building cost £300,000, its capacity just falling short of that of Drury Lane. Its stage is the largest in London. In addition, there were two extraordinary innovations: a revolving stage comprising three concentric sections that could move clockwise or anti-clockwise independently of each other; and the King's Car, a mobile lounge to carry royal parties from the entrance of the Coliseum to the Royal Box at the back of the stalls. On its first run, with Edward VII on board, it blew a fuse and refused to move. The King walked to the box and the car was never used again. The black-faced singer Eugene Stratton was on the first bill on Christmas Eve 1904. The finale, entitled Derby Day, featured real horses and jockeys galloping round the revolving stage.

The London Coliseum: for Oswald Stoll, the jewel in the crown. *(Richard Anthony Baker)*

Later, variety bills mixed music-hall stars with the likes of Sarah Bernhardt, Dame Ellen Terry and Sir Seymour Hicks. In 1926, Sir John Gielgud and Gwen Ffrangcon-Davies were hired to perform the balcony scene from *Romeo and Juliet*. Gielgud's memories of it were not happy:

We were given a terrible set with a sort of cardboard pink marble balcony. Gwen looked as if she was standing in a pink bath when she appeared and the audience did not know what to make of it. The scene went very badly, but one of the stagehands was kind enough to say to me during the last week 'You're doing it a bit better now.' The Houston Sisters used to follow us and we were preceded by a huge man called Teddy Brown. He weighed about twenty stone and played the xylophone. He was such a success with the audience that, when the revolve began to go round, they were still screaming for him as our garden scene was heaving into view. And, when the Houston Sisters came on, one of them would give a sort of imitation of me with her Scottish accent – 'A thousand times goodnight' and get a huge laugh. It was the only time I have ever appeared in a music hall.[5]

The Coliseum celebrated its last night as a variety theatre in 1931. It underwent extensive restoration in 2003 at a cost of £41 million.

Ipswich Hippodrome (1905). It opened only five months after the foundation stone had been laid. In 1959, it became a dance hall and, in 1964, a bingo hall. It was demolished in 1984.

Coliseum, Glasgow (1905). By 1929, it had outgrown its usefulness. On its conversion to a cinema, the interior was entirely transformed.

Holborn Empire (1906). It was the acknowledged home of the variety singer Gracie Fields and Max Miller. It replaced Weston's music hall, which had occupied the site since 1857. It was badly damaged by enemy action in 1941 and, although Moss Empires had plans to reopen it, they sold it instead to Pearl Assurance. It was demolished in 1960.

Willesden Hippodrome (1907). A bomb destroyed the stage and a large part of the back of the theatre in 1940. It was demolished seventeen years later and replaced by government offices.

Ilford Hippodrome (1909). Throughout the 1920s and 1930s, all of music hall's big names came here. In January 1945, the curtain had just risen on *Robinson Crusoe* when the blast of a V2 rocket, which had fallen on a nearby row of cottages, demolished the dressing-rooms and brought scenery crashing down onto the stage, showering the audience with dust and debris. Two days later, the roof collapsed, bringing down the gallery. The shell of the theatre stood intact until 1957 when crumbling masonry fell from the building, hitting a passing bus. The local council ordered its immediate demolition.

Finsbury Park Empire (1910). This theatre, the best equipped in the London suburbs, opened in 1910. During the 1920s, many American stars made their British debuts here, among them Sophie Tucker. Towards the end of the 1950s, standards started to decline. The Empire's last bill was presented in 1960. The theatre was closed that year and demolished five years later.

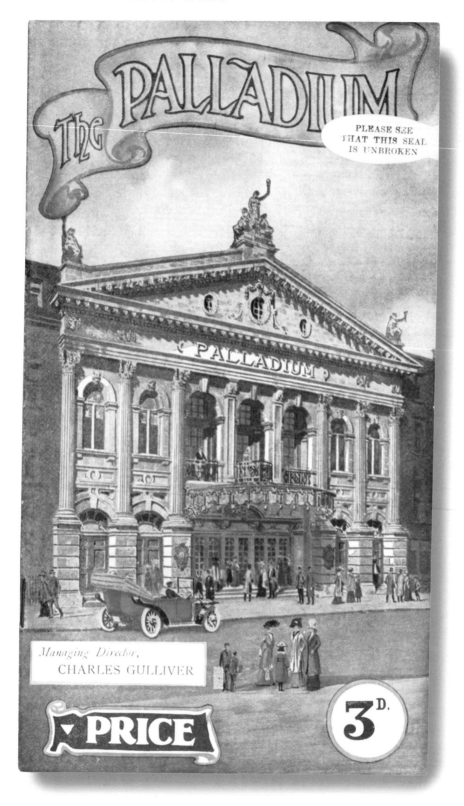

The London Palladium, the world's most famous variety theatre. *(Richard Anthony Baker)*

London Palladium (1910). The greatest variety theatre in the world. Its first owner, Walter Gibbons, the inventor of a device that removed the flicker from early moving pictures, appointed Matcham to build it in Argyle Street, not far from Oxford Circus. It was to stand on the site of a circus designed by Jethro Robinson. A unique feature of Matcham's design was the installation of phones in the boxes so that people in one box could chat with friends in others. The Palladium's opening bill on Boxing Night 1910 featured three future female music-hall stars, Nellie Wallace, Ella Shields and Ella Retford. At the outset, the Palladium largely presented music-hall bills, but, after two years, revues, plays, operetta, musical comedy and ballet were all gradually introduced. For a short time in 1928, the Palladium was used as a cinema, but, when George Black took over, the theatre moved into one of its most successful phases. Crazy Weeks were introduced, the first in 1931, featuring the comedians Nervo and Knox, Naughton and Gold and 'Monsewer' Eddie Gray. The following year, a Crazy Month was staged, this time adding Flanagan and Allen to the mix. This was the start of the Crazy Gang, the court jesters of the twentieth century.

Lewisham Hippodrome (1911). It was the largest theatre in the London suburbs with seating for 3,500 people. It was a big success until the early 1950s. The final curtain fell early in 1952; it became the Eros cinema; but closed in 1959. The following year, it was demolished and replaced by an office block called Eros House.

New Middlesex, Drury Lane (1911). It was originally the Mogul Tavern. Even though its name had been changed to the Middlesex Music Hall by 1851, Londoners knew it as the Old Mo' for many more years to come. J.L. Graydon rebuilt it in 1872 and then, with Stoll, he commissioned a further reconstruction to Matcham's designs in 1911. It became the Winter Garden eight years later. After many successes with musical comedies, it closed in 1959 after being sold to a property development company. It stood derelict until 1965 when it was demolished to make way for a complex incorporating the New London Theatre.

Victoria Palace (1911). The Crazy Gang staged a string of shows here that ended in 1962. Later, BBC Television's Black and White Minstrels gave 4,344 performances here.

Chatham Empire (1912). Its decor had a distinctly maritime flavour in keeping with a prominent naval town. After the Second World War, the Empire prospered with variety bills, but eventually closed. It was demolished in 1962.

Wood Green Empire (1912). It is mostly associated now with the death on stage of Chung Ling Soo. The final stage production took place in 1955. Then, Associated Television presented some variety shows here. The theatre was later demolished.

Chiswick Empire (1912). It was closed nearly a year after its opening by a fire, which destroyed the stage and badly damaged the auditorium. There was further drama in 1947 when a large part of the ceiling crashed down, hitting the front rail of the circle before falling onto the audience in the stalls. The Chiswick Empire staged its last show in 1959 with the outrageous American pianist Liberace as the star. It was demolished shortly afterwards and replaced by an office block named Empire House.

Bristol Hippodrome (1912). This was Matcham's last major work and it is still going strong.

BERTIE CREWE (William Robert Crew (*sic*))
Born West Ham, east London,
  2 August 1863
Married Edith Mary Lamb in Hackney,
  north London,
  15 August 1894
Died Willesden, north London,
  10 January 1937
Left £27

W.G.R. SPRAGUE (William George Robert
  Sprague)
Born Australia 1865
Married Isabel Katherine Bennett in
  Camberwell, south London, 30 April
  1900
  Son (b. 10 April 1907)
Died 4 December 1933
Left £397

You will have seen that the worst decade for destroying Matcham's work was the 1960s. We were then so preoccupied with the new that we forgot that the old deserved attention too. Fact: of the 1,100 British theatres standing in 1914, 85 per cent had been lost or irretrievably altered by 1980.

After 1912, Matcham went into semi-retirement. He moved to a house at Westcliff-on-Sea in Essex. Opposite, the town's principal theatre, the Cliffs Pavilion, was built many years later. Matcham would have loathed it. He died unnecessarily. After clipping his finger nails overzealously, he contracted blood poisoning.

Two other architects deserve mention, Bertie Crewe and W.G.R. Sprague. The theatre design expert Victor Glasstone describes Crewe as one of the most dynamic architects of the 1890s. His early work, carried out in collaboration with Sprague, was regarded as tepid in comparison with the florid and Baroque style he later favoured. Crewe planned or collaborated in the planning of nearly 200 theatres.

Sprague, who was apprenticed to Matcham for four years, was one of the first architects to eliminate columns supporting the circle. His music halls have all but disappeared.

The Opera House, Blackpool, built by Frank Matcham in 1889, shows the wealth of detail he lavished on the interiors of his theatres. (*The Frank Matcham Society*)

CHAPTER 9

MIXING WITH TOFFS

Music hall started out as entertainment for the working classes and remained so until Moss, Stoll and others saw ways of widening its appeal. Early on, certain writers, artists and Bohemians joyfully supported it. In 1865, the sheer nonsense of one of Vance's most popular songs, 'Slap bang, here we are again!' ('The School of Jolly Dogs'), seemed to have everyone in its grip. Dickens's journal, *All the Year Round*, noted:

> Everybody, old and young, male and female, grave and gay, lively and severe, sang it or hummed it . . . Well might the philosopher observe 'Let me write the songs of my country and I do not care who makes the laws.' What influence do our law-makers exercise at the present moment compared to that which is wielded by the author of 'Slap, bang, here we are again'.[1]

The article did not name the writer, but Vance felt the notice was such a good advertisement that he quoted it word for word on the front of *The Era* a few weeks later.

At the top of English society, there was mere blind disregard for music hall. Once, at Windsor Castle, Queen Victoria heard a military band playing a song she liked. She sent a Court official to find out what it was. Back came the embarrassed reply: 'Come Where the Booze is Cheaper'. The Queen's unamused response: 'I don't know the meaning of "booze", though I can guess . . . At all events, the tune is pretty enough.'[2]

Queen Victoria's idea of a rollicking night out (or, probably, in) was Barnum's famous midget, General Tom Thumb,[3] the Christy Minstrels or performing animals. Her son the Prince of Wales (later Edward VII), took a different view. The Queen despaired of him. He appeared in court twice – first, when falsely accused of having an affair; secondly, when a friend was accused of cheating at the illegal card game baccarat.

In 1868, Vance, Arthur Lloyd and the large and jovial Jolly John Nash, who specialised in laughing songs, became the first music-hall entertainers to appear before the Prince of Wales at a party given by the Earl of Carrington at Marlborough House. John S. Evalo (masquerading as Mr E.) described Nash's style: 'Jolly John Nash was a man of fine physique with a dignified appearance and with a firm belief in the importance of upholding the dignity of his profession. He sang and spoke on the stage in a clear, distinct voice, so quietly that he might have been in a drawing room . . . He could command the attention of any audience.'[4]

Nash himself recalled his Royal Command:

When I entered the room as Racketty Jack, one of the company, the Duke of R——, called out to me to take off my hat and keep it off. I had taken it off to make my preliminary bow, but had

Always laughing, Jolly John Nash. *(Richard Anthony Baker)*

resumed it to give effect to the character I was presenting and I now appealed to him in this way: 'Mr Chairman' (loud laughter from the noble audience, who appeared mightily tickled at my calling the autocratic individual 'Mr Chairman' and they called him 'Mr Chairman' for the remainder of the evening and thought it great fun). 'Mr Chairman' said I 'am I to give this song as if I were in a music hall?' 'Certainly, Nash,' from all the other noble guests 'and keep your hat on, if necessary.'[5]

Unfortunately, Nash eventually overstepped the boundaries of his friendship with the Prince. He slapped him on the back and, from then on, he was ostracised. You do not touch royalty.

After Queen Victoria died, Edward was in mourning for nearly a year and then staged his first royal 'command performance'. In November 1901, Sir Seymour Hicks and his wife, Ellaline Terriss, were summoned to Sandringham, together with Dan Leno. Hicks wrote: 'Dan Leno convulsed everyone with his songs . . . I watched the audience through a hole in the back-cloth and I never saw anyone laugh more than did the King.'[6] Leno was rewarded with a jewelled tie-pin. The coster comedian Albert Chevalier was summoned a year later.

It was not until George V became King that the owners and managers of most of London's leading halls invited him to command (as they put it) a music-hall performance either in London or Edinburgh. The King chose Edinburgh as the venue and July 1912 as the date. The show should have been staged at the Edinburgh Empire, but, after the illusionist the Great Lafayette died in a fire there, it was rearranged for the Palace Theatre in London.

When the bill was announced, there were three notable absentees, Marie Lloyd, Eugene Stratton and Albert Chevalier. Marie pretended not to care; Stratton said nothing; but Chevalier made a tremendous fuss, virtually claiming that there would have been no Command Performance at all had it not been for his efforts to cleanse music hall.

I am convinced that my name was never submitted to the King. Why not? I have already appeared by Royal Command at Sandringham. But when I ask the committee for explanation, I am declined information . . . I think I may claim without egotism that my work has helped to purify the music halls and has assisted to produce a condition of things which has made the Command Performance possible.[7]

Some years earlier, Clement Scott had felt similarly:

Albert Chevalier has had much – very much – to do with the wholesome reform of the modern music hall. An artist by instinct, he left the stage and, with laudable courage, he gave his talent to the common people. He understood that there was a warm heart under a corduroy jacket, a vein of sentiment even in the lowly costermonger and he gave us the ballads which are now household words.[8]

The appalling snobbery of those sentiments (that music hall was innately inferior to the legitimate theatre and that the working man could only appreciate or comprehend entertainment as undemanding as music hall) cannot disguise the fact that Chevalier was an entertainer and lyricist of considerable talent, even if his brand of sentimentality now renders much of his work outdated.

ALBERT CHEVALIER (Albert Onesime
    Britannicus Gwathveoyd Louis
    Chevalier)
Born Notting Hill, London, 21 March
    1861
Married Florence Isabel(la) Leybourne
    (1867–17 October 1931)
    (daughter of George Leybourne)
    at Chapel-en-le-Frith, Derbyshire,
    8 October 1894
    Son, Frederick (d. November 1909,
    aged 22)
Died 10 July 1923
Left £7,164

Chevalier appeared on the so-called legitimate stage with the likes of the Kendals and the Bancrofts before being persuaded to switch to music hall. In 1891, wearing a peaked cap, a check jacket, a necktie and bell-bottomed trousers, he reluctantly made his debut at the London Pavilion. Marie Lloyd stood in the wings, greeting him characteristically when he complained of the audience's 'row'. 'Row?' said Marie. 'Tonight, they are quiet as bloody church mice!'

One of Chevalier's supporters was Lewis Carroll,[9] who generally viewed music hall with disdain. He wrote: '[Albert Chevalier] was decidedly good as an actor; but, as a comic singer (with considerable powers of pathos as well), he is quite first-rate.'

In 1896, Chevalier repeated his success at Koster and Bial's music hall in New York, where, in spite of initial nerves, he was hailed as one of the city's idols. He returned to America in

1906 for a six-week tour in the unlikely company of the French singer Yvette Guilbert, who described him as 'rather more skilful than actually talented'.[10] Their show was seen in London by Max Beerbohm, who was equally unimpressed by Chevalier: 'He has never picked up the knack of ease and quickness . . . He makes a dozen gestures, a dozen grimaces, when one would be ample . . . His points do not need such an unconscionable amount of hammering home.'[11]

On the other hand, the ventriloquist Fred Russell, who appeared on the same bill as Chevalier at the Queen's Hall, Langham Place, in the early 1890s, was full of admiration: '[I] could never keep away from the wings, listening to his masterpiece, *A Fallen Star*. His coster idylls established him in public favour; but it was in such wonderful studies as that of the broken down actor and the old countryman – '*E can't Take the Roize out of Oi* – that I admired him most.'[12]

Albert Chevalier, the Kipling of the Halls. *(Richard Anthony Baker)*

With his younger brother, Charles Ingle, Chevalier wrote his two most famous songs, which outlived him, 'Wot cher! (Knocked 'em in the Old Kent Road)' (1891) and 'My Old Dutch' (1892). ('Old Dutch' ('Duchess of Fife') was cockney rhyming slang for 'wife'):

> We've been together now for forty years
> An' it don't seem a day too much.
> There ain't a lady livin' in the land
> As I'd swop for my dear old Dutch.
> There ain't a lady livin' in the land
> As I'd swop for my dear old Dutch.

Marie Lloyd helped Chevalier cope with his music-hall debut, but, in the dispute over the first Command Performance, she left him to fight his own battles.

Her apologists found at least four possible reasons for her omission. Some assumed her risqué reputation was to blame; others felt the selectors disapproved of her living openly with the man who was to become her third husband, Bernard Dillon, while still married to her second, Alec Hurley; or it could have been her participation in the music-hall strike of 1907, in which employers tried to force artists to work extra matinées for no extra money; or simply, she may have been invited, but decided against taking part. The comedian Wee Georgie Wood used to say that she was asked to appear, but declined because she felt that she would be too nervous and that, in any case, she would not be allowed to perform her whole act. The true reason is probably the first: she was considered too 'blue'.

Chevalier was equally angry about the snub to Marie:

Who is there more representative of the variety profession? Miss Lloyd is a great genius. She is an artist from the crown of her head to the sole of her foot. You know the range of my theatrical experience, the actors with whom I have been associated and the parts I have played. Well, I say deliberately that no woman alive can 'read' a song like Miss Lloyd – can get so much out of the lines. It is an education to hear her.[13]

On the night of the Royal Command, Marie was at the other end of Shaftesbury Avenue playing the London Pavilion. The impresario Don Ross wrote: 'She was greatly upset, but typically she put on a brave face and advertised that every one of her performances were "by Command of the British Public".'[14]

Officially, there were only two command performances – in 1912 and 1919. Those held since have been Royal Variety Performances. The bill of the first Royal Command included Wilkie Bard, G.H. Chirgwin, Cinquevalli, David Devant, Happy Fanny Fields, Barclay Gammon, Harry Lauder, Alfred Lester, Little Tich, Cecilia Loftus, Clarice Mayne, Arthur Prince, George Robey, Harry Tate and Vesta Tilley. The grand finale was entitled Variety's Garden Party, in which 142 music-hall performers appeared.

The following day, a letter from Buckingham Palace indicated that 'their Majesties thoroughly appreciated the [entertainers'] talent, so equal in excellence and varied in style'. Others were not so sure. *The Times* felt that some of the performers seemed to be overawed and lacked the sparkle of the oddity, which endeared them to music hall's nightly patrons.

Certainly, some of those appearing were seized with nerves. Fanny Fields told the audience: 'I'm suffering as much as you are.' Little Tich could not bring himself to join the finale; the *Daily Mail* called Wilkie Bard 'dreadfully dull'; and Chirgwin just seemed out of place. One fable handed down over the years was that Queen Mary, offended by seeing a woman dressed as a man (Vesta Tilley), turned her back on her. That, of course, is ridiculous: both the King and the Queen were fully aware of who they were going to see.

The most extraordinary behaviour came from the truculent Georgie Wood. He had been selected to appear in the Garden Party, but did not want to miss a night's pay at the Bedminster Hippodrome, Bristol, and so, in an act of unalloyed discourtesy to the King and Queen, found a look-alike to take his place. The day after the Command Performance, there was a review of the local bill: 'Wee Georgie Wood is the great attraction this week and two large houses on Monday evening roared with laughter at his antics in his sketch "An evening in the Nursery" . . . His impersonations of Mr Neil Kenyon, Miss Marie Lloyd and Miss Maud Allan were remarkably clever.'[15] But then, Wood's long life was punctuated by such behaviour.

Capitalising on his lack of height (he was just 4ft 9in) (145cm), Wood performed sketches as a child, first, as a young girl impersonating music-hall stars, then as a member of the so-called Black Hand Gang and, most notably, as the naughty son of Mrs Robinson, played by Dolly Harmer,[16] an association which lasted for nearly forty years. George Wood was famous in Britain, the United States, Canada, South Africa, Australia and New Zealand, but, as his star began to fade, he became one of the least popular men in show business, demanding to be treated with dignity at all times, expecting enormous favours from friends and acquaintances and, for some years, blackballed by the Water Rats, the showbiz brotherhood, founded in 1889, that works for charity. The Rats were named after a comment made about a pony called Magpie, whose owner was one of the Rats' founders, Joe Elvin. One rainy day, the animal was pulling a cart carrying several entertainers to the Epsom races. At a set of traffic lights, a bus driver asked of them: 'What have you got there?' Elvin replied: 'That's our trotting pony, Magpie.' 'Magpie!' said the driver. 'Looks more like a bloody water rat.' The founders had been searching for a name for their new organisation. Thanks to the bus driver, they found it.

George was born in a room above a pawnbroker's shop in Jarrow, owned by his father. When he was only a few weeks old, his father was appointed the manager of one of a chain of grocery shops in South Shields and the family moved there. Before the age of 4, he discovered he could commit to memory recitations of several hundred words and he was soon performing them at local Methodist Church functions. (Much later in life, he converted to Catholicism.) Between the ages of 6 and 10, he was a member of a number of concert parties and pierrot companies.

In his solo sketch, set in a nursery, he lined up his teddy bears and, seemingly oblivious of his audience, entertained them with impressions of the likes of Marie Lloyd, Vesta Tilley and Harry Lauder. In fact, he used to say that Marie helped him with his impersonation of her,

---

WEE GEORGIE WOOD (George Wood Bamlett)

Born Jarrow, Tyne and Wear, 17 December 1895

('Later in America, I legally changed my name to George Bamlett Wood.')

Married Ewing Veronica Eaton, New York, 7 April 1933 (dissolved)

Died Bloomsbury, London, 19 February 1979

Left £1,135

even ordering a miniature version of one of her dresses for him to wear. George made his London debut at the Shepherd's Bush Empire in 1909 with the melodramatic actor Bransby Williams at the top of the bill. At the age of 13, he could still pass for 5. He claimed he was soon earning £100 a week. In fact, in the run-up to the First World War, the wage book for the London Tivoli showed he was getting £28 a week, which was, even so, a big salary.

Around 1920, George teamed up with Dolly Harmer in domestic comedy sketches, in which Dolly tried to persuade George to behave properly. Between then and Dolly's death in 1956, they appeared in thirty-six different sketches. In one, George tells her about taking a girl to the cinema: 'We were sitting in the pictures and she took hold of my hand and squeezed me hard twice.

Wee Georgie Wood, blackballed by the Water Rats. (Richard Anthony Baker)

Then she whispered "Diddle-iddle". I didn't know what to do. So I said "Doddle-oddle." Then, the lights went up and the man came down the aisle and disinfected the place.'[17]

At about the same time as George began working with Dolly, he dispensed with the nursery sketch and, in addition to Mrs Robinson and her son, played in several sketches featuring the escapades of the Black Hand gang, who feature in one of his movies and on one of only two records he made.

In 1932, George was appearing on the same bill as an American entertainer, the daughter of a St Louis businessman, Ewing Eaton, who was fourteen years his junior. A romance developed between them and they married in New York the following year. It did not work out. In a brief but poignant reference to his marriage in his disappointing autobiography, he wrote: 'That is all over now, but, if she ever does read this book, it was all my fault and I have never ceased regretting it.'[18] Later, George blamed his mother: 'It was not my fault as much as my mother's, who, with a self-possessiveness amounting to cruelty, determined to wreck the marriage.'[19]

From about the age of 35, George's career was in decline. It was becoming harder to convince audiences he was still a boy and, in any case, his brand of sentimentality was going out of fashion. The Second World War helped to some extent, in particular ENSA, the Entertainments National Service Association, which organised shows for troops fighting in the Second World War, sometimes in near impossible conditions. During the war, many unknowns in uniform, such as Harry Secombe, Frankie Howerd and Benny Hill, were given their first chance to learn how to play to an audience. George and Dolly travelled some 70,000 miles to entertain the troops in the Middle East, North Africa and Sicily, as a result of which he was awarded the OBE. He was also able to adapt some of the mother-and-son sketches into similar ones featuring an officer and a difficult soldier.

In 1936, George was made King Rat, the Chairman of the Water Rats, but he then wrote a privately published book, *Royalty, Religion and Rats!*, which disclosed some of the order's secrets. As a result, he was expelled, the only time this has happened. It was not until the agent Philip Hindin was King Rat in 1970 that he was readmitted, in spite of the opposition of other former King Rats, including Bud Flanagan and Ted Ray, who disliked his superior attitude. When Philip had lunch with George at the Eccentric Club to invite him back, George burst into tears, but, within a fortnight, he was again misbehaving.

George was a self-educated man, an omnivorous reader with a prodigious memory, but he made sure people knew it. In addition, he was, according to your outlook, either a romancer or a consummate liar, claiming to have sat on Queen Victoria's knee as a child. Since she had died before he entered the profession, the story is unlikely. He frequently borrowed money without repaying it; he insisted on being called Mr Wood, never George and certainly not Georgie; and he took enormous liberties with people who tried to show him friendship. A stage-struck garage owner, Leslie Austin, offered George transport whenever he wanted it. Eventually pricked by conscience over accepting such hospitality, George gave Austin a Masonic watch to show his gratitude. Not long afterwards, George phoned Austin one night to ask where his car was. He was told it would be with him within a quarter of an hour. 'I ordered it for eight o'clock,' replied George. 'You can tell Leslie I want my watch back.'

In 1946, his mother, Georgina, died. She had long since divorced George's father and had married a policeman, whom George did not like. In a letter to the talented television journalist, writer and photographer Daniel Farson, George explained that he believed she had exploited him as a child: 'From the time I brought £3 12s 6d [£3.62] home to my mother from a concert, she put me to work and my own lost childhood is my reason for being opposed to child performers.'[20] Asked whether he loved his mother, he replied: 'I think not. I had a conscience thing about her, upsetting myself that I ought to love her, pretending I did and feeling guilty. It never occurred to her – she just accepted that I loved her and ought to give her everything. It would have been too brutal to disillusion her.'[21] When she died, George said to himself: 'Now, thank God, I can really live.'

George told fellow Rats that, in his will, he had left instructions for his body to be made available for scientific research. 'Good,' the comic Eddie Reindeer commented; 'they'll put you in a bottle and we'll come and visit you.' This was one of many jibes against midgets which George had to bear, another being Noel Coward's line that the trouble with small men was that their brains were too near their backsides.

Towards the end of his life, George's housekeeper, Ethel Adams, who had been a fan before becoming his closest friend, moved into his flat in Bloomsbury. He was by now almost completely impoverished. The Rats allowed him £10 a week and paid his electricity and telephone bills. He died a lonely and bitter man.

Given the lowly origins of music hall, the excitement of some entertainers at being accepted by nobility is understandable, but there was an amount of showing off, too. Vesta Tilley's autobiography is entitled *Recollections of Vesta Tilley* by Lady de Frece. That is absolutely accurate since Vesta married Sir Walter de Frece, music-hall proprietor and later Conservative MP. But how more straightforward it would have been to have called her memoirs the *Recollections of Vesta Tilley* by Vesta Tilley?

The most astounding example of social reinvention was the work of Millie Lindon, a minor singer and impersonator, whose music-hall career lasted little more than a decade. Her first husband was the tragic T.E. Dunville, billed as 'an eccentric comedian and contortionist'. The 'eccentric' reference related to his appearance. His coat was basically a black alpaca bodice, which had belonged to his mother. He added a white frill to the bottom of it and a white linen collar to the top. Calling it his mascot, he wore it thousands of times and resented other entertainers copying it. His appearance was once described in these terms: 'A long lean figure clad in exiguous black, with a bare, dome-like forehead, wild glaring eyes, a nervous, twitching restlessness and a mad, staccato utterance.'[22]

Dunville remained successful for more than thirty years, but, during the early 1920s, he began suffering fits of depression. In the early months of 1924, his second wife, Dora, described him as a bundle of nerves: 'the slightest thing seemed to worry him.' In March, he left her a note that read in part: 'I feel I cannot bear it any longer.' He drowned himself in the Thames; his body was found at Caversham Lock, near Reading.

> T.E. DUNVILLE (Thomas Edward Wallen)
> **Born** Coventry, 29 July 1867
> **Married** (1) Fanny Elizabeth Warriss (professionally known as Millie Lindon) at Clapham, south London, 8 April 1895; divorced 1902
> (2) Dora Cross in central London, 3 December 1909
> **Died** near Reading, Berkshire, March 1924
> **Left** £237

Dunville managed the early part of the career of Millie Lindon, his first wife, who was the daughter of a tailor. At their wedding, Millie embellished her name to become 'Florence Elizabeth Millicent Warriss' and reduced her age by nine years. She had one hit song, 'For Old Times' Sake' (1898), written by Charles Osborne.

In 1902, Millie and Dunville divorced and Millie married the Manchester newspaper magnate Sir Edward Hulton, who founded the *Daily Sketch*, bought and enlarged the London *Evening Standard* and then sold his empire to Lord Beaverbrook for £6,000,000. They had two children: a daughter, who died at the age of 22, and a son, Edward George Warris (*sic*). This marriage also failed.

> MILLIE LINDON (Fanny Elizabeth Warriss)
> **Born** King's Norton, West Midlands, 1 April 1869
> **Married** (1) Thomas Edward Wallen (professionally known as T.E. Dunville (1867–1924)) at Clapham, south London, 8 April 1895; divorced 1902
> (2) Sir Edward Hulton (d. 23 May 1925)
>   One son, Edward (1906–88); one daughter (d. 1932)
> (3) Major-General John Thompson in central London, 21 November 1928; divorced 1937
> (4) Baron Otto Sklenar von Schaniel, 7 April 1938
> **Died** Taormina, Italy, 1940.

The younger Edward became a newspaper proprietor in his own right, developing a new style of photo journalism in the hugely successful *Picture Post*. He also wrote his memoirs, *When I Was a Child*, which gives a vivid account of the highly comfortable style of living his mother enjoyed after leaving music hall. In the morning, she spent an hour or two making up her face, ate an enormous breakfast,

Below: T.E. Dunville, the Long, Lean, Lorn Loon. *(British Music Hall Society)*

Above: Millie Lindon, who reinvented herself as a minor aristocrat. *(British Music Hall Society)*

wrote letters and pottered about among her rococo furniture before driving to lunch. She was well known at all the fashionable restaurants of the day, such as Quaglino's.

For a man described as having a lively, enquiring mind, Hulton seemed curiously uninterested in his mother's past. To him, she had been a beautiful actress, whose clothes trunks were marked W-L, as she had sometimes called herself Miss Warris-Lindon. She was descended from an ancient Spanish family, de Warris, which bore a coat of arms. With apparent naivety, Hulton also described Millie's collection of 'gentlemen friends': a former President of Peru, a Uruguayan colonel and a handsome, athletic young man, who she said was the original Galloping Major from the song of the comedian George Bastow.

Millie told her son that she had a penchant for soldiers. Indeed, her third husband was a militaire, as she liked to call them. This marriage lasted eight years. There was to be one more husband, a Czechoslovak landowner, before Millie died in Italy. *The Times* reported that she had been married three times. Poor Dunville had been airbrushed out of her history.

CHAPTER 10

ACROSS THE POND

Just as the tone of music hall changed in Britain during its short history, so did that of its American counterpart, vaudeville – from working-class, inner city origins, the entertainment bawdy and boisterous, to a more broadly based audience with apparently more 'refined' tastes. The word 'vaudeville' itself is supposed to have been derived from Vaux-de-Vire, a collection of songs written in the valley of the Vire in Normandy in fifteenth-century France. If this sounds fanciful, many etymologists would agree.

As Charles Morton became known as the Father of the Halls, Tony Pastor was equally famous as the Father of Vaudeville, booking many British music-hall stars for their first visit to the United States.

Pastor started out as an entertainer himself, making his first public appearance at a temperance meeting at the age of 6. After some years in minstrel troupes and circuses, he made his debut as a comic singer in Philadelphia in 1860. The following year, billed as 'the greatest clown and comic singer of the age', he was seen at the American Concert Hall in New York and, with the Civil War about to erupt, he finished his act by singing 'The Star-Spangled Banner'.

TONY PASTOR (Antonio Pastor)
Born New York, 1832/35/37/40 (?)
Married (1) Anna —— c. 1862 (d. 18 July 1867)
(2) Josephine Foley, 1871
Died New York, 26 August 1908

Pastor first entered management in 1865 by forming a minstrel troupe, the first of many companies he sent on tour. That same year, he opened Tony Pastor's Opera House in New York. He later leased other theatres. His best known was the New Fourteenth Street Theatre, formerly Bryant's Minstrel Hall.

A proponent of black-faced minstrelsy in Britain, G.W. Moore, a friend of Pastor since the 1840s, became his unofficial agent in London and arranged trips to New York by a number of music-hall entertainers. Ten years after Sam Cowell's gruelling transatlantic trip, Moore sent Annie Adams to America. Annie was one of Britain's first female music-hall stars. In fact, during her heyday in the 1860s and 1870s, she had few women competitors.

The daughter of an innkeeper on the Isle of Wight, Annie Adams was not a pretty girl, but she had a jolly face and laughed a lot and, as she grew up, she developed a fine figure with a pronounced bust. Throughout her childhood, she lived in or near Southampton, where her parents kept various hotels. She made a name for herself locally by singing songs and ballads at theatres and concert rooms in the area. She had a strong voice and put her songs over with such vigour that glasses jumped up and down on the tables. The agent Ambrose Maynard saw potential in her and signed her up.

The first engagement he secured for her was at Barnard's music hall in Chatham. There, she met her future husband, Harry Wall. She made her London debut at Weston's, later the Holborn Empire, in 1862 and, after an engagement at the London Pavilion, her stardom was established: she went on to play every music hall in Britain. Two of her most popular songs were written by G.W. Hunt, 'Johnny, the Engine Driver' (1867) and 'When the Band Begins to Play' (1871).

Her two-year tour of America between 1871 and 1873 earned her a fortune: she was paid $200 to $250 (£40 to £50) (by today's standards, £8,000 to £10,000) a week. Billed as the Queen of Serio-Comic Vocalists (singers of both serious and comic

Annie Adams, Queen of Serio-Comic Vocalists. *(Richard Anthony Baker)*

songs), she began by playing the Union Square Theater in New York for ten weeks and then travelled on to Brooklyn, Philadelphia; St Louis, Pittsburgh; New York again; Boston; New York yet again; Philadelphia again; then Buffalo, ending with a two-month appearance in San Francisco, which, in itself, netted her more than $1,000. Most music-hall entertainers had previously been nervous at the idea of trying their luck in America, but Annie's success led many of them to cross the Atlantic for the first time.

ANNIE ADAMS (Ann Eliza Adams)
Born Newport, Isle of Wight,
  16 November 1843
Married Henry Whiting (professionally
  known as Harry Wall), Chatham,
  Kent, 22 May 1862 (d. November
  1918)
  Son, Harry, married Louie Wilmot, of
  Grand Theatre, Islington
Died London 12 May 1905

The Americans loved her. In New York, she was called 'the most original singer who ever appeared on the variety stage in America'; in Philadelphia, she was 'the centre of attraction'; and, in San Francisco, she was awarded 'the highest encomiums of the American press'.

Pastor was prevented from visiting London himself by a dread of deep water. By 1887, he had overcome his phobia and made an annual trip to London part of his professional calendar. One of the first stars he booked was the male impersonator Bessie Bonehill, who made her American debut in 1889. Two years later came Jenny Hill, music hall's most popular female entertainer before Marie Lloyd. Pastor was so worried that American audiences would not understand her London patois that he distributed special dictionaries throughout the theatre.

Jenny could mix comedy and pathos with ease and, according to the theatrical manager John Hollingshead, would have become a supreme actress, had she been properly trained as a girl. For her vivacity on stage, she was billed as 'the Vital Spark'.

JENNY HILL (Jane Hill)
Born London *c.* 1850
Married John Wilson Woodley (professionally
known as Jean Pasta), London, 28 May 1866
(d. 8 January 1890)
One daughter, Letitia Matilda (professionally
known as Peggy Pryde, 1867–(?))
Another, Jenny, married Alex Davidson in Dover,
1 August 1898
Died London, 28 June 1896
Left £2,137

Her childhood was far from easy. Her father looked after cabs in Marylebone. As a young girl, she worked at a local factory making artificial flowers. It was owned by Bob Botting, who also managed the Marylebone Music Hall in Marylebone High Street. The story goes that Botting paid her a few pennies to sing at the factory because it encouraged other workers to put in more effort. If this is true, Jenny would have been under 11 at the time as Botting did not take over the theatre until 1861.

She first appeared on stage in a pantomime produced by Joe Cave. This may have been *Goody Goose* produced at the Marylebone in 1858/9. Jenny played the legs of the goose, but, one night, she lost her way and ended up weeping and half-naked in the centre of the footlights much to the delight of an audience that roared with laughter. Her first regular engagement was at Doctor Johnson's Concert Room. Here, by her own account, she was 'a little thing in socks and shoes', earning 3*s* (15p) a night, plus refreshments.

At the age of 12, she was apprenticed for seven years to the manager of the Turk's Head Inn in Bradford. She was to learn the trade of a serio-comic singer, as well as carry out domestic duties around the pub. It was a tough regimen. On market days, for instance, Jenny had to be ready to sing and dance for the entertainment of local farmers until as late as two in the morning. Then, she had to be up again at five to scrub floors, polish pewter and bottle beer. It is unclear whether she completed the apprenticeship because, back in London in 1866, she married an acrobat, Jean Pasta. They had a daughter, who became well known in later life as Peggy Pryde, but the marriage failed and Jenny found herself out of work and close to starvation.

Shortly before Christmas 1871, she went to see Ambrose Maynard, almost begging him for work, even at £1 a week. He scribbled something on a sheet of notepaper, sealed it, addressed it to the manager of the London Pavilion, Emil Loibl, and sent her away with it. At the Pavilion, Loibl read the note and commented: 'Well, little woman, you've got a fine recommendation here. What can you do? Sing? Dance?' Jenny was offered an extra turn that night and, when George Leybourne was late, she was pushed on in his place and sang a parody of 'Old Brown's Daughter'. The audience liked her. She was told to go on again, but felt faint through lack of food. Leybourne, who had arrived by now, led her on to acknowledge the applause. Backstage once more, she was offered a glass of port and a long engagement. Loibl then handed her the 'letter of recommendation' as a keepsake. It told Loibl not to bother to see her. Maynard had sent her merely to get rid of her, adding that she was troublesome.

That is the most commonly told story about Jenny Hill's lucky break. Maurice de Frece had a different version. In a letter to *The Performer* in 1915, he claimed to have been her first agent, meeting her at his office in Liverpool and obtaining engagements for her at three London halls every night, the Oxford, the South London Palace and the Foresters. He said he argued with the Oxford manager, who did not want to retain her and then succeeded in booking her with Loibl at the London Pavilion at a good salary.

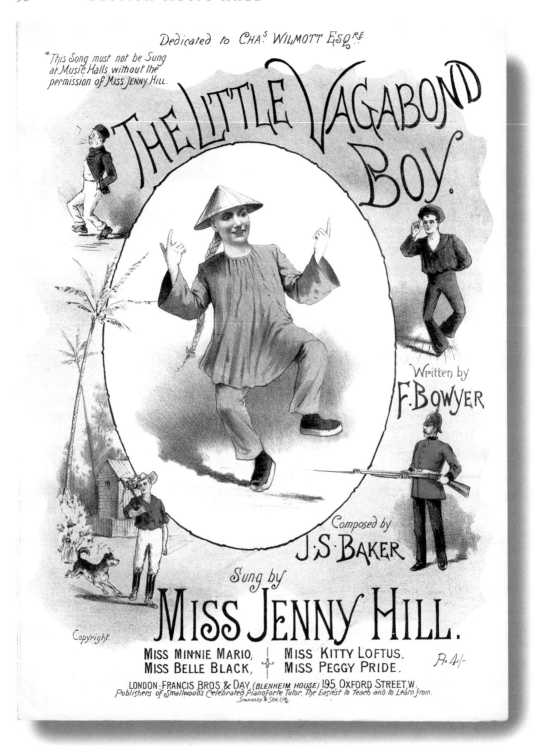

Jenny Hill, the Vital Spark. *(Richard Anthony Baker)*

One reporter described Jenny as 'trimly built, agile, nervous and energetic, with a face that is both pleasing and expressive, but often grotesque beyond description'. Her fame gathered momentum during the 1870s, with such songs as 'I've been a good woman to you' (1876):

> I've been a good woman to you
> And the neighbours all know that it's true.
> You go to the pub
> And 'blue' [squander] the kids' grub,
> But I've been a good woman to you.

At the turn of the decade, Jenny was playing the title role in *Aladdin* at the Prince of Wales's Theatre in Birmingham. Fully accustomed to the gusto of a music-hall audience, she was none too surprised when a cabbage thrown from the gallery hit her on the bosom. As she fell, she was caught by Mark Kinghorne playing the Emperor, for whom it was intended: 'She would talk to an audience like a mother and take them into her confidence . . . and, though petite, she was of a pleasing countenance with a healthy pallor . . . Above all, she was a consummate artiste and I never forget her tragic acting as Aladdin in the cavern scene. They gave you something to remember in those days.'[1]

Jenny's most famous numbers belonged to the 1880s. In 1882, there was ''Arry', written by E.V. Page, the tale of a cockney on holiday; in 1883, 'Sweet Violets'; in 1888, 'Masks and Faces' by George le Brunn and John P. Harrington, which ends with the murder of an elderly miser; and in 1889, le Brunn and Harrington's 'The City Waif', the story of a woman of easy virtue who spends her money trying to find a cure for her crippled sister. 'The City Waif' was more sketch than song, as were Frederick Bowyer's 'The Little Stowaway', first produced in 1889; 'Shadows of St Paul's'; and 'Little Gyp', the melodramatic story of a fairground child who escapes from a brutal master to marry a miner.

Jenny's health started to fail at the end of the 1880s. Unfortunately, she became embroiled in a controversy over whether sketches should form part of a music-hall bill. 'The Little Stowaway' was banned in 1889, only to reappear the following year. The controversy angered *The Era*:

> The theatres seem to forget what obligation they are under to the music halls. In pantomime and in burlesque, they steal our business and our songs and they take nearly all our leading artistes. They might in common fairness let us have our little sketches. The theatres make a great mistake if they think the sketches in the music halls do them any harm. They don't. They stimulate the taste for a better class of entertainment than is usually given in the music halls.[2]

Before the 1880s, Jenny Hill was earning big money, but the decade itself was less successful for her business enterprises. In 1879, she had become the proprietress of the Star Music Hall in Hull, which Pasta was supposed to run. For unexplained reasons, the venture collapsed. In 1882, she took the lease of a pub in south-east London, the Albert Arms, another loss-making enterprise. In 1884, she bought the Rainbow music hall in Southampton, but, two months later, it burnt down. All the same, in 1889, a reporter from the music-hall press found Jenny living in some style on an 80-acre farm, the Hermitage in Streatham, south London. On most Sundays, lavish parties were held, to which dozens of music-hall people were invited.

In the autumn of 1890, Jenny travelled to New York, where she was paid £150 (by today's standards £900) a week and enjoyed great success, but the trip proved a great strain and, for fifteen months after her return in 1891, she was practically an invalid. At one stage, it looked as though she would never appear in public again, but, when she returned to the Oxford in 1893, singing two new songs, 'That's Bill' and 'The Southend Picnic', she was given a stupendous reception with huge bouquets being passed across the footlights. To help to restore her health, she went to South Africa in December 1893, returning in May 1894, but it did little good. Just over two years later, she died at Peggy Pryde's[3] home in the Brixton Road. *The Era* summed up her appeal:

> Her free spoken characters were taken from life and their originals were to be met with any day in the vastly populated district of Whitechapel . . . The secret of her success lay quite as much in her ready wit as in the unflagging spirit with which she rendered her ditties. A dispute between two women, a discussion outside a public house, the reminiscences of a lodging house keeper or the experiences of a girl at a coffee shop she could reproduce to a nicety, interspersing comments adapted to the quarter of the metropolis in which she was for the moment appearing.[4]

Vesta Victoria first went to America in 1893 and, in time, became as popular there as she was in Britain. After one of her earliest hits, 'Daddy wouldn't buy me a bow-wow', she mainly specialised in songs depicting her as the sufferer of some romantic misfortune, such as 'Waiting at the Church'.

Vesta made her first appearance in London in 1883 when she was nearly 10. She was billed as Little Victoria, 'the most marvellously gifted child in the world'. A little later, she introduced impersonations into her act, mimicking the likes of the singer Bessie Bellwood and the male impersonator Bessie Bonehill. Her big break came in 1891 with a George and Thomas le Brunn song, 'Good-for-Nothing Nan', based on a character in a John Baldwin Buckstone play, *Good for Nothing*. According to Vesta, it trebled her earnings in a week. Joseph Tabrar's 'Daddy wouldn't buy me a bow-wow', which proved a more durable song, came the following year. She sang it on her first visit to America in 1892 when she appeared for eight weeks at Tony Pastor's theater in New York City and Shea's Theater in Buffalo, New York:

VESTA VICTORIA (Victoria Lawrence)
Born Leeds, 26 November 1873
Married (1) Frederick Wallace McAvoy, 20 September
    1897 (divorced 1903)
    One daughter, Irene Victoria Blanche
      (b. 13 November 1898)
    (2) William Herbert Henry Terry in May 1912
      (divorced 1926, d. 18 November 1929)
    One daughter, Iris Lavender (b. 1913;
      d. 11 August 1995)
Died Hampstead, London, 7 April 1951
Left £15,632

> Daddy wouldn't buy me a bow-wow
> Daddy wouldn't buy me a bow-wow
> I've got a little cat, I am very fond of that
> But I'd rather have a bow-wow-wow.

As for Vesta's other hits, she was lucky to have a brother, Ernest, professionally known as Lawrence Barclay, who proved to be a highly talented songwriter. He was responsible for

Vesta Victoria, a Vesta that will Strike anywhere. *(Richard Anthony Baker)*

'Our Lodger's such a Nice Young Man' (1897) and 'He Calls me his Own Grace Darling'[5] (1898), as well as at least ten other songs for Vesta. Her other major successes were 'It's Alright in the Summertime' (1902) by George Everard and Fred Murray; 'Waiting at the Church' and 'Poor John' (both 1906) and both written by Henry Pether and Fred W. Leigh:

> There was I waiting at the church,
> Waiting at the church, waiting at the church,
> When I found he'd left me in the lurch.
> Lor', how it did upset me.
> All at once, he sent me round a note.
> Here's the very note.
> This is what he wrote.
> 'Can't get away to marry you today.
> My wife won't let me.'

Vesta made her second trip to America in 1895; her third in 1906, when one of San Francisco's main roads was renamed Vesta Victoria Avenue in her honour; her fourth in 1907, when she made a ten-week tour, earning $3,000 a week; and many more times. Over the years, she bought a considerable amount of property in America. At the peak of her fame, she was the highest paid star in American vaudeville.

In 1897, Vesta married the manager of the South London music hall, Fred McAvoy, but, by 1900, divorce proceedings had begun. McAvoy accused Vesta of committing adultery with a number of men, including Eugene Stratton. The judge, however, found in Vesta's favour: 'with regard to the cruelty, he was satisfied that, when the petitioner was married, she was a young woman in good health, but, owing to the series of accusations that she was an immoral person, her health was seriously injured.'

Vesta's second husband was an actor-manager and dramatist, Herbert Terry, the son of Edward Terry, the owner of Terry's Theatre in the Strand. However, on marrying her in America in 1912, he committed bigamy. His first wife later died and Vesta and Terry went through a second form of marriage ceremony in London in 1920. He left her in 1926.

According to their only daughter, Iris, Vesta had a drink problem and Terry took cocaine and morphine. When drunk, Vesta had screaming fits, which became worse after her divorce from Terry. His behaviour seemed to be governed by the moon. Once, he tried to kill both Vesta and Iris by putting carbolic acid in a trifle he had made. During the Second World War, Vesta became friendly with a crook, who persuaded her to sign documents when she was drunk. Iris said Vesta once bought a non-existent gold mine in Canada from the man, a pimp who died in a brothel during the Second World War.

Vesta's solicitors told Iris that, in the 1920s, Vesta was worth about £3.25 million (by today's standards £975 million). On her death, she left £15,631 17s 5d (£15,631.87). Towards the end of her life, she contracted cancer and moved from her houseboat on the Thames to one of her houses in Hampstead, where, according to Iris, she continued drinking, keeping brandy at one end of her bedroom and gin at the other.

Alice Lloyd was as popular in the United States as her elder sister, Marie, was in Britain. The Americans preferred her less broad style of comedy. She earned even more money than

ALICE LLOYD (Alice Mary Ellen Wood)
Born City Road, London, 20 October 1873
Married Thomas William Norton (professionally known
  as Tom McNaughton), Lambeth, south London,
  16 January 1894 (d. 28 November 1923)
Two daughters, Alice Daisy Victoria (1895–1987),
  married (1) John Keller, 1953; (2) Julian Hyman, 1965
and Grace Cecilia Ida (1916–2003), married William
  Penri Thomas, 1939; one son, William Paul Lloyd
  (b. 1943); one daughter, Luanne Lloyd (b. 1946)
Died Banstead, Surrey, 17 November 1949
(She signed her will as Alice Victoria Bourne-Norton)

Marie and, whereas Marie lost hers through reckless generosity, Alice saw hers disappear in the Wall Street crash of 1929.

Marie and Alice made their first public appearance while still children. To help raise funds for the Band of Hope attached to their local parish church, Marie formed a group she called the Fairy Bell Minstrels. As part of their show, Alice read a poem entitled 'The Dead Doll':

> You needn't be trying to comfort me.
> I tell you my dolly is dead.
> She died of a broken heart
> And a dreadful crack on the head.

Many years later, Alice credited Marie's work as director: 'I recited these lines, according to Marie's minute instructions. A dramatic gesture towards the direction of the deceased doll; my hand over my heart to indicate the broken heart; and a thump on my own head to demonstrate the whack that killed the doll.'[6] A short while later, Marie and Alice appeared at a charity bazaar at the Congregationalists' City Temple at Holborn Viaduct. Afterwards, the Temple's founder, Dr Joseph Parker, called the girls over and balanced them on his knees. 'Who taught you to recite?' he asked Marie. 'No one,' she replied. 'I taught myself.' 'And who taught you, little girl?' he asked Alice. 'She did,' said Alice, pointing at Marie.

As teenagers, while Marie's fame grew month by month, Alice teamed up with another sister, Gracie, as the Sisters Lloyd, 'the talented juvenile song and dance artists'. (It was this pair of Lloyd sisters whom Walter Sickert painted.) They made their first appearance at the Foresters in Bethnal Green in 1888. Some weeks later, they were at the Albert, where a reviewer from *The Entr'acte* reminded readers of the girls' up-and-coming sister: 'The Sisters Lloyd are a pair of youthful vocalists and dancers who are making successful experiments at this hall just now. These young ladies come of very good stock and, having a bright light constantly before them, should prosper.'[7]

The act indeed prospered until Gracie married a jockey, George Hyams, in 1896 and retired from the stage. Alice then went solo, making one of her first appearances as Morgiana in *Ali Baba Or* [sic] *The Forty Thieves* at the Palace, Manchester, in 1895/6. It may be cynical to suggest how she won the part. The show was written by G.H. MacDermott, who was by then her agent. At the end of the run of *Ali Baba*, she played Brighton, Bolton, Liverpool, Cardiff, Newport, Liverpool, Bristol, Plymouth and Birmingham, before arriving in the West End of London in the middle of the summer of 1896, billed at first as the Acme of Perfection and then as the Essence of Refinement.

Alice made her American debut in 1907 in extraordinary circumstances. Percy Williams, who ran the Colonial Theater on New York's Broadway at 63rd Street, wanted a repeat of the

Alice Lloyd, the Ideal Dainty
Chanteuse. (Luanne Beaton)

successes enjoyed in America by Vesta Tilley and Vesta Victoria. His agent in Britain sent him a cable: 'Can send Lloyd by next steamer. Am confident she will make big success.' Understandably, Williams thought his agent meant Marie. He cabled back: 'Send Lloyd to open at Colonial immediately on arrival.' Williams ordered bills to be printed, but, before they were put up, Alice cabled from Liverpool, announcing that she was about to sail and signing herself 'Alice Lloyd'. In Williams's office, there was consternation. The bills were torn up; another star was booked; and Alice was put on as fifth turn, her time limited to 15 minutes.

When she arrived in New York, there was no one to greet her. She went to the Colonial the following Monday and rehearsed her songs. Williams had forgotten all about her – that is, until she reached her third song at the Monday matinée. The audience rose to its feet and would not let her go until she had sung seven songs in all, including one of the most famous of her career, 'You Splash me and I'll Splash you'. Her 15 minutes became 45.

The Americans liked her lack of brashness. The *Brooklyn Daily Eagle* reported: 'Miss Lloyd is of the pink and white, Dresden china type and renders her songs in a dainty, modest and demure manner, instead of hurling them at her audience as we have come to expect from English singers.'[8]

Within days, Alice's name was in lights outside the theatre; she was placed top of the bill; her salary was increased from $300 (£60) a week to $1,500 (£300); her stay in America was extended to three months; and she signed a five-year contract with American agents. Starting in May 1908, she was to work forty weeks a year in America at a salary of $2,000 (£400;

How Others Saw Us

A minor American double act, Ross and Lewis, once wrote of their experiences touring Britain. With surprise, they noted that some first-class music halls were to be found in badly lit back streets; that audiences would queue for an hour or more for tickets; and that Chatham had the last hall in the country to retain a chairman announcing turns as they appeared:

Perhaps the funniest experience for the raw American act is to play some of the Lancashire and Yorkshire towns. The chief industry there is cotton spinning. The mill hands usually see the first show as they have to be up early . . . All wear clog shoes, the girls with shawls over their heads. They are weary of being 'stung' and often elect a delegate to report on the show Monday night. If his verdict is 'champion', business is good for the week. A hard working lot, there is a saying that 'the act which sweats the hardest gets the most applause'. This is true all over England. They want a lot of action and the act which opens with patter is apt to hear from the gallery: 'Well, do something;' if their patience is too far tried, they are not backward in giving you 'the bird' [hissing]. A favourite expression of the Scotchman in a like case is to shout out 'Go back to your work.' But this same crowd is very staunch and, if you please them, they never forget you.*

* *Variety*, 14 December 1907.

today's equivalent of £22,000) a week. With the exception of Harry Lauder, she became the highest paid British entertainer to visit America to date. Alice liked the Americans:

> They have the most wonderful audiences there. In London, we must make our points broad – the broader the better – but in America our hearers seem to know what we're going to say before we say it. The defter and more delicate a point is and the harder to catch, the better they like it. In fact, they like to depend on themselves for at least half the humour in a song and it must be put to them in such a way that they can pick it out for themselves, instead of having it 'handed to them', as they term it.[9]

For the next twenty years, Alice Lloyd worked more in America than Britain. In 1928, she turned down an offer to appear on an all-English bill at the Palace and returned to England for the last time. Later, she joined Rosie, Daisy (and later still Marie Lloyd junior) to appear as the Lloyd Family, singing songs Marie had made famous.

The Fourteenth Street Theater became a cinema in June 1908. Pastor announced that vaudeville programmes would return that August, but, by then, his health was failing. After his death, many people were surprised that his estate, valued at $72,500, was not larger. They did not know that he had given away more than $1 million.

Daisy Wood, another Lloyd sister who went on stage, but the only one to retain the family name. *(Richard Anthony Baker)*

CHAPTER 11

BONDAGE AND MUSCLES

In the space of two months in 1904, music-hall regulars at the London Hippodrome saw two of theatre's greatest and most original showmen – the escapologist Houdini, and the strongman Eugen Sandow. It is an indication of the fame of both men that, years after their deaths, fans around the world are competing with each other to acquire what memorabilia they can find.

Harry Houdini, born Ehrich Weiss, was the son of a rabbi who moved his family from Hungary to America in 1876. In his mid-teens, Ehrich teamed up with a friend, Jacob Hyman, to form a magic act, the Brothers Houdini. The name was chosen in honour of the French conjurer Jean Eugène Robert-Houdin, the founder of modern magic. Ehrich's nickname, Ehrie, easily became Harry.

Billed as the Modern Monarchs of Mystery, the pair performed at the World Fair in Chicago in 1893, but, after some changes of personnel, the Brothers Houdini broke up when Harry married. He and his wife, who was known as Bess, then launched themselves as the Houdinis, playing chambers of horrors, waxwork exhibitions and dime museums. They perfected an escapology act, called Metamorphosis, in which Harry was tied in a sack, which was itself locked in a trunk. Knocking and shouting were heard from inside the trunk, a curtain was drawn across it, Houdini reappeared in front of the curtain, the ropes and locks were undone and – inside the sack – well, of course, Bess.

HARRY HOUDINI (Ehrich Weiss)
Born Budapest, Hungary, 24 March 1874
Married Wilhelmina Beatrice Rahmer, 22 June 1894 (d. 12 February 1943)
Died Detroit, Michigan, 31 October 1926

Houdini had to wait until the spring of 1899 to get his big break. Appearing at a beer-hall in St Paul's, Minnesota, he was seen by a party of theatre managers, including Martin Beck, who had built up the Orpheum circuit of theatres in America. He set Houdini a challenge by presenting him with a few sets of handcuffs from which to escape, a feat Houdini accomplished with ease. As a result, Beck, who was to build the flagship of vaudeville, the Palace Theater in New York, offered Houdini work at $60 a week – more than Houdini had ever earned.

New tricks were devised for the better dates he was playing: needle-swallowing and making playing cards disappear, but Houdini's escapes remained his most popular act. His business card read:

Houdini, the King of
Handcuffs. *(Richard
Anthony Baker)*

POSITIVELY

The only Conjurer in the World that [*sic*] Escapes out of all Handcuffs,
Leg Shackles, Insane Belts and Strait-Jackets, after being STRIPPED STARK NAKED, mouth
sealed up and thoroughly searched from head
to foot, proving he carries no KEYS, SPRINGS, WIRES or other
concealed accessories . . .
under management of Martin Beck, Chicago

Beck arranged for Houdini to visit Britain and continental Europe in the autumn of 1899. The plan was complicated by the Boer War and, in the event, Houdini did not set sail for Southampton until the end of May 1900. He was told that on his arrival in London he would be given contracts for dates in London. There were no contracts. Houdini was left to his own devices. So he booked the Alhambra for an afternoon and invited an audience of police officers and journalists. He performed his usual act: some card tricks, his incarceration in a trunk and some other escapes. He secured a two-week booking at the Alhambra and embarked on a provincial tour. Then, after telling Beck he was having to work as his own agent, he set off for mainland Europe, where he spent the next four and a half years, by the end of which he was an international star.

At each place he visited, Houdini cleverly generated some pre-publicity by arranging to break out of the local jail. In Sheffield, he escaped from the cell which had housed the legendary burglar Charles Peace, who was hanged in 1879. The police had put triple locks on the door, placed Houdini's clothes in another cell, which also had triple locks on it, and then fastened the iron gate leading to the cell block with a seven-lever lock. Houdini was out – fully clothed – within five minutes.

He made one of his hardest escapes at the Palace Theatre in Blackburn in 1902. As always in the provinces, Houdini offered £25 to anyone who manacled him with 'regulation' handcuffs from which he failed to escape. In Blackburn, a young man named Hodgson, who in time opened a School of Physical Culture, accepted the challenge, carrying on stage with him six pairs of heavy irons, plus chains and padlocks. Houdini noticed that some of the locks and keyholes had been tampered with and rejected the challenge. Hodgson objected and so Houdini agreed to try and, tied in chains, he got into his cabinet. His audience had to wait until after midnight. In all, it took Houdini an hour and 40 minutes to get free, his arms swollen and discoloured, his skin bleeding where he had torn against it. Houdini returned to Blackburn, but he hated the place – 'the worst of all the hoodlum towns I ever worked', he said.

At the London Hippodrome the following March, a representative of the *London Daily Illustrated Mirror* challenged Houdini with a pair of handcuffs which had taken five years to make. Even the key took a week to construct. Dressed in what had now become his uniform, a black frock coat and a high white collar, Houdini got into his cabinet as the Hippodrome orchestra began playing. The handcuffs were clicked onto his wrists. The key was inserted and turned six times. During the next hour, Houdini appeared three times: firstly, to have a better look at the lock in a strong light and secondly to stretch his knees and have a glass of water. On the third occasion, he was still handcuffed. The audience moaned. He asked to have the handcuffs removed for a moment so that he could take his coat off. This was refused – and so, edging his penknife out of his pocket and opening it with his teeth, he tore at the coat with the blade until it lay about him in strips. He went back into the cabinet only to jump out ten minutes later, holding the handcuffs in his hand. The audience went wild, the orchestra broke into Handel's 'See the Conquering Hero Comes' and Houdini left the stage weeping hysterically.

How did he do it? Some thought that he was in collusion with the Birmingham blacksmith who made the handcuffs and that he stretched out the escape to more than an hour for sheer showmanship. Another expert believed he had made the handcuffs himself merely because they fitted him: not all handcuffs would. One escapologist said he could have got out only by using the key. If so, how was it passed to him? Bess may have smuggled it to him when she gave him the water. Indeed, during some of his most difficult escapes, he was always handed water.

Unusually, Houdini revealed some of the secrets behind his escapes. When he was put in a chest or a case, the men who hammered the nails in to make it more secure were encouraged to concentrate on the top, which might have seemed the most obvious route of escape. In advance, Houdini ensured that one of the side panels was weak and did not require much pushing to let him out.

Appearing at the Regent Theatre at Salford in Greater Manchester, he disclosed how another escapologist broke out of a coffin. On stage, he lay down in a coffin made by the man who had built those of his rival. The coffin-maker then drove six long screws into the lid and poured wax into the boreholes. Houdini put his hands through two holes in the lid, where they were handcuffed. A screen was then placed round the coffin, but not for long. Houdini was out within two minutes. Other screws sealing the lid were much shorter, he explained; and he slipped out of the handcuffs easily merely by contracting his wrists. By crawling out through the weak panel and reinserting the long screws, the escape took no time at all.

In 1902, Houdini signed a contract with Moss Empires. He was to play Moss theatres for twenty weeks at £100 a week and, if Moss wanted more, he could book him for a further twenty weeks. Early in 1904, Moss decided that he would take up that option, but Houdini had already agreed to appear that spring at a Glasgow hall run by the smaller Barrasford chain at £125 a week. Having decided he would not work for less money than he could make elsewhere, Houdini was sued by Moss. The court found in favour of Houdini, ruling that, although the option forced Houdini to work twenty weeks for Moss, it did not specify which weeks. Moss again went to court to stop Houdini from appearing in Liverpool, but again lost. Moss Empires offered to pay him the same as Barrasford, but Houdini declined and it was at that point that Houdini believed Moss set out to ruin him. Moss hired another escapologist, Frank Hilbert, to appear in various towns and cities and explain how he got out of handcuffs, producing picks and other concealed instruments he said were used.

When Houdini arrived in Cardiff in 1905, he saw posters everywhere advertising Hilbert at the local Empire. Deciding to join the audience, Houdini dyed his hair grey, reshaped his nose with wax and hobbled into the theatre with a walking stick. At an appropriate moment, he called out to Hilbert that he had some handcuffs from which Hilbert would be unable to free himself, but he was promptly bundled out of the theatre by waiting policemen.

In spite of his dispute with Moss (and in spite of his loathing for Blackburn), Houdini liked Britain. He found no racial discrimination in British theatres and he relished British sport. He once said that, if he had had the opportunity, he would have become a naturalised Briton.

In 1926, Houdini was in Canada. During one afternoon, he lectured students at McGill University in Montreal. The following day, a group of them visited him in his dressing-room at the Princess Theatre. One of them asked him if he could resist the hardest blows struck to his stomach. Houdini accepted the challenge, whereupon the young man began violently pummelling him. Houdini called a halt and remarked that he did not feel well. He and his party travelled to Detroit in Michigan, where, after the opening night of his show, he was admitted to hospital. He was suffering from peritonitis and, after two operations, he died, aged only 52.

Eugen Sandow virtually invented body-building. Before him, middle-class men preferred to cultivate a pale and willowy physique if only to show they were not labourers and farm-workers for whom muscles and a suntan came with the job. Gradually, attitudes changed. As more men began working in offices, they started exercising to counter the mental strain of their work; schoolboys were told (although not in so many words) that an interest in games kept their minds off masturbation and homosexuality; an interest in sports increased; and across Europe at first and then later in America, gymnasia opened. Sandow came to represent the ideal of robust health and masculine strength.

> EUGEN SANDOW (Friedrich Wilhelm Muller)
> **Born** Konigsburg (?), 2 April 1867
> **Married** Blanche Brookes, Manchester Cathedral, 8 August 1894
> Two daughters: Helen, married Joe Strong; Lorraine married (1) James Douglas Brown, 1924 (divorced) (2) Nugent Davidson
> **Died** 14 October 1925

There are many accounts of his early life. Born in east Prussia, he stayed there until he was 17. He had decided to earn his living as a performer and went to the local gyms as often as he could. But he failed to build muscles as fast as he wanted and so he joined a circus that took him all over Europe for the next two years. In search of a stage name, he adopted the maiden name of his Russian mother, Sandov, but replaced the last letter with a 'w' to make it sound more German.

When the circus broke up in Brussels in financial disarray, Sandow found himself alone and penniless. Almost by fate, he chanced to meet a professional strongman who had adopted the sobriquet Professor Attila. As a circus acrobat and gymnast, Sandow had become lean and wiry. Attila became Sandow's mentor and encouraged him to start using heavy weights to acquire more mass. Sandow soon began staging the type of display that was to help him make his name. One day, at the Free Gymnastic Society in Brussels, he laid a large handkerchief on the floor, stood on it with his feet together and, carrying a weight of 25 kilograms (55lb) in each hand, performed a somersault, landing back on the handkerchief with his feet together.

Attila realised that Sandow was now ready to be launched before the general public. The two men paid professional visits to Rotterdam, Antwerp and other towns and cities nearby. Sandow decided to visit Amsterdam on his own, but failed to find anyone interested in seeing him. However, with an eye for publicity, he toured the city in the dead of night to test his strength on weight-lifting machines outside cafés. Each machine had a lever. Anyone putting a coin in the slot could pull the lever to see how strong he was. Sandow pulled the levers so hard that he broke every machine he tried. Eventually, the police caught up with him. Their first question was: where was the rest of the gang that helped him wreck the machines? Sandow explained there was no gang. Furthermore, he had not broken the law as he had paid his money and lawfully tested his strength – and, to prove his strength, he lifted the largest

Sandow, the Modern
Hercules. *(Tony Barker)*

policeman present, held him in the air for a moment and then gently placed him down. All the same, he was kept in prison until Attila arrived to bail him out. The trick worked: he was now a star, at least in Amsterdam. A hotel allowed him to stay for free and a theatre owner who had previously refused to book him was now ready to pay him 1,200 guilders a week.

Sandow and Attila next played the Crystal Palace in London, but, shortly after starting, Attila injured himself while training and the rest of their engagement was cancelled. While Attila stayed in London to recuperate, Sandow travelled to Paris, where he modelled for the finest work undertaken by the sculptor, Gustave Crauck, his *Combat du Centaure.*

Sandow's lucky break came in 1889 back in London, where Attila had set up a gym in Bloomsbury. At the Royal Aquarium in Westminster, two tricksters, called Sampson and Cyclops, were presenting an act of strength and chicanery. In addition, Sampson offered to pay £100 to anyone who could perform the same feats as Cyclops and £500 to anyone who could duplicate his own feats.

London audiences already knew about Sampson. When he appeared at the Canterbury, he lifted a dumb-bell marked 2,240 pounds, a ton. Before doing so, he invited members of the audience to try their luck, but none could manage it. Then, Sampson's manager gave a long speech explaining how difficult the lift was. Eventually, there was a drum roll and Sampson, grimacing and grunting, slowly lifted the dumb-bell higher and higher until it was at arm's length above his head. The audience went wild and all was well until someone tried lifting the dumb-bell after Sampson. Then, the truth was out. While the manager was giving his speech, two holes were opened in the weight to allow heavy sand inside to drain into barrels on which the dumb-bell rested. Sampson was undeterred and, when the time came for Sandow to try to win the money from Cyclops, he easily did so. He also managed Sampson's tricks, but was given only £350 of the £500 on offer.

Soon, Sandow signed a contract to appear at the Alhambra for £150 a week. Every night was a sell-out. While in London, Sandow took the opportunity to have some publicity photographs taken – photographs of him wearing only a fig leaf. These quickly circulated among groups of excited women and of some excited men, too, including the critic and biographer Edmund Gosse, and the art historian and critic John Addington Symonds.

There were suggestions that Sandow may himself have been gay. When he sailed to America in 1893, he travelled with a Dutch pianist and composer, Martinus Sieveking, who was described as his inseparable friend. They had known each other since their days in Belgium, had lived together for some time and, when they arrived in New York, set up a flat there as well. Sandow caught the eye of the renowned dancer-cum-courtesan, la Belle Otero, who was considerably more famous for her horizontal performances than her vertical ones. One night, Otero, who was appearing at the Empire, invited Sandow to a supper party at her hotel. He accepted only to find there was no party. It was just the two of them. Sandow refused champagne, asking for milk instead, and, after an hour or two, according to Otero, 'I sent him back to the young man he was living with.' Professionally, New York was disappointing for Sandow. The heat of the city in June 1893 had sent many would-be theatregoers to the beach and the countryside. Critics posted good notices, but audience figures were poor.

Sandow's fortunes improved when he was booked for the Chicago World Fair, although it was only through a fluke that he appeared at all. Musical entertainment at the Fair was to have been organised by the President of the city's Musical College, Dr Florenz Ziegfeld. His plans, involving the finest classical musicians he could hire, were all but complete when the theatre in which the concerts were to have been staged burnt to the ground. Ziegfeld had to start afresh. He set about refitting a huge armoury building, which he called the Trocadero, and sent his young son, Florenz, to Europe to find more talent. Unfortunately, father and son did not share the same tastes in the performing arts. Whereas Florenz *père* brought Johann Strauss to America for the first time, Florenz *fils* organised a show in a park featuring the 'Dancing Ducks of Denmark'.

True to form, young Florenz returned from the music halls of London, Paris and Berlin with – among others – a group of 'grotesque eccentrics' and a trio of yodellers and clog dancers. In despair, the elder Florenz dispatched telegrams to dozens of musical agents, ordering a further supply of serious musicians, but those who arrived were distinctly second-rate. The Ziegfelds needed a star attraction and, this time, Florenz junior travelled to New York and, for the first time, saw Sandow's current act – a series of poses, a display of chest expansion, juggling with a man in the place of a ball, lifting a dumb-bell from which, when lowered, two men emerged and finally lying down to allow three horses to walk along a plank placed across his chest.

To appear in Chicago, Sandow demanded $1,000 a week. Ziegfeld persuaded him to take 10 per cent of the box office instead and Sandow ended up collecting $3,000 a week. On his first night in Chicago, the Trocadero was packed out. Martinus Sieveking strode onto the podium and the orchestra played a rousing march especially composed for the occasion. The audience was enthralled by Sandow's act, particularly the matron ladies of Chicago to whom Ziegfeld made a special offer. Any woman prepared to donate $300 to charity would be admitted to Sandow's dressing-room after the show to run her fingers over his muscles. There were many takers.

So, more than a few ladies were grief-stricken in 1894 when Sandow married Blanche Brookes, the daughter of a Manchester photographer, who had produced a fine set of studies of him. Ziegfeld, who was by now Sandow's manager, did all he could to keep the wedding a secret, but gave up when the new Mrs Sandow decided to accompany her husband on his next tour of America. There were to be changes to his way of living, too. Sieveking disappeared and the backstage muscle-feeling sessions were discontinued. The tour, lasting seven and a half months, was arduous and, after about six months, Blanche decided she wanted no more of it. Pregnant with their first child, she returned to England. In fact, in time, Blanche decided she did not like theatre life at all. She refused to watch Sandow's act and increasingly the couple grew apart.

Blanche had a brother, Warwick, who was determined to exploit Sandow. First, he set himself up in business as chairman of the Sandow Grip-Bell Company, the grip-bell being a kind of dumb-bell. Then, he marketed Sandow's Cocoa, but the big cocoa companies cut their prices and forced Sandow's Cocoa out of business. Next came Sandow's corsets – just at the time when corsets were beginning to go out of fashion.

Sandow died in 1925 apparently from the strain of single-handedly pulling a car from a ditch. There was some confusion over when the accident occurred, but Sandow's followers were more concerned when it was discovered that his grave in Putney Vale cemetery in south-west London was to be left unmarked – and, for many years, no stone commemorated him. Blanche, now mentally unstable, could not cope with incessant newspaper enquiries about Sandow. But did she also resent affairs he may have had? Had Sieveking continued to play a part in Sandow's life? Were there other lovers, gay or otherwise? Did he, as many have suggested, die of syphilis? Today, a black marble gravestone maintained by a Sandow worshipper marks his last resting place, a sign of his continuing fame.

CHAPTER 12

MORE LONDON HALLS . . .

Between about 1740 and 1840, additions were made to tea-rooms which stood in Highbury Park, Islington. A former clown, Edward Giovanelli, built a large theatre in the grounds, naming the whole place the Alexandra Theatre and Highbury Barn. Many famous artists appeared there, including the tightrope walker Blondin[1] and the trapeze artist Leotard. The popularity of the spot became its undoing. Prostitutes gathered there and noisy revellers left the place singing at all hours of the night. After Guy Fawkes' night in 1869, the Highbury Riot broke out: up to 200 people left the theatre, smashing nearby windows, pulling down shop blinds and shouting 'Fire'. The disturbances grew worse; the theatre was closed in 1871 and it was demolished the following year.

A rowdy tavern in an alley just off Cable Street in Whitechapel was known as the Old Mahogany Bar since it was the first pub in London to introduce mahogany fittings. From about 1846, some form of entertainment was staged here and, when John Wilton[2] took over in 1850, he set about making the place respectable and lending it his name: Wilton's. In 1858, he built a new hall that could accommodate 1,500 people and, four years later, from the stage of his theatre, he mused over the changes wrought by music halls all over Britain:

> They have created a great moral and social improvement amongst the working classes of this country. You refer to the statistics of drunkenness and breaches of the peace now and twelve or fifteen years back and you will see a wonderful decrease in these offences . . . To what then, I would ask, is to be attributed the decrease of this offence? Why, to nothing else but the establishment of cheap and rational entertainment which these music halls have provided for the working classes.[3]

After being all but destroyed by a fire, Wilton's closed in 1877. Eight years later, the East End Mission of the Methodist Church took it over, reopening it as a church in 1888. The Mission used Wilton's until 1956 when the building was sold and used as a rag warehouse. In 1964, the poet John Betjeman led a campaign to save it from demolition and, two years later, it was bought by the Greater London Council. It is now run by an opera company.

Six years after its opening in 1854 as the grandly titled Panoptican of Science and Art, the Alhambra, situated in Leicester Square, became a music hall. Leotard was one of the first entertainers to appear there. Ballet once formed part of the Alhambra's entertainment, but Middlesex magistrates refused the theatre a music and dancing licence on account of indecency: the cancan had been danced there. A series of promenade concerts was then

Wilton's, a surviving East End hall. *(British Music Hall Society)*

arranged, but they were deemed to have infringed licensing regulations. The Alhambra was forced to close at the beginning of 1871, but for only four months. It was destroyed by fire in 1882. Another Alhambra was built, but it was demolished in 1937 to make way for an Odeon cinema.

Marie Lloyd made her debut at the Eagle Tavern music hall in the City Road in 1885. Her father, known as 'Brush' Wood, worked there in the evenings as a barman. The hall is immortalised in the nursery rhyme, 'Pop Goes the Weasel': 'Up and down the City Road, In and out the Eagle'. It had ceased to be a music hall by 1888 and, together with the adjacent Grecian theatre, it was demolished in 1899. A police station was built on the site.

Hoxton Hall in Hackney is one of the most important survivors of an early music-hall building in that it was a purpose-built hall that was not attached to a pub. At one time known as Mortimer's Hall and then McDonald's Music Hall, it lost its licence in 1871. A temperance movement bought it in 1879. The Quakers took over in 1893 and incorporated it into new buildings in 1910. It has been excellently restored.

The Bedford, a lovingly remembered music hall in Camden High Street, enjoyed a history lasting about 150 years. Originally the Bedford Arms Tavern and Tea Garden, it opened in about 1824. It became the Bedford music hall when a theatre proper was built in 1861 and, with slight variations of name, remained so until 1941. Between 1896 and 1898, it was rebuilt to the designs of Bertie Crewe. It closed in about 1950 and was demolished in 1969.

Before the first London Pavilion took shape in Tichborne Street, Westminster, in 1861, the site had accommodated a hall built next to a tavern called the Black Horse Inn. In 1859, it became a saloon where songs were performed, but, after £12,000 had been spent on it, it reopened as the Pavilion, seating at first 2,000 people. This first London Pavilion lasted until 1878 when the Metropolitan Board of Works bought it so that it could be demolished for road improvements. The second London Pavilion emerged in 1885. After twice being rebuilt, it was converted into a cinema in 1934.

At one time the Boar and Castle inn, the Oxford in Oxford Street became central London's first purpose-built hall under the aegis of Charles Morton in 1861. Twice destroyed by fire (in 1868 and 1872), the third Oxford was demolished in 1892. A fourth theatre was opened the following year, but, by 1913, touring revues and musical comedies were being staged there. It shut in 1920 for partial reconstruction, but was closed for good in 1926 before being demolished.

The Players' Theatre in Villiers Street off the Strand was the last theatre in the world offering a modern representation of Victorian music hall. Before Charing Cross railway station was built in 1863, the site was occupied by Hungerford Market, where Carlo Gatti, his brother, Giovanni, and their partner, Guiseppe Monico, ran coffee and ice-cream rooms. When the market was demolished in 1862, the two Gatti brothers used the compensation they received to move to Westminster Bridge Road to open first a restaurant and then a music hall.

In 1867, Carlo Gatti applied for a music licence for two of the arches built under the new station at Charing Cross. Despite objections from people living nearby, the licence was granted and, by 1875, the arches, popularly known as Gatti's under the Arches (as opposed to Gatti's in the Road, south of the river), were recognised as one of the leading music halls in London. By 1903, however, the hall had closed. Between 1910 and 1923 it was a cinema and was not used again for live entertainment until 1946 when the Players' Theatre, a club founded by Peter Ridgeway and Leonard Sachs in 1936 in premises in Covent Garden which had once housed Evans's Supper Rooms, moved in.

The Players' was so successful that Moss Empires invited Sachs to undertake a long tour of major variety theatres, resulting in *The Good Old Days*, a music-hall show which ran on BBC Television from 1953 to 1983 with Sachs as its sesquipedalian chairman. Sandy Wilson's musical *The Boy Friend* also started at the Players'. After disclosing long-standing debts of more than £500,000, the club closed in 2002. Two years later, it was announced that it would reopen not as a music hall, but as a venue for off-Broadway transfers, revues and small-scale musicals.

Known locally as the Fleapit, the Scratcher, Harwood's Abode of Love and the Sods' Opera, the Variety was built in Pitfield Street in 1869 to the design of C.J. Phipps. When George Harwood owned the hall during the 1870s and 1880s, he described his audiences as the most unmanageable in the world. Fortunately, he was able to break up fights in the gallery even when the police failed. He dispensed with the idea of a box office and even of tickets. He stood at the entrance to the pit and his wife at the entrance to the circle, each of them throwing their customers' admission money into satchels. Harwood dressed immaculately with a diamond cluster pin always in his tie. He died in 1903, leaving £136,982. After 1910, the theatre became a cinema and was demolished in 1981.

On the site of a tennis court built in the middle of the eighteenth century, the Trocadero opened as the Royal Trocadero Palace of Varieties in 1882. It was not a success and, after the owner, Robert Bignell, a wine merchant, died in 1888, his trustees let it to Sam Adams, who had run the London Pavilion. Albert Chevalier and Hugh Jay Didcott took over in 1894, but their company went bankrupt and they closed it. The following year, Bignell's daughter sold a ninety-nine-year lease to the caterers, J. Lyons, who converted it into a restaurant. Charles Cochran staged cabaret here and in 1936 Charles Coborn appeared with Wilkie Bard and the daughters of Little Tich and Marie Lloyd. In 1965, Mecca reopened the restaurant as Tiffany's. Later, a casino and a bowling alley were added. It is unclear how much of the Trocadero's original fabric remains.

CHAPTER 13

... AND OTHERS ACROSS BRITAIN

In the late 1840s, inns in Bristol started advertising amateur 'harmonic meetings' and 'convivials'. The best of these is said to have been the Angel at the bottom of the High Street. Professional music hall was introduced to Bristol by James Doughty and his two sons, who ran the Cider House tavern in Cider House Passage, off Broad Street. A concert room was opened, which, by October 1844, was attracting visiting artistes. Several music rooms began to emerge at about this time: the Ship and Castle in Marsh Street, which was destroyed by fire in 1859; the Canterbury between Maryleport and Bridge Street, which became a refreshment room in 1868; and the Rose Inn in Temple Street, of which there were no reports after 1866.

In Newcastle, the Oxford music hall opened in a first-floor room of the Wheatsheaf Inn in the Cloth Market in 1848. Here, a crippled ex-miner, George Ridley, sang his own composition, 'Blaydon Races' (1862), with its reference to Balmbra's, another name for the pub, as it had been owned from 1840 by John Balmbra. The annual race, in which first-rate athletes and ordinary joggers take part, is started by the Lord Mayor of Newcastle, using a handbell; it is mentioned later in the song.

> I went to Blaydon races.
> 'Twas on the ninth of June
> Eighteen hundred and sixty two
> On a summer's afternoon.
> I took the bus from Balmbra's
> And she was heavy laden.
> Away we went along Collingwood Street
> That's on the road to Blaydon.

The success of Balmbra's was partly due to the position John Balmbra held in the city. He was a founder member and twice president of the local Licensed Victuallers' Association and quartermaster of the Northumberland Yeomanry Cavalry. He retired from public life in 1864 and died in 1868. After the hall was enlarged in 1865, it reopened as the Oxford. It was destroyed by fire in 1899.

The New Wear in Drury Lane, Sunderland, opened in 1871. George Leybourne appeared here in 1875 at a salary of £80 a week. The theatre collapsed in ruins in 1902. Its foundations had been greatly affected by a strong spring of water, which had to be pumped out every day. Durland's Star music hall in Upper Sans Street was entirely destroyed by a fire which broke out one evening in 1883. The owner, Henry Durland, and a police officer who was on duty urged the audience, numbering between 1,000 and 1,300, to leave quietly. The roof of the theatre fell in only half an hour after the fire was discovered. There were no casualties. Durland, a builder by trade, rebuilt the theatre and reopened it in 1885. It closed in 1892.

Durland was a local character. In spite of financial difficulties, he drove around in an open landau, throwing money to the poor, providing blankets for striking miners and allowing free use of his theatre for meetings of the unemployed:

> One winter, when trade in Sunderland was very bad and hundreds were on the verge of starvation, Durland opened a soup kitchen and gladdened the hearts and homes of many of the 'out-of-works'. Long after, when trade was booming again, he went on to make one of his customary speeches, when a voice from the back of the pit cried out the familiar 'Get yer 'air cut!' Durland, with the air of a tragedian, answered back: 'Ah, my friend, when you were starving, you didn't say "Cut the supply of soup!"'[1]

In Dover, the Phoenix music hall, situated in Market Square, was built on the site of the Hero tavern, which had been destroyed by fire in 1863. It opened the following year. Charles Coborn came here in the mid-1870s for a salary of 30 shillings (£1.50) a week. Throughout the 1870s and 1880s, the proprietor was Isaac Kemp. He did every job at the hall, even polishing the brasswork on the front doors. The songwriter F.V. St Clair wrote: 'All the best artistes of the day appeared at Kemp's. It was wonderful how the little place paid; but then he had the town to himself or nearly so . . . If any of the soldiers got a bit too boisterous, he would warn them and, if they didn't mend their ways, he would remove them all "on his own".'[2]

In 1897, the Phoenix was rebuilt and reopened as the Empire Palace of Varieties, a name it kept until 1910 when it became the Palace and Hippodrome Southern. During the First World War, it was loaned to the East Surrey Regiment. The Palace reopened after the war, but not for long. By 1926, it was closed again. Even so, its licence was renewed every year until 1942 when it was destroyed by enemy action.

A railway terminus built by the London, Chatham and Dover Railway Company at Margate was never used and so, in 1867, it was converted into the Hall-by-the-Sea. Seven years later, 'Lord' George Sanger (1825–1911) bought the hall and its surrounding land to use as the headquarters for his circus empire. The hall became the home of music-hall shows, concerts and dancing, while the nearby land housed a menagerie, exhibitions and waxworks. A skating rink was added in 1893 and, by the time Sanger retired to a farm in Finchley in north London in 1910, the hall was used for cine-variety and concert parties. The following year, Sanger was shot dead by one of his employees who had nurtured a grievance against him. His body was buried in Margate with municipal honours beside that of his wife. George Sanger left £29,349, including £50 to his murderer, Herbert Cooper, who was found dead by a railway line.

With the exception of the hall and a ballroom, which the skating rink became, the whole complex was destroyed by fire in 1930. In its place, a huge new Dreamland amusement park, modelled on new German designs, was developed, comprising, among other attractions, a theatre complete with full stage facilities. By 1975, however, it had been converted into a bingo hall. Dreamland is still a major sight on Margate's seafront.

The City Varieties in the Headrow and Swan Street, Leeds, the home of *The Good Old Days*, had its origins in the singing room of a pub, the White Swan Inn, which was built at the end of the eighteenth century. In 1865, it was billed as Thornton's New Music Hall and Fashionable Lounge. The Varieties opened in 1898 with Alec Hurley at the top of the bill. Three leather-bound ledgers, which recorded acts booked for the hall between 1898 and 1904, have survived. Vesta Victoria earned £50 a week; G.H. Chirgwin £75; but Charles Coborn was rated 'not worth the money'. Between the First and Second World Wars, the City Varieties was run by several companies. After the 1939–45 war, girlie shows were staged with such titles as *Taking off Tonight* and *Fun and Dames*. It must have been hard work dreaming up new titles for these shows. The author's favourite is *See Nipples and Die*. The agreement in 1954 to allow the BBC exclusive use for radio and television broadcasts ensured the hall's survival.

At Barrow-in-Furness, the Royal Alexandra Music Hall and Theatre of Varieties in Forshaw Street was opened at the end of 1867. Five years later, the 'Old Alex', as it had become known, changed its name to the Royal Star Theatre of Varieties. After a fire in the early months of the twentieth century, it was partially demolished, rebuilt and renamed. It reopened as the Tivoli Theatre of Varieties. Many of music hall's most famous names appeared here, as well as Lofty, the Dutch Giant, in 1927: he stood 9ft 3½in tall (283cm). On another occasion, the call went out: 'Is there a doctor in the house?' A yodeller had collapsed on stage and died. The advent of the talkies spelt the end of the Tivoli. Although tickets were made cheaper in 1931, the theatre closed in May of that year. The Regal Cinema, which was built inside its shell, showed movies until the end of 1956. After that, the building was used as an increasingly ramshackle warehouse, overrun by rats and pigeons.

The Argyle Theatre of Varieties at Birkenhead came into being when it was built onto a pub of the same name in Argyle Street in 1868. Between 1876 and 1890, it was run as a legitimate theatre, the Prince of Wales. Its new manager, Dennis Clarke, who restored the name the Argyle, was a fine talent spotter. It was Clarke who in 1898 hired an unknown Harry Lauder for £4 for a week's work to sing Irish songs in the first half of the programme and Scottish ones in the second. Clarke persuaded Lauder to sign a contract guaranteeing him a booking every six months, his salary starting at £8 a week and rising to £15. For the next forty years, Lauder returned time and again to the Argyle. Clarke chose to forget the terms of the original contract and generously paid him more each time. In the 1930s, when variety was beginning to fail at the theatre, regular BBC radio shows entitled *Saturday Night at the Argyle* helped to revive its fortunes. After Dennis died in 1934, his son, Tom, took over, but, in September 1940, the Argyle was destroyed by a wartime bomb.

Designed by W.G.R. Sprague, the Norwich Hippodrome opened as the Grand Opera House in 1903. It became a music hall within a year. When Marie Lloyd appeared there in 1907, the manager reminded her that Norwich was a cathedral city and so nothing offensive was required. Marie told him she would immediately return to London. In the event, everything was smoothed over and Marie gave a performance that offended no one. The theatre was converted into a cinema in 1930 and, from 1937, it alternated between being a theatre and a cinema. It closed in 1960 and was demolished six years later.

The Middlesbrough Hippodrome, which opened in 1908, was built on the site of a Quaker burial ground in Wilson Street. To prepare for it, gravediggers exhumed bodies in the middle of the night so as not to offend anyone. Even so, many people stayed up late to watch the coffins being carried away. On the first night, the bill was topped by the chorus singer Florrie Forde. In 1911, panic was caused by someone shouting 'Hip on fire' after an electric fan at the back of the gallery fused. In the stampede that followed, two girls were killed, one aged 15, the other 4. Gaumont Cinemas took the theatre over in 1928, but it closed as a cinema in 1956. Three years later, it reopened as the Astoria Ballroom and played host to many rock and pop groups, including the Beatles. It is now a nightclub.

The City Varieties, Leeds, pictured in 1949, four years before BBC Television's *The Good Old Days* began its thirty-year run. *(Leeds Library and Information Service)*

CHAPTER 14

WIZARD OF OZ

arry Rickards started out as a comic singer and, if Mr E. (John S. Evalo) is to be believed, he was not very good: 'He never had what could be called a good song . . . and no-one could credit him with being an artiste . . . He was simply a bawler of comic and topical ditties and, when he tried to be funny, it was a dismal failure.'[1]

Through a misguided management venture, Rickards fell into financial difficulties, but vowed to pay back every penny he owed. He kept his promise. He set himself up as a music-hall entrepreneur in Australia, importing British performers and giving some Australian entertainers, such as Florrie Forde and the debonair Albert Whelan, their first opportunities. Single-handedly, he set the style and tone of Australian vaudeville from late Victorian times to the early 1930s. When he died, he left a small fortune.

The son of an engineer who had worked in Egypt, Harry Rickards was the eldest of a family of three sons and six daughters. As such, he was expected to follow his father's trade and indeed he worked for some time as a mechanic in Woolwich, but his heart was always set on a stage career. After singing in pubs in the East End of London, Rickards auditioned for Wilton's and, in 1864, he was engaged there for a long run as a comic vocalist earning £2 a week.

HARRY RICKARDS (Benjamin Henry Leete)
Born 1845 (?)
Married (1) Caroline Tudor at Bromley
    16 March 1862 (divorced 1879)
    (2) Kate Roscoe (Roscow?) (professionally
    known as Katie Angel) in the United
    States
    Two daughters, Noni and Madge
Died Thornton Heath, London,
    13 October 1911
Left £135,000

Harry Rickards became Australia's greatest music-hall impresario. *(Tony Barker)*

At about that time, Rickards chose to appear from then on as a *lion comique*, a young man about town, singing about the high life. It helped him towards his first big break, a rollicking song, which he wrote with Tom MacLagan, 'Captain Jinks of the Horse Marines'. By the late 1860s, he was earning £20 a week and appearing in the best halls in London, particularly the Oxford, where he sang another favourite, 'Oxford Joe', in which he dressed in cap and gown.

By 1870, he may have started to believe that he was, in fact, a young toff, since he gave an interview to *The Entr'acte*, in which he stated he was the son of a Norfolk gentleman, Benjamin Plantagenet Rickards, that he had been born in Cairo, and that he was educated at Eton and was intended for the Church. *The Entr'acte* threw some doubt on the account and there was an unpleasant scene at the Cambridge, when Rickards spat at the paper's owner, Samuel Barrow. He was charged with assault and fined £1.

Harry Rickards first tried his hand at management in 1871 by taking control of the Swiss Cottage pub at Hackney in east London, which had a concert hall on the first floor over the bar. It was not a success and Rickards ran into debt. It was to make amends that he set sail for Australia, a country still in its music-hall infancy, with the Rickards London Star Comique Company, which included his first wife, Carrie Tudor. On their Australian debut in Melbourne, they attracted good notices.

The company played throughout Australia and New Zealand and in 1874 toured across America from San Francisco to New York, but Rickards's financial difficulties were not over. Back in London, he leased a hall with his second wife, an Australian dancer, Kate Roscoe (or Roscow). At a meeting of creditors at the start of 1880, a statement of accounts showed that his debts amounted to £1,500, while his assets stood at £15. At the time, he was singing 'I Never Go East of Temple Bar' ('I stick to St James and Belgravi-ah'). One night, someone in the gallery shouted: 'How did you get to Basinghall Street, then?', the site of the former bankruptcy court.

After two more tours of Australia (in 1885 and 1887), Rickards decided to settle there. He took the lease of the Opera House in Sydney with his grand-sounding New Tivoli Minstrel and Grand Specialty Company of Forty Great Artists. Its success led him to taking a long-term lease on another theatre, which he renamed the Tivoli and which he operated along the lines of an English music hall.

By now, Rickards was appearing as a performer less and less and devoting most of his time to management. He extended his operations to the Prince of Wales Opera House in Melbourne, which he leased in 1895. Four years later, he bought the freehold of the Tivoli and, although it was destroyed by fire within six months, he rebuilt it. He also took on a theatre in Adelaide in 1900, all the time importing the world's finest stars, including Marie Lloyd, Little Tich and Harry Tate. Katie Lawrence, who popularised 'Daisy Bell', found him a bit of a show-off:

I remember him strutting round the theatre with his chest sticking out and diamonds, instead of buttons, down his shirt front. He had a car that he brought from England, complete with its chauffeur. It was a Rolls, I think. In those days, you bought the chauffeur with the car! Before that, he had imported a carriage that had once belonged to Disraeli. It had a crest on the side. He'd spend money on his artistes, he'd spend money on himself and his family, but, if anybody tried to take him down, he'd fly into a terrible rage.[2]

Rickards was hopelessly superstitious. He had a lifelong fear of the number thirteen, and refused to hire a performer on either a Friday or the thirteenth of the month. He would not print playbills with black letters on a yellow background and was similarly opposed to green wallpaper. No one was allowed to sing Tosti's 'Goodbye', as it had been sung on the night the Tivoli burnt down. Rickards reckoned all sorts of actions heralded bad luck:

An imported star, from whom great things were expected, attended band-call to rehearse his music. It was a pouring wet day and the star, carrying an umbrella, had it partly open and was shaking off the water as he walked on to the stage. 'That's done it,' cried Rickards. 'You're ruined before you open.' And, sure enough, the hoodoo worked . . . The artiste's somewhat unconventional style failed to please the critical Tivoli gallery . . . Rickards declared the opening of that umbrella on that stage cost him a thousand pounds.[3]

Inevitably, Rickards died on the thirteenth of the month.

Florrie Forde, one of the first stars Rickards discovered, was born in Melbourne, the sixth child of an Irish mason, Lott Flannagan (*sic*), and his American-born wife, Phoebe. Her professional career began at the Polytechnic in Sydney in 1893. She then joined a vaudeville company and played principal boy in a pantomime, *The House that Jack Built*. After a year-long engagement with Rickards, she appeared in three plays before returning to Rickards for another two and a half years, her last engagement in Australia.

Florrie arrived in London in 1897 totally unknown, but carrying with her a letter of introduction from an Australian newspaper proprietor addressed to Charles Morton. After an audition, he told her he thought she would be a great success, but not with his audience. He gave her a letter to take to Frank Glenister at the London Pavilion, who engaged her at £8 a week to sing two songs, 'Not an M-U-G', written by Joseph Tabrar, and 'Only a Working Girl', which she had brought with her from Australia. She made her British debut at three London halls, the Oxford, the Pavilion and the South London over the following August Bank Holiday weekend.

> FLORRIE FORDE (Flora Flannagan)
> **Born** Melbourne, 16 August 1875
> **Married** Laurence Barnett at Paddington,
>   London, 22 November 1905
>   (d. Worthing, west Sussex,
>   22 October 1934, aged 58)
> **Died** Aberdeen, 18 April 1940
> **Left** £4,863

Florrie Forde was billed as Australia's premiere comedienne. During the following month, *The Era* twice commented on her, saying that she had a 'serviceable voice and expressive declamation' and that she had 'a fascinating appearance and a finished style'. She went on to appear at the Canterbury, Paragon and Tivoli and, from that moment, she was barely out of work.

In time, Florrie became music hall's greatest chorus singer. When she arrived in Britain, she was a slight figure, weighing just under 8 stone (112lb), but, as the years went by, she ballooned to something like 15 stone (210lb). Florrie decided then that she needed to slim. She found a diet that worked and, within a short time, lost weight dramatically. So many people wanted to know how she had done it that she decided to print her diet, charge for it and send the money to charities she supported:

Florrie Forde, the world's greatest chorus singer. *(Richard Anthony Baker)*

The company was playing at Bradford when one of the purchasers, an exceedingly stout woman, known locally as Yorkshire Pudden, went to the theatre and demanded her money back. Florrie, who at that time believed her remedy to be infallible, had the complainant escorted to her dressing-room and proceeded to cross-examine her. 'You knew you had to follow a strict diet, I suppose?' 'Certainly.' 'Did you follow the instructions faithfully?' 'Oh, ah.' 'Did you eat the lettuce, tomatoes and brown bread and drink the orange juice every day?' 'Of course.' 'Did you eat anything else?' 'Only my meals.'[4]

On stage, Florrie dressed elaborately in jewels and furs and, carrying a pompadour stick, she paraded up and down as if she were instructing her audiences in the lyrics of her songs. She had one rule about a new song: if her audiences were not singing along with her by the middle of the first week, she dropped it. She had an almost unerring ear for a hit, however, and made a number of songs her own, particularly 'Down at the Old Bull and Bush' (1903), an archetypal British song, although written by three Americans, Percy Krone, Russell Hunting and Harry von Tilzer.

Summer after summer, she appeared on the Isle of Man, where she became a great celebrity. She always stayed in a boarding house, where, towards the end of each afternoon, her gleaming open carriage, drawn by horses, arrived to collect her. Cheering crowds lined the route between there and the theatre and Florrie, almost regally, waved back to them.

For three years running early in her career, C.W. Murphy provided Florrie with songs whose popularity swept the country. The first was 'Oh! Oh! Antonio' (1908), written in association with Dan Lipton. Florrie called it her latest and greatest chorus song. In 1908, during Glasgow Fair Week, thousands of Scots were said to have become frenetic over the song. 'Holiday-making Scots' were, according to one report, 'singing the ditty at all hours everywhere':

> Oh! Oh! Antonio, he's gone away.
> Left me alone-io,
> All on my own-io.
> I want to meet him with his new sweetheart.
> Then, up will go Antonio and his ice-cream cart.

C.W. MURPHY (Charles William Murphy)
Born Manchester 1871/5 (?)
Married Margaret Alice ——
Died Blackpool, Lancashire, 18 June 1913
Left £3,882

With Florrie back on the island in 1909, Billie Murphy wanted to repeat his success. He liked the idea of 'lost lovers', which he had used in his first hit, but the Italian setting of 'Oh! Oh! Antonio' was too far away to guarantee a second year's success. The sequel 'Has anybody here seen Kelly?' placed the Isle of Man itself at the centre of the action. Murphy, this time working with Will Letters, wrote the chorus first, introducing a reference to the previous year's hit:

> Has anybody here seen Kelly?
> K E double L Y. Has anybody here seen Kelly?
> Find him if you can.
> He's as bad as old Antonio.
> Left me on my own-i-o.
> Has anybody here seen Kelly?
> Kelly from the Isle of Man.

Murphy said he believed no song had ever attained a more instantaneous success. Within a few weeks of it first being sung, it became the rage all over England, its sheet music selling by the thousand: 'With this song, as with all the songs I write, I never tackled a word or a note of the verses until I had the refrain exactly to my liking. To find a refrain which will go with a swing is the secret of success in popular song-writing for the general public . . . It must have a melody in which "something sticks out", so to speak.'[5]

On the Isle of Man, it was difficult to know where to escape the song. It could be heard on the trams, in the trains, on the steamers and among holiday-makers driving donkeys and traps. At Derby Castle, where Florrie was appearing, she received 'an ovation that happens to few in a lifetime'. Away from the island, the songwriter Edgar Bateman, who was making a tour of Brighton, Eastbourne, Ramsgate, Margate and Broadstairs, on behalf of the music publishers Francis Day and Hunter, reported 'the overwhelming success of the song'.

When it reached the United States, it was sung first by Emma Carus, one of the stars of the original Ziegfeld Follies, but American audiences, not understanding the references to Antonio and not caring much for the Isle of Man either, decided it was a flop. However, William J. McKenna rewrote it for Norah Bayes to sing in a Raymond Hubbell show, *The Jolly Bachelors*. By setting it in New York and making it basically an Irish song, he turned it into a success.

In 1910, Florrie waited to see whether Murphy and Letters could give her a hat-trick of hits. They kept her waiting until the end of April before handing her their manuscript, 'Flanagan'. Two days later, she sang it for the first time at the Duchess music hall in Balham, later to become the Balham Hippodrome. The theatre was reported to have been almost 'wrenched from its foundations' by the chorus. The fans who cheered Florrie that summer probably did not realise the private joke that was being played. Florrie had been born Flora Flannagan (*sic*):

> Flanagan, Flanagan, take me to the Isle of Man again.
> Take me where the folks all cry
> K E double L Y
> Flanagan, Flanagan,
> If you love your Mary Ann
> Oh oh oh oh Flanagan
> Take me to the Isle of Man.

Florrie was as generous as her music-hall predecessors. When the unidentified body of a young serviceman was washed up on the coast of the Isle of Man during the First World War, there was talk at first of burying him in a pauper's grave. Florrie intervened, paying for a grave and tombstone etched with the words 'Some Mother's Son'.

She formed her own company, Flo and Co., in which she toured all over the country with a company of youngsters just making their start in show business, including, at one stage, Bud Flanagan and Chesney Allen, the mainstays of the Crazy Gang.

Her dinner parties often ended with a game of poker with a pot of money at the centre of the table. At some point during the evening, Florrie invariably reached into the pot and scooped out a handful of silver, which she described as her table money. No one knew at the time, but this money, supplemented every week by some of Florrie's own, was put into a Post Office account for Bud Flanagan's young son, Robert, who was known as Buddy. By the time

'Death of An Actress' by Louis MacNeice

I see from the paper that Florrie Forde is dead –
Collapsed after singing to wounded soldiers,
At the age of sixty-five. The American notice
Says no doubt all that need be said

About this one-time chorus girl; whose role
For more than forty stifling years was giving
Sexual, sentimental or comic entertainment,
A gaudy posy for the popular soul.

Plush and cigars: she waddled into the lights,
Old and huge and painted, in velvet and tiara,
Her voice gone but around her head an aura
Of all her vanilla-sweet forgotten vaudeville nights.

With an elephantine shimmy and a sugared wink
She threw a trellis of Dorothy Perkins roses
Around an audience come from slum and suburb
And weary of tea-leaves in the sink,

Who found her songs a rainbow leading west
To the home they never had, to the chocolate Sunday
Of boy and girl, to cowslip time, to the never-
Ending weekend Islands of the Blest.

In the Isle of Man before the war before
the present one she made a ragtime favourite
Of 'Tipperary', which became the swan-song
Of troop-ships on a darkened shore;

And during Munich sang her ancient quiz
Of 'Where's Bill Bailey?' And the chorus answered,
Muddling through and glad to have an answer:
Where's Bill Bailey? How do we know where he is!

Now on a late and bandaged April day
In a military hospital Miss Florrie
Forde has made her positively last appearance
And taken her bow and gone correctly away,

Correctly. For she stood
For an older England, for children toddling
Hand in hand while the day was bright. Let the wren
   and robin
Gently with leaves cover the Babes in the Wood.

he was 21, a considerable amount had accrued. Buddy unfortunately had a troubled life and died of leukaemia in 1956 at the age of 30.

Florrie turned down one song, the American hit of 1923, 'Yes, we have no bananas'. It was taken up, instead, by Lupino Lane. All the same, Florrie persuaded Fyffe's to let her have thousands of bananas free to sell for charity.

James Agate saw her in pantomime (*The Forty Thieves*) at the Lyceum in 1935/6:

> This great favourite of an older day still holds us in the hollow of her hand and it is good to hear the old songs reminiscently sung, even when the singer, discarding boyish livery, presents them from a matronly ambuscade of puce and gold draperies, surmounted by a confection of obsequious and heliotrope plumes. Let it be put down in black and white that, unlike the principal boy a la mode, Miss Forde can sing, that, when she opens her mouth, the issuing sound is not a rillet, but a spate, and that you can hear every word and every syllable of every word. The artiste has the power to dominate and, when she is on the stage, you cannot look anywhere else, even if there be room.[6]

At the start of the Second World War, Florrie began entertaining the troops, but collapsed and died shortly after a concert in 1940. Pathetically, the last song she sang was 'Good-bye-ee'.

Billy Williams was another Australian singer who found greater fame in Britain than in his home country. Styled as the Man in the Velvet Suit (usually a blue one, but sometimes grey or claret), he was one of music hall's most prolific recording artists, making dozens of discs between 1906 and 1914. Billy, the son of an Irish draper Richard Banks, worked first at a racecourse, but, by the age of 18, he was singing at a working men's club in Melbourne, where he was heard by the comedian Tom Woottwell. So impressed was Woottwell that he granted Williams the right to sing sixteen of his songs. Towards the end of the 1890s, a rich horse-racing entrepreneur, George Adams, gave Williams £100 and a one-way ticket to London. Williams left Sydney on board the SS *Afric* in November 1899 and arrived in Britain in late December. He worked first as assistant manager at the Marylebone music hall and in March 1900 made his London debut there, billed initially as Will Williams.

BILLY WILLIAMS aka William Holt Williams
(Richard Isaac Banks)
Born Melbourne, Australia, 7 February 1878
Married Amy Robinson, 30 September 1901
(d. near Sydney 1976, aged 97)
Four children
Died Shoreham-by-Sea, west Sussex,
13 March 1915

Williams became a great self-publicist, travelling on trams around London dressed in one of his velvet suits. He was instantly recognised not only by this raffish style of clothing, but by his relentless chuckle, something that on his recordings now sounds irritating. Passengers began calling him the Little Boy Blue and regarded it as a lucky sign if they caught the same tram as him.

In 1906, encouraged by Florrie Forde, Williams began his recording career. He reached a three-year agreement with Edison that he would make cylinders for a flat fee of £2 10s (£2.50) each. His first, 'John, Go and Put your Trousers on', proved a hit and Williams tried to renegotiate his contract with Edison. They refused, but Williams spotted a loophole. The agreement referred only to cylinders. This allowed him to start making gramophone records with many other companies.

When he renewed his contract with Edison, he made some extravagant demands, all of which were met: that, on the day of a recording, he would arrive at any time he chose, although he expected a well-rehearsed orchestra to be in place by 8 a.m.; he would sing each song only once; his fee would be £100; if a player in the orchestra made a mistake, he would record another take, but only for another £100.

Williams and his wife set up home in Brixton in south London, but he was soon doing well enough to buy a string of bungalows in Shoreham-by-Sea in west Sussex, a popular spot for entertainers. In 1910, under the management of Rickards, who had seen him perform at Margate, he returned to Australia for a highly successful tour, also visiting South Africa en route. He opened in Melbourne Opera House before going on to the Tivoli Theatre in Sydney: 'He taught the audience three comic songs

Billy Williams, the Man in the Velvet Suit. *(Tony Barker)*

in a few minutes and then for 20 minutes put them through a practice. At a wave of Billy's hand, "the committee", as he styled the people in the gallery, sang as obediently as a choir, while everyone who was not singing was laughing at the comedian's droll sayings and antics.'[7]

Billy Williams made his final appearance in London at the Islington Empire in 1915. After routine surgery two weeks later, he died and was buried in Shoreham cemetery next to his father, who had died while visiting him the previous year.

Albert Whelan also preferred to pursue his career in Britain rather than his home country. That career began when Queen Victoria was on the throne and ended in Britain as the Beatles were about to enjoy their first success. His first records were cylinders; his last recording was on a long-playing record. Whelan's was an original act. Immaculately dressed, he spent three minutes making his stage entrance, strolling on whistling a German waltz, 'The Jolly Brothers', so becoming the inventor of the signature tune. During the three-minute entrance, he removed his gloves (they took a minute and a half in themselves), overcoat, scarf and hat. Once he had completed his act, he spent another three minutes putting his clothes back on again and strolling off, again whistling 'The Jolly Brothers'.

Whelan was the son of a Jewish pawnbroker. At the age of 18, he went gold-prospecting at Coolgardie in Western Australia. He and a friend set up a store in a huge tent to sell clothes and other necessities to the miners. After a while, he disposed of his tent and its contents to a

ALBERT WHELAN (Albert Waxman)
Born Melbourne, 4 May 1875
Married (1) Florence Agnes McRae in Sydney 1897
   (d. London, 26 July 1927, aged 52)
   Three sons, Cyril (b. Collingwood, Victoria, 1899);
   Ronald Albert (b. Fulham, London, 2 November
   1905); and Gordon Albert (b. Fulham, London,
   9 February 1909)
(2) Violet Doris Chard (the divorced wife of William
   Joseph Bleach; professionally known as Dainty
   Doris[8]), London, 2 November 1929 (d. London,
   5 February 1936, aged 39)
(3) Irene Tabitha Taylor McIntosh, also known as Rene,
   Marylebone, London, 1 April 1938
Died west London, 19 February 1961.

Albert Whelan, who invented the signature tune. *(Tony Barker)*

man already established in Coolgardie and joined a show there, playing the violin in the orchestra and later on appearing on stage.

He arrived in London in 1901, making his British debut at the Empire, Leicester Square, as an eccentric dancer – that is to say, his dancing was made up of odd or comical steps. (The greatest practitioner was the variety comedian Max Wall.) Soon, the act in which he played a smartly dressed man-about-town took over, its centrepiece his best-known song, 'The Preacher and the Bear' (1904), written by Joe Arzonia. His other famous songs included 'The Butterfly and the Bee' and 'The Old Top Hat'.

After the London Coliseum opened at the end of 1904, Whelan was booked to appear there for four weeks. He told the stage staff his act ran for 18 minutes. Ordered to cut it to 7, he did just that, strolling on and whistling in the usual way and then, when he had done that, strolling off again, without singing even one song. He fully expected to be sacked by the autocratic Oswald Stoll, but Stoll saw the funny side of it and Whelan got his way.

He made his American debut in 1908 and appeared both there and in Australia and Britain regularly throughout the 1920s. His last American tour took place in 1924/5 while on his way back to Britain from Australia. It culminated in New York in 1925 when Whelan introduced a song new to American audiences, 'Show me the Way to Go Home'.

All the time, Whelan continued releasing records, often cover versions of other entertainers' famous songs.

In 1914, Albert Whelan was a central figure in a divorce case. Its details reveal much about the morality of the day and the social lives of theatre people. A jealous barrister, John Hissey, sued for divorce from his wife, Elsie, whose stage name was Queenie Merrill. (Later in life, as Mary Merrall, she appeared in many films, largely as a dithery, scatterbrained woman. She married three times in all and died on 1 January 1973.)

Hissey alleged improper conduct between her and Whelan. While she was working in America, he wrote to her:

Is it true that you were seen on the front at Brighton with Albert Whelan? How you could mix your name up with that man I don't know. You know I did not care for you knowing him, but you were so young and foolish. [Miss Merrill was 23 at the time.] A wife is her husband's property until she makes herself so no longer. I know a lot has been my fault. I should have been firmer and refused to let you go about with the people you did.*

Queenie replied:

I swear to you, Jack, dear, I have never been seen on the front at Brighton with Whelan or at any other place with him . . . I saw him in Birmingham. I told you about it. I saw him in London. I told you about it . . . Oh, God, I wish I were on my way home. I loathe this country. I am frightfully homesick. The life is so different and the people are so objectionable. New York is so gawdy. It reminds you of Earl's Court all the time.†

Queenie had been introduced to Whelan by his wife in the wings at the Palace Theatre in 1913. When they found they were both staying in Birmingham the following month, they had supper each evening in Whelan's suite at the Grand Hotel. His valet was always present. At the end of each evening, Whelan saw Queenie home to her digs. They did not even address each other by their Christian names. Whelan's barrister addressed the jury: 'Things have changed. The world has gone ahead . . . The theatrical profession claims and enjoys a far greater amount of freedom than ordinary people and it is inevitable owing to their calling. Were they [the jury] going to sit in judgment on the respondent because she is young and fond of life and society?'§ After 35 minutes' deliberation, the jury agreed there had been no misconduct and the petition for divorce was dismissed. Even so, Whelan's costs were not allowed.

*   *Daily Telegraph*, 16 July 1914.
†   *Ibid*.
§   *Daily Telegraph*, 17 July 1914.

He attributed his long-running popularity to his ability to adapt: 'So many old-timers cannot or will not adapt themselves to modern requirements and then resent it because modern managements won't accept them. Because I have appreciated that new methods, faster and more expert, are used on the music hall today, I am able to go on where most of my famous contemporaries are now in retirement.'[9]

When Daniel Farson took over the Metropolitan music hall, Edgware Road, for a day in 1960 to record a long-playing record, he invited Whelan to join the company. Farson later admitted wincing when he listened to his introduction of Whelan: '. . . and tonight at the age of 85, he is still going strong, having thankfully recovered from an operation in which he lost his leg. He is still whistling his signature tune – Albert Whelan.'[10] Undaunted, Whelan went on to give a spirited rendition of 'The Preacher and the Bear', the song he first sang at the start of his long career.

Not 'Good-bye-ee', but another valedictory song from Florrie Forde.

CHAPTER 15

BEHIND THE LAUGHTER

The history of music hall is littered with stories of tragedy. In less safety-conscious times, terrible accidents occurred. In 1868, a faulty gas chandelier caused a panic at the Victoria, Manchester, killing twenty-three people, most of them teenagers; in 1878, the lives of thirty-seven people were lost after part of the ceiling fell into the pit at the Royal Colosseum, Liverpool; in 1884, fourteen people were trampled to death as the result of a false fire alarm at the New Star Theatre of Varieties in Glasgow; and in 1891, seven children were crushed to death after another false alarm at the Gateshead Hippodrome.

Less stringent fire regulations led to many music halls being destroyed by fire: in 1852 and 1857, Burton's, Brighton; 1859, the Ship and Castle, Bristol; 1863, the Phoenix, Dover; 1865, the Surrey, Sheffield; 1866, the Olympia, Shoreditch; 1867, the Brighton Empire; 1868 and 1872, the Oxford in the West End of London; 1869, the South London Palace of Varieties; 1875, the Albert, Glasgow, and the Tivoli, Liverpool; 1877, the Rotunda, Liverpool; 1878 and 1890, the South of England/Barnard's in Portsmouth; 1882, the Alhambra, London; 1882 and 1900, the Philharmonic/Grand, Islington, north London; 1883, the Star, Stockton-on-Tees, Durham, and the Victoria, Grimsby; 1885 and 1934, Barnard's, Chatham; 1889, Pullan's, Bradford, the Cardiff Empire and Paul's, Leicester; 1891, Vento's Temple of Varieties, Portsmouth; 1896, the Royal Cambridge in Shoreditch; 1900, the Oxford, Newcastle; 1908, Accrington Hippodrome; 1921, the Garrick, Edinburgh; 1922, the Gateshead Hippodrome, Tyne and Wear, and the Grimsby Hippodrome; 1932, the Grand, Hanley, Staffordshire, and the Hippodrome, Stockton-on-Tees; and 1942, the Sheffield Empire.

The relative infrequency of fires in the twentieth century is directly attributable to the world's worst theatre tragedy, a fire at the Iroquois Theater in Chicago in 1903, in which no fewer than 602 people, mostly women and children, lost their lives.

The theatre, advertised as absolutely fireproof, had been open for only five weeks. The show was a popular musical, *Mr Blue Beard*, the greatest stage success of one of America's most famous song-and-dance men, Eddie Foy. He had just walked on stage at the start of the second act when an overhead light shorted, propelling hundreds of sparks onto a curtain and some props. When some burning scenery fell on stage, the chorus rushed into the wings. Foy tried to set the audience at ease by announcing 'Everything is under control', but, when some debris fell at his feet, it was clear he was not telling the truth. Foy called for the safety curtain to be lowered, but, as it came down, it stuck.

The singers and dancers waiting backstage decided to run for it. Outside the temperature was −18°C and, as the stage door was opened, a rush of freezing air pushed the flames under the asbestos curtain and over the heads of the audience in the stalls; they reached the circle within seconds. Many in the audience were asphyxiated in their seats. Others rushed for the exits only to find that they were covered by iron gates, some of which were locked. An inquest revealed incredible negligence by theatre and city officials whose job it was to guarantee public safety. Many people were charged, but every case was eventually dismissed on technicalities.

At least lessons were learned. Anyone now pushing a door open or following an exit sign at a theatre or a cinema does so as a result of that tragedy.

The grisliest accident at a British music hall occurred at the Oxford Theatre of Varieties in Brighton just after Christmas 1881. George Smythe, who was 15, was in the gallery with a group of friends to see the Great Chinese Salamander, Ling Look, Lord of Fire, Cannon and Sword. The climax of his act was the firing of a cannon into the theatre, its elevation adjusted so that it pointed towards the top of the proscenium. The audience were warned to stay in their seats, but, while George's friends crouched down, he leaned over the bar at the front of the gallery, keen to witness everything on show. The orchestra played a dramatic chord as the cannon was fired, but the next sound to be heard was shouting and screaming from the gallery. The cannonball had blown George's brains out. Ling was arrested and stood trial at Lewes Assizes, charged with manslaughter. His solicitor argued that his very living depended upon the safety of the performance. Ling was acquitted, but nothing was heard of him after that.

Some entertainers suffered dramatic ends to their lives, too. Charles Sloman was one of music hall's pioneers. He worked in many of the early halls in London, billed as 'the only English improvisatore', making up songs on the spot about subjects suggested to him by members of the audience.

He began singing in taverns in London at the age of 8. The first place at which he appeared where he was paid to sing was an inn, known as the White Conduit House in Islington. (Situated in what is now Barnsbury Road, the White Conduit Gardens or the Flower Gardens of Islington had their origins in a ale- and cake-house built in 1641. In 1826, they reopened as the Minor Vauxhall, incorporating the Apollo Room. By 1841, its new pavilion could accommodate up to 8,000 people at a meeting.) Sloman made his second professional appearance at the Rotunda, later the Britannia music hall, in Southwark. He regarded this as London's first music hall in 1825.

Thackeray, who frequented the Coal Hole as a young man, used Sloman as the model for his character, little Nadab, in *The Newcomes*. In fact, Thackeray was greatly hurt when Sloman declined a dinner invitation because he had a prior engagement. In addition to improvisations, Sloman wrote dozens of songs for music hall's earliest entertainers, such as W.G. Ross, Sam Cowell and J.W. Sharp. He also wrote much of the material used by Baron Renton Nicholson at the Judge and Jury Society.

Sloman's heyday was the 1840s and 1850s. In 1866, as the father of the profession, he was invited to attend a meeting called to set up a Provident Society. In a passionate speech, he urged everyone there to do all they could to help entertainers who had fallen on hard times:

I have in my time seen the beginning and decadence of many a professional man; and many a one, who has stood at the height of popularity in his day, has fallen afterwards so much into decay and desuetude as to be obliged to ask assistance from his brother professionals. It's to avoid this that the instigators . . . of the . . . meeting . . . have brought us together to found an institution which should give to the decayed professional man . . . some rest and relief in his declining days.[1]

Ironically, only four years later, Sloman was admitted to the Strand workhouse. In July 1870, seven weeks after his admission, the man who had refused dinner with Thackeray died a pauper.

The fate of J.W. Sharp (c. 1820–56), another of music hall's earliest stars, was similarly unfortunate. He chose not to specialise in any particular style of song: his repertoire included risqué and topical songs, as well as parodies. Little is known of his early life. He was mostly associated with the Vauxhall Gardens, the Cremorne[2] and Evans's, where he was paid £1 a week, plus free drinks. He supplemented his income by selling manuscript copies of his songs to the audience. At the Vauxhall Gardens, he sang a Robert Glindon song, 'A Guide to Travellers', which was crammed with puns:

> Gossips go to Chatham.
> Tall folks to Lankyshire,
> Watermen to Rowhampton
> Should werry wisely steer.
> Pork butchers to Hogsnorton
> Or Hogsdon to make merry,
> Undertakers to Gravesend
> At Blackwell or at Bury.

E.W. Mackney and E.L. Blanchard both asserted that Jack Sharp was the greatest comic singer of his day. Drink was his downfall and, although he was appearing every evening at the Grecian in the autumn of 1855, he died while still young at a workhouse in Dover only a few months later.

In the twentieth century, Mark Sheridan was blessed with a good ear for a song. He had three enormous successes. The first was 'Here We Are! Here We Are!! Here We Are Again!!!' (1914), written by Charles Knight and Kenneth Lyle and described at the time as the battle cry of the British Army. The second was 'Who were you with last night?' (1912), which Sheridan wrote with Fred Godfrey:

> Who were you with last night?
> Who were you with last night?
> It wasn't your sister. It wasn't your ma.
> Ah! Ah! Ah! Ah! Ah! Ah! Ah! Ah!
> Who were you with last night
> Out in the pale moonlight?
> Are you going to tell your missus when you get home
> Who you were with last night?

Sheridan's third big hit was 'I do like to be beside the seaside' (1909),[3] written by John A. Glover-Kind:

MARK SHERIDAN (Frederick Shaw)
Born Hendon, Tyne and Wear, 1865/6 (?)
Married Ethel Maud Salisbury Davenport
   in Wandsworth, south London, 16
   March 1889 (d. February 1951,
   aged 88)
   Sons
Died Glasgow, 15 January 1918
Left £12,802

Oh, I do like to be beside the seaside.
I do like to be beside the sea.
I do like to stroll along the prom, prom, prom,
Where the brass band plays Tiddley om pom pom.
Oh, I do like to be beside the seaside.
I'll be beside myself with glee.
There are lots of things besides
I would rather be beside
Beside the seaside, beside the sea.

Sheridan created a furore with 'I do like to be beside the seaside'. Wearing a battered top hat, an ancient frock coat and bell-bottomed trousers, he strutted up and down, swinging his cane and banging the stage with it to underline each 'do' in the lyric. The painted backdrop usually depicted holiday-makers at the seaside. Sheridan often made out that one of them was Maud Allan, commenting 'So much on, she's nearly suffocated, poor girl'. The seaside entertainer Clarkson Rose was a fan:

When you saw Mark Sheridan, in his distinctive music hall dress, sing *I Do Like to be Beside the Seaside*, it was something more than someone singing a good, rousing song. He *became* a man who really *did* like to be beside the seaside. As he strode across the stage, singing lustily in his Tyneside voice and slapping the back-cloth with his stick, he was a man, full of fresh air and vigour and health, striding along the promenade.[4]

By 1917, Sheridan had switched to revue. He wrote the sketches and composed the songs for *Gay Paree*, which played a number of towns and cities, including the Coliseum in Glasgow, a city in which he had enjoyed some of his earliest successes. During one performance at the Coliseum at the start of 1918, there was some booing and whistling; the following morning, the reviews in the Glasgow papers were, at best, lukewarm.

As his popularity waned, Mark Sheridan killed himself.
(Richard Anthony Baker)

That afternoon, two men found Sheridan's body, shot through the head, in Kelvingrove Park. A Browning automatic was discovered nearby. Since inquests are not held into sudden deaths in Scotland, most people assumed he had killed himself. Only recently, it has been suggested that he may have been murdered, possibly by someone who resented the success of his two wartime hits, 'Here We Are! Here We Are!! Here We Are Again!!!' and 'Belgium put the kibosh on the kaiser', written by Alf Ellerton. (To 'put the kibosh on' meant 'to halt' or 'to prevent from continuing'.) The theory is fanciful.

On his death, *The Era* summed him up as: 'a breezy and spirited favourite of the public and a witty commentator on passing events with his own sunshiny smile, his delightful dance, his irresistible hat and his famous bell-bottomed trousers. Mark was one of the most successful comedians of the variety stage.'[5]

Another entertainer who died by his own hand was Frank Coyne, the son of a music-hall performer and one of the most successful light comedians of his day. A man known for his geniality and impeccable appearance, he had the knack of picking chorus songs that were hummed on every street corner.

Coyne started his working life in Derby as a travelling salesman in jewellery, but he enjoyed enough success as an amateur comic singer at local concerts to make him decide to turn professional. On arriving in London, he soon had a hit with 'The Tiddley at the "Fountain"' (also sung by a teenage Ernie Wise) and followed it with 'The Horse the Missus Dried the Clothes on'. After returning from a successful tour of South Africa in 1906, he suffered a mental breakdown and killed himself by cutting his throat.

> FRANK COYNE (Josiah Harris)
> **Born** *c.* 1867
> **Married** —— (professionally known as Carrie Joy)
> **Died** Brixton, south London, 18 April 1906
> **Left** £1,097

Fred Barnes, the original singer of 'Give me the Moonlight' (1917) and 'On Mother Kelly's Doorstep' (1925), was among the most popular entertainers of his day. But his career was ended by heavy drinking and his homosexuality. Having earned thousands of pounds, he finished his days in poverty.

> FRED BARNES (Frederick Jester Barnes)
> **Born** Birmingham, 31 May 1885
> **Died** Southend-on-Sea, Essex, 23 October 1938

Frederick Jester Barnes owed his appropriate middle name to his mother, born Mary Alice Jester. His father, Thomas, was a butcher and Fred was born above his shop in Birmingham. Fred's interest in music hall began when he was 10: Vesta Tilley arrived in the neighbourhood in a carriage and pair to visit her sister, who lived nearby. At the time, Tilley was appearing in the pantomime *Dick Whittington* at the local Prince of Wales Theatre and Fred persuaded his mother to take him there, his first visit to a theatre. So smitten was he that, for weeks afterwards, he tried impersonating Tilley's gestures and mannerisms in the privacy of his bedroom.

He first sang in public in the local church choir. In his teens, he became friendly with Dorothy Ward, who became one of pantomime's most popular principal boys. After she had appeared in panto at the Alexandra Theatre, Birmingham, in 1905/6, she encouraged Fred to audition for the following year's show. Despite opposition from his father, he did so, landing a small part with just one song to sing and a short dance to go with it.

Better than that, he was spotted by the singer George Lashwood, who styled himself the Beau Brummel[6] of the Halls, the last of the *lions comiques*. Lashwood told Fred's father: 'I have seen an artist to take my place. It is your son.' Fred began modelling himself on Lashwood and, in the spring of 1907, made his London debut at the Empress in Brixton. At about that time, he wrote his own song, 'The Black Sheep of the Family', but did nothing with it for some months. In Leeds, he played it to some fellow entertainers, who were convinced he had a potential hit on his hands. With some misgivings, he tried it out on the first night of an engagement at the Hackney Empire. Even though he was first turn, he was encored, and, on the second night, he was given a second song and moved up the programme. His real success began that week.

Some time later, he was given an audition at the London Pavilion. Nervous enough already, his trepidation grew when he walked onstage to find George Robey sitting on one side of the manager and the dapper light comedian Whit Cunliffe on the other. Scarcely audible, his clothes wet with perspiration, he did his best and succeeded. He was booked to appear at the Tivoli and the Oxford, although only at £4 a week, considerably less than the £12 he had been earning in the provinces. But he went from strength to strength, appearing at the Coliseum, the Holborn Empire and the Palladium and soon earning £100 (by today's standards £5,500) a week. Fred Barnes rose very quickly indeed.

It is impossible to tell how many people knew Fred was gay. (Homosexual acts were then illegal.) At first, it became known within the profession. Fred was derided for wearing more stage make-up than most and he earned himself the nickname Freda. Quentin Crisp has recounted that, on making visits to Portsmouth as a young man, friendly sailors jokingly asked him if he knew Fred. It is probable that Fred's father knew of his predilection. Whatever the truth, Fred's store of good luck started to run out in 1913 when his father committed suicide by cutting his throat. One account speaks of Fred's father arriving with a meat axe at the stage door of a theatre Fred was playing, determined to kill him. When he was thwarted, he went home and killed himself. Fred dated his own downfall from that moment, although he still

Fred Barnes, ruined by alcohol and his homosexuality. *(Richard Anthony Baker)*

had many more years ahead of him as a star. In 1914, he said he had no vacant dates for three years and even had contracts booking him as far ahead as 1924.

Fred's success went to his head. He kept four cars; he employed a butler, a valet and two maids; he gambled, getting through as much as £1,500 in one night in Monte Carlo; and he began drinking. His dressing-room drinks bill sometimes totalled £30 a week. By 1922, his drinking had become a problem. He was booked to appear in Australia at a salary of £200 a week, more than he had ever earned before, but, every day, he said, he drank more than was good for him and, during the middle of his second week at the Tivoli, Melbourne, he missed a performance. The rest of the run was cancelled, although the shock was diminished by a booking from South Africa: on the way home, he played Johannesburg and Cape Town at a salary of £130 a week. Back in Britain, theatre managers soon got to know of his unreliability. In Brighton, he was taken off the bill of the Hippodrome after being drunk on stage.

Things came to a head in 1924 when he was arrested for drunken driving in Hyde Park after knocking a motorcyclist off his bike. He was sentenced to a month's imprisonment. One account said that, immediately after the accident, his boyfriend, a sailor, quickly left the car and disappeared, although this was not made public at the time. Fred's incarceration did not immediately affect his popularity. At first, he carried on earning big money, but his drinking again became a problem. He missed a performance at the Holborn Empire and, little by little, he started slipping down the bill, until he was again appearing as first turn, singing only one song. He was still spending as much; a tour he financed failed; and it was only after mixing with down-and-outs that he finally decided to sober up.

In the early 1930s, he appeared in Lew Lake's company, Stars that Never Fail to Shine, but, by the mid-1930s, his health was failing. Stricken with tuberculosis, he moved to Southend-on-Sea and was often seen in the bar of a pub, singing his old songs. In 1938, he was found dead in a gas-filled room at his lodgings, although the tap to the gas fire had been turned off. Suicide was ruled out.

Harry Daley, a gay policeman, who had an affair with E.M. Forster, summed Fred up:

Fred Barnes had been one of those young men, who, with straw hat and cane, stepped about rhythmically on the music hall stage, singing about moonlight and girls . . . He was good natured and silly and the appearance of his Rolls Royce was a welcome sight to many an unemployed man – especially to those in the know. His good nature was his downfall for he never did harm to anybody.[7]

LETINE (George Thomas Gorin)
Born 1853 (?)
Married Olga Caroline Moralt
(daughter of the music director of
the Opera Theatre, Munich),
Kennington, south London,
22 September 1884
Died Lambeth, south London, 21 June
1889
Left £279

George Gorin, known professionally as Letine, was remembered more for the manner of his death than for anything he did on stage. He was stabbed to death at the stage door of the Canterbury.

The Wonderful Letine Troupe (of Bicyclists), comprising Gorin, his wife, an adopted daughter, another child and three young women, appeared at the Paragon early one evening in 1889. Their carriage took them on to the Canterbury and Gorin let the women get out first. Then, as he left, a man emerged from the shadows, saying: 'I've been waiting a long time and now I've got you.' He plunged a knife into Gorin's stomach and ran across the road, where he produced a gun and shot himself in the mouth. Both men were taken to hospital. Gorin died within half an hour, but the bullet the murderer used lodged in his palate and he survived.

The attacker was Nathaniel Curragh. His daughter, Beatrice, had been part of Letine's troupe. She left the previous year and died before Christmas. Curragh believed Gorin had used cruelty to train his daughter and was therefore responsible for her death. At the Old Bailey, a jury agreed that he was insane and therefore unfit to plead. He was given an indefinite prison sentence.

As for the act, a commentator wrote:

> Perhaps the most remarkable thing about Letine was the fact that he was adept at teaching others to do what he had never learnt to do himself. He was a tall, fine-looking man, but merely one of the stage ornaments in the troupe of which he was the proprietor; the performers in it were a number of attractive young ladies and the feats they accomplished while gyrating on the whirling wheels were well ahead of anything previously done by the fair sex.[8]

Frank Leo, ostracised after his lover's husband shot himself dead. *(Richard Anthony Baker)*

Up to 1913, Frank Leo, the son of a clerk, wrote songs especially for Wilkie Bard, among them 'My Little Deitcher Girl' and 'Let me Sing'. (The arrangement ended when Bard refused to pay the fees Leo was demanding.) Leo also wrote for Sable Fern, who in 1896 married Walter Allen, a comedian, professionally known as Watty Allan (*sic*). The marriage was unhappy and, after a time, Fern set up home with Leo close to the Kennington Theatre in south London. One morning in 1903, Allan arrived at the house with a loaded revolver. He shot Leo in the arm and wounded Fern in the hand. He then turned the gun on himself and blew his brains out. He was 34. People queueing at the Kennington Theatre, alerted by the shooting, crowded into the front garden of Leo's home as the police arrived. An hour before the inquest into Allan's death, further crowds lined nearby streets. As Leo and Fern arrived, there were cries of 'You wretched woman' and 'Shame on you'. Some of Fern's evidence was greeted by catcalls from the public gallery. A jury returned a verdict that Allan had committed suicide while temporarily insane. On the day of his funeral, thousands of people turned out to watch the cortège. The mourners included Dan Leno, Kate Carney and Alice Lloyd.

> FRANK LEO (Ernest Vincent Peers)
> **Born** Chatham, Kent, 10 September 1874
> **Married** Alice Steward (professionally known as Sable Fern), Southwark, south London, 26 June 1905 (d. 20 July 1942)
> **Died** Twickenham, Greater London, 25 October 1940

For a time, Leo and Fern were ostracised by the music-hall profession, but in 1905, they married and formed a double act called the Song Shop. Leo wrote a number of popular songs for his wife, including 'You Can't Stop the Sun from Shining', 'My Lily of the Valley', 'Where is the Heart?' and, most successful of all, 'What is the Use of Loving a Girl?' (1902).

Harry Fragson was a much more celebrated songwriter than Leo. His biggest hit was 'Hello! Hello! Who's your lady friend?' a few months before it became a gruesome comment on his own life.

> HARRY FRAGSON (Leon Philippe Pot (*sic*))
> **Born** Soho, central London, 2 July 1869
> **Married** Elise Delisia (professionally known as Alice Delysia)
> **Died** Paris, 31 December 1913

Fragson used to make out he was a cockney, but he was not to be believed. He was born in the heart of London's Soho, where his father, Victor, ran a hotel. As a young man, he was a devotee of the halls. His idol was Alfred Vance. Although he showed some musical talent, his father did not encourage him. In fact, Fragson was 18 before he even touched a piano. At about this time, he moved to Paris, where he lived the life of a pauper, often surviving on the equivalent of twopence a day, enough to buy a crust of bread and a piece of sausage.

He was determined to become an entertainer and, building on a boyhood gift for mimicry, he perfected an impersonation of the French music-hall singer, Paulus (Paul Habans (1845–1908)). With other impressions, he put together an act, which he eventually tried out at La Cigale, a hall in Montmartre. He proved a success and, going from strength to strength, he gradually dropped the impersonations and replaced them with songs he had written himself, accompanying himself on the piano.

By 1905, he had established himself as a well-known and successful entertainer in Paris. That year, Arthur Collins, the manager of the Theatre Royal, Drury Lane, saw him at the Folies Bergère. He was so impressed that he offered him a role in *Cinderella*, the pantomime he was planning for the Lane that Christmas. Fragson was to play Dandini in the French manner, Dandigny.

Fragson had a naturally comic look. He was tall, with large expressive eyes, a drooping lower lip and long strands of hair which he plastered over his otherwise bald head. He was an inveterate practical joker. Switching between a thick London accent and the near perfect French he had learned, he might say to a newcomer:

Of course, you know George Insimsimsin, the jeweller in the Rue de la Paix. The reply, inevitably, was 'George who?' 'Why, George – blessed if I haven't forgotten his name. But he

Harry Fragson, killed by his demented father. (Richard Anthony Baker)

Bon Souvenir,
Harry Fragson

told me he met you last season at the Exspinachi Hotel and you . . .'. 'Met me where?' 'At the Monte Carlo hotel and you promised to send him some eskerfudel when you got to town.'[9]

By this time, his victim usually realised his leg was being pulled.

Cinderella was a great success. 'Whispers of love', a song Fragson had written for the American entertainer May de Sousa, who played the title role, was the hit of the show. The reviews hailed Dandigny as 'a triumph of artistic treatment'. By the time the panto had finished its run, Fragson was as big a star in Britain as he was in France.

He continued writing his own songs, including a witty send-up of department stores, 'Other Department, Please' (1910) and 'All the Girls are Lovely by the Seaside' (1913), which he wrote with Worton David and Bert Lee.

Fragson was now in the big time. His earnings were at least £10,000 (by today's standards £550,000) a year; he moved his elderly father out to live with him in his apartment in the Rue Lafayette; and, in spite of his looks, women loved him. Fragson, was, in fact, either gay or bisexual. He once hosted a party with Proust's first lover, the composer Reynaldo Hahn. One of Proust's biographers insists Fragson was known to be gay.[10] However, for a time, Fragson was married to the French revue artiste Alice Delysia, and, by the end of 1913, he had apparently fallen in love with a 24-year-old dancer, Paulette Franck.

At the onset of that winter, he sang his most famous song, 'Hello! Hello! Who's your lady friend?'

> Hello! Hello! Who's your lady friend?
> Who's the little girlie by your side?
> I've seen you with a girl or two.
> Oh! Oh! Oh! I am surprised at you.
> Hello! Hello! Stop your little games.
> Don't you think your ways you ought to mend?
> It isn't the girl I saw you with at Brighton.
> Who, who, who's your lady friend?

It seemed life could not have been better for Fragson, but his new song proved to have a macabre significance. Fragson's father had grown incurably jealous of Mlle Franck; he did not like being left on his own in the Paris apartment; and he suspected that he was going to be put into an old people's home.

When Fragson returned home on New Year's Eve, 1913, his father produced a revolver and shot him dead. Fragson was 44 and, according to friends, had amassed a fortune of about £80,000 (by today's standards more than £4 million). His body was buried in the cemetery of Montmartre. So many thousands of people turned out in his honour that the police could not keep control. Six weeks later, his demented father died in an asylum.

CHAPTER 16

SUNG HEROES

In the heyday of music hall, the top singers were paid fabulous money. By contrast, songwriters earned a pittance. Herman Finck, who used to conduct the orchestra at the Palace Theatre, London, noted: 'People would say to one another "Have you heard Dan Leno's new song? It's magnificent – tremendously funny." They give all the credit to the man who sang the song and forget about the poor fellow who wrote it.'[1] Charles Coborn, who both wrote and bought songs, felt the same: 'When people remark "Have you heard Bill Jones's great new song?" they should give a thought or two to the author and composer of that "great song". We owe an immense debt of gratitude to those who write our good things for us.'[2]

Oscar Wilde used to visit the halls, as did the man who eventually stood beside him in the dock at the Old Bailey, Alfred Waterhouse Somerset Taylor, although in Taylor's case, the attraction was not so much the show as the rent boys he found there. One of the boys, Frederick Atkins, had ambitions to go on the halls himself. During the first of Wilde's trials, he was questioned about his generosity towards the boy:

Did you give Atkins any money?
   Yes. £3 15s [£3.75] to buy his first song for the music hall stage. He told me the poets who wrote for the music hall never took less.[3]

Wilde was being hoodwinked. The going rate was nearer a guinea (£1.05) a song. Not many of the 'poets' made a proper living from songwriting. Many died in penury. Those who did earn big money either published their works themselves or became involved in other more lucrative theatrical enterprises.

In ignorance of the economics of the business, the journalist and poet T.W. Crosland once composed a music-hall song for a female singer. The woman and her husband met Crosland, read the song through and decided they liked it. Then, the discussion turned to money. Crosland thought he should receive at least £10. 'What do you usually pay?' he asked. 'A guinea,' replied the star's husband. 'A guinea?' Crosland yelled. 'Don't be so silly. I could borrow that.'

The music-hall song was criticised ruthlessly. It was an easy target. As it addressed issues an uneducated audience could understand and presumed to do no more than amuse and entertain, it was attacked as either banal or immoral. In 1889, one songwriter, Harry Dacre, spiritedly defended his trade when it was denounced by Henry Arthur Jones, one of the most popular playwrights of the time.

Harry Dacre, who wrote *Daisy Bell*. *(Richard Anthony Baker)*

In a lecture in Manchester, Jones characterised the popular music-hall song as:

Pert, catchy, empty, leering – its only wit lying in some cloaked and yet quite palpable indecency with a jingling refrain that is at once caught up and ground out by the barrel organs, while the poor white-faced morsels of humanity, the children of our towns . . . the poor, deformed rickety mites of children swarm out of their dens and garrets and alleys and dance round to the jingling, foolish strains. It's a death dance, believe me, it's a death dance.[4]

> HARRY DACRE (Frank Dean)
> **Born** possibly in the Isle of
> Man, *c.* 1855
> **Died** Marylebone, London,
> 22 July 1922
> **Left** £7,670

Dacre argued that any amusement enjoyed by poor children was better than none: 'Are these children any more demoralised or any less happy for their terpsichorean efforts? Would the sun shine any brighter on their lives, would more bread be their portion, if they were to refrain from this exercise?'[5]

Dacre was a good-humoured, alert and businesslike man. He spent some time in Manchester, but was living in Preston in 1882 when he decided to try to make a career from songwriting. In his first two years, he claimed to have written more than 700 songs and to have sold around 600 of them.

His first big hit was also the first success of Harry Randall. The song was 'The Ghost of Benjamin Binns', which Randall first sang at the Oxford in Brighton in 1885. Dacre temporarily abandoned Britain soon after this success, complaining that the strain of writing a song a day for two years was beginning to affect his health. He emigrated to Australia, where he stayed for four years. Two years after returning, he left again, this time for America. He took with him a song that proved more durable and more popular than any other music-hall composition: 'Daisy Bell' ('Daisy, Daisy, give me your answer do'). The original lyric referred not to 'a bicycle built for two', but 'a donkey-cart made for two'. However, Dacre found that donkey-carts in America were known as mules and wagons. He needed to change the words.

The story goes that he took his bicycle with him and, on reaching New York, was surprised to be made to pay import duties. A friend remarked that he was lucky he had not taken a tandem with him or he would have had to pay double. So, Dacre easily amended his lyric:

> Daisy, Daisy, give me your answer, do!
> I'm half crazy, all for the love of you!
> It won't be a stylish marriage.
> I can't afford a carriage.
> But you'll look sweet on the seat of a bicycle built for two.

At first, Dacre could not persuade any singer to buy the song, but he eventually induced Katie Lawrence to try it. Towards the end of 1892, she was at Tony Pastor's theatre in New York and was due to return to London to open at a number of halls on Boxing Day. In later years, Lawrence and Dacre disagreed over what she first thought of the song. She said she had liked it instantly; he said she was not keen, but decided to sing it anyway. As it turned out, the song was not an immediate success in London. Lawrence said:

When I reached London, I sang it for four or five weeks, but it never seemed to catch on or go at all well. I sang it in the provinces with a not much better result and I made up my mind to drop it. I returned to London on the afternoon of Whit Sunday, having to open on the Whit Monday. Suddenly, whilst at the station getting together my luggage and putting it on a cab, I heard someone humming 'Daisy'. A few minutes later, I heard it again and found that it was all over London. I was completely surprised and, as you may imagine, I did not drop the song. I sang it on the Monday and it went simply magnificently.[6]

'Daisy Bell' was Katie Lawrence's greatest success, but her fame was short-lived. At the height of her career, she lived in a large house in Regent's Park in central London. Twenty years after 'Daisy Bell', she died in poverty and obscurity, meriting only one line of obituary in *The Stage*.

In 1895, Dacre set up his own publishing house, Frank Dean and Co. and, in 1899, he was able to follow 'Daisy Bell' with a song that has withstood the test of time almost as well, 'I'll be your sweetheart', sung by Lil Hawthorne:

> I'll be your sweetheart, if you will be mine
> All my life I'll be your Valentine.
> Bluebells I've gathered.
> Keep them and be true.
> When I'm a man, my plan
> Will be to marry you.

By the turn of the century, publishers were suffering badly from the work of pirates, people who copied and printed the sheet music of popular songs and sold it cheaply and illegally. When it was found that the law could do little to stop them, Dacre withdrew from the business in disgust. He did not return until a new Copyright Bill was steered through the Commons by the Liverpool MP, T.P. O'Connor. It received Royal Assent in 1906. Thereafter, Dacre was able to live in some comfort. His home, a short walk from his office, was a charming house in Langham Place in the West End of London. For those trying to emulate his success, he had this advice: 'An average musician can turn out hundreds of songs more or less after a pattern and that is the pattern that will neither wash nor last . . . Dozens of songs are written which, without being a direct imitation of something else, is so much like it that the public won't have it . . . Originality is what is wanted.'[7]

The prodigious output of songs by George le Brunn and John P. Harrington earned them the nicknames the Gilbert and Sullivan of the Halls. For Marie Lloyd alone, they wrote more than thirty songs.

Le Brunn was born plain George Frederick Brunn, the son of a Brighton coach-builder. Young George added the 'le', thinking he would be taken more seriously as a musician. He was educated at a private school in Brighton, studying piano, violin, harp and harmony. For most of the 1870s, he played in the orchestra pit at music halls both in London and the provinces. He last worked at the Shoreditch hall, Harwood's, where he played the piano, but he was sacked for reading a newspaper.

From 1883, le Brunn devoted himself entirely to songwriting. After a brief partnership with Harry

GEORGE LE BRUNN (George Frederick Brunn)
Born Brighton, 20 June 1864 (?)
Married Eliza Hewer, St Pancras, London, 23 October 1883
Died Lambeth, south-east London, 18 December 1905
Left £183

George le Brunn, prolific melodist.
(*Richard Anthony Baker*)

Adams, he joined forces with Harrington, who, until then, had been working with Joseph Tabrar. One of their first clients was Charles Chaplin, the father of the king of silent movies. Over the next twenty-one years, they wrote for practically every music-hall star.

John Harrington, a tailor's son, began work at the age of 12 as an office boy with Tabrar, later becoming his secretary and then manager. He sold his first song to Harry Rickards: 'May God protect our soldiers in the Transvaal War', but Rickards never sang it. Harrington received his music-hall education from Tabrar, who first took him to the wine bar of the York Hotel, where much music-hall business was transacted. In a welter of cliché, he wrote:

> I can still feel the glow of awed rapture that thrilled me to the marrow that glorious day of days that I first stood within the sacred precincts of the wine bar. I arrived under the sheltering wing of Joe Tabrar, the most popular song-writer of that particular period . . . He certainly taught me more about the art of writing a successful song than I could ever have learnt on my own.[8]

Harrington worked with Tabrar until he was 19. He then tried to work on his own as a song-writer:

> To my intense surprise, [the stars] were not at all eager to be made famous by my song offerings and it was not until I fell in with George le Brunn that I really came into my kingdom at all . . . I have worked with a number of famous composers of popular songs . . . but, without fear of contradiction, I boldly assert that George le Brunn was the daddy of them all.[9]

J.P. HARRINGTON (John Harrington)
Born London, 1 May 1865
Married Jane Eliza Arthur, Wolverton, Buckinghamshire, 26 December 1887
Died Barnet, Greater London, 23 August 1939

For more than twenty years, Harrington and le Brunn tailored their songs to suit a wide range of entertainers. Le Brunn memorised their pitch and range; Harrington worked on the subject matter that matched their style. Harrington, the lyricist, was amazed at the speed with which le Brunn, the melodist, worked:

> George could compose songs as easily and deftly as another man might write a letter. A rapid glance at the lyric, a grunted 'This in six-eight time, eh?' and, after my nod of acquiescence, presto! His fluent pen would positively fly over the sheet of music paper ere you had time to gasp 'Gee-whiz!'. Seldom, if ever, was so much as a note altered afterwards and never once was the piano touched, until the melody was completed . . . Some of our most popular songs were composed in ten or fifteen minutes. Foolishly, at first, I was a little indignant that George earned his money apparently so easily, whilst the lyric took me perhaps an hour or two to write.[10]

Le Brunn was quick, but also erratic. When he was writing for the singer of comic and patriotic songs Charles Godfrey, they often called at a number of pubs on their way to a hall, only to find they had left the band parts somewhere en route. Someone was then sent from pub to pub to try to find them.

One le Brunn–Harrington song shows how readily composers turned to contemporary events. In the summer of 1887, a respectable young dressmaker, Elizabeth Cass, who had arrived in London from her native Stockton only six weeks previously, was arrested in the West End and charged with being a prostitute. The policeman who apprehended her, the wonderfully named Bowden Endacott, gave evidence that he had seen her soliciting a number of men. She had, in fact, done nothing of the sort, but the publicity surrounding the case turned it into a minor cause célèbre, raising such issues as the extent of prostitution in London, the morals of young women in general and the probhity of the police. With questions being asked in Parliament, the Home Secretary was forced to set up a public inquiry. Endacott was charged with perjury, but was acquitted on the grounds that he may have been mistaken.

J.P. Harrington, one of Marie Lloyd's favourite lyricists. *(Richard Anthony Baker)*

Public interest in the case inspired Harrington and le Brunn to write a song about it during the course of one weekend. On the following Monday morning, they took it to one of pantomime's finest principal boys, Harriett Vernon, who liked it, but did not think it was a woman's song. She suggested it would suit Charles Godfrey better; Harrington and le Brunn went to see him; he bought it at once; le Brunn arranged the band parts there and then; and Godfrey sang it at the London Pavilion that night to thunderous applause – with Harriett Vernon standing in the wings, since she was appearing next.

In 1888, Harrington and le Brunn wrote a descriptive song for Godfrey, 'The Seven Ages of Man'. It was such a success that they had a request for something similar from Jenny Hill. Harrington wrote for her a story of double standards, 'Masks and Faces' (1888), so named after a play by Charles Reade. Le Brunn set it to music and the couple set off to see Hill at her home in Streatham in south London. It was the first time either of them had written for Jenny Hill and they were both delighted with their new song. Hill seemed happy, too. She spent more than an hour playing it over on the piano in what Harrington called a hoarse, croaking little voice, quite different from the clear tones in which she sang at night. Hill was prepared to pay 2 guineas (£2.10), twice the going rate, but Harrington refused. He set a new standard of 5 guineas. Hill paid up and the song proved one of her most popular.

Bessie Bonehill was another female star who bought a Harrington–le Brunn song in 1888: 'The Girls of Today'. Bessie sang it at practically every engagement for eighteen months. She was so impressed by its success that she asked Harrington and le Brunn to bring her three or four songs every month. The two men looked forward to their visits, not least for the steak puddings, some with kidneys, others with oysters, made by Bessie's mother, who was known to everyone in music hall as Granny.

Two of le Brunn's most lasting melodies, sung by Gus Elen, were written not with Harrington, but with Edgar Bateman. They were 'If it Wasn't for the Houses in Between' and 'It's a great big shame' (both 1894). Together with W.T. Lytton, le Brunn also wrote the song that made Marie Lloyd's name, 'Wink the Other Eye'. Marie explained:

> There was a convivial little gathering in progress and George le Brunn sat at the piano, playing anything and everything. I said to him in the way of a joke about something that was going on 'Oh, wink the other eye, George' and he repeated the words playing a sort of accompaniment. Well, it just occurred to us 'What a good song that would make'.[11]

Marie's first big success is not remembered today, but a song le Brunn wrote with his brother, Thomas, in 1892 did stand the test of time, 'Oh, Mr Porter', a plea to a railwayman to be returned to London from Crewe as quickly as possible. George Bernard Shaw did not like it. 'Though very funnily sung,' he wrote, '[it] is not itself particularly funny'. Max Beerbohm differed: 'The flurry, the frantic distress of it . . . Marie was bursting with rapture and made us partakers of it.' Eight years later, le Brunn and Harrington wrote another song for Marie: one that introduced a new saying into the language: 'Everything in the Garden's Lovely'.

By 1893, Harrington had become a comparatively wealthy man. He bought a large house in Bedford, which he named Lyric Lodge. Each day, he travelled to London by train in top hat and morning coat, his buttonhole filled in summer with a single bloom from a hollyhock in his garden. Having been brought up in London, Harrington relished his garden. On returning home, he often took a late-night walk round his lawn, striking matches so that he could check the progress of his plants.

Le Brunn died at the age of 41. Because of piracy, his widow, Eliza, was left virtually penniless. The composer of musical comedies, Leslie Stuart, was incensed: 'George le Brunn . . . was . . . the most prolific popular melodist of the time. His songs are being sung in every corner of the earth and he has probably had more current songs in prominence than any living composer. Through the monstrous depredations of the music pirate, he died in financial difficulties.'[12]

To help le Brunn's widow, a benefit concert was arranged at the Oxford. Many stars who had sung his songs appeared, Marie Lloyd among them. In all, £600 was raised. In addition, a fund was set up to which Marie contributed 100 guineas (£105).

Harrington's prosperity began to falter with the outbreak of the First World War, as music hall started losing its appeal. He moved from his comfortable home in Bedford to rented accommodation in Finchley. There, he mourned music hall's passing, precipitated by an influx of American talent: 'Let English publishers give English song-writers the same monetary backing as they at present put behind the American songs and then see which country produces the most successful song-writers.'[13]

> FRED W. LEIGH (William Frederick Bridgen)
> **Born** Shoreditch, London, 21 October 1869
> **Married** Kate Louisa Berry, Hackney,
>   London, 16 December 1894
>   (d. 4 September 1959; left £3,596)
> **Died** Edmonton, north London,
>   21 August 1924
> **Left** £71

Another of the halls' most successful writers was Fred W. Leigh, the son of a cook. At the age of 13, he worked as an errand boy at the offices of the humorous magazine *Punch*, and later began writing stories for boys' magazines. In 1901, he joined the staff of the music publishers Francis, Day and Hunter, as literary editor, a post he held until his death. By nature, he was a literary man, given to reading the Bible and Shakespeare long into the night. He was not a churchgoer, but his Christian demeanour led Marie Lloyd to tell him that he ought to have been a clergyman.

In 1906 alone, Leigh had three hits. One was 'The Galloping Major', which he wrote with George Bastow, who also sang it while prancing around the stage on a wooden horse:

> Bumpity! Bumpity! Bumpity! Bump!
> As if I was riding my charger.
> Bumpity! Bumpity! Bumpity! Bump!
> As proud as an Indian rajah.
> All the girls declare that I'm a gay old stager.
> Hey! hey! clear the way.
> Here comes the galloping major!

The other two were sung by Vesta Victoria. The first, 'Poor John', is the tale of a man introducing his girlfriend to his mother, who is entirely unimpressed. Leigh wrote that with Henry E. Pether. The second song was the even more successful 'Waiting at the Church', all about a would-be bride abandoned at the altar. This song helped to make Vesta's name in America.

In 1907, Leigh and Kenneth Lyle wrote 'Jolly good luck to the girl who loves a soldier' for Vesta Tilley, and, in 1910, there came 'Put on your tat-ta, little girlie', sung by the winsome Clarice Mayne:

> Put on your tat-ta, little girlie.
> Do, do what I want you to.
> Far from the busy hurly-burly,
> I've got lots to say to you.
> My head's completely twirly whirly.
> My girl I want you to be.
> So, put on your tat-ta, your pretty little tat-ta
> And come out a tat-ta with me.

Five years later, Leigh and George Arthurs came up with 'A Little of what you Fancy' for Marie Lloyd, and in 1917, he and Charles Collins produced 'Why am I always the bridesmaid?' for the comedienne Lily Morris:

> Why am I always the bridesmaid,
> Never the blushing bride?
> Ding dong! Wedding bells
> Only ring for other girls.
> But some fine day,
> Oh, let it be soon,
> I will wake up in the morning
> On my own honeymoon.

In 1919, Leigh and Collins wrote one of Marie Lloyd's last hits, 'Don't Dilly Dally', all about a couple fleeing their home by dead of night to avoid paying back rent.

Another writer, Felix McGlennon, had a low opinion of the music that earned him a comfortable living:

Assume, if you like, that what I write is rubbish. My reply is 'It is exactly the sort of rubbish I am encouraged by the public to write' . . . All my life I have tried to produce an article for which there is a public demand. If I visit a music hall, it is with the single object of instructing myself as to the class of thing that is pleasing the public. Then, I try to write it – and write nothing else.[14]

As a young man, Felix McGlennon, the son of an Irish shoemaker who died of excessive drinking, set up a business in Manchester printing penny songbooks.

FELIX MCGLENNON
Born Glasgow, 30 January 1855
Married (1) Louisa Wilson, Chorlton, Lancashire,
      14 December 1886 (d. Lambeth, 11 January
      1915, aged 52)
   Two sons, Felix Cornelius (b. 1888; as Lance
      Corporal, killed in action 9 September 1918)
      and Herbert (1891–1964)
   Two daughters, Marie Louise (1890–1903) and
      Louisa, b. 1895
   (2) Edith Louisa Jury, Edmonton, north London,
      17 May 1915
Died 1 December 1943
Left £79,217

During the 1880s, he went to America, where he enjoyed his first success as a songwriter. Some of these songs found their way back to Britain, including 'And her Golden Hair was Hanging down her Back' (1894), sung first by Alice Leamar and amended for Seymour Hicks to sing in *The Shop Girl* at the Gaiety Theatre.

McGlennon did not always follow the popular trend. He sometimes set it. In an advertisement in 1890, he described himself as the originator of the current style of serio-comic song-writing: as he put it, the first composer to have rescued the modern serio-comic from 'Strolling in the fields with Charlie'. McGlennon was also the first to use black humour in comic songs with 'His Funeral's Tomorrow' (1888), which Tom Costello sang, using an axe, a brick and a pistol as props. It was Costello's first big success.

In 1890, Costello introduced a song by McGlennon, first heard in the United

Felix McGlennon demeaned his own songwriting abilities. *(Richard Anthony Baker)*

States three years previously. It was 'Comrades', the story of the friendship of two old soldiers. It provided both McGlennon and Costello with the greatest success of their careers:

> We were comrades, comrades
> Ever since we were boys,
> Sharing each other's sorrows,
> Sharing each other's joys.
> Comrades when manhood was dawning,
> Faithful whate'er might betide
> When danger threatened, my darling old comrade
> Was there by my side.

McGlennon was not a trained musician. He used to pick out his melodies on a toy piano, but he wrote hundreds of songs. He lived to a ripe old age, remaining active until his mid-eighties. One memory is of him chasing his panama hat across a busy road near his publishing business in north London at the age of 85.

The comedian Arthur Rigby once paid E.W. Rogers this compliment: 'His songs took the town and country more than once or twice and he supplied more jokes and patter than many can know.' All that was true, but, as Rogers was known for his reticence, not all his music-hall colleagues realised just how industrious a figure he was.

In his early years, Teddy Rogers appeared on stage himself in sketches written by the singer-songwriter Harry Pleon. He started writing songs in the 1880s. His first big success is still known today, 'Ask a Policeman' (1888), which he wrote with A.E. Durandeau and which was sung by James Fawn:

E.W. ROGERS (Edward William Rogers)
Born Newington, London, 6 January 1864
Married Amelia Ann Ayres, 1 October 1895
Died Wandsworth, London,
    21 February 1913

If you want to know the time, ask a policeman.
The proper Greenwich time, ask a policeman.
Every member of the force
Has a watch and chain, of course.
If you want to know the time, ask a policeman.

Within three years, 'Ask a Policeman' sold half a million copies of sheet music. Rogers's next success was a drinking song for Charles Godfrey, 'Hi-Tiddley-Hi-Ti' (1890), which was set to music by George le Brunn. In about 1891, he began working as an accompanist to George Robey, but, characteristically modest, he made no mention of his songwriting prowess. Robey wrote: 'He was a fine accompanist. He also wrote music hall songs, though I didn't know that then. All I knew was that he played my accompaniments just as I liked them played. And all the time he was quite a famous person, turning out some of the best ditties of the day.'[15]

Rogers wrote Robey's best-known patter songs, as well as material for Robey's character, the Mayor of Mudcumdyke, a garrulous local dignitary, dressed in top hat, robes and old-fashioned glasses and known to his friends as Sebastian – 'that's my Christian name on my mother's side'.

For Vesta Tilley, Rogers wrote 'Following in Father's Footsteps' (1902):

I'm following in father's footsteps.
I'm following the dear old dad.
He's just in front with a fine big gal
So I thought I'd have one as well.
I don't know where he's going,
But when he gets there, I'll be glad.
I'm following in father's footsteps.
I'm following the dear old dad!

In her autobiography, Tilley dismissed in just a few sentences the man

E.W. Rogers, shy about his songwriting
prowess. (Richard Anthony Baker)

who provided her with one of her greatest successes: 'It was a rare thing not to see Rogers at my home in London every day with a batch of new numbers. He turned them out so quickly and they were all more or less successful.'[16]

Lady de Frece devoted little more space to Harry B. Norris, whom she paid a guinea for an enormous hit, 'Algy, the Piccadilly Johnny with the Little Glass Eye' (1895). Norris ended his days in a lunatic asylum at Cheadle in Greater Manchester.

Joseph Tabrar was one of music hall's greatest self-publicists. No one had a higher opinion of him than he did himself, but most entertainers of his day sang his songs and he wrote one of music hall's most durable, if not silliest songs, 'Daddy wouldn't buy me a bow-wow'. His advice about how to write a comic song was: 'Think of a catchy refrain. Think of the damned silliest words that will rhyme anyhow. Think of a haunting pretty melody and there you are. The fortune of your publisher is made.'[17]

Joe Tabrar, of Spanish and Italian extraction, was introduced to music hall early. At the age of 13, he was one of the choristers singing at Evans's. He was presumably one of the group of boys described by the drama critic Clement Scott as 'poor pale-faced little urchins, who were kept up miserably late, [but whose] singing was a treat'. Later in life, Tabrar used to say that his singing was praised by Wagner, whom he described as an Evans's regular, but, as Wagner made only three trips to London (1839, 1855 and 1877) and as there is no evidence that he went anywhere near Evans's, Tabrar must be suspected of being economical with the truth.

Here lies the main problem in recounting Tabrar's life. He was, by all accounts, a colourful character much given to hyperbole. He claimed all sorts of things, some true, others patently not. He was also contemptuous of other musicians: he often boasted that he could 'knock Sir Arthur Sullivan into a cocked hat'. For the record, this is mostly his account of his early life: as a boy, he sang sacred songs at the Italian church in Hatton Garden; he played the violin at St James's Hall; he was a clown, a minstrel singer, an acrobat, a pianist, a comic singer and a musical director.

When his voice broke, Tabrar said, he began work as a mechanic. But he made sure he was seen

> JOSEPH TABRAR[18]
> **Born** Holborn, London, 5 November
>   1857
> **Married** Emily Cox, known as Lilla or
>   Lila, Bermondsey, south London,
>   29 July 1878
>   Five children: Joseph (b. 1878);
>   Eleanor (b. 1880); Walter
>   (b. 1885); Lily (b. 1887); and
>   Alfred (b. 1889)
> **Died** Camberwell, south London,
>   August 1931

regularly near Poverty Corner, the spot outside the York Hotel near Waterloo Bridge, where, every Monday morning, out-of-work entertainers hung around in the hope of being signed up by agents whose offices were nearby: 'Not that they were all in a state of poverty who congregated there. Many a time I have hobnobbed there with the leading men of the stage, George Leybourne included . . . It was really a sort of exchange and mart. Many a small proprietor would come there and fill up his week's programme to commence that very night!'[19]

Tabrar often sat in the York Hotel, writing songs, which he sold for as little as a shilling (5p) apiece. He was in the hotel one day in 1880 when he was greeted by G.W. Hunt and eventually joined by George Leybourne. Hunt was reprimanded by Leybourne for failing to supply him with a song that had been promised; Hunt replied that he had decided to give up

Joe Tabrar, who wrote 'Daddy wouldn't buy me a bow-wow'. *(Richard Anthony Baker)*

writing altogether (certainly he wrote little after 1880); someone then laid a bet that Tabrar could write a song there and then more quickly than Hunt could. Hunt agreed to take part in the bet and the two men retired to another room.

Tabrar recalled:

As soon as the door was shut, Hunt leaned across the table and said: 'Look here, young man. I'll confess to you now that I couldn't write a song on the spur of the moment if you offered me £100. Still, if you think you can write one, go ahead.' So, I sat down and began to scribble. In a quarter of an hour, I had finished the song, complete with three verses, chorus and music. Leybourne was dubious. But, when I played it over to him on the piano in the smoking-room, he was delighted and bought it. Within a week, it was being sung all over London. It was *I Am a Millionaire* (1880).[20]

This was the first of many songs Tabrar wrote for Leybourne. In fact, he wrote Leybourne's last success, 'Ting Ting, That's How the Bell Goes' (1883).

Tabrar enjoyed his greatest success in 1893. He was at a theatre to hand over a song to Ada Reeve, one of the Gaiety Girls, who appeared in George Edwardes's musical comedies at the Gaiety Theatre. While waiting for her, he was approached by Joe Lawrence, who was known as the Upside Down Comedian because he did his act standing on his head. Lawrence reprimanded him for forgetting to write a song for his daughter, who was just starting on the halls. Thinking quickly, Tabrar said that he had not forgotten and showed him the song he had written for Ada Reeve:

He read it through and said it was rubbish. I persuaded him to let his daughter try it over at home, so that his wife could hear it. The girl, whose name was Vesta Victoria, seemed to like it, but her mother was strongly against it. In the end, I decided to tear it up, but, seeing my disappointment, they bought it out of kindness, giving me two guineas (£2.10) for it. Not long afterwards, that song was being sung all over the world. It was *Daddy Wouldn't Buy Me a Bow-wow*.[21]

That was how Joe Tabrar remembered it. Vesta Victoria's account is somewhat different. She said she took a fancy to the song as soon as Joe had sung it to her. She had just been given a black kitten and so put it in a basket and took it on stage with her when she sang the song. It was an instant success.

By 1894, Tabrar reckoned he had written 17,000 songs. His office housed twenty-four manuscript books, each containing 300 songs. So, he had written at least 7,200. They seemed to come easily to him: 'My most successful ditties have been written on the dead wall between this house and the Canterbury music hall. An idea will strike me as I walk along. Out comes half an envelope and a pencil; down goes the song with a dead wall for a desk.'[22]

In 1916, Tabrar felt obliged to defend his honour. The *Sporting Times* had suggested that he needed help in writing songs:

Old Joe Tabrar in his day contributed some good songs to the Foundry [the Gaiety Theatre] and, after Lionel Monckton had added two or three notes to the end of the chorus and corrected the spelling, some of them became quite popular in the musical comedies he composed. George Edwardes generally stood Joe Tabrar a bottle of fizz water and handed him a fiver for these little efforts that were composed somewhere near the Tankard in the Kennington Road. Afterwards, Joe would treat two or three of his pals to a 3s 6d [17.5p] table d'hote . . . As Joe used to describe these little feasts: 'I know it ain't as classy as the Savoy, but blimey, what a gorge for three and a tanner.'[23]

In a libel action against the paper, Tabrar testified that nobody had ever added a note to or corrected the spelling of any of his songs. He won the case and was awarded £500 damages.

Later in 1916, a benefit concert was arranged for him. It turned out to be an embarrassing affair. It was postponed once because Tabrar was suffering from a nervous illness. When it was eventually held at the Oxford music hall, Charles Coborn, Joe Elvin and Alice Delysia appeared, but there were plenty of empty seats and, when Tabrar stood up to give his speech of thanks, he criticised the tune of the National Anthem and played the audience his setting of the words: a British tune, he stressed, not a German one. One account said he was given 'a saddening reception for his misguided patriotism'.

Tabrar continued writing up to his death at the age of 74. In 1931, he produced a book of children's songs for the BBC, but he died before it could be published. He should have been rich, but he was yet another music-hall writer who ended his days with scarcely a penny to his name. 'I have made thousands for other people, but not for myself,' he recalled. 'I am the most Bohemian of all the Bohemians you ever met . . . I don't value money. I never valued money.'[24] As *The Era* commented: 'an odd, whimsical gentleman is Mr Tabrar with a many-sided genius.'

R.P. Weston and Bert Lee may be better-known songwriters as they were the subject of the Roy Hudd stage show, *Just a Verse and a Chorus*. Weston and Lee were writing partners for twenty years, mining a seemingly inexhaustible vein of comic invention. They produced more than 3,000 songs and hundreds of sketches for music hall, revue, musical comedy and the cinema.

Bob Weston was a heavily built man with a round, innocent face and a dry, caustic wit. In contrast, Bert Lee was small and cheery. As a young man, he was a piano tuner, but then he joined a troupe of pierrots, working first at Hoylake in Merseyside and then at Barmouth in Gwynedd.

R.P. WESTON (Robert Harris)
Born Islington, north London,
7 March 1878
Died Twickenham, Greater
London,
6 November 1936

Bob Weston first worked for an engineering firm, but was sacked for writing songs on the backs of pieces of emery paper. For the sake of his wife's health, he moved to Weston-super-Mare in Somerset. There, like his future partner, he too joined a concert party and became half of a knockabout Irish act, Conway and Weston. This was the first time he used the name Weston, probably borrowing it from his new town.

Weston and Lee were introduced to each other by the music publisher David Day of Francis, Day and Hunter. It was Day's suggestion that they should work together. There was never a contract, merely a handshake and a promise that their word was their bond. They were both exempted from service in the First World War, Bob because of poor eyesight and hearing and Bert through rheumatism. Instead

BERT LEE (William Herbert Lee)
Born Ravensthorpe, Yorkshire,
11 June 1880
Died Llandudno, Conwy,
23 January 1946
Left £36,934

of fighting, they wrote a string of wartime hits, the most famous of which was 'Good-bye-ee' (1917), sung by Florrie Forde; another of Marie Lloyd's younger sisters, Daisy Wood; and Charles Whittle. They got the idea while watching a crowd of factory girls shouting 'Good-bye-ee' (in the comic way that Harry Tate used to say it) to a regiment of soldiers marching to Victoria station in London:

Good-bye-ee! Good-bye-ee!
Wipe the tear, baby dear, from your eyeee
Tho' it's hard to part, I know
I'll be tickled to death to go.
Don't cryee. Don't sighee!
There's a silver lining in the skyee
Bonsoir, old thing. Cheerio. Chin chin ('Goodbye')
Nah-poo! [based on the French *il n'ya plus* ('it no longer exists')]
Toodle-oo
Good-bye-ee!

Weston and Lee developed a strict routine. Bert travelled each morning from Barnes to start
work at Bob's house in Twickenham at 10.30. They had a cup of coffee and then worked until
early afternoon when they finished the day with a glass of whisky. Sometimes Bob wrote the
tune and Bert the lyric; sometimes it was the other way round. Bert used to say: 'Bob has the
brains. I put the laughs in.' The comedian Clarkson Rose, who knew them well, described
Weston as blinking like a frustrated butterfly while thinking out ideas. Lee he found to be 'a
short quizzical Northern character with no high-falutin' ideas about inspiration or urges'.

They wrote two hits for the monologuist Stanley Holloway, who rounded off his career by
playing Alfred Doolittle in *My Fair Lady*. One was 'My Word, You Do Look Queer' (1922), all
about a man who is told by a succession of friends that he looks ill; and a song about Anne
Boleyn, 'With her head tucked underneath her arm' (1934), which was banned by the BBC
because it used the word 'bloody', as in the Bloody Tower.

One of their last songs was the mock melodramatic ballad 'And the Great Big Saw Came
Nearer and Nearer' (1936). Towards the end of that year, Weston died of a brain tumour. Lee
commented: 'Twenty years and we never had a quarrel. My old pal was so deaf he couldn't hear
what I used to call him.'

CHAPTER 17

. . . AND MORE

Many people think that music-hall songs dealt only in domestic humour: henpecked husbands, domineering wives and fearsome mothers-in-law; young lovers trying to find somewhere quiet; food and drink (of the latter, generally too much), holidays by the sea and so on. Certainly, those topics were given a music-hall treatment night after night, but, in an age when the British were proudly patriotic, a rousing song about Britain's international power could be cheered to the rafters. Topical songs were enjoyed too. There were several about the Tichborne case. Even when William Holland staged a contest between barmaids at the North Woolwich Gardens, George Leybourne was soon singing a song about it.

The hit songs of music hall were written by a surprisingly small number of men – no more than twenty – and their names were unknown outside the profession. Some could not read a note of music. Others, such as James W. Tate, had had a thoroughgoing musical education. Tate was equally at home in music hall, revue and musical comedy. As well as writing songs, he appeared on stage, playing the piano. He had one unhappy marriage and one tempestuous one. He was wildly extravagant and overwork appears to have contributed to his early death.

> JAMES W. TATE (James William Tate)
> **Born** Wolverhampton, west Midlands, 30 July 1875
> **Married** (1) Charlotte Louisa Collins (professionally known as Lottie Collins), 16 August 1902
> (2) Clarice Mabel Dulley (professionally known as Clarice Mayne), London, 19 March 1912
> **Died** Longton, Staffordshire, 5 February 1922
> **Left** £8,803

Jimmy Tate was the son of Catholic parents. His sister, Margaret, became the distinguished soprano Dame Maggie Teyte. Music flowed through the family home, Dunstall House. Jacob, the father of James and Maggie, was a dedicated amateur pianist, who had studied under the Polish teacher Theodor Leschetizky. Their mother, Maria, was a fine amateur singer.

At the age of 8, James was sent to Cotton College near the Staffordshire town of Cheadle. There, he achieved distinction as a brilliant pianist and a choirboy who sang with ease and assurance. A school record of 1887 states simply: James Tate, praestantissimus (supreme). He had been intended for the Church, but it was clear he was better suited to a musical career. After ten years in the United States, he returned to Britain as musical director of the Carl Rosa Opera Company, but, all the while, he maintained an interest in music hall. Jimmy went to the halls with his friends, wearing the standard insignia of the contemporary gay blade, a brightly coloured waistcoat and a monocle; and he even sang and played at some of them. It was all too much for his puritanical father and there were furious rows.

Clarice Mayne – and That. *(Richard Anthony Baker)*

Jacob was further angered when Jimmy married Lottie Collins, whose outstanding success with 'Ta-ra-ra-boom-de-ay' had been a high point of the 1890s. The marriage did not work. Lottie began drinking heavily and, within a few years, the couple were hardly seeing each other.

At about the same time, Tate teamed up professionally with Clarice Mayne, who had an almost doll-like quality in the songs she sang. Tate, still wearing his monocle, accompanied her on the piano, making a display of doting on her every move. Mayne introduced their act dismissively: the next song would be sung by this, she said, indicating herself, and accompanied by that, indicating Tate. They were soon billed as Clarice Mayne and That.

In 1912, the couple appeared at the first Royal Command Performance four months after they had secretly married. Their joint income allowed for a lavish honeymoon, travelling to Paris, Brussels, Vienna and Berlin. They were back in good time to rehearse for the Command Performance. In a crinoline and hat reminiscent of the 1860s, Clarice sang 'I'm Longing for Someone to Love Me', with Tate supplying the customary squirming and swooning. In 1914, Tate supplied Clarice with one of their most lasting songs, 'I was a good little girl till I met you', the lyrics by F. Clifford Harris:

> I was a good little girl till I met you.
> You sent my head in a whirl, my poor heart, too.
> Oh, how you told me the tale you always do.
> I was a good little girl till I met you.

Tate now began diversifying. Sensing that music hall was losing its appeal, he involved himself in revues, appearing in some and supplying material for others. In 1916, *The Maid of the Mountains* opened at the Princes Theatre, Manchester, starring Tate's stepdaughter, Jose Collins. Some alterations were made to it before it reached Daly's Theatre in London in 1917, most notably the addition of two songs by Tate, 'My Life is Love' and 'A Paradise for Two', and, at a later stage, two more, 'A Bachelor Gay' and 'When You're in Love'. Later that year, an entire show he had written, *Beauty Spot*, opened at the Gaiety. It brought a 17-year-old Evelyn Laye to the West End stage for the first time.

Tate could not have been working harder; he was also earning prodigiously; but it did not help his marriage. Although he overwhelmed Clarice with extravagant presents, she merely fretted that their money was disappearing too quickly. Their arguments were punctuated by the smashing of crockery. Clarice began investing in jewellery, but Tate saw this as an affront to his generosity and merely showered her with more lavish gifts. He also gave Clarice another hugely successful song, 'A Broken Doll' (1916), although, this time, Clifford Harris's lyric had an edge to it:

> You called me Baby Doll a year ago.
> You told me I was very nice to know.
> I soon learned what love was.
> I thought I knew,
> But all I've learnt has only taught me how to love you.
> You made me think you loved me in return.
> Don't tell me you were fooling after all.
> For, if you turn away, you'll be sorry some day.
> You left behind a broken doll.

After the First World War, Tate and Mayne appeared in the second Command Performance. Tate wrote for more revues, *The Peep Show* with Stanley Lupino and *Round in Fifty* with George Robey, both at the London Hippodrome. At Christmas 1921, Tate contributed to Robey's first London pantomime, *Jack and the Beanstalk*, also at the Hippodrome. Clarice played Jack and Robey Dame Trot. It was a tremendous success. Robey wrote: 'I honestly doubt if Londoners have ever seen a pantomime which evoked more laughter.'

But for Jimmy Tate and Clarice Mayne, the laughter ended early in 1922. Jimmy caught a cold, which turned to pneumonia, and he died at the age of 46. At Golders Green cemetery, his marble headstone takes the form of a book of music open at a page inscribed with the melody of 'A Broken Doll'.

EDGAR BATEMAN (Edgar Davies)
Born Marylebone, London, 15 February 1860, the illegitimate son of Ann Davies, who later married William Bateman
Married Margaret Griffiths, Middlesex, 25 December 1887
Two children: William (b. 1891) and Cicely (b. 1898)
Died Finchley, north London, 17 August 1946

The pressures of music hall turned many to drink. Most of them died young. Edgar Bateman, who went from hall to hall each evening in pursuit of his work as a talent scout for Francis, Day and Hunter, was known as a toper, but he defied the trend by living to the age of 86.

Bateman began his working life as a printer, but he was stage-struck from an early age. When he was 16, he waited at the stage door of the Theatre Royal, Drury Lane, to catch a glimpse of the Vokes family, the mainstay of pantomimes there during the 1870s.

Bateman enjoyed his greatest successes with two songs set to music by George le Brunn and sung by Gus Elen. In 1894, Bateman was sitting at home in Clerkenwell, idly picking out distant landmarks. In one direction, he could see Crystal Palace and in another a newly built terrace of houses in Bethnal Green. Bateman sensed the germ of an idea that became 'If it Wasn't for the Houses in Between'. Elen sang it dressed as a Covent Garden porter:

> Oh! it really is a werry pretty garden
> And Chingford to the eastward could be seen
> Wiv a ladder and some glasses
> You could see to 'Ackney marshes
> If it wasn't for the 'ouses in between.

A year later, Bateman and le Brunn produced another hit for Elen, 'It's a great big shame', 'as quaint and interesting as any Mr Elen has given us', according to *The Era*. Bateman and Elen both believed there was life away from the theatre. Elen enjoyed breeding poultry and game. Bateman fished off Southend Pier and, on occasions, inspiration for a song came to him there.

He was by now an established songwriter, but, ever cautious, he continued working as a printer. In 1897, however, he was made an offer he found too attractive to refuse. David Day asked Bateman to work for him. He was to tour the halls and bars each evening, meeting singers and writers and reporting any new talent to Day the next morning. Calling himself the Shield of David, he was said to be able to drink beer by the gallon and still remain sober. Each morning, he made his report to Day with a remarkably clear head.

In 1900, there was a reminder that music hall still had its critics when this letter appeared in a national paper: 'Most [music-hall songs] glorify drink, licentiousness, greed, theft, in fact, vice in its worst aspects. The "patriotic" songs are a compact of bombast and bloodthirstiness.'[1] Bateman was quick to respond:

If the writer's statements are correct, our managers foolishly jeopardise their licences and pander to the vilest tastes; our firms of publishers are aiders and abettors; our music hall reporters are unfit for their posts in not calling attention to the badness of the songs; and the public is degraded by tacitly accepting what is offered . . . As I have paid 400 visits [to music halls] this year, I may be allowed to know something of a matter in which the writer appears to be totally in the dark.[2]

GEORGE ARTHURS (George Alfred Jones)
Born Chorlton, Manchester, 13 April 1875
Married Lyra Ione Rewse White, 19 August 1903 (d. 1944)
One son, two daughters
Died Harrow, Greater London, 14 March 1944

By day, George Arthurs worked in an accountant's office. By night, he was in the box office of the Metropolitan, where he got to know most performers appearing there. The jokes and songs he began writing for them marked the first step in his life's work.

His songs were first published in the early years of the twentieth century, but he had to wait

In spite of appearances, George Arthurs was a great comic songwriter. *(Richard Anthony Baker)*

until 1910 before he enjoyed great success. In that year, he and Bert Lee wrote 'Joshu-ah', which suited Clarice Mayne ideally:

> Joshu-ah, Joshu-ah,
>   Why don't you call and see Mama?
>   She'll be pleased to know
>   You are my best beau.
> Joshu-ah, Joshu-ah,
>   Nicer than lemon squash you are
>   Yes, by Gosh you are,
>   Joshu-osh-u-ah.

'I want to sing in opera', which Arthurs wrote with Worton David, allowed Wilkie Bard to poke fun at the operatic world. Over the years, it proved to be Bard's most successful song:

> I want to sing in opera.
> I've got that kind of voice.
> I'd always sing in opera
> If I could have my choice.
> Signor Caruso
> Told me I ought to do so.
> That's why I want to sing in opera
> Sing in op-pop-pop-popera. Hoorah!

In 1915, Arthurs and Leigh wrote 'A Little of what you Fancy', a summary of Marie Lloyd's music-hall philosophy. It was Arthurs's last big music-hall success.

In 1939, he was involved in a misunderstanding that could easily have come from the plot of a musical comedy. He met the comedian Albert Burdon in a pub in the West End of London to discuss a new show. Someone who overheard them talking about 'the plot' phoned the police and, within minutes, they were being questioned on suspicion of being IRA terrorists.

Harry Castling was one of the many songwriters who could not write a note of music. Even so, the songs he produced over twenty-five years provided music hall with several outstandingly successful compositions, including 'Just like the ivy', 'Let's all go down the Strand' and 'Don't have any more, Mrs Moore'.

Harry Castling was the son of a street musician. He began writing songs in the 1890s, enjoying his first hit with 'What-Ho! She Bumps' (1899), which he wrote with A.J. Mills. Castling and Mills could move easily between comic and sentimental songs. A love song they wrote for Marie Kendall proved to be the most successful song of her career, 'Just like

HARRY CASTLING (Henry Castling)
Born Newington, London, 19 April 1865
Married 1897
    Four daughters
Died Camberwell, south London,
    26 December 1933

the ivy' (1902). Seven years later, Castling and C.W. Murphy set themselves the task of writing a chorus song without the word 'girl' in the title. They were not misogynists, they explained; they were just certain that people were becoming tired of such titles as 'Put me amongst the Girls' and 'When there isn't a Girl About'.

One evening, the two men were leaving the Lyceum Theatre near the junction of Aldwych and the Strand. Murphy was about to cross the road and head for Waterloo Bridge when Castling called him back, suggesting 'Let's go down the Strand'. He maintained later that, as soon as he had said it, he realised it would make a good song title, but neither of them could expand the idea into a full lyric until they added the word 'all'. 'Then', said Castling, 'both the words and the music came to us as though we had been singing them all our lives':

> Let's all go down the Strand
> Oh, what a happy land.
> That's the place for fun and noise
> All among the girls and boys
> Let's all go down the Strand

The song was bought by Charles Whittle. Castling's last major success was another song that has stood the test of time, 'Don't have any more, Mrs Moore' (1926), sung by the plump and bouncy Lily Morris:

> Don't have any more, Mrs Moore
> Mrs Moore, please don't have any more.
> The more you have the more you want they say
> And enough is as good as a feast any day
> If you have any more, Mrs Moore,
> You'll have to rent the house next door.
> They're alright when they're here,
> But take my advice, old dear.
> Don't have any more, Mrs Moore.

Once, Castling teamed up with Percy Edgar to write a sentimental song for Lily Morris. Outside her dressing-room, the two men discussed how much they should charge. Castling thought it was worth £5; the cautious Edgar, two guineas (£2.10). They went in and Castling sang the song to Lily in his cracked voice. Halfway through, Edgar nudged him and whispered, 'Ask for five. She's crying.'

T.W. Connor began writing songs in the early 1890s. His most successful was George Beauchamp's 'She was One of the Early Birds' (1895):

> She was a dear little dickey bird.
> 'Chip, chip, chip', she went.
> Sweetly she sang to me
> Till all my money was spent.
> Then she went off song.
> We parted on fighting terms.
> She was one of the early birds
> And I was one of the worms.

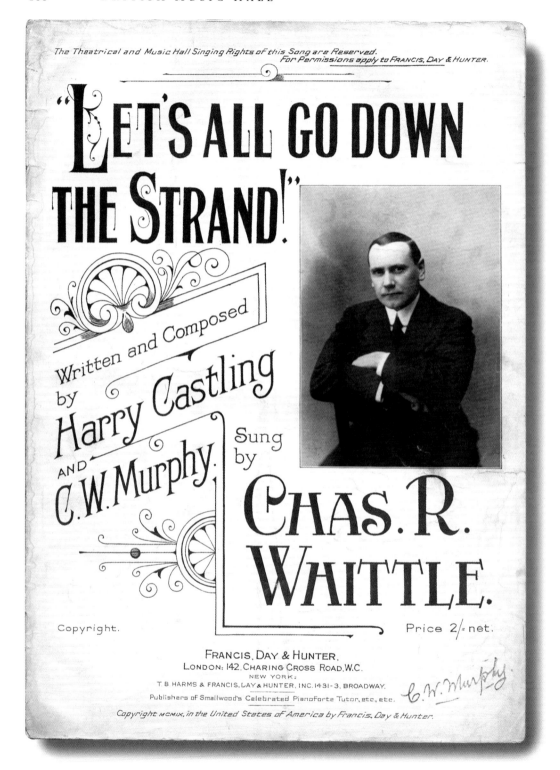

An immortal hit, written by Harry Castling and C.W. Murphy. *(Richard Anthony Baker)*

Connor also worked with the variety comedian Billy Bennett on many of his monologues.

Worton David was described by the publisher Lawrence Wright as the best lyric writer in Britain. His first job was in a solicitor's office, but he spent all his spare time writing stories, some of which were accepted by the *Leeds Mercury*. David was an adept cartoonist, too. So, when he joined the staff of the Mercury, he was given the job of visiting the Leeds Empire every Monday night to draw cartoons of entertainers appearing there. He came to know some of them well and persuaded them to buy one or two of his songs. Saving the money he earned from songwriting, he eventually travelled to London with his wife and baby son, Hubert. They took £50 with them. The idea was that, if they spent it without David earning anything from writing, they would return to Leeds. They never returned.

WORTON DAVID (Ernest Worton David) (his mother's
    maiden name was Worton)
Born Rawmarsh, near Rotherham, 17 October 1872
Married Gwen Rees 1928
    Son, Hubert Worton (1904–99; Hubert David, a
    leading light in the Performing Right Society, was
    also a songwriter; he produced his first million-seller,
    'Felix Kept on Walking', when he was only 17)
Died Worthing, West Sussex, 15 November 1940
Left £35,626

David's first success was a song he wrote with Norman Reeve, 'Bobbing Up and Down Like this' (1899), not to be confused with the now better-known American song, 'Bobbin' Up and Down' (1913). In 1909 and 1910, he teamed up with George Arthurs to write two songs for Wilkie Bard, 'I Can Say "Truly Rural"', the story of a man trying to pretend he is sober, and 'I want to sing in opera'.

David and Arthurs also wrote for Marie Lloyd. In 1912, they provided her with 'Piccadilly Trot', the first song Marie sang with the syncopation of the new craze, ragtime. With C.W. Murphy, David also wrote one of Florrie Forde's greatest choruses, 'Hold your hand out, naughty boy!' (1913):

> Hold your hand out, naughty boy.
> Hold your hand out, naughty boy.
> Last night, in the pale moonlight,
> I saw you, I saw you,
> With a nice girl in the park.
> You were strolling full of joy
> And you told me you'd never kissed a girl before.
> Hold your hand out, naughty boy!

In 1914, David joined up with Lawrence Wright to produce a string of hits, including 'Are we Downhearted? – No!' and, in 1919, '[That Old-Fashioned] Mother of Mine', but the partnership ended when David objected to the number of American songs Wright was starting to import. For £30,000, Wright bought him out of all the songs they had written together. With the money, David started his own publishing firm.

At the age of 22, Bennett Scott placed an advertisement in a music-hall paper claiming that he knew just what audiences wanted: 'the principal requirements today are good songs and catchy melodies. These I am prepared to supply at a guinea a time.' For more than twenty years, Scott had a hand in dozens of catchy melodies. Largely by forming his own publishing company, the guineas piled up.

As a young man, Scott worked in a warehouse in the City of London, but, within a few years of turning to songwriting for a living, he had his first major success, 'I've Made up my Mind to Sail Away' (1902), sung by Tom Costello. His best songs were written in collaboration with A.J. Mills; in 1906, they supplied Happy Fanny Fields with her most successful song, 'By the Side of the Zuyder Zee'.

In the autumn of 1906, Scott and Mills established the Star Music Company, which published one new song every week. Three years later, they persuaded Hetty King to listen to a song they had written with Fred Godfrey, 'Ship Ahoy'. She liked it and sang it first either at the Hackney Empire or the Liverpool

BENNETT SCOTT (Barnett Scott)
Born London, 12 October 1871
Married Daisy Kathleen —— (d. 1962)
Died north London, 1 June 1930
Left £4,178

Empire. Hetty was not sure. Within a week, it was being sung, hummed and whistled all round Hackney (or Liverpool), but, strange to relate, it was not an immediate success everywhere:

> All the nice girls love a sailor.
> All the nice girls love a tar
> For there's something about a sailor.
> Well, you know what sailors are.
> Bright and breezy, free and easy,
> He's the ladies' pride and joy.
> Falls in love with Kate and Jane,
> Then he's off to sea again
> Ship Ahoy! Ship Ahoy!

In London that autumn, Hetty gave greater prominence to a Herman Darewski song, 'In the Park, Park, Park'. While detailing the likely pantomime winners in 1909, Scott placed Hetty's 'bright and breezy sailor song' well down his list. Even so, *The Era* noted: 'There is no getting away from the lilt of the chorus.' Within a year, it was a surefire hit and it remained in Hetty's repertoire for the rest of her life.

In 1910, Scott and Mills wrote an equally strong song for Charles Whittle, 'Fall in and follow me': *'Fall in and Follow Me . . . is destined to take the place of Ship Ahoy* as the bright and lively number of the year. After the first choruses, the audiences made the song their own and, even after Mr Whittle had retired, certain merry folk broke into the refrain at intervals during the evening.'[3]

> Fall in and follow me.
> Fall in and follow me.
> Come along and never mind the weather.
> Altogether, stand on me boys.
> I know the way to go. I promise you a spree.
> You do as I do and you'll do right
> Fall in and follow me.

At Christmas, 1910, every pantomime in Britain was featuring the song.

Twice within its first four years, the company had to move to larger premises. Scott spent the summer travelling round seaside resorts to assess the public taste in songs. Many singers insisted on including a Scott–Mills song in their act, believing it would bring them good luck.

By the First World War, Scott was more involved in publishing other writers' songs than in composing his own. There was no shortage of work from which to choose. In 1916, he told an interviewer that his reputation would be ruined if he published 99 per cent of the material brought to him. Scott also knew that, if he failed to keep abreast of changing public taste, demand for his work would diminish. 'Again and again,' he said, 'I have to explain that what went in 1910 won't go in 1916.' Scott noted that, as the First World War dragged on, even the taste in war songs changed. He noted:

> A new species is now demanded. The flag-waving ballad so popular two years ago is rapidly on the wane; so is last year's Bravo, Tommy! type. The great change that is taking place in public taste is that it is identifying itself with the taste of the Army and Navy. The public wants the things the soldiers and sailors want; they prefer real fun and real sentiment to wordy boasts and disconcerting praise.[4]

Mills, Scott and Fred Godfrey encapsulated that mood with 'Take me Back to Dear Old Blighty' (1916), sung by Florrie Forde. Scott wrote: 'That song comes straight from the trenches. Two years ago, it could not have existed.'

A few months before the outbreak of the war, Scott, Worton David and Henry Pether were among the founders of the Performing Right Society, the organisation that collects and distributes copyright payments to composers, writers and publishers. It grew from the Copyright Act of 1906, which halted the piracy of sheet-music publishing. After a time, some songwriters left the PRS, believing their work would not be performed if copyright payments had to be made, but they realised their mistake and eventually rejoined. In 1917, the Society made its first distribution of royalties among members, totalling £11,000 over its first three years. It formed an alliance with the Mechanical Copyright Protection Society in 1998 and, in 2003, it distributed £242 million.

One of the most popular songs of the First World War was the work of Felix Powell and his brother, George, who adopted the curious pseudonym George Asaf. Entering a competition for a rousing wartime song, they pulled one from a drawer they had written some time before. 'Pack up your troubles in your old kitbag' (1915) was sung by Florrie Forde and by thousands of young men on their way to fight:

> Pack up your troubles in your old kitbag and smile, smile, smile.
> While you've a lucifer to light your fag, smile, boys, that's the style.
> What's the use of worrying?
> It never was worthwhile.
> So, pack up your troubles in your old kitbag and smile, smile, smile.

During the Second World War, Felix Powell served as a staff sergeant with the Home Guard at Peacehaven in Sussex, but, complaining that the war was preventing him from carrying on his work as an estate agent, he took a service rifle and shot himself dead. George Asaf, a baker and confectioner, died nine years later.

FELIX POWELL (Felix Lloyd Powell)
Born *c.* 1879
Died Peacehaven, east Sussex,
    10 February 1942
Left £148

GEORGE ASAF (George Henry Powell)
Born 1875 (?)
Married Rachel ——
Died Coventry, 11 May 1951
Left £1,001

JACK JUDGE (John Thomas Judge)
Born 1873 (?)
    Son, Tommy (b. 1902) (?)
Died West Bromwich, West Midlands,
    28 July 1938

Another of the most successful songs of the First World War was 'It's a long, long way to Tipperary', but whether Jack Judge wrote it on his own or with his one-time friend Harry Williams has been a matter of dispute ever since.

Henry (Harry) Williams, an invalid from childhood, started composing at an early age. His last song was 'Eileen', which was published in 1923. He died on 21 February 1924, apparently aged 50.

Judge ran a fish stall at Oldbury market in Hereford and Worcester. In his spare time, he was a semi-professional music-hall performer. That much is certain. Much of what follows is contested.

At the end of January 1912, Judge was appearing at the Grand at Stalybridge in Greater Manchester, a theatre which stayed open until 1954. (It was demolished ten years later.) Just after midnight one night, while leaving a club, he accepted a bet that he could compose and sing a new song before the day was over. On his way back to his lodgings, he heard someone say 'It's a long way to . . .' somewhere or other. The following morning, he chose Tipperary, sat down and (he said) wrote the whole song.

> It's a long way to Tipperary.
> It's a long way to go.
> It's a long way to Tipperary
> To the sweetest girl I know.
> Goodbye, Piccadilly.
> Farewell, Leicester Square.
> It's a long, long way to Tipperary,
> But my heart's right there!

The conductor of the orchestra at the Grand Theatre wrote out band parts for the song and Judge sang it that night. By the end of the week, it had become such a success that it formed the centrepiece of a grand finale, which the whole company sang. Bert Feldman's firm bought the publishing rights from Judge and Williams for 5 shillings (25p). It was published in October 1912 and, by the outbreak of the First World War, it had become such a hit that Feldman agreed to pay the two men £5 a week for the rest of their lives. By the end of 1914, 10,000 copies of the sheet music were being sold every day. The song was translated into seventeen languages and, by the end of the war, it had sold eight million copies.

From the outset, Bert Feldman believed the song was a winner. He persuaded Florrie Forde to sing it in 1913 during her annual summer season on the Isle of Man, but Florrie found it was unpopular and dropped it from her act. Judge recorded the song in 1915, but Florrie waited until 1929 and then merely included it in a medley.

Published copies of the song name its writers as Judge *and* Williams, but, after Williams's death, Judge claimed that he alone was responsible for the song. One account said Judge had promised Williams that, if he ever published a song, he would say they both wrote it and would share the royalties. Another account said Judge was repaying a loan by agreeing to publish the song jointly, but Williams's family has always insisted that the song really was a joint collaboration. A niece, calling Judge 'the biggest liar that ever was', said that Williams had written the song in 1910 and that Judge, who could not write music, helped out with some of the words: 'It was catchy and rhythmic; its qualities soon made it into a marching song of the troops and the combination of nonchalance and sentiment in the words reflected the emotions of the moment . . . The refrain . . . can recall more immediately than anything else the spirit and excitement of the early days of the war.'[5]

CHAPTER 18

HERE'S TO THE LADIES WHO WERE . . .

One of the most endearing female entertainers in British music hall was Bessie Bellwood. Her studies of working-class characters were loved by audiences and, if she was occasionally vulgar, they loved her even more.

BESSIE BELLWOOD (Kate Mahoney)
Born Monkstown, Cork, 1856 (?)
Baptised Southwark Cathedral, south
  London, 4 June 1856
Married her agent, John (known as
  Jack) Nicholson, Leeds,
  24 September 1884
Died London, 24 September 1896

Bessie's upbringing was untypical of a popular London entertainer. Born in the Irish Republic, the daughter of a builder, she was educated at a convent. She remained a strict Catholic, always wearing a small gold cross round her neck. Her great-uncle was Francis Mahoney (1804–66), who abandoned the priesthood to become a humorist, writing under the name Father Prout.

It is unclear how and why Bessie moved to Britain, but, while still in her teens, she became a protégée of the songwriter J.W. Cherry. At first, he appeared unable to choose a stage name for her: in May 1876, she was Elsie Bellwood; in August, Amy; but, by Christmas 1876, when she had already played some of the smaller London halls, she was Bessie Bellwood, singing ballads at first, but soon switching to comedy, which she found more popular. It was at Lusby's that she first attracted attention, singing the wondrously titled 'E's Got a Wooden Leg and a Tall White 'at'. Her fame dated from that point, her greatest success coming in 1884 with her impersonation of a factory girl who wore feathers and garish skirts: the song was 'What Cheer 'Ria!' written by Will Herbert, a match seller on the streets of Liverpool.

One reviewer wrote of her 'rollicking style . . . effectively exercised in her sketches of lowly character'. Another said, 'Her fun is broad, but it is supremely funny.' The songwriter Richard Morton provided one of the best descriptions of her rapport with an audience:

Onto the stage she would bounce to a roar of welcome. 'All right' – to an admirer in a private box – 'don't open your mouth so wide. You'll cut your throat with your collar.' The result was a louder guffaw than before. 'That's wider. Now I can see what you had for your dinner.' Sometimes she was smart; sometimes just a little vulgar. But always, she enjoyed a licence that would be permitted to no performer today.[1]

Many stories were told of her knack for quick repartee both on and off stage. Jerome K. Jerome, the author of *Three Men in a Boat*, witnessed a slanging match between Bessie and a heckler at the Star, Bermondsey. For nearly six minutes, Bessie wiped the floor with him:

Bessie Bellwood, the Comedy Queen.
(Tony Barker)

At the end, she gathered herself for one supreme effort and hurled at him an insult so bitter with scorn, so sharp with insight into his career and character, so heavy with prophetic curse, that strong men drew and held their breath while it passed over them and women hid their faces and shivered. Then, she folded her arms and stood silent and the house, from floor to ceiling, rose and cheered her until there was no more breath left in its lungs.[2]

The *Daily Telegraph* commented pompously: 'Having regard to her early life and surroundings, which had familiarised her all too well with expressions not quite of the "drawing room order", it is perhaps hardly to be wondered that, in the excitement of "gagging the gods", phrases to which she would have hesitated to give utterance in her calmer moments sometimes fell spontaneously from her lips.'[3]

At a party, Bessie overheard a fellow music-hall entertainer giving a false account of her family tree. She interrupted: 'Well, your grandfather may have been a bloomin' emperor, but your mother sold coke to the man who ran away with my aunt.' Bessie enjoyed mixing with the gentry, although she rarely tempered her behaviour. In the presence of the Duke of Manchester, she bit the ear of a boxing manager she accused of slander. She had affairs with titled men. Once, when she switched from a duke to a marquis, a friend remarked: 'A marquis, eh? You do find 'em, Bess.' 'Finding 'em is easy,' came the reply. 'Keeping 'em is the trouble.'

Arthur Roberts described Bessie as a Jekyll and Hyde character: within hours of discussing some Catholic charity with Cardinal Henry Manning, she would be arrested for knocking down a cabman she accused of insulting her latest beau. In fact, Bessie had a number of brushes with the law. When the controversy about the alleged salaciousness of music-hall songs was at its height in 1889, a London magistrate claimed she had been sacked from three halls because her act was indecent. Bessie threatened to sue him, but he eventually conceded that he had been misinformed. Later that year, she was accused of assault and was ordered to keep the peace. Things turned rather more serious in 1890, when she was sentenced to twenty days' imprisonment for failing to settle a debt.

At this point, Bessie's career started to fail. Marie Lloyd, another artiste skilled in quick-fire cockney badinage, had arrived, and audiences became fonder of the younger woman. Even so, Bessie's early death not only shocked her many followers; it provoked encomia from the unlikeliest quarters. The *Daily Telegraph* could be forgiving: 'Kind, tender-hearted, hospitable, generous . . . and, at the same time, impulsive, heedless, headstrong and impatient of counsel and advice, even when knowing they were tendered for her own good.'[4]

There can have been few entertainers who achieved stardom so rapidly as Cissie Loftus, described by the American showbiz paper *Variety* as 'one of the most versatile women on the stage'. Within a month of her first appearance as a mimic in London, she was the most talked about woman in Britain. From then on, she switched between the variety stage and the legitimate theatre, at one point playing opposite Sir Henry Irving, and commuted between Britain and America, where she was equally adored. Although in later life she developed a drink problem and became dependent on drugs, she worked virtually to the end.

CISSIE LOFTUS (Marie Cecilia Loftus Brown)
Born Glasgow, 22 October 1876
Married (1) Justin Huntly M'Carthy, Edinburgh,
    29 August 1894 (divorced 1899)
(2) Dr Alonzo Higbee Waterman, Kensington,
    west London, 9 June 1909 (divorced)
    Son
Died New York, 12 July 1943

Cissie Loftus was practically born in a trunk. Her mother was the singer Marie Loftus, her father, Ben Brown, of the blackfaced act, Brown, Newland and le Clerq. After being educated at the Convent School of the Holy Child in Blackpool, she became her mother's dresser, a job that allowed her to stand in the wings, studying stage technique. She made her theatrical debut at the Alhambra in Belfast in October 1892. Her London debut came the following July when she was still only 16. She was reviewed at the Oxford:

The debutante scored an immediate success in imitations of such leading professional entertainers as Eugene Stratton . . . and Marie Lloyd and, during the week, has been the heroine of popular demonstrations of approval . . . The young lady has not really left the schoolroom, but whether she will return to her studies at a convent school in Lancashire has not yet been decided.[5]

She probably did not return as, within weeks, she was appearing at the Tivoli and the Gaiety, as well as the Oxford. In fact, she became so popular so quickly that George Edwardes of the Gaiety sought a court injunction to try to restrict her performances to his theatre alone. He believed that an agreement he had reached with Cissie and her mother, under which Cissie was to be paid £15 a week, was

Cissie Loftus, an impressionist who was virtually an overnight success. *(British Music Hall Society)*

exclusive. The judge, referring to the poor grammar of the agreement, refused to grant the injunction.

Many men fell under her spell, including Max Beerbohm, who was infatuated with her. Toulouse-Lautrec made a lithograph of her. There was then, understandably, an outcry, when, in 1894, Cissie broke off an engagement at the Palace to elope with the novelist and playwright Justin Huntly M'Carthy, who was sixteen years her senior. A civil marriage was contracted in Scotland and later solemnised according to the Roman Catholic ritual in London. M'Carthy announced that Cissie was tired of the music hall and, when they arrived in New York, he disclosed that she had been engaged by Augustin Daly of Daly's Theatre to appear as an actress.

But Daly's plays failed to materialise: in 1895, Cissie made her American debut at Koster and Bial's music hall in New York. Again, she was a sensation, continually adding to the repertoire of personalities she impersonated. Eventually, the list included such diverse entertainers as Fanny Brice, Mrs Patrick Campbell, Caruso, Noel Coward, Harry Lauder, Beatrice Lillie and Eugene Stratton.

Of her appearances on the legitimate stage the most startling was that with Irving in 1902: an eleven-week season as Margaret in W.G. Wills's adaptation of *Faust*. Irving decided that Ellen Terry, who had played the part many times, was now old, but his choice of Cissie surprised many, as he abhorred music hall. She was paid £100 (by today's standards £6,000) a week, about half the money she could have earned on the halls. She attracted mixed reviews, but was honoured by being impersonated herself by Marie Lloyd and Harry Tate. Cissie's career enjoyed a further landmark in 1905 when she appeared as only the second Peter Pan. J.M. Barrie was sufficiently impressed to agree to be the godfather of her son.

Cissie's problems began in about 1914. Her growing taste for alcohol and drugs started to make her unstable and unreliable. In 1922, a month after topping the bill at the Coliseum, she was charged with possessing atropine and morphine. A magistrate accepted that the drugs were for her sole use and placed her on probation for a year.

The following year, she left Britain for the last time to play the Palace in New York. Her turn was supposed to last 20 minutes, but the audience would not let her go. She was on stage for a full hour. *Variety* noted that she could entertain both the masses and the classes. Cissie returned to Britain in 1938; her final stage appearance was in a 1942 tour of *Arsenic and Old Lace*.

The most successful coster comedienne on the halls was Kate Carney, a small, dumpy, red-haired woman. She once said: 'What Chevalier and Elen have done for the male I have endeavoured to do for the female. I have shown the English public types of the flower girls, the coster girls, the factory workers and the other toilers from the slums, not as she might be supposed to be, but as she is. I know the London working girl. I ought to, for I was one.'[6]

Kate Carney was the daughter of half of a popular double act, the Brothers Raynard. Her mother, Hannah Baker, was also on the halls, although not as successfully. It was as part of her mother's act that Kate first appeared on stage in 1880. At first, her mother tried to dissuade her from becoming a music-hall singer. In fact, she paid £5 to get Kate apprenticed to the silk hat trade, but Kate was sacked after being caught doing a sword dance with a couple of broomsticks. The foreman who fired her suggested she took up the stage, adding: 'anybody'd give you £2 a week'.

KATE CARNEY (Catharine Mary Pattinson)
Born south London, 15 August 1869
Married George Shea (professionally known as George
    Barclay), London, 6 October 1886 (b. 7 June 1868;
    d. 30 January 1944; left £10,927)
    Five children: eldest son, George, married Gladys
        Mavius, 27 June 1908
Died Streatham, south London, 1 January 1950
Left £2,290

While still in her early teens, Kate was taken to the South London music hall, where she saw such stars as Jenny Hill and Nelly Farrell, whose songs she started to learn. Towards the end of 1885, she appeared under the name Kate Paterson at the Castle music hall in south-east London. In the wings of the Royal Victoria, she met a young man who sold bags of sawdust to publicans, but who had aspirations to become a comedian and step dancer. This was George Shea, who had assumed the stage name Barclay. His real surname, O'Shea, had been shortened so that it did not appear to sound Irish. At the age of 17, Kate married him.

Kate then left the stage for a time, reappearing as Kate Carney towards the end of 1889. Earlier that year, Nelly Farrell had died of typhoid. Kate had asked if she might sing her songs and the request was granted. At the end of 1889, she began appearing at the Montpelier music hall in Newington, billed as Ireland's Gem, but she dated her real music-hall debut as January 1890 when she appeared at the Royal Albert in Canning Town at first as an extra turn and then staying for some weeks at a salary of £1 5s (£1.25) a week. She was immediately successful.

Her husband was also doing well. He teamed up with another comic, Walter Bentley, the pair calling themselves Barclay and Perkins, the Brewers of Fun (warranted XXX). Barclay and Perkins were also the names of well-known London brewers.

Little by little, Kate began dropping Irish songs from her act, replacing them with cockney numbers. In 1893, Harry Bedford wrote for her 'Sarah' or 'A Donkey Cart Built for Two', but her first big success came in 1895 – 'Three Pots a Shilling', also written by Bedford:

When the summer comes again
And the pretty flowers are growing.
The sunshine after rain.
The summer breezes blowing.
Then to roam around the country with a
    girl who's ever willing.
I can buy and she can cry 'Three pots a
    shilling.'

Kate Carney, the Coster Queen. *(Tony Barker)*

By now, Kate was in such demand that her husband abandoned his act to start work as an agent. In time, he was to manage, among others, Ted Ray and the Houston Sisters, but Kate was his main interest. She used to say she was the only music-hall singer who slept with her agent and could still hold up her head in public.[7]

Two more hits were to follow, both of them sung for the first time in 1901: 'Our Threepenny 'Op', written by Harry Castling, and 'Liza Johnson', written by Edgar Bateman and George le Brunn. Kate's success brought her great wealth: besides the eleven-bedroom house at the top of Brixton Hill, there were racehorses and expensive cars. After the First World War, she worked only when she wanted to. Come the 1930s, her stage act assumed a somewhat opulent air, with a butler accompanying her on the piano and a housemaid joining in the choruses.

Kate appeared in three Royal Variety Shows: in 1912, 1935 (in which she sang 'Are we to Part like this, Bill?' requested by the Duchess of York, later the Queen Mother) and 1938. During the Second World War, air-raid warnings often interrupted Kate's shows. She always ignored them, often extending her performance until four o'clock in the morning, talking to members of the audience and inviting them up on stage. Given her humble beginnings, she had an odd attitude towards her followers. 'Sod the people in the stalls,' she used to say. 'What they're paying only keeps the theatre open. Play to the people in the circle. They're paying your salary.'

A bomb dropped near Kate's house during the war. Barclay put up a notice saying that Hitler had tried to kill him, but had failed. Barclay did not see the end of the war. He died in 1944. Kate carried on performing until April 1949 when she was taken ill after a BBC broadcast.

Marie Kendall, who popularised 'Just like the ivy' (1902) and sang it more than 5,000 times, seemed destined for a career as a singer from her twelfth birthday. To celebrate the day, her mother took her to the Three Cups at Bow in east London (later the Bow Palace). Marie so much enjoyed the chorus of a song called 'Don't Look Down on the Irish', sung by the Sisters Brigg, and sang it so loudly that everyone else stopped, leaving her to sing it on her own. Afterwards, the Sisters Brigg told Marie's mother that she ought to make singing her career. Marie's mother was not keen on the idea, but did agree to let her have singing lessons at J.W. Cherry's so-called Music Hall Academy.

Marie made her debut at the Three Cups in a benefit concert for a local tradesman. As a male impersonator, she sang three songs written for her by Fred Bullen, the leader of the orchestra at the Sebright in Hackney.

MARIE KENDALL (Mary Ann Florence Holyome)
Born Bethnal Green, east London, 27 July 1873
Married John Joseph McCarthy (professionally known as
    Steve McCarthy), east London, 5 February 1895 (d.
    3 April 1944)
    Two sons, Justin (known as Terry) (b. south Hackney,
    20 January 1901) and Shaun, and two daughters,
    Moya and Pat. Justin married
    (1) Gladys Drewery, 1923; she bore him Terry
    (b. 1923); Patricia Kim Kendall (b. 1925; married in
    USA Ludlow Stevens January 1952); and Justine
    Kay Kendall (professionally known as Kay Kendall,
    the film star, 1927–59) (Justin and Pat formed a
    double act, which appeared in Noël Coward's revue
    On with the Dance); Justin married (2) Dora
    Spencer and formed a successful comic dance act
    with her
Died Clapham, London, 5 May 1964

Thirty years after becoming a star, Marie Kendall was still drawing crowds. *(Richard Anthony Baker)*

Under the name Marie Chester, she then appeared at the Star, Bermondsey, and the Royal Albert in 1888 and in the pantomime, *Whittington and his Cat*, at the Pavilion, Mile End, in 1888/9.

After a spell in mainland Europe, Marie returned to Britain to join a pantomime company travelling through Wales. In 1893, it was suggested that she gave up male impersonation. She was appearing at the Bedford, where Charles Deane was enjoying great success with a song called 'One of the Boys'. Marie's mother thought that an 'answer' song would suit her and, when she met Deane at Poverty Corner one morning, he agreed to write the song, 'I'm One of the Girls', for half a guinea (52.5p). It provided Marie with the breakthrough she had been seeking. Soon, she was on George Foster's books and her salary rose from £1 10*s* (£1.50) a week to £27 10*s* (£27.50). After 'I'm One of the Girls', Marie had a string of successful songs, the most memorable being 'Just like the ivy'.

> Just like the ivy on that garden wall
> Clinging so tightly, whate'er may befall.
> As you grow older, I'll be constant and true
> And just like the ivy I'll cling to you.

One night in 1902, Marie's husband, Steve McCarthy, was walking along the Embankment in London with Harry Castling when he mentioned that Marie was looking for a new song. Castling replied that he and A.J. Mills had recently sold to David Day of Francis Day and Hunter 'Just like the ivy', but he felt it was unsuitable for Marie. McCarthy persuaded Castling to hum it and quite liked it. When he got home, he woke Marie to tell her about it. She paid little attention at the time, but, the next morning, she made a few changes to it and immediately went to see Day, who gave her permission to sing it. When she gave it its first public airing at the Stratford Empire, it was an immediate success and Marie sang it for the rest of her career. At the 1932 Royal Variety Show, it was the centrepiece of the finale, with Marie accompanied by Jack Hylton's 120-piece orchestra.

In 1934, Marie took part in the movie *Say it with Flowers*, in which she sang another of Castling's songs, 'Did your First Wife Ever Do That?' Marie always credited Castling with having 'a great brain'. In 1951, she sang 'I'm One of the Girls' in Michael Miles's television show *Life Begins at 60*, staged at the Bedford, where she had first sung it nearly sixty years earlier. When Collins' music hall was demolished a few months before she died, she appeared in a TV programme reminiscing about the theatre and the entertainers who had appeared there. *The Times* reported: 'Her death made those days seem suddenly more distant.'

Ada Reeve spent an amazing seventy-five years dodging between music hall, musical comedy, straight plays, movies, radio and television. Coming from a theatrical family, she played many child parts on stage before making her music-hall debut, billed as the Juvenile Wonder and appearing with her father in a sketch.

Ada's breakthrough came in 1892 with a Richard Morton–F.W. Venton song, 'What Do I Care?' in which she performed cartwheels to the audience's refrain of 'Over, Ada!' After singing the song for the first time at the Metropolitan, she was able to demand an increase in her salary from £5 a week to £30 almost immediately.

ADA REEVE (Adelaide Mary Isaacs)
Born 3 March 1874
Married (1) Gilbert Hazlewood (professionally known
 as Bert Gilbert), Nottingham, 5 May 1894
 (divorced) (Hazlewood then married
 F. Humphreys (professionally known as Dolly
 Daintree), Cardiff, 1 December 1900)
 Two daughters, Bessie, and Goodie (b. 1897)
 (2) Albert Wilfred Cotton, Maidenhead, Berkshire,
 14 July 1902
Died Kensington, London, 26 September 1966
Left £549

She enjoyed her first success in musical comedy in the George Edwardes show, *The Shop Girl*, which ran at the Gaiety Theatre from November 1894 until May 1896. She appeared in many other musical comedies, including Leslie Stuart's *Florodora* (1899–1901), in which she created the role of Lady Holyrood. During the First World War, she was an enthusiastic entertainer of the troops, introducing the song 'There's a Long Long Trail A-winding'.

Ada Reeve made her American debut at Koster and Bial's music hall in New York in 1893. After that, she frequently topped the bill at the Palace in New York, the flagship of the B.F. Keith vaudeville circuit, making her last appearance there in 1928 when she ended her act with a character study of a cockney mother talking to her baby.

She toured South Africa three times (1906, 1911 and 1913) and was in Australia in 1897, 1914, from 1922 to 1924 and from 1929 to 1935. In 1897, she toured with her first husband, Bert Gilbert, a comic, playwright and song-writer, whose infidelities with several young women were gleefully reported by the Australian press. During the 1920s, Ada herself had an affair with Tom Holt, the father of the future Prime Minister Harold Holt. The senior Holt ran a film studio, for which Ada recorded a great comic song, 'I Never Forget I'm a Lady'.

When she returned to Britain in 1935, many thought she would quietly retire. Instead, she made her first appearance in cabaret and embarked on the final stage of her career, playing eccentric old women in such plays as *The Shop at Sly Corner*.

In private, Ada Reeve could be difficult. She had a razor-sharp tongue and treated her friends abysmally, using them more like servants and

Ada Reeve, the World's Most Popular Comedienne.
(Richard Anthony Baker)

losing several of them. She loathed her daughter Goodie, calling her the biggest bitch of all time and blaming her for the break-up of her second marriage to her manager, Wilfred Cotton. One of her friends, Gwen Adeler, wrote: 'It may seem strange that we were so attracted to a cantankerous old woman, but it's hard to convey the complexity of her character. She was a teenage star in musical comedy at the Gaiety and then idolised in three countries and had that wonderful charisma until the very end of her life.'[8]

Nellie Wallace was a contemporary of Marie Lloyd. They were born in the same year; they were both comediennes; they both reached the top of their profession; and they were both greatly loved for who they were, as well as what they did on stage. There the similarities end. Whereas Marie traded to a large extent on her joy of sex, Nellie made a feature of her lack of success, blaming it on the plainness of her looks. Marie was a star at the age of 20. Nellie had to wait until she was over 30 before her name became widely known, but she went on making audiences laugh for another twenty-five years after Marie's early death.

The daughter of a professional singer, Nellie, billed as the Essence of Eccentricity, was an integral link in a chain of what used to be called grotesque comediennes: women who poked fun at their own sex, their lack of appeal and their inability to catch a man. Nellie made herself look as ugly as possible. A typical outfit was elastic-sided boots; a tight dress, which required her to lie on the floor to pick up anything she dropped (the trombones in the pit making inelegant noises as she tried to regain her balance); a mangy stole, which she referred to as her little bit of vermin; and a hat topped by either a long feather, a flower or the skeleton of a fish.

> NELLIE WALLACE (Eleanor Jane Tayler)
> **Born** Glasgow, 18 March 1870
> **Married** William Henry Liddy, Salford, Greater
>   Manchester, 18 November 1895 (d. 5 March
>   1921)
>   Daughter, Nora (b. Darlington, 29 September 1896;
>   married Lionel Graham, Wandsworth, south
>   London, 1923; d. 24 March 1948)
> **Died** Highgate, north London, 24 November 1948
> **Left** £8,439

She was, in any case, exceedingly plain, as Don Ross acknowledged: 'Poor Nellie had a nose like Mr Punch, no chin at all and very prominent teeth . . . She'd only got a little skimpy bit of hair. She always put a little dot of pink on the end of her nose and made no attempt to beautify herself. You couldn't do anything with that face.'[9]

Less was made about the strangeness of Nellie's voice. Although she had perfect enunciation, she spoke on stage in a quaint, constrained, confidential voice, sometimes sounding as though she were talking to herself as she muttered 'Dear, dear, dear'. As her career progressed, she perfected her own rules about the art of comedy: 'Many years ago, when I was a kiddy, a man said to me "Nellie, when you get older, you will have a big pull because you are never at a loss for by-play, which means that one can be a comic without ever opening one's mouth".'[10]

Nellie first appeared on stage at the age of 12 as a clog dancer at the Steam Clock Music Hall in Birmingham. She toured as a dancer for a while, billed as La Petite Nellie. Then, while still in her early teens, she joined forces with her two sisters, Fannie and Emmie, to form the Sisters Wallace. In later life, Fannie was her understudy. After that, Nellie joined a drama company, taking part in every kind of play, but attracting laughter in all the wrong places,

Nellie Wallace, the Essence of Eccentricity. *(Richard Anthony Baker)*

especially as Joan of Arc and in the death scene in the melodrama *East Lynne*. Before long she left.

In 1894, she appeared at the Comedy Theatre in Manchester as second girl and understudy to a pregnant Ada Reeve in *Jack and Jill*. As the show ran into 1895 and Ada increased in girth, it looked more and more as though Nellie would get her chance. In March, she finally took over as principal girl for the last weeks of the run. As Ada remarked all too pointedly: 'She [Nellie] had not developed her own distinctive style at that time, but was still trying to compete with prettier girls in ordinary show business.'[11]

It is hard to say exactly when Nellie switched to eccentric comedy, but it was before she reached London in 1902. By the summer of 1903, she was becoming well known. Over the next few years, she undertook more panto work and a trip to America. Then, at the end of 1910, she featured on the very first bill of the new London Palladium: 'Of present day low comediennes, one cannot recall a single one who indulges a broader vein than Nellie Wallace. Everything with this vivacious entertainer is subservient to laughter-making – no costume can be too ludicrous, no make-up too extravagant.'[12]

At the Palladium, she sang 'Oh! The Hobble!' written by Charles Collins and Fred Murray, which satirised the craze for the hobble skirt, an ideal item for Nellie: a skirt made tight by a band below the knee. After the First World War, she appeared in a number of revues, the most successful of them, *The Whirl of the World*, again at the London Palladium in 1924/5. Here, she played several roles, including Juliet to Billy Merson's Romeo in a skit on the balcony scene and a boarding-house landlady who manages to fit twenty-four people in one bed. *The Whirl of the World* ran for 627 performances, a Palladium record which remained unbroken for twenty years. When she topped the bill at the Coliseum, Nellie gained a new fan, a 7-year-old Alec Guinness:

She appeared in a nurse's uniform ready to assist a surgeon at an operation. The patient, covered with a sheet, was wheeled on stage and the surgeon immediately set about him with a huge carving-knife. Nellie stood by, looking very prim, but, every now and then, would dive under the sheet and extract with glee and a shout of triumph quite impossible articles – a hotwater bottle, a live chicken, a flat-iron, and so on. Finally, she inserted, with many wicked looks, a long rubber tube which she blew down. The body inflated rapidly to huge proportions and then, covered in its sheet, slowly took to the air. Nellie made desperate attempts to catch it, twinkling her boots as she hopped surprisingly high, but all in vain. The orchestra gave a tremendous blast as she made her last leap; and that is when I fell off my plush seat and felt faintly sick.[13]

Nellie could sometimes be mildly risqué, pronouncing 'ridiculous' as 'ridicu-larse' and 'treacherous' as 'tretcher-arse'. Only the prudish BBC was worried. Appearing on *Garrison Theatre* in 1940, she introduced new lines into her patter: 'I remember I was walking down Piccadilly. It was one of my quiet nights. That's the end of the gag. It's been blue pencilled.'

A weary Controller of Programmes sent a memo to the Assistant Director of Variety, commenting that there were some artistes 'you must either take or leave without much possibility of modification'. During another broadcast, Nellie met the singer/actress, Betty Driver: 'I'll never forget drooling over her diamonds . . . She said "That's all I've got left." Her husband had taken everything – the bank account, her furs, her home, everything. "Thank God I never took my jewels off," she added. That's why she started working again.'[14] Even given Nellie's bizarre sense of humour, it was a curious remark to have made. There had never been any other suggestion of difficulties in Nellie's marriage.

In 1948, Nellie joined Don Ross's company of veterans, *Thanks for the Memory*. It toured Britain to great success, but, during the course of its run, Nellie's widowed daughter, Nora Graham, on whom she doted, died after a short illness and, as a result, Nellie lost the will to live. *Thanks for the Memory* was selected as part of that year's Royal Variety Performance at the Palladium. As Nellie left the stage, she collapsed and died three weeks later.

Fortunately, BBC Radio made a recording of *Thanks for the Memory*, now released on CD, and Nellie's extraordinary song 'My Mother's Pie Crust' is probably the best thing in it. Between 1920 and 1936, Nellie made commercial recordings of twelve of her songs, including 'The Blasted Oak' (1934) and Harry Castling's 'Under the Bed' (1929):

> My mother said:
> 'Always look under the bed.
> Before you blow the candle out.
> See if there's a man about.'
>
> I always do.
> But you can make a bet.
> It has never been my luck
> To find a man there yet.

CHAPTER 19

HERE'S TO THE LADIES WHO WEREN'T... AND THE MEN WHO WERE

Male impersonation belonged to Britain and to music hall. Few male impersonators succeeded in other countries, and, once music hall had faded away, the art of the remaining practitioners seemed anachronistic.

Bessie Bonehill, who was among Britain's first male impersonators, made her stage debut at the age of 6 in a pantomime in her home town of West Bromwich. Her first salary was 3 shillings (15p) a week. On her London debut at Christmas 1873, she secured favourable reviews and, within a year, she was being described as a favourite at the Metropolitan.

It is difficult to establish when Bessie decided to switch to male impersonation, although her career was greatly assisted by her portrayal of William in a revival of F.C. Burnand's burlesque, *Black Ey'd Susan*, at the Alhambra in 1884. This helped to establish her reputation on the legitimate stage. In fact, one of her early successes in America was her portrayal of Christopher Columbus at the Garden Theatre, New York. In Britain, she was a particular success in pantomime, especially in Sheffield.

> BESSIE BONEHILL (Betsey Bonehill)
> **Born** West Bromwich, west Midlands, 17 January 1855
> **Married** (1) Louis William Abrahams, Shoreditch, London, 20 September 1877 (d. 1890)
> Eldest son, Jack (of double act, Seeley and West)
> (2) William Robert Smith (professionally known as Billy Seeley, of the Four Emperors), 14 September 1890
> Son, Henry Washington Bonehill Seeley
> **Died** Portsea Island, Hampshire, 21 August 1902

Bessie made her American debut in 1889, scoring an immediate hit. As an expression of thanks, she added a new song to her repertoire, 'How I like America', written by Arthur West. One reviewer wrote: 'She looks like a handsome boy and dances like a sprightly girl.' Her turn consisted of four songs: two sung in male evening dress, the third decked out as a young newsvendor and the fourth as a naval attaché. This was the first of several American tours, all of which made Bessie a wealthy woman. She bought a large farm on Long Island, which comprised an orchard, a granary, a dairy and a cheese-making plant, which she helped to supervise.

Of her songs, she introduced her best known, the nationalistic 'Here Stands a Post' (1888) at the Oxford. It was written by Clement Scott, who was devoted to her. Her other songs included 'Old Tattered Flag' (1887) and Harry Dacre's 'Playmates' (1890).

Bessie Bonehill, England's Gem. *(Richard Anthony Baker)*

Her convincing male guise was not a complete asset. She received on average a dozen marriage proposals from girls every week. One girl fell in love with her when she was playing the Alhambra, Nottingham, and wrote to her, suggesting a meeting-place. Bessie turned up, dressed in her usual offstage clothes. The girl was indignant at first, but Bessie gave her a sound talking to. There was a similar incident at a wedding party in Glasgow. On this occasion, Bessie was dressed in men's clothes. She escorted home a pretty girl only to meet her angry boyfriend when she got back. Bessie had to do some quick talking to avoid getting into a fight.

After Bessie, there were three main female cross-dressers, one of whom, Hetty King, went to extraordinary lengths to perfect her impressions of the working man. During a career that lasted seventy-five years, she twice recorded her most famous song, 'Ship Ahoy' ('All the nice girls love a sailor'), once in 1910, the year after she had first sung it, and secondly in 1960, when she appeared in a show at the Metropolitan, staged by Daniel Farson.

HETTY KING (Winifred Emms)
Born New Brighton, Merseyside,
   21 April 1883
Married (1) Ernest Lotinga (professionally
   known as Ernie Lotinga), 20 November
   1901 (divorced 1917)
   (2) Alexander Lamond at Roker, Tyne and
   Wear, 18 June 1918
Died Merton, south-west London,
   28 September 1972

Hetty was born into a showbiz family. (Her birth appears not to have been registered. As her family was itinerant, that is perhaps unsurprising.) 'So much has been written about me that isn't true . . . and that includes where my real home is. It was never New Brighton. I just happened to be born there when my father had a touring act of minstrels. My parents rented a house there for the season and then we moved on around the country.'[1] Her father, a comic and multi-instrumentalist, ran a travelling troupe, Uncle Billy King's Minstrels. Longevity was evidently a family attribute. Hetty's father, Will King (Emms), was born in Barrow-in-Furness on 3 June 1856 and died at Banbury in Oxfordshire on 14 January 1954. They had a portable theatre and lived in a caravan. Hetty had two sisters, Mary Florence, known as Florrie, who was older, and Olive, her dresser all her life, who was younger. The family travelled constantly. Hetty went to school in whichever town the caravan stopped. When a representative of the School Board called, she hid under her mother's crinolines. Hetty did everything in her parents' show. At the age of 5, she mimicked a red-nosed Irish comedian. Then, she imitated popular stars of the day, but she wanted in particular to perfect an impression of the dapper George Lashwood. She saved her money to have a suit made and spent 10 shillings (50p) on two new songs.

Hetty used to say that she made her name in one night, when she switched to male impersonation full time. She said that during one week she was among the 'wines and spirits' (a theatrical phrase meaning that her name appeared in print that was as small as the typeface used for advertising drinks) and at the top of the bill at the start of the next. Her money, she maintained, went up from £6 to £50 a week, but some of the detail of her early career is difficult to work out.

She said that the first night of her new career was at the Palace in Bradford in 1902. Lily Burnand, who was topping the bill, told her that she looked good, but that a pair of white gloves would make her look even better. Lily found some long ladies' gloves, shortened them and gave them to Hetty. It is a good story, but Lily and Hetty did not share a bill in Bradford in 1902. In any case, Hetty took rather longer to establish herself.

It was not until after she had appeared in *Dick Whittington* at the Kennington Theatre in 1905/6 that she began to appear regularly at the top of provincial bills. During 1907, two of her songs were widely recognised: 'I Want a Gibson Girl' (a Gibson Girl was an elegant young woman, as depicted by the American artist, Charles Dana Gibson) and 'When I Get back to Piccadilly'. Then, in the autumn of that year, she and R.G. Knowles sailed from Liverpool to New York, the first of many trips she made to America. The publicity at home made out that she was a sensational hit. She broke all records at the New York Theater and had a six-week stay extended by fourteen weeks, but her success did not come straight-away. A review in *Variety* said that only one of her five songs, 'I'm Going Away', was universally approved by audiences and that she was unfortunate in having to stand comparison with Tilley. Two weeks later, however, a further review said:

> She is a little woman with a world of personal magnetism – the magnetism that goes out over the footlights in its effect and literally draws the audience to her . . . Her songs are clean and wholesome . . . She believes that the stage artist who deserves popularity will win it by work of high quality with songs bright, witty and tuneful . . . She never loses the charm of her femininity.[2]

This is one of the most interesting aspects of Hetty King's act. She went on board ship to watch how a sailor cut his tobacco, rolled it and put it in his pipe.

The Immaculate Hetty King. *(Richard Anthony Baker)*

For three months, she went every morning to the Knightsbridge Barracks in London to learn how to handle a rifle, how to march and how to salute and, when she carried a kitbag on stage, it was no prop: it had to be the right weight so that she could swing it convincingly onto her shoulder. All the same, as the *Variety* critic noted, she made sure that her femininity shone through, sometimes winking at the audience as if to let them in on the subterfuge.

In a film of her career, *Hetty King, Performer*, made by the movie historian David Robinson, she said that she first sang 'Ship Ahoy' at the Liverpool Empire. It did not go well and she dropped it until she found the right uniform in which to sing it. Hetty was at the Liverpool Empire in July 1909, but the song did not feature in the advertisements of its publishers, the Star Music Publishing Company, until September, when it was dubbed Hetty King's great winner. By December 1909, it was described as the biggest panto hit for four years.

Hetty married Ernie Lotinga, but, in 1917, he divorced her. The judge hearing the case summed it up by saying: 'There are some wives whom it is better to lose than to keep.' The American singer-songwriter Jack Norworth, was named as the co-respondent. Lotinga told the court that, when they married in 1901, he was the star comedian of the Six Brothers Luck, earning £30 a week, while Hetty was a mimic earning £5. He had given up his work to support her. He had advised her to become a male impersonator as a result of which her salary rose to between £150 and £200 (by today's standards £8,000) a week. Towards the end of 1915, they became friendly with Norworth and his wife, but, at the Nottingham Empire, Lotinga saw Norworth leave Hetty's dressing-room with greasepaint on his lips. It happened again at the Holborn Empire. Lotinga told Hetty her friendship with Norworth had to stop. She refused and went to stay with her father the following day.

In court, a letter written by Lotinga was produced, in which he admitted '[messing] about with those girls', an apparent reference to Hetty's two sisters. He explained that the sisters lived with them and that there were always joking and laughter in the house. At one point, Hetty had encouraged him to get under their bed to frighten them. The case made lurid reading in the papers, but Hetty's career was unaffected.

Naturally enough, she attracted a lesbian following. In a somewhat ingenuous interview, she said that she, too, got love letters from girls: 'Some of the letters I get are terrible. They frighten me . . . They declare that they can't eat or sleep or are going to kill themselves for love of me. It sickens me.'[3] Don Ross saw proof of that. Whereas Ella Shields treated her lesbian fans kindly, Hetty would slam the door on them. She refused to see Marie Lloyd's lesbian biographer, Naomi Jacob, and she was spiteful to Ella. One week, they shared the bill at the Bristol Hippodrome. During the whole week, Hetty spoke only two words to Ella. By contrast, David Robinson, writing in *The Times* in 1979, referred to the two artistes sharing a bill at a hall in Brighton. Hetty invited Ella to her dressing-room, but was met with a curt reply. 'An icy chill', Robinson wrote, 'pervaded the theatre for the rest of the week'.

Don, though, did find Hetty difficult to do business with. At her funeral, he delivered the eulogy with one hand on the coffin: 'Hetty, old girl, you can rest at last. No more fighting about your billing or your salary or your dressing room or who you will follow on the programme. It's all over now and you can rest in peace.'[4]

An entertainer of charm and elegance, Ella Shields was fortunate enough to weave her career around one of music hall's most delightful songs, 'Burlington Bertie from Bow', written by her husband, William Hargreaves. American by birth, Ella Shields began her career in Pennsylvania in 1898, singing black-faced songs. She came to Britain six years later, appearing first in Newcastle and making her London debut at the Foresters two weeks after that. She was soon accepted as an English performer, although she always retained a slight transatlantic accent.

It was when Ella was booked to appear at the opening night of the London Palladium in 1910 that she decided to perform her entire act in male dress for the first time. The show was a bitter disappointment for her. It wildly overran and, when Ella appeared at 11.45 p.m., she was told there would be time for her to sing only one song.

> ELLA SHIELDS (Ella Catherine Buscher)
> **Born** Baltimore, Maryland, 27 September 1879
> **Married** (1) Theodore Darwin Middaugh (divorced)
> (2) William Joseph Hargreaves, Lambeth, south London,
>   5 December 1906 (divorced 19 November 1923;
>   d. Clacton-on-Sea, Essex, 25 January 1941)
> (3) —— Buck (divorced)
> **Died** Lancaster, Lancashire, 5 August 1952

The man I first approached to help me dress (as a man) was Leslie Stuart, a correctly groomed man no matter whether it was morning, afternoon or evening. He would never wear diamond studs; he wore nothing that was showy. When he introduced me to his tailor, the latter thought a practical joke was being played on him and, when he was taking my measurements, he was decidedly embarrassed. So was I, for that matter.[5]

Ella first sang 'Burlington Bertie from Bow' at the Argyle at Birkenhead in 1914, depicting its subject more accurately than many who have sung the song since – not as a man-about-town, but as a broken-down toff, who is too proud to accept dinner invitations:

> I'm Burlington Bertie, I rise at ten thirty
> And saunter along like a toff.
> I walk down the Strand with my gloves on my hand
> And then walk down again with them off.
> I'm all airs and graces, correct easy paces,
> So long without food, I forgot where my face is.
> I'm Bert, Bert, I haven't a shirt,
> But my people are well off, you know.
> Nearly everyone knows me from Smith to Lord Rosebery.
> I'm Burlington Bertie from Bow.

The song is possibly the only case of a parody or 'answer' becoming more famous than the original. Vesta Tilley had a song about a swell prepared to die for his country, 'Burlington Bertie'. Hargreaves's version was written for the character comedian J.W. Rickaby, but he turned it down, believing it to be too similar to a song he was already singing.

Ella had married Hargreaves[6] in 1906, but they were divorced in 1923. She alleged cruelty by him, accusing him of beating her about the face and body and seizing her throat so hard that she was unable to sing. She admitted misconduct with an army colonel during the First World War, but maintained she had been weakened by Hargreaves's treatment of her.

Ella Shields travelled widely. She returned to America as a star at the Palace in New York in 1920 and went again in 1924 and 1928. During the first of those bookings, she was, of course,

Ella Shields, the Ideal of Ideals. *(Richard Anthony Baker)*

a complete stranger to most of her audience, in spite of being born in America:

> Yet before she was half through, the audience sat up and took notice of everything she did. It couldn't help it. Miss Shields was giving the folks an act worthy of their attention and appreciation. True, she reminded us of the day of Vesta Tilley when she sauntered on in male attire, but her style, voice, unaffected way of working and gracefulness when tripping a few steps a la light fantastic were such that she was accepted as an artiste worth while.[7]

Ella made her first visit to South Africa in 1905; and she was in Australia in 1921, 1925 and 1947. When she was part of Don Ross's *Thanks for the Memory* team in the 1948 Royal Variety Show at the London Palladium, it was a poignant comeback for one who had been on the opening bill thirty-eight years previously.

So, to Vesta Tilley herself, the greatest male impersonator in music hall, but, more than that, one of the most loved figures on the popular British stage: in her act, she impersonated through song the men of her day: the man about town, the curate, the cheeky boy, the policeman, the sailor, the Guardsman and, especially during the First World War, the soldier. It was all done with humour, pathos and immense charm. Don Ross, who saw her perform many times, said that when she toured Britain, whole families who seldom visited music halls would turn out en masse to see her. She was not merely idolised, according to Don. She was revered.

Vesta was the second of thirteen children of a Worcester pottery worker. Her father, William, had another life too. As Harry Ball, he was the Chairman at the local music hall. As a very young girl, Matilda, her name usually abbreviated to Tilley, was taken along

VESTA TILLEY (Matilda Alice Powles)
Born Worcester, Worcestershire, 13 May 1864
Married Abraham Walter Defrece (*sic*)
    (professionally known as Walter de Frece),
    6 August 1890 (b. Derby, 7 October 1870;
    d. Monaco, 7 January 1935; left £69,000)
Died London, 16 September 1952
Left £84,945

Vesta Tilley, the London Idol.
(Richard Anthony Baker)

as well and, back home at the end of each evening, she sang some of the songs she had heard and mimicked the singers. After a time, her father put together a medley of the songs she had learned and accompanied her on the violin. He was then offered a better job as manager and chairman of St George's music hall in Nottingham. He had been popular in Worcester and, before he left, he was given a benefit night at his hall there. On that evening, little Tilley sang her medley in public for the first time, her music-hall debut. In Nottingham, while still only 4 and billed as the Great Little Tilley, she sang regularly at the St George's and began getting invitations to appear at Leicester, Dudley, Derby and other towns nearby. At first, a neighbour took her, but eventually her father gave up his job and travelled with her. They were two distinct acts: Harry Ball, the tramp musician, and the Great Little Tilley.

In time, Vesta decided she wanted to try a song dressed as a man; her father bought her a little evening dress suit; and she made her debut as a male impersonator at Day's concert hall in Birmingham. In her autobiography, published in 1934, Vesta Tilley said she was then 5 and earned £5 a week. Unfortunately, her recollections of her early days are unreliable: understandably so, since she was writing about events that had occurred sixty-five years previously. So, from now on, this account of her life is based on what the theatrical press reported she had done rather than what she herself recorded.

When she was 13, she secured four weeks' work in the run-up to Easter 1878 at two London halls, Lusby's and the Royal Music Hall in Holborn. She was advertised as 'The Great Little

Tilley, impersonator of male character and burlesque actress'. The *Entr'acte*, reviewing her at Lusby's, noted: 'A clever and realistic entertainment is given by a youthful lady, Little Tilley, whose impersonations of male character command sincere approbation. Not only is this little artist exceptionally good in the assumption of character, but her acting and speaking are forcible and enchanting and, when necessary, truly pathetic.'[8]

The Era's critic saw her that week at the Royal: 'This is a little lady not very far into her teens who has a pretty face, a sweet voice and a captivating style. Tilley prefers to appear in male costume and, as she dresses remarkably well and conducts herself like a lady, we are ready to admit the claim she puts forward in one of her impersonations as "A Perfect Little Gentleman".'[9]

As Vesta approached 14, it became clear that her days as Little Tilley were numbered. Audiences were sometimes confused over whether she was, in fact, a boy or a girl. A new name was needed. According to her autobiography, her father went through a dictionary; three words were written on slips of paper and placed in a hat. Tilley made the selection and, accordingly, on 14 April 1878, *The Era* proclaimed: 'The Great Little Tilley will in future be known as Miss Vesta Tilley.' She continued touring and, as word of her successes spread, she added to her billing: No vulgarity; Genuine Talent; All imitators notice: Tilley stands unrivalled.

In 1880/1, she played the title role in *Robinson Crusoe* at the Theatre Royal, Portsmouth, the local press noting that she had 'a pretty face, a beautiful figure and an abundance of vivacity'. The following Christmas, she was in *The Beauty and the Beast* at the Theatre Royal, Birmingham, reaching the pinnacle of pantomime venues in 1882/3, when she was cast as Captain Tra-lala in *Sindbad* (*sic*), Augustus Harris's third and E.L. Blanchard's thirtieth panto at the Theatre Royal, Drury Lane. Here, Tilley, scoring a personal success with F.V. St Clair's song, 'When Will Old England Be Herself Once More?' played alongside some of the greatest music-hall luminaries of the time, Nellie Power, whom she understudied, Arthur Roberts, James Fawn, Herbert Campbell and Harry Nicholls. In 1883, she adopted her main billing matter, the London Idol.

Over the years, Vesta Tilley had a string of successful songs. Among the best known were 'After the Ball' (1893), written by the American songwriter Charles Harris and rewritten by Frederick Bowyer and Orlando Powell; 'Algy, the Piccadilly Johnny with the Little Glass Eye' (1895); 'Burlington Bertie' (1900) (both written by Harry B. Norris); 'Following in Father's Footsteps' (1902) (E.W. Rogers); and 'Jolly good luck to the girl who loves a soldier' (1906) (Fred W. Leigh and Kenneth Lyle):

> Jolly good luck to the girl who loves a soldier!
> Girls, have you been there?
> You know we military men
> Always do our duty everywhere.
> Jolly good luck to the girl who loves a soldier!
> Real good boys are we!
> Girls, if you'd like to love a soldier,
> You can all love me.

Vesta made her American debut at Tony Pastor's music hall in 1894. She returned to America in 1905 and was invited again in 1912, but turned down the offer of $4,000 a week rather than work on Sundays.

Walter de Frece, impresario and husband of Vesta Tilley. *(Richard Anthony Baker)*

After her husband, the theatre owner Walter de Frece, was knighted in 1919, he begged her to retire. He was going into politics and he wanted her by his side. She had been working for about fifty years. Some of her followers told her that they remembered having seen her mother on stage. She had to tell them that her mother had never been on the stage; the woman they had seen was, in fact, a much younger version of herself. In August 1919, she began her farewell tour, earning £500 (by today's standards £12,000) a week. At the end of each week, she presented a local children's hospital or a disabled children's home with a cheque for that amount. The tour culminated in a four-week season at the London Coliseum in May 1920. On the last night, the theatre was packed.

Dame Ellen Terry went on stage hand in hand with Tilley and paid her a glowing tribute: 'She made us laugh when, God knows, England wanted to and now she deserves a crown.'[10] Tilley began making a speech, but broke down in tears. When she sang 'Jolly good luck to the girl who loves a soldier' and reached the last line 'You can all love me', a loud roar went up from the audience: 'We do!'

Male cross-dressers were more daring. People knew that men who dressed as women were probably gay. The molly houses (gay bars) of eighteenth-century London were frequented by homosexuals in drag. The rent boys spotted by Wilde outside Swan and Edgar's in Piccadilly Circus wore make-up. So, music hall's female impersonators had a difficult course to follow. Three deserve mention. Bert Errol began his career as a concert singer and after-dinner entertainer. He joined a concert party and then a minstrel troupe, where his versatile voice, ranging from tenor to falsetto, was put to good use. He made his London music-hall debut at the London Pavilion in 1908, billed as the Famous Male Soprano and Double-Voiced Vocalist: 'Bert Errol, new to London, made a successful debut here . . . and scored an immediate success in his business. He burlesques the operatic solo, *Nobil Signor*, just sufficiently and, although wearing his skirts, he knows how to be refined and artistic.'[11]

BERT ERROL (Isaac Whitehouse)
Born Birmingham, west Midlands, 11 August 1883
Married Ray Isaacs (professionally known as Ray Hartley), Lambeth, south London, 28 April 1910
Daughter, Betty
Died Brighton, east Sussex, 29 November 1949

Although Errol sang some of his songs completely straight, he enjoyed his greatest successes impersonating musical comedy actresses. He first

Bert Errol, the Famous Male Soprano. *(Tony Barker)*

visited America in 1910 creating a sensation when he paid $1,000 customs duty on his gowns. Between then and 1921, he was frequently in the United States. He also toured extensively throughout Australia, New Zealand, South Africa and Canada. To try to avert any hint of homosexuality, Errol's wife always appeared with him at the end of his act.

Julian Eltinge had another way of dealing with any such gossip. He made sure that stories circulated of him physically attacking anyone who questioned his sexual preferences – a stagehand, for instance, who called him 'Lucy' and suggested he was more than just friends with the founder of a cutlery company in Sheffield.

The early career of Eltinge is another which is hard to verify. His father travelled to California to prospect for gold, but, when he failed, he opened a barber's shop in Montana. Encouraged by his mother, Eltinge began to dress in drag and perform in local bars while he was still in his teens. When his father found out, he was beaten within an inch of his life. In 1899, his mother sent him to live with her sister in Boston, where he entered a cakewalk contest and won. Having enrolled in a dance class, he then appeared with the Cadet Theatricals at the Tremont Theater in Boston, where he was a tremendous success. His big break came in the musical comedy, *Mr Wix of Wickham*, at the Bijou Theater in New York in 1904. It managed only forty-one performances, but the critics singled Eltinge out for particular praise. After that, he moved into vaudeville, undertaking a European tour that took him to London, Paris, Berlin and Vienna. He made his London debut at the Palace Theatre in 1906, billed merely as Eltinge:

With an effeminate face and an adaptable figure, he wears the short skirts and evening bodice of the soubrette of musical comedy with considerable grace and without a trace of vulgarity. He is decidedly clever and has quite an air of dainty coquetry both in song and dance. Female impersonators in this country scarcely ever reach the first rank as artists, but Eltinge is certainly entitled to do so.[12]

JULIAN ELTINGE (William Dalton)
Born Newtonville,
Massachusetts,
14 May 1883
Died New York, 7 March 1941

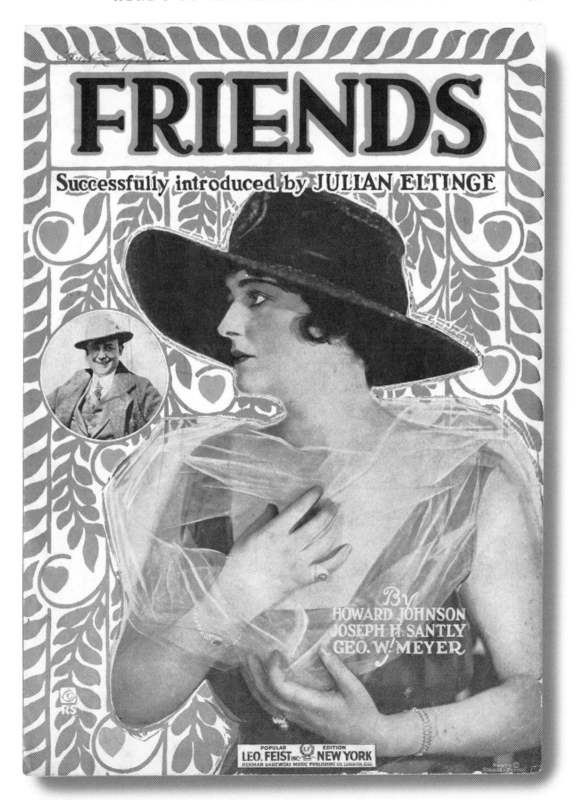

Julian Eltinge marketed his own cold cream. *(Richard Anthony Baker)*

Eltinge's first appearance in vaudeville in New York came a year later: 'The audience was completely deceived as to Eltinge's sex until he removed his wig after the second song. Eltinge will be liked. He is artistic in everything he does and his act is far and away above what is described as female impersonation.'[13]

Eltinge had a good singing voice, wore beautiful gowns and was meticulous about his make-up. He and his Japanese dresser spent two hours on the transformation, including an hour on his make-up. He forced himself into 4-inch heels and a corset that reduced his waist to 23 inches. In fact, he was a spokesman for a firm of corsetières; he published a beauty magazine and created a line of cold cream. One advert proclaimed: 'See What The Julian Eltinge Cold Cream Does For A Man. Imagine What It Will Do For A Woman.' By 1912, he was the best-paid vaudeville entertainer in history, earning $1,625 a week.

Eltinge made a number of movies, one of them, *The Isle of Love*, featuring Rudolph Valentino, with whom he was rumoured to have had an affair. But, by his early forties, he was drinking heavily and his figure had filled out. In 1923, he was accused of smuggling alcohol from Canada, but, in spite of a sensational trial, he was acquitted. It was, though, the start of his decline. In the 1930s, he appeared in a Hollywood nightclub with a gay clientele. As by-laws prohibited men from wearing women's clothing, he had to perform his act in a tuxedo. He lived his last years with his mother on a ranch in southern California. According to his death certificate, he died of a stroke, but, in *Hollywood Babylon*, Kenneth Anger claimed he killed himself with an overdose of sleeping pills.

The leading female impersonator in Britain, Malcolm Scott, billed as the Woman Who Knows, did not try to look feminine. In whichever role he took (Elizabeth I, Boadicea, Catherine Parr, Nell Gwynn and many others) he always retained a masculine face in the style of some pantomime dames.

MALCOLM SCOTT (Malcolm Dalkeith Scott)
Born Bloomsbury, central London, 7 March 1872
Died Burgess Hill, west Sussex, 7 September 1929
Left £947

The son of a solicitor, Malcolm Scott was stage-struck as a child, even though the only shows he saw in childhood were panto-mimes. His life was thrown into disarray when he was orphaned at the age of 14. He was sent to Canada, where he worked successively on a farm, in a jeweller's and on a railway. On doctor's orders, he was soon back in England and made his way to Margate, where he found work at the Theatre Royal. About five years later, he was working at a small German music hall, singing Millie Hylton's song 'The Rowdy Dowdy Boys'. Back in England, he appeared with several theatrical companies and, during the summer, with a party of pierrots at New Brighton in Merseyside.

In the early years of the new century, he determined to become a female impersonator, presenting 'a feminine character of a higher tone than the average dame study'. He started in the provinces, appearing in *Cinderella* at the Comedy Theatre, Manchester, in 1902/3. At the end of the show's run, he made his London debut at the Pavilion, taking the place of Dan Leno, who was ill. By 1904, he was to be seen regularly in London. In 1906, his engagements included a visit to South Africa. Otherwise, his year divided neatly between the pantomime season and music-hall bills in London, most notably those at the Pavilion.

A man of ready wit, he once crossed swords with Oswald Stoll. When appearing at the London Coliseum, he was ordered to cut his version of the Dying Swan because the ballerina

Malcolm Scott, the Woman Who
Knows. *(Richard Anthony Baker)*

Anna Pavlova was due to appear at the theatre shortly. Scott gave Stoll a withering look and swept towards the office door, pausing just long enough to say: 'Oswald Stoll, you are the sort of manager who would book a giant and not let him stand up.'[14]

Anecdotes about Scott's wit circulated throughout the profession. Everyone knew that he was not friendly with his brother, Admiral Sir Percy Scott. The pierrot leader Edwin Adeler recalled that, on Sir Percy's death, it became known that he wanted to be cremated and that his ashes were to be scattered from his old flagship in the Solent:

> One afternoon, Rogers (a mutual friend) met Malcolm in Charing Cross Road with a tall hat, black frock coat and trousers and necktie and said 'Good Lord, Malcolm. What's this? Oh, of course, you have been to Sir Percy's funeral. What was it like?' 'Oh, it was fearfully windy,' replied Scott, as he flicked an imaginary speck of dust off his coat collar. 'My lapels are covered with Percy.'[15]

In 1917, Malcolm Scott appeared in his first revue, replacing Wilkie Bard in *The Bing Girls*, starring Violet Loraine. He visited Australia in 1922 and returned to South Africa the following year. He continued performing throughout the 1920s, although he retired gradually from the stage as a result of a malignant growth, which affected his chest and throat.

A cultured man, he snobbishly resented being sent to the Hackney Empire in the 1920s. As the audience ate peanuts during his portrayal of Catharine Parr, he told them that, although he was loved at the London Coliseum, it was obvious that he was not at what he called 'the Hacker-nee Empire'. He then invited them to carry on eating.

In retirement, Malcolm Scott kept a sweetshop at Brighton in east Sussex, where Fred Barnes once paid him a visit:

As I entered the shop, Malcolm, attired in a white apron, was struggling with a bottle of sticky humbugs. A little boy, his mouth watering in anticipation, was holding up a penny. There was something so incongruous about this picture of Malcolm that I burst out laughing. Malcolm looked up and saw me . . . 'I've got enough humbugs in my shop,' he rallied. Though he had now retired, it was the same Malcolm. At one time, [he] had a house in Hounslow. He called it Malcolm Scottage. He had to have his little joke.[16]

Innocent Times

In 1912, Malcolm Scott took a 16-year-old newspaper boy with him to Canada. He had been sitting in the Royal Court Hotel, Liverpool, when the boy tried to sell him a copy of the *Liverpool Express*. They began chatting and Scott learned that the boy was without both friends and family. Scott bought him some new clothes and a ticket for Canada and, once there, found him a job in Winnipeg.

Hetty King in civvies.
(Richard Anthony Baker)

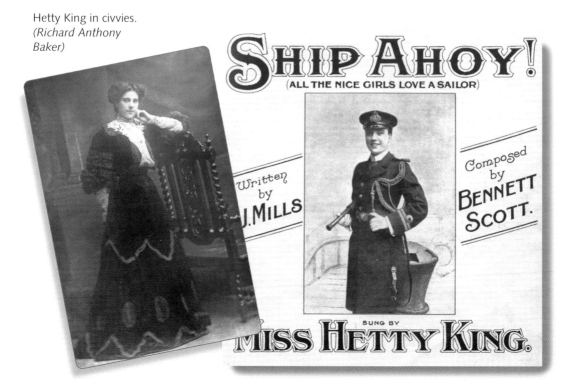

CHAPTER 20

WAL THE RIPPER?

The impressionist artist Walter Sickert loved music hall. Taught by James Whistler in London and heavily influenced by Degas in Paris, he was to British music hall what Toulouse-Lautrec was to its French counterpart.

Sickert favoured the lesser halls, such as the Bedford and the Middlesex, and mostly favoured the lesser stars. He painted the eccentric comedienne Ada Lundberg, at the Marylebone and Katie Lawrence at Gatti's under the Arches. Katie was unimpressed. On being offered one of Sickert's life-size paintings of her, she replied: 'What! That thing? Not even to keep the draught from under the scullery door!'[1]

Sickert also painted the singer Minnie Cunningham, whose career rested on the offering, 'It's Not the Hen

WALTER SICKERT
Born Munich, 31 May 1860
Married (1) Ellen Cobden, 1885 (divorced)
(2) Christine Angus, 1911 (d. 1920)
(3) Therese Lessore, 1926
Died Bathampton, Somerset, 22 January 1942
Left £145

that Cackles the Most (that lays the golden egg)', the Sisters Lloyd (this was hung in Ten Downing Street when John Major, of music-hall provenance, was Prime Minister) and Talbot O'Farrell, who sang Irish ballads. Sickert was also fond of T.W. Barrett, billed as the Nobleman's Son. He made two etchings of him, inscribed: 'To T.W. Barrett, in grateful and affectionate hommage [*sic*] for countless hours between 1885 and 1922, cheered and sweetened by his gentle and reticent wit, his exquisite and lovable personality.' When Victoria Monks (she of 'Bill Bailey, Won't you Please Come Home?') died in 1927, Sickert wrote: 'Victoria Monks will remain in the memory of all that ever heard her for the rare quality of resonant sincerity . . . To hear her sing at the New Bedford *We've Got A Navy, A British Navy* was to feel that Nelson was sitting in the Royal Box. The fury of controlled vituperation in her *Kaiser Bill* must have been worth an army corps to us.'[2]

But, at one point, Sickert's art seemed to be in danger of being overshadowed by the possibility that he was Jack the Ripper. Since the disembowelling of five prostitutes in east London in 1888, still the biggest unsolved murders of all time, many scenarios have been sketched out, some wilder than others. It has, for instance, been suggested that the killings were perpetrated by Queen Victoria's physician, Sir William Gull. The aim, apparently, was to silence the first victim, Mary Jane Kelly, and prevent her friends from blackmailing the government. Kelly had told them of a potentially huge scandal which she had heard about while working as a nursemaid to the Duke of Clarence, Prince Albert Victor, who, as the elder son of Edward VII, was heir presumptive to the throne. It was said that Albert had secretly

The Sisters Lloyd, as depicted by Walter Sickert. *(Richard Anthony Baker)*

married Annie Crook, who had borne a son by him. After the murders, highly placed Masons in the government and the police were said to have organised a cover-up of Gull's identity. Much of this theory has since been discredited. The main source was a man calling himself Joseph Sickert, who said he was an illegitimate son of Walter and the grandson of Annie Crook.

In 1990, rumours emerged that Walter Sickert himself was the murderer, a hypothesis tested by the American novelist Patricia Cornwell, who published her findings in 2002. Using highly sophisticated DNA tests, Cornwell maintained that a letter apparently sent by the Ripper to a London newspaper matched the notepaper Sickert used at the time of the killings; she argued that a defect in Sickert's penis had made him impotent, a characteristic he shared with many serial killers; and that he had left clues about the murders in several of his paintings.

Her critics seemed to resent her wealth. Having amassed a fortune of about £100 million from her novels, she was able to spend £2 million buying more than thirty Sickert paintings, some of his letters and even his writing desk. Naturally, she tells her story well. Her research seems impressive, until, that is, she touches a subject that has been investigated more deeply before: music hall, for instance. Gatti's under the Arches was one of the most vulgar halls in London, she says; Katie Lawrence exposed more flesh than was deemed decent; girl singers as young as 8 imitated sexual awareness that invited paedophiliac excitement: all wrong. Since then, a new biography of Sickert accuses Cornwell of using selective facts and poor scholarship to support her case. According to the writer, Matthew Sturgis, Sickert was, in any case, abroad when the murders took place.

Forever keen on a meaty crime, Londoners were equally enthralled by the trial of a quack doctor who married, then murdered, a minor music-hall entertainer, Belle Elmore.

The daughter of a Polish grocer, Belle was still in her teens when she decided she wanted to be an opera singer. She took singing lessons in New York

> BELLE ELMORE (Kunigunde Mackamotzki)
> **Born** c. 1871
> **Married** Peter Hawley Harvey Crippen,
> Jersey City, NJ, 1 September 1892
> (b. Coldwater, Michigan, 1862;
> hanged Pentonville prison, London,
> 23 November 1910)
> **Died** north London, 1 February 1910

and, in 1892, when she was 19, she met Hawley Crippen, who was running a homeopathic surgery in Brooklyn. He had wanted to become a family doctor and had studied at the University of Michigan and the Homeopathic College in Cleveland. He met and married an Irish nurse who bore him a son before she died of apoplexy. He deposited the boy with his grandparents and moved to New York.

Belle and Crippen married two months after they met, but problems lay ahead. Crippen's business began to falter and Belle learned she could not have children. In 1894, Crippen turned to quackery while Belle helped out as his cashier. Here, he fared better, moving to Philadelphia and then to Toronto, but leaving Belle behind. She started taking singing lessons again and, after Crippen's new employers, Munyon's Homeopathic Remedies, asked him to open a branch in London, the couple arrived in Britain in 1897.

By then, Belle had decided to abandon opera for vaudeville, a move Crippen opposed. Frictions arose with Belle accusing him of trying to sabotage her career. Their marriage started to cool. Billed as Cora Motzki and partnered by an Italian tenor, Belle made her music-hall debut in a mini-operetta, *The Unknown Quantity*. She was not a success. Her plump figure led to her being dubbed the Brooklyn Matzos Ball. At the end of a week, her contract was not renewed. In 1899, Crippen was recalled to Philadelphia, shown a copy of a playbill which named him as Belle's business manager and was sacked. By the time he returned to London, Belle had started seeing a former boxer, Bruce Miller. She told Crippen she did not love him any more and intended to go on seeing Miller.

Crippen started working for a rival of Munyon's, the Sovereign Remedy Company, which collapsed after eight months; then he tried marketing a nerve tonic, but it did not sell; in despair, he put up a notice outside his flat reading: Belle Elmore, miniature painter. The work was farmed out to others.

Towards the end of 1901, Crippen became 'consulting physician' for another quack outfit, the Drouet Institute for the Deaf. Full details of the racket emerged during hearings of the Commons Select Committee on Patent Medicines. But, before that, a doctor testified at an inquest into the death of a locksmith that inflammation the man had been suffering from was probably exacerbated by plasters manufactured by Drouet, as they contained a powerful

Belle Elmore, the Brooklyn Matzas
Ball, mercilessly mutilated. *(The
Mander and Mitchenson Theatre
Collection)*

irritant. One of Drouet's employees was a shorthand typist, Ethel le Neve, the daughter of a drunken railway clerk.

Belle was still getting music-hall work and came to know many of the leading female entertainers of the day through the Music Hall Ladies' Guild, whose President was Marie Lloyd. Belle became its treasurer. Crippen began an affair with le Neve and told her he would marry her as Belle was about to leave him for Miller. In the event, Miller returned to his wife in Chicago in 1904. By then, Crippen had bought Drouet's, running it as the Aural Remedies Company. Ethel, who was keeping his books, could see he was heading for bankruptcy. At the same time, Belle was becoming more and more extravagant. Both the marriage and the business deteriorated until February 1910 when the Music Hall Ladies' Guild received a note, seemingly from Belle, saying she was resigning as she had to go to America at short notice. The Guild's officers were perplexed; the letter seemed to be a forgery; Elmore, for instance, was spelt with two 'l's.

In February, Crippen attended a dinner of the Music Hall Railway Association accompanied by le Neve, who was wearing Belle's coat and some of her jewellery. In March, *The Era* printed a short paragraph saying that Belle had died in California. The Guild's office started making enquiries, all of which heightened their suspicions. At the start of July, Lil Hawthorne's husband, John Nash, a theatre manager, went to see Crippen at his home in Finsbury Park, where le Neve was now also living. Crippen admitted he had lied. He said that he and Belle had quarrelled and that she had left him. Ethel said they were both going to America to try to find the man who had sent the cable.

That same day, Crippen and le Neve went to see the wigmaker, Willie Clarkson, saying they wanted to play a trick on some friends. Ethel was to be dressed as a boy and, in that guise, she and Crippen set off for Quebec on board the SS *Montrose* as Mr and Master Robinson. The following day, some human flesh and hair were found under the floor of the coal cellar of the house in Finsbury Park. A medical examination showed that the remains were those of a stout woman who bleached her hair and who had undergone a stomach operation. Traces of hyoscine, a poison which Crippen had bought earlier that year, were found in various organs.

For a few weeks in the summer of 1910, music halls resounded to a topical song:

> Inspector Dew is waiting, Miss le Neve.
> Inspector Dew is waiting, Miss le Neve,
> But Miss le Neve is sitting
> On the knee of Dr Crippen
> Boarded on the *Montrose*
> Dressed in boy's clothes.
> Oh! Miss le Neve!

But that was nothing to an execrable musical comedy, *Belle or The Ballad of Doctor Crippen*, which opened at the Strand Theatre in 1961. Reviewed by the *Daily Express* as 'a practically unsalvageable mess' and by the *Daily Mail* as 'a sick joke with music', the tastelessness of its songs was exemplified by the lovesick le Neve warbling 'Will I ever hear him call me Ethel?' *Belle* closed after six weeks.

A hundred and fifty miles off the Irish coast, the captain of the *Montrose* sent a wireless message to Scotland Yard saying he believed Crippen and le Neve were on board, the first time the wireless had been used to intercept a suspected criminal. A Scotland Yard inspector, Walter Dew, who had been put in charge of the case, set off in pursuit and, off the coast of Quebec, he arrested Crippen.

At the Old Bailey, in November 1910, le Neve was acquitted of being an accessory to murder. Crippen's defence was that there was no proof that the remains in the cellar were those of a woman, let alone his wife. But, if they were not the remains of his wife, whose were they? Crippen also argued that he had bought the hyoscine because it was a sexual depressant and both his wife and le Neve were making physical demands of him that he could not meet. (In addition, a television documentary[3] has since claimed that there was evidence that Belle was living in America at the time of the trial and had, in fact, written two letters to the police in London, both of which were kept from the defence.)

Within half an hour, the jury found Crippen guilty and he was hanged at Pentonville Prison.

Walter Dew (represented as Sherlock Holmes) being mocked in the American press for not preventing Crippen's escape. *(Cleveland Plain Dealer)*

CHAPTER 21

THE QUICKNESS OF THE HAND

Conjurers sometimes tried to deceive their audiences not only with their tricks. Chung Ling Soo, for example, went to great lengths to prove an Oriental ancestry. Unfortunately, there were too many people who remembered him as Billy Robinson. The last trick of his life, however, contained genuine mystery. He was killed on stage at the Wood Green Empire in north London when something went wrong.

CHUNG LING SOO (William Elsworth Robinson)
Born New York City, 2 April 1861
Married Olive Path
Sons, Elsworth and Hector
Daughter, Mary (married George Nye)
Died Wood Green, north London, 24 March 1918
Left £5,832

Chung Ling Soo, who was billed when young as 'Robinson, the man of mystery', toured the eastern states of America as a solo act from 1880 to 1887. Then he met Olive Path, a soubrette with a company in Massachusetts. They worked together on an act based on 'Black Art', magical parlance for a black stage setting in which lights are directed out towards an audience, dazzling them so much that they believe they can see tables floating about, heads severed from bodies, ghosts appearing and disappearing, and so on. Working then as Achmed Ben Ali, Robinson was signed up by a showman, Harry Kellar, who persuaded him to introduce other illusions he had devised, such as the spinning cylinder of silk, which, as it slowed down, revealed itself to be a beautiful girl.

In 1899, Robinson and Olive became a double act. At first, work was hard to find, but, at the Folies Bergère in Paris, Robinson reinvented himself once again, this time, as a Chinese equilibrist, Hop Sing Loo; however, by the time he reached the Alhambra in London in 1900, he was Chung Ling Soo. He and Olive, who had been transformed into Suee Seen, had a 20-minute spot at each house. They stayed at the Alhambra for three months and were a big success, but it was the London Hippodrome that became Chung's showplace in London. He returned there every year. After a three-month booking in 1904, he produced a new act and went on tour with it. Everything went well until the start of the following year when another company appeared in London, 'The Ching Ling Foo troupe of Oriental magicians, contortionists, equilibrists, jugglers, acrobats and vocalists', all appearing at the Empire, a hundred yards from the Hippodrome. Ching was real, the great Chinese magician of the American theatre. He was born in a suburb of Beijing and had been appointed Conjurer to the Empress of China.

Music-hall fans were confused. Within days, Ching offered to pay Chung £1,000 if he could perform ten of Ching's new tricks. A Sunday newspaper invited the couple to fight it out and a

Chung Ling Soo, Chinese Magician Extraordinary. *(Tony Barker)*

time and date were set. Chung and Suee Seen arrived in a red Daimler, but there was no sign of Ching. He later said he would appear only if Chung could prove he was Chinese. The press loved it, asking 'Did Foo fool Soo? And can Soo sue Foo?'

Robinson continued trying to explain his Oriental lineage. He used to say his father was a Scottish missionary, called Campbell, who married a native girl in Canton. He was given the name, Chung Ling Soo, which meant extra good luck, because, after five girls, he was the first boy to be born in the family. He went to great trouble to try to convince his followers that he was Chinese: 'Always Chung Ling Soo travelled with a Chinaman and his wife, who acted as interpreters . . . The Chinaman and his wife would listen to the question put by the Westerner and then turn to Chung Ling Soo and put it to him in the native language. Chung would nod and smile and indicate that he understood.'[1]

At the start of 1909, Robinson's company enjoyed a highly successful tour of Australia and New Zealand. He stopped in Egypt on his way back to Britain and, in 1911, produced a new trick, A Dream of Wealth. Milk, which was poured into a casket, turned into flurries of silver, then a continuous shower of five-pound notes and finally an enormous five-pound note, which covered the backdrop. Other tricks involved a drum which yielded fish bowls, flowers, baskets and Chinese lanterns; an iron pot suspended high above the stage, from which ducks, doves, rabbits and a woman were produced; as well as potted plants which grew dozens of carnations.

There was also an old established gun trick, in which bullets marked by members of the audience were loaded into rifles. A squad of volunteers then fired them at Robinson, who caught the bullets on a china plate. The bullets were then returned to the audience to be reidentified and the plate was given to someone as a memento. At the Wood Green Empire one night in 1918, Robinson called for the curtain to be brought down after the rifles had been fired. He had been hit by a bullet, which penetrated his right lung.

There were many rumours. Had Robinson committed suicide? He was not in financial trouble. Did Olive have him killed? There was no reason why she should. At the inquest, it was decided that the trick had failed. Billy Robinson had suffered death by misadventure.

Considered by many to have been Britain's greatest illusionist, David Devant was the obvious choice to be the first President of the Magic Circle. Born David Wighton, the son of a Scottish landscape painter, he acquired his new name from a visit to an art gallery. He was impressed by a biblical painting entitled *David Devant Goliath* and, misunderstanding the meaning of the French word 'devant' ('in front of'), he decided that one day David Devant would make a good stage name.

As a youngster, Devant worked successively as a page boy, a telephone operator and a gas fitter, all the time buying tricks and watching other conjurors. At the outset, he presented his act at parties, making his music-hall debut at the Albert Palace near Battersea Park.

DAVID DEVANT (David Wighton)
Born Highgate, London, 22 February 1868
Married Annie Marion Goslin
(professionally known as Marion
Melville), Steyning, Sussex, 1904
Daughter, Bedelia, known as Vida
Died in Wandsworth, south-west London,
13 October 1941

One of his earliest illusions was the Vanishing Lady trick, which required the participation of two women of identical looks. After a long search, he found the right couple, who agreed to appear with him. The trick involved Devant covering one of the women with a cloth and then whisking it away to show that she had disappeared. When Devant

David Devant, a sense of wonder. *(Tony Barker)*

asked where she had gone, the second woman stood up in the gallery and made herself known. To make the trick work, only one woman could be seen entering and leaving the theatre while the other had to be smuggled in. The arrangement worked until the woman on stage refused to disappear while the other still called out from the gallery. The pair had quarrelled about who had eaten most of a box of chocolates sent to them by an admirer. After that, Devant used only one woman, but never explained how the trick continued to work.

In 1891, Devant made his first appearances at the London Pavilion and the Oxford, but was sacked from the Oxford after he dropped a rabbit he was about to make disappear. It meant the loss of twenty-four weeks' work. His agent, Hugh J. Didcott, pleaded with the manager of the Oxford to let him stay, but to no avail. The manager had been looking for an excuse to dismiss Devant as he had booked another conjurer and did not want two on the same bill.

In 1893, John Maskelyne, an illusionist who had been presenting shows with George Cooke at the Egyptian Hall in Piccadilly for the previous ten years, saw Devant's turn at the Trocadero. Devant was presenting one of his most successful tricks, 'Vice Versa', inspired by F. Anstey's novel of the same name. In Anstey's book, a man is changed into a boy and back again. Devant's trick changed a man into a woman. Maskelyne was so impressed that he asked Devant to join his company at the Egyptian Hall. In time, Devant was made a managing partner of the firm Maskelyne and Devant, at St George's Hall in Langham Place.

In 1912, Devant was chosen to represent magicians at the first Royal Command Performance. Appearing with his young daughter, Vida, and Maskelyne's grandson, Jasper, he borrowed a bowler hat from a member of the audience and began producing eggs from it. The eggs were passed to Vida and then to Jasper, but, when Devant produced them faster and faster, Jasper started dropping them on the stage, proving, of course, that they were real. The floor around him quickly became covered with yolks and egg white.

John Fisher, of the Magic Circle, believes there was more to Devant than sheer showmanship:

His success as a public figure was due in no small part to something about the man. From the moment he made his entrance on stage, audiences responded to the quiet command and the impish twinkle in the eye of this lovable uncle. Even when presenting his larger illusions, he was able to project the intimacy of the drawing-room in the largest of theatres. He allowed nothing unnecessarily gaudy or shoddy on his stage. The result was that no magician ever exerted a greater sense of wonder.[2]

In 1913, a testimonial evening was held in Devant's honour. He was presented with a service of plate and an address printed and signed by most of the outstanding conjurers in Britain, as well as many from overseas. Maskelyne was apparently jealous of the accolade paid to Devant and in 1915 their partnership was dissolved.

Appearing in Manchester in 1919, Devant was again joined on stage by a small boy, whom he asked to copy everything he did. Devant could not understand why the child was shaking the handkerchief he had been given until he looked down at his own hand shaking. He was suffering the first stages of nervous palsy. There was no worse fate a magician could suffer. After 1920, he could no longer perform on stage and he ended his days in the Royal Hospital for Incurables at Putney in south-west London.

The Great Lafayette, an eccentric and unsociable man, who became the highest paid conjurer of his day, is remembered, if at all, for the manner of his death, rather than the achievements of his life. He perished in a fire at the Edinburgh Empire, together with eight other people and a number of animals.

Lafayette moved to New York from his native Germany when he was just 12. As a young man, he dreamed up a sharp-shooting act with a bow and arrows and, billed as the Crackshot with the Bow, launched himself on the vaudeville stage. In 1892, he travelled to London to present the act at the Alhambra. He was not a success and returned to America, where he augmented the act with quick-change impersonations and conjuring and resolved to make his stage appearances as spectacular as possible.

> THE GREAT LAFAYETTE (Siegmund Ignatius Neuberger)
> **Born** Munich, 25 February 1871 (this is the date of birth given on Lafayette's marble tablet at Piershill cemetery, Edinburgh)
> **Died** Edinburgh, 9 May 1911

So, booked for the London Hippodrome in 1900, he arrived on stage by car, performed some quick impersonations, including those of the composer John Philip Sousa, and Ching Ling Foo, and produced from under a cloth a small child; his beloved dog, Beauty; a turkey; and twenty-four pigeons in a bowl. He then rolled two thin pieces of cardboard into tubes, placed one over the child and made it move from one tube to the other.

This time he was acclaimed and, from then on, his act became more and more outlandish. He was in great demand, although his show could be performed only at theatres with large stages. Lafayette invented a pigeon-catching trick which is still performed today. It involved him sweeping a net attached to a pole over the heads of the audience and catching pigeons which were invisible until the moment they landed in the net.

His most famous illusion was the Lion's Bride. In it, a woman is thrown into a lion's cage. Lafayette dresses in her clothes to trick the lion into thinking he is the woman so that he can save her life. Soldiers fling Lafayette into the cage and the lion leaps at him. Then, it becomes apparent that the lion is, in fact, a man dressed in a lion's skin. The man removes the skin: he is, of course, none other than Lafayette himself.

Lafayette, the Lion's Bride. *(Tony Barker)*

Lafayette was a perfectionist. He designed the costumes for his shows, supervised the layout of the programmes and forbade any theatre staff, even stage hands, from going anywhere near the stage when he was performing. Outspoken, anti-social and intolerant, he had few friends. In fact, he reckoned he had eight. At his home in Tavistock Square in central London, a typewritten note was pinned behind the front door: 'These are my friends: [followed by a list of eight names]. They are to be admitted at all times whether I am at home or not. My house is their house and everything in it, except my dog.'[3]

Each guest room was equipped with pyjamas, hairbrushes, new toothbrushes, tooth powder and paste, shaving tackle and scented bath lotion. Any of the eight who stayed were tended by an all-black staff. Lafayette's dog, a present from Houdini, was well looked after too. It had its own bathroom and was served only the very best food. Lafayette told a number of people that, when Beauty died, he would die shortly afterwards. The dog, in fact, died of epilepsy when Lafayette was appearing at the Edinburgh Empire. Greatly distraught, he went to enormous difficulties to arrange for the animal to be buried in a cemetery. Officials at Piershill cemetery agreed only after he had promised that his own remains would be interred there too, flown there from wherever in the world he happened to be.

Three days after Beauty had been buried in an oak coffin with silver handles under a marble slab, the fire broke out at the Empire during the second house performance of the Lion's Bride. The stage curtain was lowered and one of Lafayette's musicians played the National Anthem to try to stop a stampede by the audience. All 3,000 members of the audience left the building safely, but backstage, three musicians, two stage hands, two midgets and a man who appeared as Lafayette's double all died, as well as the lion and several dogs and horses. Three days later, Lafayette's remains were found among the debris, identifiable only by rings on his fingers. Even then, some believed that it was a publicity stunt – that he had arranged the whole affair so that he could reappear a month later, walking round the battlements of Edinburgh Castle, dressed in purple robes. But Lafayette had died and, in a service conducted by a Presbyterian clergyman, his ashes were placed between Beauty's paws.

CHAPTER 22

I CAN SEE YOUR LIPS MOVE

Ventriloquism was revolutionised by Fred Russell, who became the first vent to use only one dummy in his act: Coster Joe. Previously, ventriloquists had worked with rows of dolls. By concentrating on just one, Russell was able to make more of the interplay between him and Joe and, by treating Joe as the more important figure, he was able to introduce more comedy into the act. Thereafter, every vent copied Russell's style and he became known as the father of modern ventriloquism.

> FRED RUSSELL (Thomas Frederick Parnell)
> **Born** Poplar, east London, 29 September 1862
> **Married** Lilian —— (The Water Rats' Queen Ratling in 1929)
>   Five sons, Frederick Russell (professionally known as Russ Carr), ventriloquist and later variety agent (1889?–1973)
>   Valentine Charles (professionally known as Val Parnell), Managing Director of Moss Empires (1894–1972)
>   Archibald (Archie), general manager of the Variety Theatres Controlling Company and later an agent; married Violet Little (professionally known as Dolly Denton), 29 September 1910; d. 27 February 1942
>   Wallace, manager of the Australian Tivoli Circuit of Theatres; shot himself dead, 20 May 1954
>   and Arthur, booking manager for Walter de Frece and general manager of the Newsome Theatres
> **Died** Wembley, Middlesex, 14 October 1957

Russell, the son of a shipwright, taught himself ventriloquism as a boy. When he left school, he worked first as a journalist, although, at evening concerts, he performed his vent act, sometimes appearing at the Crystal Palace, using the then customary row of dummies. In 1896, he was one of the entertainers at a dinner attended by Charles Morton, who offered him an engagement at £10 a week to appear at the Palace Theatre. Russell, until then known by his real name Thomas Parnell, accepted, adopted the surname of his local MP, Charles (later Lord) Russell, and made his debut at the Palace in April 1896.

During the next two years, Russell tried to run parallel careers as both journalist and ventriloquist, but, in the end, he gave up the former, from then on confining his writing to the routines he devised for himself and Coster Joe. He travelled the world with Joe and achieved respect at home for the work he contributed for the good of the music-hall profession. For more than fifty years, he was a member of the Water Rats; he was also one of the founders of the Variety Artistes' Federation; and he helped to set up its paper, *The Performer*.

As a teenager, Arthur Prince was inspired by the performances of Fred Russell. After seeing one of Russell's shows, Prince met him and was given some advice. Russell also introduced

Fred Russell, who revolutionised ventriloquism. *(Tony Barker)*

ARTHUR PRINCE (Arthur John Prince)
Born London, 17 November 1880
Married (1) Amelia Bottomley (professionally known
    as Ida Rene, whose bill matter was 'the
    charming singer of charming songs') Dewsbury,
    Yorkshire, 1900
(2) Julie Arthur-Prince, Marylebone, London,
    9 August 1944 (she had changed her name
    from Julie Milburn by deed poll) (d. 14
    September 1949)
Died Marylebone, London, 14 April 1948

Prince to a doll maker, who made him a boy figure, first known as Jim James, but later as Sailor Jim, a cheeky cockney.

Details of the early career of Arthur Prince are difficult to disentangle, but it is known that he began to obtain provincial bookings, the first at the Royal Empire, Leicester, in 1901. The following year, he made his London debut. His skill was quickly recognised and he was soon appearing at every important music hall in London and the provinces and making tours of America and Australia. Prince's signature tune was 'A Life on the Ocean Wave'. As the curtain rose, the deck of HMS *Seaworthy* was to be seen, with Jim, a cabin boy, on his own. Soon, the first mate entered and warned Jim that he was in trouble with the admiral. Prince then appeared as the admiral and began his repartee with Jim. He was, incidentally, the first ventriloquist to drink a glass of beer as his dummy continued talking.

Prince took good care of his voice. He recommended the would-be ventriloquist to undertake deep-breathing exercises at an open window every morning, as well as an elaborate routine of oral hygiene, including a thorough cleaning of the nostrils and massaging the throat and jaws.

Prince made his last appearance at the Finsbury Park Empire in north London in February 1948. On his death, he received warm tributes from his peers. The ventriloquist A.C. Astor wrote: 'London audiences during the first three decades of this century particularly loved him and awaited with quickened interest that moment when he emptied his glass of beer, while his sailor boy, Jim, commented acidly on being overlooked in the dispensing of this refresher, a beautifully timed trick that will remain Arthur Prince's trade mark.'[1]

Arthur Prince and his Sailor Boy, Jim. (*Richard Anthony Baker*)

Tommy Mitchell, who began his working life at a mill, had a naturally good singing voice. After he made his first public appearance as a boy soprano, he joined a band as a cornet player. While still a boy, he amused his friends by routines he devised involving two Chinese puppets. This led to him practising his skills as a ventriloquist on the sands at Morecambe.

After many years working in northern England, Coram (as he now called himself) made his London debut in 1905 with his dummy, Jerry Fisher. At the start of the act, Jerry was seen on his own. Then, he drove on stage in a car. Throughout the act, Coram remained in the car, operating Jerry's movements remotely and conducting a duologue between them. At the end, he drove off-stage, leaving Jerry to receive the applause.

> CORAM (Thomas Mitchell)
> **Born** Halifax, west Yorkshire, 1882/3 (?)
> **Married** Patricia —— (d. 17 March 1949)
>   One daughter
>   Two sons, Ralph and William (professionally known
>   as Billy Whittaker, who married ——
>   (professionally known as Mimi Law; d. Isle of
>   Wight, November 1994; during the 1950s, Billy
>   Whittaker and Mimi Law toured in the revue,
>   Hi-Diddle-Diddle; they also appeared regularly in
>   pantomime)
> **Died** London, 25 March 1937

Coram continually improved Jerry's technology, eventually enabling him to walk, smoke, cry, wink and even spit. In time, the act adopted a military theme with Jerry cast as Private Fisher, who had his own song:

I'm Jerry Fisher,
One of the old militia.
I'm Jerry Fisher in the morning,
One of the rank and file.
No wonder the ladies smile,
But I'm every inch a soldier.

Coram, with Jerry Fisher, who walked, smoked, cried, winked and spat. *(Richard Anthony Baker)*

CHAPTER 23

BURNT CORK

lack-faced minstrel shows, now discredited by the sensitive elite, ran separately from music hall, although individual minstrels, such as Eugene Stratton and G.H. Elliott, became big stars in Britain, while Al Jolson achieved fame around the world.

It is impossible to identify exactly when white men first daubed their faces with burnt cork to impersonate black men. However, a crucial character in the history of minstrelsy was a young light comedian, T.D. (Thomas Dartmouth) Rice, who could tell a story, sing and dance a hornpipe. One account relates how, in 1828, he was employed at a theatre at Cincinatti in Ohio and, while strolling through the streets one day, he heard a black man singing 'Jump Jim Crow':

> Come listen, all you girls and boys, I's just from Tuckyhoe.
> I'm going to sing a little song. My name's Jim Crow.
> Wheel about and turn about and do just so.
> Every time I wheel about and jump Jim Crow.

It struck Tom Rice that he could build an act based on Jim Crow and he launched his impersonation at Pittsburgh later that year, wearing a wild black wig, an old straw hat, a dilapidated coat and a pair of trousers covered in patches. The success of Jim Crow was instantaneous and, as Rice began to travel with the act, he added verses that told of local events and items in the news.

From Pittsburg, Rice went to Philadelphia, Boston, New York and then to London, where he made his first appearance at the Surrey Theatre in 1836. 'Jump Jim Crow' quickly became the rage with men wearing Jim Crow hats and smoking Jim Crow pipes. Rice introduced burlesques, playing the same character. One of them was 'The Black God of Love': 'The whole piece depended almost entirely upon the inimitable acting of T.D. Rice as the enamoured negro . . . There was something inexpressibly comic in his delineation of the Black God and, though his audience at first did not appear to understand him, he soon secured their undivided attention.'[1]

Rice appeared in London three times in all and enjoyed enormous popularity in America until 1858, when he was stricken with paralysis. Two years later, comparatively poor, he died in New York at the age of 53. His success inspired a circus performer, Dan Emmett, to form the first minstrel troupe, the Virginia Minstrels, who comprised only four men: Emmett himself and Bill Whitlock, both playing banjo; Frank Brower on bones (a pair of spoons or rib bones that rattled); and Dick Pelham, a dancer, who also played the tambourine. After making their debut at the Bowery Amphitheatre in New York in 1843, they came to Britain, appearing first in

Liverpool, then in Manchester and finally at the Adelphi Theatre, London, where they had a month's engagement earning a phenomenal £100 (by today's standards £5,500) a week: 'Dressed in plantation costume, they gave an original entertainment that was distinctly odd and amusing. The dancing was good and the combination on the whole a capital one.'[2]

Emmett joined Bryant's Minstrels in 1859 and wrote '(I wish I was in) Dixie', which became the battle hymn of the Confederate army in the American Civil War. Emmett, in fact, condoned slavery, as did the man who promoted the craze for minstrel shows, Phineas T. Barnum. His black valet, whom he suspected of stealing some valuables, was given fifty lashes and was sold at auction.

After the Virginia Minstrels, who disbanded after their British tour, there came the Christy Minstrels, who set the pattern of minstrelsy for the following century. Edwin Christy, a talented dancer, singer and burlesque performer, divided his show into three sections: in the first, the troupe sat in a semicircle with the host (or interlocutor) at the centre and Mr Bones and Mr Tambo at either end (the end men); in the second, known as the olio, there were variety acts and miscellaneous songs; and in the third, a one-act musical was staged, usually making fun of a current novel or play. From 1847 to 1854, Christy's Minstrel Hall rivalled Barnum's museum in New York as the city's main attraction. The original Christy Minstrels disbanded in 1854. Eight years later, Edwin Christy, troubled by the effects the Civil War might have on his investments, killed himself by jumping out of a window.

The original Christy Minstrels never appeared in Britain, but another troupe, using the same name and including four of the original members, came to London in 1857. In the middle of their run, one of the troupe's finest comedians, Earl Pierce, died at the age of 36. An American comedian heard of their difficulties, booked himself a passage to Britain, sought them out and was immediately given a contract.

This was George Washington Moore, who became a leader of black-faced minstrelsy in Britain. He was born in New York, the son of an Army bandsman. He ran away from home to join a circus and became so adept with its ponies that everyone called him 'Pony', a nickname which stuck for the rest of his long life. After three years with the Christy Minstrels, he joined

Two rival minstrel troupes in Britain led to the formation of Francis Day and Hunter, the main publishers of music-hall songs. The Mohawk Minstrels, run by two brothers, William and James Francis, former employees of the music publishers Chappell, appeared at Berner's Hall, later the Islington Palace. The Manhattan Minstrels, seen at suburban halls and occasionally in London itself, were led by Harry Hunter, who wrote many of the troupe's songs, jokes and sketches. In 1874, Hunter joined the Mohawks. As their popularity grew, they moved to another Islington hall that seated about 3,000 people and formed the company that gave them a publishing outlet for all the songs made famous by the Mohawks. David Day, who worked for another publishing firm, Hopwood and Crew, was appointed to run what was first W. and J. Francis and Day, then Francis Brothers and Day and finally Francis Day and Hunter.

forces with Frederick Burgess to form the Moore and Burgess Minstrels, whose rule at St James's Hall in Piccadilly stretched from 1862 to 1904.

In 1881, Moore helped to write the sentimental song 'The Blind Boy', which G.H. Chirgwin sang in a high falsetto. For the next forty years, wherever George appeared, he was not allowed to leave the stage until he had sung 'The Blind Boy':

GEORGE WASHINGTON MOORE
Born New York, 1820
Married —— Mynott
  Three daughters: one, Annie Matilda Rosina, married
    Eugene Augustus Ruhlmann (professionally known as
    Eugene Stratton); one married the middleweight boxer
    Charlie Mitchell (1861–1918), whom Moore managed;
    the other, Martha Isabella, married Frederick Mortimer
    Vokes (professionally known as Fred Vokes), central
    London, 25 March 1873
Died north London, 1 October 1909
Left £10,422

> I am but a poor blind boy. Still my heart is full of joy,
> Tho' I never saw the light or the flowers they call so bright.
> I can hear the sweet bird sing and the wild bee on the wing,
> Bird and bee and summer wind, sing to me because I'm blind.
> They love me, yes, they love me and to me they are so kind.
> They love me, yes, they love me because I am blind.

At the age of 6, George appeared with members of his family as a minstrel troupe. He made his solo debut in about 1868 at a small hall in Margate. He was hired to sing the tear-jerking ballad 'Come Home, Father' to accompany one of a series of tableaux vivants depicting a temperance theme. The engagement, originally intended to last only a week, was extended for the whole summer. His London debut followed nine years later at the Oxford. He proved a great success, moving up the bill after only two days and being allowed to extend his act from about 10 minutes to 45.

By now, George had practically perfected the solo act that he was to perform for the rest of his career. His appearance was purposefully odd. He wore a cloak,

G.H. CHIRGWIN (George Chirgwin)
Born Seven Dials, London, 13 December 1854
Married (1) Clara Ann Grayston, Liverpool, 3 June
    1878 (d. London, 13 July 1892, aged 37)
  One daughter, Clara (b. London 1880)
(2) Rose Rendle, Brighton, 17 February 1893
    (d. Shepperton, Middlesex, 16 June 1952,
    aged 76)
  Four sons, George Edward, John Lundy (d. 1898),
    Thomas (d. 1898) and James
  Two daughters, Marguerite Norah, and Josie
    Caroline (d. 1903)
Died Streatham, south London, 14 November 1922

covering a jersey and tights, and a tall hat to exaggerate his height (nearly 5ft 11in) (180cm). He appeared in black face, but with a large white triangle painted over one eye. A frequently told anecdote explained the origin of his make-up. During an open-air fête near Gloucester, he rubbed some burnt cork from his face while trying to remove a particle of dust from his eye. The audience found it funny – and he resolved to retain the white eye as part of his appearance. From 1877, he was billed as the White-Eyed Kaffir.

A reviewer, writing in 1909, said George was like no one else on the music-hall stage; he talked to his audience as if he were addressing a select circle of old chums at his club; in the

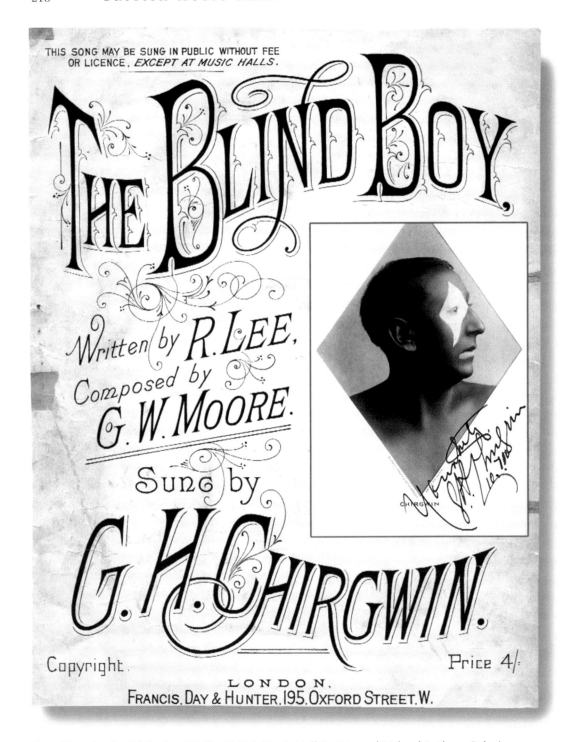

G.H. Chirgwin, the White-Eyed Kaffir. *(British Music Hall Society and Richard Anthony Baker)*

intervals between dashes of smart repartee, George sang a snatch of a topical song of his own making; many of his topical verses dealt with news that was still being shouted by the newsboys; George was nothing if not up to date.

He also became a popular figure in pantomime, although he often changed his lines to suit himself. Appearing in *Aladdin*, he once said 'Hi, cocky, 'alf a mo, hand up that there lamp, dya 'ear me? Pip pip, come on out and 'ave one. 'Urry up, cocky. What? You won't? All right, well stay there and die of hunger and thirst. I'm going to have a couple.'

In 1895, G.H. Chirgwin bought Burgh Island, a 26-acre tidal island 200 yards off the coast of South Devon, and built a nine-bedroom timber hotel there. For a time, it was called Chirgwin's Island. Whit Cunliffe, Gus Elen and others stayed there. Chirgwin's widow, Rose, sold it in 1927 and it was replaced by a building resembling an art deco cruise liner stranded on dry land. Its guests have included Noel Coward, Agatha Christie and Amy Johnson. One of the suites is named after Chirgwin. He continued to perform until 1919 when ill health forced him to retire.

Brown, Newland and le Clerq were a black-faced act best known for their sketch, 'Black Justice', in which Ben Brown played a judge, George le Clerq, a police officer (PC Boozer) and James Newland, a confused barrister. Much of the humour derived from the contrast between the bulky Brown and the short and thin-voiced le Clerq.

In the late 1860s, Brown and Newland worked in the jewellery trade in Birmingham, but they were so enthusiastic about the stage that they resigned and became a pair of black-faced entertainers. After playing minor halls for several months, they were booked to appear at Day's in Birmingham. By their own account, they were so successful that they performed an encore, delaying the ballet that was to follow them. Day was furious and it was many years before they appeared there again.

During the early 1870s, the couple appeared in three halls in London, but were paid so little that they could not afford a brougham to carry them between venues. They returned to the provinces; their earnings gradually grew; and they were eventually able to return to London. Technically, their act, lasting between 20 and 30 minutes, was known as a chair turn, consisting of songs, dances, instrumental performances and stump oratory. In 1877, they joined a party of entertainers bound for Australia. When the company broke up, the two men joined

---

BEN BROWN (Benjamin Brown)
Born Cirencester, Gloucestershire, 23 November 1848
Married Sarah Butts, Birmingham, 1869
   Daughter, Flora (b. Birmingham, 1874)
   Ben also had a daughter by Marie Loftus: Marie Cecilia Loftus (professionally known as Cissie Loftus; b. Glasgow, 22 October 1896; d. New York, 12 July 1943)
Died West Norwood, south London, 16 December 1926

JAMES NEWLAND (James George Spiers)
Born Birmingham, 1848
Married Caroline Margaret Walton, Edinburgh, 23 December 1876 (d. Harold Wood, Essex, 20 January 1939)
Died 20 March 1931

GEORGE LE CLERQ (George Henley)
Born Irish Republic, 1847/8 (?)
Married (1) Annie ——
(2) Georgina Howard (d. 20 April 1937)
   Children Arthur and Cissie
Died Brixton, south London, 16 January 1911
Left £1,885

a minstrel troupe, which came to Britain in 1881. As a sketch act, they were teamed at first with Charles Wallace, but, in 1888/9, he was replaced by le Clerq.

From time to time, the music-hall press gently criticised them for returning to popular sketches year after year. 'Black Justice' dates from about 1885. When it returned to the Middlesex in 1891, a reviewer noted that, although it had 'done good service for the last few years . . . it [possessed] plenty of vitality':[3]

JUDGE.	What case is this?
LAWYER.	Boy charged with stealing bread.
JUDGE.	Transformation for life.
LAWYER.	What life?
JUDGE.	Yes – and you sit down or I'll give him ten years longer.
POLICEMAN.	Come on. Get out of here.
LAWYER.	I'll appeal.
JUDGE.	I'll peal your nose.[4]

Not all humour travels well.

There was nothing particularly original about G.H. Elliott's act as a black-faced entertainer, but his charming, soft voice, his agile soft-shoe dancing and a repertory of tuneful songs ensured him stardom over many years under a billing that would now be deemed completely unacceptable, 'The Chocolate-Coloured Coon'.

> G.H. ELLIOTT (George Henry Elliott)
> **Born** Rochdale, Greater Manchester, 3 November 1883
> **Married** (1) Emilie (Emily) Hayes, Southwark, south London, 3 May 1913 (d. Edinburgh, 17 February 1940)
> Daughter, died in infancy
> Son, George Thomas (b. 1917)
> (2) Florence May Street (known as June), 28 July 1943
> **Died** Brighton, east Sussex, 19/20 November 1962
> **Left** £20,911

George came from Rochdale, where his parents kept a small pub. When he was 3, they moved to the larger Assembly Rooms hotel in Nottingham, but, a year later, they emigrated to America, settling at Newark, New Jersey. Mother and son landed parts in a melodrama at the local theatre. Later, in New York, George was billed as the Wonderful Boy Soprano. While there, he learned the rudiments of his dancing skills. After some touring, the family returned home, settling in Birmingham.

Walter de Frece heard George at a trial performance at the Gaiety Theatre in Birmingham, on the strength of which he gave him a £5 a week contract for fifteen weeks' work starting at the Birmingham Empire:

When I returned to England with my parents, I started to sing coon (black-faced) songs with a white face . . . but very soon afterwards, Tom Barrasford gave me some advice. He said to me: 'George, if I were you, I would stop singing with a white face. I would blacken it . . .' For weeks and weeks, I tried this and that concoction and, in the end, I got a really good make-up. I became a chocolate-coloured coon.[5]

G.H. Elliott, the Chocolate-
Coloured Coon. *(Michael Parker)*

In London, George at first played only very minor halls, but gradually his career improved. In 1901, he enjoyed one of his earliest successes with 'Honeysuckle and the Bee' (1901). At the Hackney Empire, eight years later, he sang for the first time 'I Used to Sigh for the Silvery Moon' (1909), written by Lester Barrett and Herman Darewski. The song stayed with him for the rest of his career.

George met his first wife, Emilie Hayes, when they appeared in pantomime in Liverpool (1911/12), but, towards the end of the First World War, when George was entertaining the troops in France, Belgium and Germany, she developed drink problems. In 1933, George and Gertie Gitana successfully toured with their own show, *George, Gertie and Ted*, the third member of the team being the comedian Ted Ray, then a newcomer. Within a few years, however, Emilie's drinking was making George's life a misery:

> In February 1940, I was appearing in Edinburgh when she arrived at the theatrical digs where I was staying. In the early morning, I woke to find her sitting in a chair in the bedroom, smoking. Without success, I tried to persuade her to come back to bed. She assured me she was quite all right and I fell off to sleep again. When I next awoke, she was lying on the side of the bed and obviously not well. I called the landlady, who came at once, examined her and exclaimed 'Good God, Mr Elliott. The poor soul is dead.'[6]

When it was confirmed that Emilie had died of cirrhosis of the liver as a result of chronic alcoholism, there was considerable publicity. Emilie had had her successes. One reviewer wrote: 'Emilie Hayes, who is winning all hearts at the London Pavilion by her artistic rendering of ballads in character, is engaged for the part of Cinderella at the Wimbledon Theatre. The value of a winsome personality and a charming voice in so delightful a part can scarcely be over-estimated and Miss Hayes possesses both.'[7]

George appeared in three Royal Variety shows: in 1925, in 1948 and in 1958 in an excerpt from Sir Harry Secombe's London Palladium show, *Large as Life*. Elliott, Hetty King and Dick Henderson closed the first half. Secombe wrote:

> All came on to do their party pieces and proved that they could still bring audiences to their feet . . . There was . . . a lot to learn from Hetty, Dick and G.H. Elliott. On the first night, as the curtains came down on the finale, all the cast left the stage as the orchestra played the National Anthem – except for the three old-timers, who stood to attention as the 'Queen' was played. I saw this and felt ashamed and on the second night I joined them. The third night saw the whole company on parade until the orchestra had finished . . . Every Saturday, between the second and third performances, I used to send a bottle of champagne to G.H. Elliott's dressing-room for the three veterans to share . . . G.H. would save the cork for applying his black face make-up, a ritual he kept secret.[8]

Among solo black-faced singers, Eugene Stratton was the most successful. He was lucky enough to have two songs from the pen of Leslie Stuart, music hall's most lyrical composer: 'Little Dolly Daydream' (1897) and the lilting 'Lily of Laguna' (1898). They should have made Stuart a rich man, but, as a result of wild extravagance and a costly campaign against sheet-music pirates, he died a virtual bankrupt and an alcoholic.

As a child, Leslie Stuart learned to play the piano. After his family had moved to Manchester, he became well known for concerts he both gave and staged. Up to 1888, he had

LESLIE STUART (Thomas Augustine Barrett)
Born Stockport, greater Manchester, 15 March 1863 (?)
Married Mary Catherine 'Kitty' Fox, Failsworth, greater
    Manchester, 9 March 1886
  Six children: Mary Catherine ('May') (1886–1956);
    Thomas Leslie (1888–1970); Bernard Vaughan
    (died before adulthood); Marie Roze ('Dolly')
    (1891–1949); Stephen (1894–early 1950s);
    Constance Lola (1896–1988)
Died Richmond, south-west London, 27 March 1928
Left £300

used his own name, T.A. Barrett, but, as the comedian T.W. Barrett became better known, he decided he needed a stage name:

> There was a copy of *The Era* lying on a table and, picking it up, I turned to the back page. There, numerous cards of people on the stage were published, being alphabetically arranged. In the middle of one column I saw the name 'Fanny Leslie' and the name after that was 'Cora Stuart.' I saw the combination of the last names in each case. That is how Thomas Augustine Barrett became Leslie Stuart.[9]

In the mid-1890s, Stuart moved to London and took with him some songs he had written. He was introduced to George Edwardes, whose production of *The Shop Girl* was running at the Gaiety Theatre. Stuart played Edwardes one of his songs, 'Louisiana Lou'. Edwardes liked it so much it was added to *The Shop Girl* for Ellaline Terriss to sing.

Another song he brought down from Manchester has something of a history. Stuart wrote it when he was 17 for an exhibition in Blackpool and then rewrote it for Hayden Coffin to sing at Daly's Theatre. This time, its sarcastic lyric told of lazy soldiers who preferred to stay at home, rather than fight. Again, it had little impact. Third time round, it changed course completely and became the rousing and patriotic 'Soldiers of the Queen':[10]

> It's the Soldiers of the Queen, my lads
> Who've been, my lads, who've seen, my lads
> In the fight for England's glory, lads
> When we have to show them what we mean.
> And when we say we've always won
> And when they ask us how it's done
> We'll proudly point to every one
> Of England's Soldiers of the Queen.

The song and lyric could not have been better timed. Soldiers were being recruited for the Boer War and, by the time celebrations were launched for Queen Victoria's diamond jubilee, it was adopted as both marching song and anthem.

Eugene Stratton was the perfect choice for Stuart's two momentous hits. Although his voice lacked power, he more than compensated for it with his effortless soft-shoe shuffle. One critic likened him to a feather blown hither and thither by Stuart's melodies. The first of the songs was 'Little Dolly Daydream':

> Little Dolly Daydream, pride of Idaho,
> So now you know and when you go,
> You'll see there's something on her mind
> Don't think it's you
> Cos no-one's got to kiss that girl but me.

Leslie Stuart: supreme melodist. *(Richard Anthony Baker)*

Stuart explained how he had got the idea for the song and how quickly he had written it. His young daughter had just started school and was upset at being parted from her mother. One night at dinner, she was particularly quiet. The silence was broken by Stuart's wife saying, 'Come, little dolly daydream, you must find your voice.' Stuart said that, by the time dinner was over, he had mapped out the song in his mind. He set to work on it at eight o'clock that evening and, by four o'clock the next morning, it was complete. At ten o'clock the same morning, he set out for Birmingham to meet Stratton, who declared himself delighted with the song. A year later, he was equally delighted with 'Lily of Laguna':

> She's my lady love.
> She is my dove, my baby love.
> She's no girl for sitting down to dream.
> She's the only queen Laguna knows.
> I know she likes me
> I know she likes me
> Because she says so.
> She is the Lily of Laguna.
> She is my lily and my rose.

Stratton began his working life as a draper's assistant and then as a telegraph messenger, all the time maintaining a private interest in dancing and acrobatics. At the age of 10, he made his stage debut in his home town of Buffalo as one-half of the Two Wesleys, an acrobatic and tumbling act. He later joined a minstrel troupe, which came to Britain in 1880. When the company returned to America, Stratton accepted an offer from G.W. Moore to stay in Britain and join the Moore and Burgess minstrel troupe.

EUGENE STRATTON (Eugene Augustus Ruhlmann)
Born Buffalo, New York State, 8 May 1861
Married Annie Matilda Rosina Moore (daughter of
    George Washington Moore), Marylebone, London,
    15 November 1883 (d. 9 January 1954)
Died Christchurch, Hampshire, 15 September 1918
Left £3,113, mostly to Joe Elvin

Stratton went solo in 1892, making his debut at the Royal, the Trocadero and the Paragon. His lucky break came with the song 'I Lub a Lubbly Girl, I Do', and, in 1896, his partnership with Leslie Stuart began. For some years, they were good friends, but their relationship came to an end on the racecourse. After arguing about the merits of a particular horse, they fell out with each other. Stratton was prepared to forget their difference of opinion, but the obstinate Stuart was not. From then on, they never spoke to each other again.

In the late 1890s, Stuart contributed songs to other writers' shows, but in 1899, he wrote his own musical comedy, *Florodora*, with its hit song, 'Tell me, Pretty Maiden'. The show became the rage of London and New York, running for over 400 performances at the Lyric Theatre in London and for more than 500 performances at the Casino Theater in New York.

Between the turn of the century and 1911, Stuart wrote seven more shows, which, together with *Florodora*, earned him enormous amounts of money. But he spent it unwisely, building himself a luxurious house, furnishing it regardless of cost and generally living well above his means. The star of *Florodora*, Ada Reeve, once spent a week with him. She had a lovely time, she wrote later, but it was a little strenuous having to drink champagne at breakfast-time. Stuart's generosity was legendary. He allowed any friend to have a meal at the Savoy Hotel on his account.

Of course, he should have been earning royalties from his songs for Stratton and others, but he suffered more than any other composer at the hands of pirates. In 1897, some 2,000 pirated copies of 'Soldiers of the Queen' were seized and burnt. In 1903, pirates sold a million

Eugene Stratton, the Dandy-Coloured Coon. *(Richard Anthony Baker)*

copies of the song within a few months, while his publishers sold just 100,000 authorised editions.

Stuart made an impassioned appeal for the law to be strengthened: 'I am an Irishman and a Catholic. I have fought side by side with Parnell. I yield to no man in loyalty to the cause, but I draw the line at martyrdom in this struggling age, when I see my roof in danger of collapse and my bread thrown to thieves and vagabonds.'[11] He called on the Attorney General to crack down on the pirates; he hired detectives to try to find the printers; his efforts cost him hundreds of pounds; and he reckoned his losses amounted to about £20,000 until 1906 when the Copyright Act came into force.

By 1909, Stuart was in deeper financial difficulties. He resorted to professional money-lenders and from 1910 he lived on borrowed money. In 1911, a receiver was appointed. Stuart put his liabilities at £8,573 and his assets at £125. In the end, he went on stage himself to try to raise some money. He looked out of place. When the curtain went up on a small, greying man, seated at a piano, many in the audience did not know who he was. It was not until he started playing his old tunes that they cottoned on and, by the time Stuart had finished his act, they were singing along with him. James Agate saw him in 1923:

Mr Leslie Stuart played the symphonies and accompaniments of his old songs to the singing of Mr Harry Barratt. How good these old melodies were in their day and how much better than the negroid cacophony of the present! A hush which could almost be felt on the crowded house for *The Lily of Laguna* and *My Little Octoroon*.[12] And then the audience began to hum under its breath for old times' sake. Altogether, this was a very perfect quarter of an hour.[13]

But the money Stuart was earning was a pittance. He wrote no more music. He could not match the ragtime, jazz and syncopated song that had arrived in the First World War and he died a virtually penniless alcoholic.

CHAPTER 24

Your Own, your Very Own . . .

In the early halls, the most prominent men were the chairmen, whose two main jobs were to announce the acts and, more importantly, to temper the worst excesses of his audience. They were, after all, his audience. In the 1860s and 1870s, a music-hall chairman wielded enormous power. He needed a commanding presence and a stentorian voice to be able to quell the rowdy element. To be allowed to sit at the chairman's table was a great honour; to be allowed to buy him a drink – well, you almost fainted with joy. Until 1983, some idea of the chairman's work was given by Leonard Sachs, who presided over the *Good Old Days* on BBC Television with the same sort of grandiloquent alliteration that was favoured by the music-hall proprietor of the 1880s and 1890s, George Belmont. He once described Marie Lloyd as 'tasty, trippy, twiggy, timely, telling, tender, tempting, toothsome, transcendent, trim, tactical, twinkling, tricksy, triumphal and tantalising' and a warning to entertainers who chose risqué material was similarly worded: 'The proprietor will peremptorily punish all performers playing putrid programmes by promptly prohibiting their performance and pocketing all promised pounds and pence.'

A record of how one Liverpool chairman gained the approval of his audience was given by J.H. Booth, who wrote for the *Sporting Times*. At the start of one week's show, this particular chairman asked:

'What did you think of Professor Rumble's monkeys?' Simian screams and observations as to the Professor's past, present and future . . . 'Then, what about the Brothers Boodle, Boxing and Clog Dancing Kings? Boxing! There's not a gent here that couldn't spit 'em to death. And Bella Bellow, the serio-comic queen and world-renowned male impersonator?' Prolonged discussion as to Bella's figure. 'Blimey, she'll never rinse her hands in my dressing-rooms again, I give you my word!' Interruptions and singing of 'Poor Old Cow' by the entire audience. 'And now, seeing that we are in accord, may I ask for your kind sympathy for one who is doing his best under difficult and personally trying circumstances to win your generous approbation and kind word? At fabulous expense, I have employed a new London agent, who is fighting like a bull-terrier with our moneyed rivals and their bribes to secure talent which has never been seen north of Crewe station and which I modestly hope will meet with your approbation and keep the ball a-rolling for the next six nights.'[1]

In London, Harry Fox was the much-loved Chairman of the Mogul Tavern, later the Middlesex music hall, for more than twenty years. His face and voice alone captivated audiences. The former was described as 'of purple hue, thickly veined and emphasised by a big bulbous boko [nose]'; the latter, rich and mellow, was likened to 'unlimited mountain dew'.

At one time, Fox was part of the bill. An advertisement in 1855 described him as 'the Great Rustic', suggesting he was a yokel comedian. Ten years later, he and his wife were black-faced entertainers.

Clearly, Harry Fox knew how to adapt to public whim. Even when his performing days were over and there was a lull in proceedings at the Middlesex, he could fill the pause with a song that reflected on his most prominent feature, 'Jolly Nose'. By the mid-1870s, he was recognised as an authority on the early music hall. He relinquished his full-time post at the Middlesex in 1876 and died later that year at the age of 59.

The Harp at Ramsgate was the only music hall in Britain where the occasional chairman was a member of the aristocracy, the Hon. Hubert

Harry Fox, much-loved Chairman of the Middlesex.
(Richard Anthony Baker)

Duncombe, who was then courting Nellie Leamar, of the Sisters Leamar. Bob Gear ran the Harp and, for many years, all the London stars appeared here, often working for about a quarter of their salary.

Baron Courtney, sporting large diamond cuff links and diamond studs in his dress shirt, his fingers covered with rings, was Chairman of the South London music hall from the mid-1860s to the mid-1890s. In his younger days, he had been President of the Kensington Dramatic Club. According to the agent George Foster, Courtney had several business interests in the City, but regarded his work at the South London as paramount.

Courtney drank constantly. Lined up on his table, there were usually twelve or so glasses, the offerings of admirers. Audiences called him 'Bob' and, if there was a pause between acts, would call on him to sing. He generally gave them Arthur Lloyd's song, 'Take it, Bob' (1873).

NELLIE LEAMAR (Mary Nellie Lewis)
Born 1857 (?)
Married (1) the Hon. Hubert Ernest Valentine
    Duncombe, central London, 12 April
    1883 (divorced 25 October 1892;
    d. 21 October 1918)
    (2) Robert James Spurney, Brighton, 1893
    (d. 1900)
Died 5 July 1938

BARON COURTNEY (Henry Blackwell)
Born c. 1835
Died Southwark, south-east London,
    30 October 1901

The Era once noted:

> The Baron with flowing curly hair and centre diamond stud was the darling of the gallery in the seventies and eighties and the cry of 'Bob!' all over the house was the playful way in which juvenile inhabitants of Walworth and Newington showed their affection. In his announcements, he was always oratorical and was not content with the mere mention of an artist's name. 'That great popular favourite and renowned serio-comic, Miss Nelly Farrell, will appear next' may be taken as a specimen of the Courtney method.[2]

After music halls dispensed with their chairmen, Courtney found work hard to come by. For a while, he was part of a theatre company, but he fell on hard times. About a year before his death, he was in a workhouse, but, when word of his plight reached the music-hall world, he was transferred to the Music Hall Home, where he spent the last nine months of his life. One of his last visitors was Dan Leno, who took a bottle of champagne with him.

Tom Tinsley, the Chairman of the two Gatti music halls in London, gave Harry Lauder his first London engagement. He started his working life as an engineer before becoming a comic singer at Nuneaton in Warwickshire, where he sang sixteen songs a night for 30 shillings (£1.50) a week. Fred Gilbert 'discovered' him and found him work at both the Royal, Holborn, and Harwood's Hall in Hoxton. A sturdy, thick-set man, Tinsley was named the 'Young John Bull' and, at one time, he sang a song of this title, although his most popular song, which he performed as a comic yokel, was 'All Among the Apples and Pears'. At the time of his death, he managed a cinema in the Potteries.

> TOM TINSLEY (Thomas Tinsley)
> **Born** Burslem/Longton, Staffordshire,
>   9 May 1853 (?)
> **Died** Wolstanton, Staffordshire,
>   20 December 1910

At another stage at Gatti's in the Road, the chairman was John Watkins. From 4 a.m. to 8 a.m. each day, he was head porter at Billingsgate fish market. He also worked at a pub he owned in Bishopsgate. Each evening, he arrived at Gatti's promptly and seldom left the theatre before midnight. Of flamboyant appearance, he wore an enormous buttonhole of flowers and a large red silk handkerchief. The ends of his moustache were waxed and stood out by four or five inches. And, if he blew his nose, the hall shook to its foundations.

Jack Knowles was Chairman of the Cambridge. He always sang his opening song from the stage, holding a roll of music, which was never unfolded. Although he had one of the loudest voices to be heard on the halls, he was frequently goaded by his audience, who pretended they could not hear him: 'This sort of baiting only ended when Knowles, shaking with rage, purple in the face, lips forming words, though silently, which were perfectly understood by the audience, at last subsided, beaten, into his Chairman's chair.'[3]

The singer-songwriter John Read, a dark, handsome man, usually seen in public with a gleaming white shirt front and a huge diamond stud, was at one point the Chairman of Collins'. He was a stern disciplinarian ready to deal with the rowdiest audience. 'Less noise, please', he shouted. 'Less noise, be blowed. This ain't a bloomin' church' was one of the politer ripostes.

John Read wrote hundreds of songs. More than 1,000 were published by Charles Sheard alone. His heyday as a singer was in the 1870s. His most famous song was 'Grandmother's Chair' (1879), not to be confused with 'My Grandfather's Clock'. Read's song told the story of a man who was left a chair in his grandmother's will and who was derided by other members of the family until £2,000 was found hidden in it. During his career, Read sang it between 10,000 and 12,000 times.

> How they tittered, how they chaffed,
> How my brother and my sister laughed,
> When they heard the lawyer declare
> Granny had only left to me her old armchair.

JOHN READ
Born *c.* 1839
Married Beatrice Bermond,
    11 November 1857 (?)
Died Edmonton, north London, June
    1920

The last chairman to work in London was Walter Leaver, who sported bushy grey hair and a long beard. In 1906, he left the chair at the Royal Albert in the Canning Town area of east London after forty-three years. *The Era* reported:

John Read, who tried to discipline the audience at Collins. *(Richard Anthony Baker)*

He revels in a mighty uproar. During the daytime, he follows the trade of blacksmith [Mr Leaver was 75]. To him, the sharp, imperative clanging of the sledge-hammer is as sweet music. It seems a curious and violent change – this discarding every evening of the dirt-begrimed smock of Vulcan [the Roman God of fire and metal-working] for the spotless starch and the silken suit of a Thespian president.[4]

Leaver took his place in the hall seated in a finely carved armchair in the centre of the orchestra, facing the auditorium and with his back to the stage. In front of him was an adjustable mirror to watch the artistes. Attached to it was a small clock by which he timed each turn. He began each show himself, singing a song he had written himself, 'The Political Shoemaker'. He made both the chair and mirror himself. As a hobby, Leaver carved pipes out of lumps of coal.

When the Tichborne claimant appeared at the Royal Albert, Leaver announced him as Sir Roger, but he knew different. When they were younger, Orton used to help him weigh out bags of nails.

CHAPTER 25

AGENTS: BULLIES AND DESPOTS

In the 1870s, music-hall entertainers resented the work of agents so deeply that they formed an anti-agency group, quickly renamed the Music Hall Artistes' Protection Society. Their first secretary, Walter Burnot, who liked to be called the comic Poet Laureate, couched his grievances in verse:[1]

> A stands for Agents, who grind down the pros
> B stands for Bullies, who everyone knows
> C's their Commission, uncertain per cent
> D stands for Despot on swindling intent
> E's our Endeavour those agents to beat
> F is our fight against fraud and deceit
> G is the Greed that to feed we refuse
> H is a letter the agents abuse
> I's Indignation at 'farming' and fees
> J is our Joy at abolishing these
> K is the Kindness that pro renders pro
> L is the Littleness all agents show
> M is the Money they take with much fuss
> N is the Nothing the agents give us
> O is the Opulence we make for them
> P is the Poverty we have to stem
> Q stands for Queer 'Quisby' tricks they have done ['doing
>   Quisby' meant 'being idle']
> R the reward their injustice has won
> S our Success that will put them all down
> T for Tyrants at York end of town [a reference to York Road,
>   Battersea, where most agents had their offices]
> U's for the Unity Pros so desire
> V is our Vengeance, both certain and dire
> W the Way we at length have found out
> X the X-press to drive agency out
> Y is the yearning we have to succeed
> Z is the Zany on whom agents feed.

There is only one first-person account of the life of a music-hall agent and that is *The Spice of Life* (1939), the memoirs of George Foster, who represented, among others, Harry Lauder, George Formby senior and Charles Chaplin. By 1939, names added to the list included Evelyn Laye, Ben Lyon and Bebe Daniels, Ray Noble and his orchestra and Wilson, Keppel and Betty.

GEORGE FOSTER
Born Bow, east London, 1864 (?)
Married Phoebe —— 1889 (?)
   Two sons, one, who died aged 3, and Harry,
     who became a partner in Foster's agency
   Two daughters, Lucy and Anne
Died south-west London, 26 July 1946
Left £44,951

But they grew less successful as Lew and Leslie Grade became more powerful.

The son of an East End builder, Foster had been expected to follow his father into the trade, but after he had visited his first music hall (a penny gaff, the Alhambra in Shoreditch) on his tenth birthday, he had other ideas. On leaving school, he worked for six months for a stationer and then began his apprenticeship in his father's building business. After work, he used to visit the Sussex Club, next door to the Pavilion Theatre in the Mile End Road. The club was run as a free-and-easy, its doorkeeper, Joe Lyons, who was to become Britain's best known caterer in years to come.

Foster's father was furious when he found out that he was spending time there and, on learning that his son had ambitions to become a comic singer, he severely thrashed him. All the same, Foster secured his first engagement in working men's clubs in east and north London, usually appearing on a Saturday or Sunday night for a fee of 5 shillings (25p).

As a teenager, George was employed in a charming piece of deceit perpetrated by the comic Fred Albert. Each evening, George rode in Fred's brougham to the three halls Fred was playing. With him, he carried a bouquet which he bought each morning with the 10 shillings (50p) Fred gave him. Once inside the theatre, George would try to position himself near the prettiest woman in the audience and throw the flowers on stage at a given moment. Fred then picked them up, smelt them and threw a kiss towards the woman, a gesture that always earned him an extra round of applause. The job ended when George tried to make each bouquet last three days. In spite of this trickery, the two men remained friends until Fred's death.

As an entertainer, George soon realised he was not going to become a star. For a while, he worked for his father again, but one night, the manager of a pub asked him if he could recommend a comedian for just one performance. This was to be the start of Foster's career as an agent. He opened offices at York Road in 1886.

On Boxing Day 1887, Foster saw Marie Lloyd perform for the first time at Collins'. A few months later, they were introduced to each other and, although Marie was still in her teens, they became engaged to be married: that was until Foster introduced her to the dashing Percy Courtenay in the bar of the Cambridge music hall. Courtenay became Marie's first husband.

GEORGE WARE
Born, Shoreditch, London, 1829 (?)
Married Isabella ——, November 1853 (?)
   Son, George Anthony, music-hall agent, whose
     business failed (married Mary Jane ——, daughter,
     Marie Adams; George Anthony died
     25 August 1908, aged 54, after swallowing oxalic
     acid; evidence given at inquest that he was a
     chronic dipsomaniac; verdict of death by
     misadventure returned)
Died Holborn, London, 30 December 1895
Left £2,259

The incident apparently inspired the A.E. Durandeau song, 'Never Introduce your Donah to a Pal' ('Donah' was slang for 'girlfriend'), which was taken up by Gus Elen, then a rising star.

George Ware was primarily an agent, representing Marie Lloyd during the early years of her fame. He also wrote the ever popular 'The Boy in the Gallery', which Marie sung, even though Nellie Power had bought the rights.

George Ware, singer, songwriter and agent. *(Richard Anthony Baker)*

In his younger days, Ware had been a singer, too; before that, he was a sailor and, for a time, a soldier, who entertained his barrack-room mates with ballads he had written himself. Ware made his first stage appearance in 1845 at Moy's music hall, now the Victoria Palace, but it was not until the late 1850s that he made a name for himself as 'the extraordinary three-voiced singer' on account of his ability to sing alto, tenor and bass.

He wrote many songs, including 'The House that Jack Built' for Sam Cowell. His first major success was 'The Whole Hog or None' (1855), which he wrote with E.W. Mackney, who also sang it. It was a song to which topical verses and choruses could be added. George Belmont once said that, if all 250 or so verses were ever printed, they would provide 'a valuable retrospective of events that stirred party strife and agitated the public mind during a long period'. In 1862, the following version was sung with references to Blondin and the American Civil War:

Since I've been in London
Some fine sights I have seen
And to the Crystal Palace
A few times I have been.
Mr Blondin on the rope
I've seen him take a run
If he should fall, he's bound to go
The whole hog or none

The northern and the southern states
Are picking of a bone
But who shall get that bone at last
It shortly will be shown.
They had a bit of fighting
At a place they call Bull Run
But John Bull would make 'em go
The whole hog or none.

Ware began work as an agent in 1850, booking acts for, among others, Phineas Barnum. He specialised in novelties. At various stages, he represented Katie Lawrence, Arthur Lloyd, E.W. Mackney, Tom MacLagan, J.H. Milburn, Mrs F.R. Phillips and Nellie Power – as well as Tiny Pau, billed as the smallest man in the world; an act called The Three Tiger Ladies; the Tichborne claimant; and such boxing personalities as Jem Mace and Dick Burge. By the spring of 1885, he could boast that he was in regular contact with music-hall proprietors throughout Europe, the Americas, Africa and Australia.

His biggest discovery, however, was the 15-year-old Marie Lloyd. Once she had been firmly told that Nellie Power owned the rights to 'The Boy in the Gallery', Ware wrote another song for Marie, called 'Whacky Whack Whack', in which she played a girl complaining of being caned at school. George Ware led a multifarious life at the centre of music hall from its meagre beginnings in the 1840s to its big business zenith in the 1890s.

Fred Gilbert was also primarily an agent. His songs were a sideline, but one proved to be an enormous success, 'The Man that [*sic*] Broke the Bank at Monte Carlo'.

> FRED GILBERT (Frederick Younge
> Gilbert)
> **Born** Charing Cross, London,
> 2 March 1850
> **Married** Emma Hudson,
> 21 December 1873
> **Died** Eltham, Kent, 12 April 1903
> **Left** £15

Fred was the son of a comedian of the same name. As a child, he appeared at the Adelphi Theatre and was later in the choir at Evans's supper rooms. In his teens, he joined the office of Ambrose Maynard, the first music-hall agent, but moved later to Charles Roberts's agency. While there, he began writing songs, advertising in 1872 that he was available to compose comic and serio-comic songs and duets. His first success came four years later, a song called 'Did you Ever See an Oyster Walk Upstairs?' He eventually set up as agent on his own account, although for a few months he was the general manager of an agency run by G.H. MacDermott.

'The Man that Broke the Bank at Monte Carlo' (1890) was based on the true story of Charles Wells, who, in three days, turned £400 into £40,000 at the Monte Carlo casinos. He was a renowned confidence trickster and later, in connection with another venture, he was sentenced to eight years' hard labour for obtaining nearly £30,000 by false pretences. Later still, he served another three years for a similar swindle.

Gilbert submitted the song to a number of entertainers, including Albert Chevalier and Walter Munroe, but they were not interested. Possibly, they thought that some of its phraseology, such as 'sunny Southern shore' and 'great Triumphal arch', was beyond the reach of a music-hall audience. Charles Coborn, who was the last to see the song, certainly felt that, but, as soon as he had sent the manuscript back to Gilbert, he relented: 'No sooner than the letter and song had been posted that I began to fear I had made a mistake. I went up and down the house humming the chorus, which I could not get out of my mind . . . Early next morning, I . . . found Fred Gilbert's address and went after him.'[2] Coborn paid Gilbert £10 for the song and sang it for the rest of his long life.

Gilbert still had two major successes to come: 'Down the Road' (1893) for Gus Elen and 'At Trinity Church I Met my Doom' for Tom Costello (1894). In 1898, he contracted consumption. He was admitted to hospital, where he continued writing songs. Then, for the sake of his health, he moved to Sandgate in Kent, but he quickly ran out of money.

Hugh J. Didcott, the leading music-hall agent of his day, did much to improve the salaries and working conditions of those on his books. Known as Diddy, he was the first agent to act as a negotiator between entertainers and theatre owners. Immaculately dressed, he was regularly seen at first nights with a new female companion by his side and smoking an expensive cigar.

> HUGH J. DIDCOTT (Hubert Joseph Morice)
> **Born** 1835 (?)
> **Married** Rose Fox
>   Two daughters, Violet Raye, actress, who married
>   the actor/manager, H. Nye Chart (d. 1876); and
>   Maudi Darrell (d. October 1910), actress, who
>   married Ian Bullough[3] (1885–1936) of the cotton
>   machinery manufacturers, Howard and Bullough,
>   1909.
> **Died** Marylebone, London, 26 November 1909

As a young man, Didcott had been an actor and a comic singer, but he was clever enough to realise he had not discovered his niche. As an agent, he was an excellent judge of talent. Alfred Vance and George Leybourne were among his earliest clients and, at the height of his career, he represented two-thirds of music hall's big stars. In spite of his success, many artists resented his power. In his autobiography, George Mozart wrote:

At one time, he controlled the entire professional world . . . We were all afraid of him. He was compared to the spider and the fly, for once Diddy got you into those wonderful offices of his [in York Road, Battersea], God help you, he could make you sign anything . . . Diddy stuck at nothing to gain his own ends . . . I knew him well. I was once on his books – and I had to go to the Law Courts to get off them.[4]

Didcott was no stranger to litigation. He once alleged libel against the weekly journal *The Pelican*, in which references were made to a shady agent named Mr York Road. Didcott claimed the publication was referring to him. Counsel for the paper argued that Didcott had no character to clear.

Undoubtedly, some of the antagonism directed against him had its roots in anti-Semitism. When G.H. MacDermott opened his agency near Didcott, H. Chance Newton wrote an anonymous piece about them, referring to 'the great Jingo songster' and 'the dapper little Semite'. Each imagined the other was the author and nearly came to blows, but Newton confessed.

Didcott's autocratic career ended when he quarrelled with one of the most powerful West End syndicates and was barred from every music hall in its control. With the glittering array of stars he represented, he thought he would win the dispute, but the syndicate proved stronger than him. Gradually, his clientele left him for other agents and he was left with only minor acts on his books. Although he maintained an impressive façade, he was soon penniless and died a broken and disappointed man.

'The Boy in the Gallery', composed by the agent George Ware. (Richard Anthony Baker)

CHAPTER 26

Midnight – and Still no Dick

When music-hall stars took over pantomime from about the start of the 1870s, there was an outcry. One influential theatre writer complained of 'offensive songs, vulgar and inane dances [and] deplorable gags'. The man who was most upset was E.L. Blanchard (1820–89), who wrote every Drury Lane pantomime from 1852 to 1887. In his 1875 diary, he set out his objection to the story being 'spoilt by music hall artistes introducing their own songs and business'. By 1882, things were even worse (or better, depending on your point of view). The Lane's strong cast included Arthur Roberts and James Fawn, Herbert Campbell and Nellie Power, but, to Blanchard, it was no more than a 'very dreary music hall entertainment . . . and the good old fairy tales [were] never again to be illustrated as they should be'.

E.L. Blanchard, who wrote the Drury Lane panto-mimes for thirty-five years. *(Richard Anthony Baker)*

The man who introduced music hall to Drury Lane was Augustus Harris, who, at the age of 28, masterminded scenes of lavish spectacle that pantomime-goers had not seen before and would not see again. Reviewing one of his productions, a critic wrote of a double staircase and a huge minstrels' gallery; girls gathering in every conceivable hue, in armour, in glittering chains, in headdresses of astonishing shape; gongs sounding from the wings; a band on stage; and another in the pit.

The regular Drury Lane panto-goer was taken aback. For, in the ten years before Harris's arrival, the Christmas show was a far more modest affair. Throughout the 1870s, the pantomime had been the monopoly of the extraordinary Vokes family, four children of a theatrical costumier, plus an actor, Walter Fawdon, who changed his name to Vokes. As the decade progressed, it was clear that the family was never going to modernise. Reviewers

AUGUSTUS HARRIS (Augustus Henry
    Glossop Harris)
Born Paris 1852
Married Florence Edgecombe Rendle,
    8 November 1881
Died Folkestone, Kent, 22 June 1896

said the Vokes troupe had been on the stage for far too long.

Harris's first pantomime was their last. In no time at all, he indicated that he meant to spare no expense. His brainwave was teaming the wiry and nervous Dan Leno with Herbert Campbell, a huge man with a voice to match. The two men performed their annual double act at the Lane for sixteen consecutive years.

Harris's most star-studded show was *Robinson Crusoe* in 1893. Both Marie Lloyd and Little Tich joined Leno and Campbell. George Bernard Shaw formed a dislike for Campbell. When he saw *Aladdin* in 1896/7, he quickly found fault, partly on account of the accent Campbell chose to play Abanazar: 'Mr Campbell can say "face" instead of "fice", "slave" instead of "slive", "brain" instead of "brine", if he likes; and yet he takes the greatest possible pains to avoid doing so, lest his occupation as a comically vulgar person should be gone.'[1]

HERBERT CAMPBELL (Herbert Edward Story)
Born London, 22 December 1844
Married Elizabeth Ann Mills, Shoreditch, London,
    20 April 1867 (d. 1884)
After 1884, Campbell lived until his death with
    Ellen Bartram
Died London, 19 July 1904
Left £4,477

Shaw saw *The Babes in the Wood* the following year, but the evening was no happier for him: 'I hope I may never have to endure anything more dismally futile than the efforts of Mr Leno and Mr Herbert Campbell to start a passable joke in the course of their stumblings and wanderings through barren acres of gag on Boxing-night.'[2]

Whatever Shaw thought, Campbell and Leno were supreme in pantomime and were upstaged only once. While preparing for a performance towards the end of the 1899/1900 run of *Jack and the Beanstalk*, word reached the theatre of a decisive moment in the Boer War, the relief of Ladysmith. Campbell and Leno worked out when they would break the news to the audience: Scene Seven, Part Two, but they figured without a messenger boy, who ran on in Scene One, Part One, giggled and said, "Aven't you heard? I've just relieved Ladysmith'. It caused a sensation among the audience, but Campbell and Leno were furious.

Harris worked tremendously hard. Even so, his death at the age of 44 shocked many people. As for Blanchard, the last Drury Lane pantomime to which he made any contribution was *Babes in the Wood* in 1888. Just before Christmas that year, he noted in his diary: 'Go through the distasteful libretto . . . giving Augustus Harris permission to use my name in consideration that he uses some lines from my old annual of seventeen years ago.' There was no further panto work for Blanchard. The following September, he died, having earned just £200 that year.

Harris's years at Drury Lane were regarded as the theatre's zenith, but, starting in 1897, the work of the Lane's assistant manager, Arthur Collins, showed that he had learned a lot. A tall, good-looking man in his early thirties, he was first employed at the theatre painting scenery, but, as the Lane's long-time conductor, Jimmy Glover, noted, Collins had the eye and pen of an artist, brilliant vision and the advantage of youth.

In his first production, *Babes in the Wood*, he wisely retained the partnership of Leno and Campbell, but, in 1900, he stamped his own style on the shows by hiring J. Hickory Wood to write the book. Wood was originally an insurance clerk, who began his theatrical career by

writing sketches and lyrics; he produced the script of *Cinderella* for a provincial company; he then moved to the Garrick, where his book of *Puss in Boots* was interspersed with songs from Leslie Stuart; and, on arriving at Drury Lane, he wrote his first script for Collins within a fortnight. Previous writers had been happy to leave all comic dialogue to the comedians, but Wood wrote the whole script, cleverly capturing the style of Leno and Campbell and ingeniously introducing new twists to the old stories. Wood's *annus mirabilis* came in 1911 when no fewer than thirty-three of his pantos were produced in Britain, South Africa, Australia and other parts of the world.

The deaths of both Leno and Campbell in 1904 delivered a potentially lethal blow to Collins' shows, but he assembled a strong cast for the next panto, *The White Cat*, which included Harry Randall, Tom Woottwell and a famous principal boy, Queenie Leighton. Collins continued introducing novelty and pageantry to the Drury Lane pantomimes until ill health forced him to retire in 1924.

After Collins, the Lyceum established itself as the leading pantomime theatre in London. Oscar Barrett, who lived to the age of 95, had been in charge of the Lyceum pantos, writing book and music for them, as well as directing. In 1910, the Melville brothers took over – Walter and Frederick, the sons of a manager of the Grand Theatre, Birmingham.

Comedy was the keynote of the shows during the Melville regime, George Jackley supplying most of the fun. In yellow and black tights, he persuaded even the coyest member of the audience to join in the choruses and his strong voice could be heard in every corner of the theatre, which seated nearly 3,000 people. Clarkson Rose was often an imposing, dignified dame and Naughton and Gold, of the Crazy Gang, supplied the

Dan Leno, Johnny Danvers (Leno's uncle, himself a panto stalwart) and Herbert Campbell. *(Richard Anthony Baker)*

slapstick, throwing flour all over the place in one scene and drenching themselves with water in others. In those years, the greatest threat to the theatre was a disagreement between the Melville brothers over management policy. For some time, they refused to speak to each other and it looked as though the dispute was going to be taken to court. Then, during the run of one pantomime, Jackley stepped down to the footlights to announce that the argument had been settled. Walter walked on from one side of the stage, Frederick from the other and the pair of them shook hands. Peace – and big profits – were restored.

The Lyceum had staged a pantomime as early as 1809, the same year as the Surrey in Lambeth. The Surrey, in which Dan Leno made his pantomime debut, was destroyed by fire (for the second time) in 1856 and was rebuilt by William Holland, invariably seen in a shiny top hat, a velvet collar and a red silk handkerchief hanging from his waistcoat. He staged many popular pantos at the Surrey with ornate transformation scenes and plenty of comedy.

In 1888, George Conquest, more commonly associated with the Grecian Theatre in Shoreditch, took over the lesseeship and produced pantos full of robust fun and handsomely staged, although without the extravagance of Drury Lane. As Conquest explained: 'If Augustus Harris wants a steam engine, he buys a steam engine. I look round the theatre for a few tables and paint the tops like wheels.' In pantomimes at the Grecian, George Conquest appeared each year in some new and weird disguise – a crab, for instance, or a spider or octopus – and still managed to sing, dance, jump through windows and appear through trapdoors.

The Britannia in Hoxton was another old London theatre with a proud pantomime tradition. Its owner, Sara Lane, insisted on appearing each year in black silk tights. Charles Dickens saw many shows at the Brit, as it became known, and compared them favourably with those at the Haymarket and Covent Garden.

In more recent times, the London Palladium became the home of spectacular pantomime. The more prestigious shows began in the 1940s and the really star-studded ones in the 1950s. In 1953, Julie Andrews and Max Bygraves appeared in *Cinderella*. Bygraves returned the following year in *Mother Goose* with Peter Sellers. The 1987 panto, *Babes in the Wood*, with Barbara Windsor and John Inman, was the last Palladium panto, although, hopefully not *the* last.

CHAPTER 27

ONE-HIT WONDERS

They spent their whole life on the halls, but they were each remembered for just one song. Lottie Collins, for instance, was associated with only one routine, her 'Ta-ra-ra-boom-de-ay' dance, based on the cancan. She caused a sensation with it, although the physical exertion of it probably hastened her death.

> LOTTIE COLLINS (Charlotte Louisa Collins)
> **Born** London, 16 August 1865
> **Married** (1) Stephen Cooney (d. Saratoga, California, 1901, although not confirmed by the County Clerk Recorder, County of Santa Clara, San Jose)
> (2) James W. Tate, Nottingham, 16 August 1902 (d. 1922)
> Three daughters, Josephine, Cleopatra and Lucia.
> **Died** London, 1 May 1910

The details of Lottie's private life are difficult to work out, although it is known she was the daughter of an accomplished step dancer and a member of a minstrel troupe. With two younger sisters, Marie and Lizzie,[1] Lottie formed the Sisters Collins, who began working in 1877.

Ada Reeve worked with them in pantomime. Nine years younger than Lottie, Ada was one of a troupe of small children who supported the sisters in a song, 'Three Jolly Waggoners'. Unconsciously, she imitated Lottie's movements, causing her to fall over and make the audience laugh: 'Turning her back on the house, Lottie scowled at me and muttered something about the brat who had spoilt their number; but nothing could have been more angelic than her smiling face when she turned round again with me in her arms, murmuring sweetly "Did it hurt itself, the little darling?"'[2] This is a typical Ada Reeve anecdote, portraying herself in the best possible light, while behaving unpleasantly to others: which entertainer, however young, wants to be upstaged by an even younger one, who has yet to learn stagecraft?

Lottie appears to have left the act in about 1880. She said she had grown too tall to be able to continue working with her sisters. Marie and Lizzie carried on as the Sisters Collins until they married. Lottie began singing black-faced songs ('Whistling Coon' was one) and performing what was known as skirt-dancing, dancing with more than one petticoat. She paid her first visit to America in 1890, getting caught for nine days in snowdrifts up to 25 feet deep in the Sierra Nevada mountains in California. While her train was cut off, a theatre manager, Stephen Cooney, with whom she was travelling, proposed marriage and, once they reached St Louis, they became man and wife.

Before the end of 1891, Cooney, while still in America, heard the song that was to change her life: 'Ta-ra-ra-boom-de-ay'. He sent a copy to Britain; Lottie, by now back home, liked it too; but she asked the songwriter, Richard Morton, to write her a new lyric. She performed

Lottie Collins, the Flower of Dancers.
(Tony Barker)

it for the first time at the Tivoli in November 1891, but it was not a success straightaway. Lottie persevered, continuing to perform it throughout the run of Geoffrey Thorn's pantomime *Dick Whittington*, at the Grand Theatre in Islington and, at eleven o'clock each night, as part of George Edwardes's burlesque, *Cinder-ellen up too Late*, at the Gaiety Theatre.

By the start of 1892, 'Ta-ra-ra-boom-de-ay' had clicked, and, for the next few years, music-hall audiences could not have enough of it. Lottie herself believed that it was 'the mad rush and whirl of the thing that made it go'; a reviewer said 'no other woman in the halls could have made of it as much as she did'; and even George Bernard Shaw praised her 'sang froid and [her] unsparing vigour'.

Lottie took the song back to America and earned $1,000 a week. In fact, for the next few years, she visited America again and again, but her daughter, Jose, who became an even bigger star in the 1916 musical comedy *Maid of the Mountains*, witnessed the song's drawbacks:

Mother worked at top pressure and it *was* top pressure for no-one was more generous, as I have been told, with her encores. The result of it was that mother's health broke down. At first, it appeared as if a short rest would completely restore her. But actually the excessive strain of her dancing had done damage far more serious and undoubtedly sowed the seed of the heart trouble from which she died at so early an age.[3]

Lottie was a troubled soul. When she was only 21, she was living with a married man, whose wife and daughter (she once claimed in court) had assaulted her. In 1897, she was termed vulgar by a weekly paper called *Society* and was awarded £25 damages. The following year, she inexplicably tried to kill herself by opening veins in her throat and wrist with a pen knife. On Cooney's death in 1901, she was annoyed to learn that he had left his money to a sister to be held in his trust for a daughter of a previous marriage.

Leo Dryden's big song was 'The Miner's Dream of Home'. Although he sang it countless times during a career of forty years, its brand of nostalgia eventually became outmoded and Dryden faded into obscurity:

> I saw the old homestead and faces I love.
> I saw England's valleys and dells.
> I listened with joy, as I did when a boy,
> To the sound of the old village bells.
> The log was burning brightly.
> Twas a night that should banish all sin.
> For the bells were ringing the old year out
> And the new year in.

(Herbert Campbell introduced a clever spoof:

> Pa was boozing nightly
> And mother was shifting the gin
> The lodger was taking the old girl out
> And the old man in.)

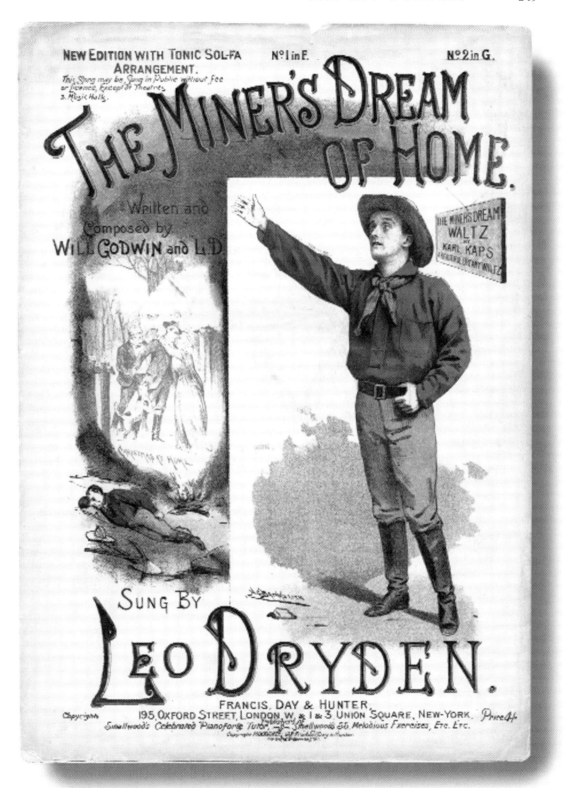

Leo Dryden built his career on one song. *(Tony Barker)*

LEO DRYDEN (George Dryden Wheeler)
Born east London, 6 June 1863
Married (1) Amy Fenton (divorced)
(2) Marian Louise Slater (professionally known as Marie
    Tyler), Lambeth, south London,
    3 November 1897 (a serio-comic, Marie Tyler
    (d. 1905, aged 30) made her name at the
    Alhambra while still in her teens; her descriptive
    song, 'When London's Fast Asleep', was reckoned
    by many to be on a par with Jenny Hill's 'Masks
    and Faces')
(3) Ada Mary Cohen, Wandsworth, 14 February 1906
Died Twickenham, 21 April 1939

While still a boy, Dryden began appearing at free-and-easies as a black-faced comedian and dancer. Precise details of his early career are difficult to work out, but at the end of 1889, he began singing two songs that became his first hits, 'Drink, Boys, Drink' and ''Twixt Love and Duty'. It was at the start of 1891 that he bought the first draft of 'The Miner's Dream of Home'.

The song was an enormous success and Dryden sang it continually during the early 1890s. By 1894, he was introducing other patriotic ballads. At each new outbreak of hostility, Dryden rose to the occasion. The Boer War brought from him 'Bravo, Dublin Fusiliers'; the war between Russia and Japan, 'For Freedom and Japan'; and, at the outbreak of the First World War, 'Remember Louvain'. (German troops destroyed medieval buildings in the Belgian city of Louvain in retaliation for civilian attacks on occupation forces.) But after the war, Dryden, in company with many music-hall entertainers, suffered badly and he began singing on the streets, earning at times about £5 a week. It was a reverse of fortune that appalled John P. Harrington: 'Why such an artist, in the maturity of his powers as an entertainer, a good comedian, as well as a fine vocalist and actor, should be overlooked by booking managers passes my comprehension.'[4]

But Fred Russell insisted that Dryden chose to sing on the streets: 'It was never necessary. Leo had only to accept the offer repeatedly made by the V.A.B.F. [the Variety Artistes' Benevolent Fund] to pass the autumn of his days in security, but it was not until comparatively recently that he agreed to become a guest at Brinsworth [the variety artistes' home at Twickenham].'[5]

Dryden's private life was, to say the least, convoluted. In the autumn of 1891, he began an affair with Lily Harley, the wife of Charles Chaplin and the mother of Charlie. In 1892, she gave birth to his son, also George Dryden Wheeler. The affair did not last long after the birth of the boy. Lily, whose real name was Hannah, began bringing him up with as much love as she devoted to Charlie and his other half-brother, Sydney, to whom Hannah had given birth before marrying Chaplin. But, in the following spring, Dryden went to her lodgings and abducted the boy. Later in life, after several unsuccessful attempts to make contact with both Charlie and Sydney, George Wheeler Dryden became a regular member of the Chaplin studio staff in 1939, acting as assistant director on *The Great Dictator* and assistant producer on *Limelight*.

Randolph Sutton was a first-rate light comedian with a repertoire of fine songs that included his one big hit, 'On Mother Kelly's doorstep' (1925). The youngest of nine children, Ran Sutton regularly spent his pocket money on trips to the Bristol Empire. Back home, his brothers and sisters persuaded him to sing them the songs and tell them the jokes he had heard. After leaving school, he took a job with a firm of printers and, during one holiday, went to Burnham-on-Sea in Somerset, where he got to know a pierrot troupe, who were working on the beach. His offer to sing a song as an extra turn at a benefit concert for a comedian in the company was readily accepted. He was such a success that the leader of the troupe invited him to join them the following week at Evesham in Worcestershire at a salary of 35s (£1.75).

Much to the annoyance of his father, Ran resigned from the printers to begin life as an entertainer. By 1930, he was topping bills at Oswald Stoll's halls. He

> RANDOLPH SUTTON (John Randolph Sutton)
> **Born** Bristol, 24 July 1888
> **Married** (1) Kitty —— (d. Coventry, 23 July 1914, aged 20)
> (2) Nellie le Breton at Fulham, south-west London, 1 December 1915 (separated)
> Sutton spent the last years of his life with Ernest (Terry) Doogan, to whom he left the bulk of his estate
> **Died** Lambeth, south London, 28 February 1969
> **Left** £26,887

believed in an immaculate appearance. Playing late at night at the Holborn Empire with a midnight appearance at the Trocadero restaurant to follow, he stood all the way in the taxi, explaining: 'I don't want creases in my crutch.'

George Stevens wrote 'On Mother Kelly's doorstep' for either Fred Barnes or Sutton to sing. Barnes tried it, but found it did not suit him. Ran Sutton paid £2 for the performing rights, but never owned the copyright of the song that virtually became his signature tune:

Randolph Sutton, Premier Light Comedian. *(Tony Barker)*

> On Mother Kelly's doorstep,
> I'm wondering now
> If little girl, Nellie,
> Remembers Joe, her beau,
> And does she love me like she used to
> On Mother Kelly's doorstep
> Down Paradise Row?

Many years later, someone phoned Ran to say that he had heard a man with a French-sounding name (was it Danny La Rue?) sing it on the radio. In tears, Ran phoned Don Ross to vent his fury. Ross calmed him down and six weeks later invited him to join his table at a Water Rats' ball. After dinner, Ross introduced Ran to La Rue. The two men got on famously and spent half an hour chatting. When Ran returned to Ross's table, he announced: 'He's the nicest man I've met in a very long time and I've told him he can use any of my songs.'

As Ran Sutton approached 60, he became gripped by stage nerves. Each day, from about four in the afternoon until the time he had to leave for the theatre, he kept looking at the clock, hoping that time would stand still or praying that something might happen to prevent him from appearing. His fears reached their climax after first house at the Chiswick Empire one Monday evening. He refused to play the second house, walked out of the theatre and did no work for about nine months. It was Ross's invitation to him to join *Thanks for the Memory* that got him working again and, from then on, he continued working right up to his death.

Some entertainers were lucky enough to enjoy two major successes. An eccentric comedian who adopted a somewhat academic air, Wilkie Bard, sang one song that will never die, the mother of all tongue-twisters, 'She sells sea-shells' (1908) and 'I want to sing in opera' (1910).

There are several accounts of why William August Smith decided to become Wilkie Bard.

WILKIE BARD (William August Smith)
Born Manchester, 19 March 1874
Married Nellie Stratton, central London, 28 July 1895 (d. 8 September 1947)
Died Hughenden, Buckinghamshire, 5 May 1944

Wilkie Bard, who turned failure in America into a big success. *(Richard Anthony Baker)*

One is that the first stage name he chose was Will Gibbard (or Gebard) and that, on receiving a parcel at a theatre addressed to Wilkie Bard, he preferred the mistaken spelling. Another is that he won so many amateur talent contests as a young man he was told 'You ought to be barred', but that sounds too facile. A third account is that he chose 'Bard' because his high forehead reminded people of Shakespeare. He usually painted two black spots above his eyes to make his forehead look even higher.

Wilkie Bard was the son of a chartered accountant. His first job was in a cotton spinner's warehouse, but, in his spare time, he sang at clubs in the City, specialising in coster songs. It is not clear when he changed track. But it may have coincided with the start of his association with the songwriter Frank Leo, who wrote many of his songs in his early professional years, including the one that he reckoned to be the turning point of his career, 'It was B-E-A-U-T-I-F-U-L' (1898).

Bard built up a range of characters. He sang 'I want to sing in opera' as an elderly dame with a shawl round her shoulders and a towering red wig. As with other character comedians, his songs became little more than introductions to each character, patter then making up the large part of his act. He returned to the song to round off the character study. Bard introduced something of himself in all the characters he played: 'In his sketches, he was a benevolent philosopher, slightly puzzled at the vagaries of his fellow men, but not above exercising his natural cunning and scoring off them in the end.'[6]

In 1908/9, Bard appeared in his first Drury Lane panto, *Dick Whittington*. Playing Idle Jack, he sang 'She sells sea-shells', written by Harry Gifford and Terry Sullivan and established the pantomime tradition for tongue-twisting lyrics. (This was followed in 1913 by Jack Norworth's 'Sister Susie's sewing shirts for soldiers'.)

In pantomimes at the London Palladium, Bard (as Pantaloon) and Will Evans (as clown) were responsible for reviving the old tradition of the harlequinade. During the First World War, Bard helped to boost business at the failing Palladium by persuading the management to play three shows a day.

In 1913, he made his American debut, accompanied on the trip by George Arthurs. Hammerstein's theatre in New York paid him $6,500 for two weeks' work. He could have suffered from other singers performing his songs before he arrived, but he attracted rave reviews. His second visit to New York did not begin well. A Monday matinée at the Palace turned into a major flop, largely because the first character he portrayed was a Welsh miner — and Americans could not understand the accent. He was booed offstage and, sobbing in his dressing-room afterwards, he threatened to return home as soon as possible, but the influential editor of *Variety*, Sime Silverman, intervened. Bard changed his whole act, replacing it with two sketches, 'The Scrub Woman', in which he played a charwoman at a theatre, exchanging comments with a dresser, played by Nellie Stratton, and 'The Night Watchman', in which he played a watchman sitting in his hut and chatting with the principal boy of a pantomime, who is on her way home. By the second week, his American audience wanted more from him. So, he supplemented the sketches with ragtime parodies of 'Sally in our Alley' and 'Alice, Where Art Thou?'. The visit turned into a success. Bard returned to America in 1923, but that was his last appearance there.

He continued working in Britain, but his material was becoming dated mainly because some of the characters he played (a bathing-machine attendant, for instance) no longer existed. There is also evidence that his mental health started to decline. When the cabaret artiste Douglas Byng played Dame in pantomime at the New Oxford Theatre in London in 1924, he found that Bard would sometimes walk offstage in the middle of a song and leave the audience to sing it themselves. There were similar problems when Bard appeared in Lew Lake's show *Stars that Never Fail to Shine*, in the early 1930s. When Florence Smithson sang 'Roses of Picardy', scattering rose petals on the stage, Bard went berserk, insisting they were Flanders poppies.

Gus Elen, one of the greatest coster comedians of music hall, also enjoyed two monster hits: 'If it Wasn't for the Houses in Between' and 'It's a great big shame', both written by Edgar Bateman and George le Brunn in 1894:

GUS ELEN (Ernest Augustus Elen)
Born Pimlico, London, 22 July 1862
Married Myrtle Warner, Birmingham,
    28 September 1887
Died Balham, south London,
    17 February 1940
Left £10,756

It's a great big shame and, if she belonged to me,
I'd let her know who's who,
Nagging at a feller wot is six foot free
And 'er only four foot two!
Oh, they 'adn't been married not a month nor more
When underneath her fumb goes Jim
Isn't it a pity as the likes of 'er
Should put upon the likes of 'im?

As a boy, Elen sang the songs he heard organ grinders playing in the street. At first, he worked as an egg packer and a shop assistant, but he also sang at smoking concerts and sing-songs in pubs. By 1893, with an accent that was pure Sam Weller, he was top of the bill on a provincial tour with another fine song, ''E Dunno Where 'E Are', all about a Covent Garden porter, who patronises his colleagues after inheriting some money. (It was written by Harry Wright and Fred Eplett.) Elen's fame spiralled during the 1890s and in the early years of the twentieth century. He scored a big success in America in 1907 and retired during the First World War.

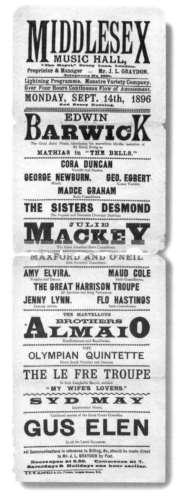

Gus Elen, the Inimitable Coster Delineator. *(Richard Anthony Baker)*

BILLY MERSON (William Henry Thompson)
Born Nottingham, 29 March 1881
Married —— (professionally known as Babs Valerie)
Died Westminster, London, 25 June 1947
Left £220

Billy Merson also had several fine songs, but there was one he was always required to sing, his greatest success, 'The Spaniard that Blighted my Life' (1909). Away from music hall, Merson also excelled as the original Hard-Boiled Herman in *Rose Marie* (1925), which ran for 851 performances at Drury Lane, a record for an American musical comedy in Britain that was unsurpassed for more than twenty years.

There are many discrepancies in accounts of the early life of Billy Merson, but, as a young man, he appears to have spent most of his spare time singing at concerts around his native Nottingham, albeit with little success because, by his own admission, he could not sing in tune. He switched ambitions and decided to become an acrobat instead, appearing at first with six other boys at fêtes and galas.

All the time, Merson's dream was to make his name in music hall. For six years, he visited most halls in the provinces, writing songs for other entertainers, including Wilkie Bard and the character comedian Harry Ford. He finally obtained a week's work at the Oxford in 1909.

Billy Merson, who wrote his biggest hit himself. *(Richard Anthony Baker)*

Merson wrote 'The Spaniard that Blighted my Life' for a pantomime in which he was appearing. (In one account, he said it was staged in Brighton; in another, Glasgow.) He had wanted to use Bard's song, 'I want to sing in opera', but was refused permission. So, he decided to write his own song in operatic style. During the pantomime, it was sung as a duet, but it was so successful that Merson decided that he would continue using it as part of his solo act. The song tells of a man who takes his girlfriend to a bullfight, but 'while I'd gone out for some nuts and a programme', she is whisked away by a toreador:

> If I catch Alphonso Spagoni, the toreador,
> With a mighty swipe, I will dislocate his bally jaw!
> I'll find this bullfighter, I will.
> And when I catch the bounder, the blighter I'll kill.
> He shall die! He shall die! He shall die tiddly i ti ti ti ti ti ti.
> He shall die! He shall die!
> For I'll raise a bunion on his Spanish onion
> If I catch him bending tonight.

The song twice became a million-selling record for Al Jolson, first in 1913 and secondly in 1947, when he rerecorded it as a duet with Bing Crosby. When Jolson sang the song in the movie *The Singing Fool*, without either permission or payment, Merson claimed compensation. He was offered £2,000, but took the case to court. He won, but on appeal the outcome was reversed on a technicality: the song could be sung only by Merson in theatres, but no mention was made of cinemas. The two hearings, costing him £15,000, left him bankrupt.

Charles Coborn's extended career was based almost entirely on two songs, 'Two lovely black eyes' (1886) and 'The Man that Broke the Bank at Monte Carlo' (1891).

Coborn made his professional music-hall debut in 1872 at a small hall, the Alhambra, attached to a pub on the Isle of Dogs. The breakthrough came in 1879 when he was taken on for six months at the Oxford, billed as the Comic of the Day. Coborn was a stout defender of music hall: 'Our patrons want "nonsense" as it is termed and it is absurd in the extreme to imagine that they can be lectured or preached into avoiding our "habitats" or accepting from us any other staple. Refine it as much as you like (or rather *can*), but nonsense they require and will have.'[7]

CHARLES COBORN (Charles Whitton McCallum)
Born Stepney, east London, 4 August 1852
Married Ellen Stockley, Belfast, 26 January 1882 (b. 29 November 1857; d. 23 March 1941)
    Four sons (the eldest, Major Duncan McCallum, MP for Argyll)
    Three daughters
Died London, 23 November 1945

In 1886, Coborn heard 'My Nellie's Blue Eyes', a song written by an American comedian, William J. Scanlan, who died in an asylum in New York in 1898. He liked the melody, which Scanlan had purloined from a Venetian ballad, 'Vieni sul mar', but he found the lyric trivial. So, he wrote his own, retitling the song 'Two lovely black eyes' and singing it in a faded frock coat with a battered umbrella – and his eyes blackened:

> Two lovely black eyes.
> Oh, what a surprise!
> Only for telling a man he was wrong
> Two lovely black eyes.

Coborn enjoyed singing the song in other languages, too. However, his French version did not convey the proper meaning. The Duke of Clarence wrote a better translation for him:

> Deux beaux yeux pochés!
> Me v'la épaté.
> Je n'ai que dit.
> 'T'as tort, mon petit.'
> Deux beaux yeux pochés.

Coborn sang the English version for the first time at the Paragon in 1886: 'It was an instantaneous success. The manager of the hall was standing at one of the bars, smoking cigars and telling funny stories, and did not observe the fact that music hall history was in the making, but *I knew*!'[8] Oddly enough, Coborn thought very little of his first major hit. He told

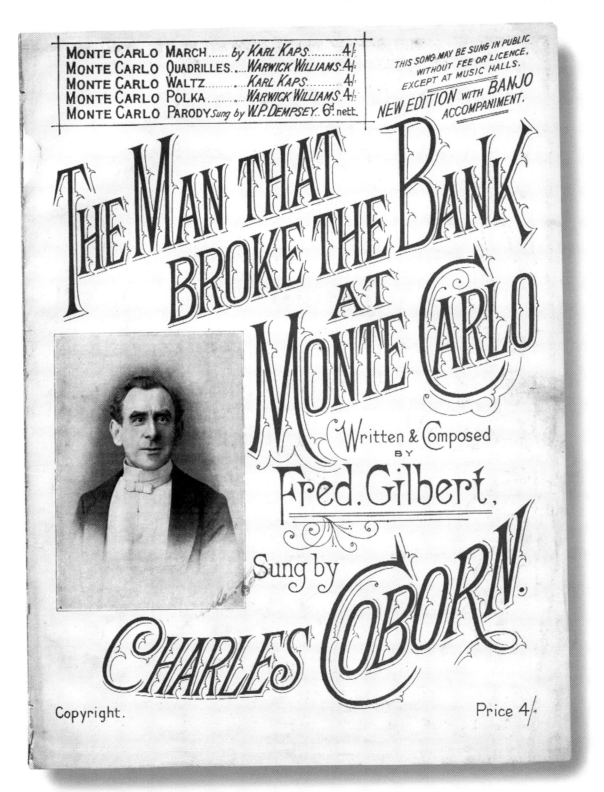

Charles Coborn: the Grand Old Man of Music Hall. *(Richard Anthony Baker)*

a reporter with the London *Evening News* in 1888 that he had other songs that were 'a great deal better'. His second major success, Fred Gilbert's 'The Man that Broke the Bank at Monte Carlo', which was all about a real-life conman, came five years later:

> As I walk along the Bois Boo-long with an independent air,
> You can hear the girls declare 'He must be a millionaire!'
> You can hear them sigh and wish to die
> You can see them wink the other eye
> At the man who broke the bank at Monte Carlo.

As with 'Two lovely black eyes', Coborn sang the song for the rest of his long life. He reckoned he sang it more than 250,000 times and could render the chorus in fourteen languages.

Coborn's repertoire was not confined to his two major songs. He sang dozens of others, but never found one that equalled the success of his hits. By the end of the 1890s, his career was in decline and, before the end of the next decade, a newspaper was able to report: 'Of late years, Charles Coborn's appearances on the West End boards have been few and far between.'[9]

Coborn's decline was caused not just by a dearth of new material. A literate man of high principles, he made enemies of some theatre managers and owners. After singing 'Two lovely black eyes' at the Trocadero for fourteen months, Coborn found that he was slipping down the bill. Instead of appearing at 10 p.m., he was going on stage at about midnight, by which time many in the audience had gone home. Coborn approached the London Pavilion, where he was immediately offered twice his Trocadero salary. Having found a loophole in his Trocadero contract, he defected, infuriating the Trocadero's proprietor.

In 1894, Coborn was appearing at the Palace and was about to go on stage one night when one of the theatre's directors asked him not to sing 'I've Never Turned Money Away', which Coborn sang as a Jew. Some of the directors are Jews, he was told, and they don't like it. Coborn abruptly told the man to mind his own business, but, halfway through his act, found he was being hissed by a section of the audience and broke a golden rule of music hall by addressing them from the stage. Afterwards, he apologised to the Palace's manager, Charles Morton, but was told that the directors had decided that he was never to be admitted to the theatre again. And, apart from a walk-on appearance in the Garden Party scene at the end of the first Royal Command Performance in 1912, he never was.

He was never invited to any subsequent Royal Variety Show. In addition, he was awarded no honour, in spite of a considerable amount of charitable work in the First World War and his efforts to improve the working conditions of music-hall entertainers in such organisations as the Music Hall Artists' Protection Association and the Music Hall Benevolent Fund.

Coborn never retired and, always ready to help a good cause, he became the Grand Old Man of Variety. When he attended Harry Tate's funeral, he found himself standing at the graveside with the comedian Charles Austin:

> 'Dear old Harry,' said Coborn. 'I can't believe we shall never see him again.' Austin shook his head, looked at the grand old man beside him and said: 'You're getting on a bit yourself, Charlie.' Coborn agreed: 'Yes, I'm over ninety.' Charlie Austin patted his shoulder and without a flicker of a smile said: 'Blimey, it's hardly worthwhile going home, is it?'[10]

CHAPTER 28

TWO'S COMPANY

Of the double acts on the halls, the Two Macs, originally Frederick Maccabe and J.P. MacNally, claim credit for introducing slapstick comedy to Britain. It had previously been highly popular in America, but unheard of here. They were also the best-known cross-talk comedians in Britain and, in time, became much imitated.

They were 'discovered' by Walter de Frece's father, Harry,[1] who ran the Sanspareil, a wooden music hall in Liverpool, which opened in the late 1860s, and the Cooperative Hall, which he reopened as the Gaiety in about 1875. When the Two Macs appeared at the Gaiety, they were billed as 'Maccabe and MacNally, Irish comedians'. Dressed in knee breeches and tailcoats, they opened their act with a song while they twirled shillelaghs:

> We're the pair at every fair to tipple all the
>   whisky.
> We can keep the girls alive. We're full o' fun
>   and frisky.
> Here, there and everywhere, such capers ne'er
>   were seen.
> Yes, we're the boys the girls enjoy when dancing
>   on the green.

There followed a wild dance and then a sketch in which they appeared as two bricklayers. They created such a storm among the audience that de Frece renamed them the Two Macs and promoted them to the top of the bill for the following week.

The Two Macs introduced slapstick to Britain.
(Richard Anthony Baker)

MIKE MAC (Frederick Michael Maccabe)
Born Newcastle 1851 (?)
Died Westminster, London, 3 April 1894

J.P. MACNALLY (John Patrick MacNally)
Born Dublin 1859 (?)
Married Alice Maydue
Died Hednesford, Staffordshire,
    20 September 1908

After that, they became the rage of Britain, every part of America and most big cities on the European mainland. When the act split up, each of them took on a new partner and, for a time, there were two turns both billing themselves as the Original Two Macs.

Maccabe and MacNally inspired the McNaughtons, Tom and Fred, to go on the halls. Known at the outset as the Brothers Parker, they first appeared together in 1886. After answering a number of advertisements in the music-hall trade papers, they joined a company at Penge in south-east London with a turn that combined black-faced song and dance, some knockabout comedy and a clog dance.

TOM MCNAUGHTON (Thomas William Norton)
Born 1866 (?)
Married Alice Wood (professionally known as Alice Lloyd), Lambeth, south London, 16 January 1894
Died St Albans, Hertfordshire, 28 November 1923

FRED MCNAUGHTON (James Frederick Norton)
Born 1871 (?)
Married Georgina Preston
Died Lambeth, south London, 24 February 1920

Tom and Fred split up when Tom joined his wife in America in 1909. Tom was succeeded by Gus Howard (1881/4?–1969), who, as Gus McNaughton, made more than seventy movies, including three George Formby comedies, *Keep Your Seats, Please* (1937), *Keep Fit* (1938) and *Trouble Brewing* (1939), Alfred Hitchcock's *The 39 Steps* (1935) and, in his best role, a James Mason film, *A Place of One's Own* (1945).

Unusually, the McNaughtons were flesh-and-blood brothers, unlike the Six

The McNaughtons: some knockabout comedy and a clog dance. *(Richard Anthony Baker)*

Brothers Luck, a comedy sketch act that, at various times, featured Ernie Lotinga and Shaun Glenville. They toured with the act all over Britain, America, Australia and New Zealand.

In 1909, Lotinga broke away from the act to present his own comedy sketches, featuring a character known as Josser. According to Philip Hindin, he was constantly in trouble with local Watch Committees for using risqué material.

ERNIE LOTINGA (Ernest Lotinga)
Born Sunderland, Tyne and Wear,
      7 December 1876
Married (1) Winifred Emms (professionally
      known as Hetty King), 20 November 1901
      (divorced 1917)
      (2) Kathleen Barbor (d. Twickenham, Middlesex,
      20 April 1952, aged 58)
      Son, Paul
Died Hammersmith, west London, October 1951

SHAUN GLENVILLE (Shaun Glenville Browne)
Born Dublin, 16 May 1884
Married Dorothy Ward, London,
      13 May 1911 (d. 30 March 1987)
      Son, Peter Patrick Brabason Browne (1913–96)
      (professionally known as Peter Glenville)
Died London, 28 December 1968

BELLE BILTON (Isabel Maude Penrice Bilton)
Born London, 29 October 1866
Married William Frederick le Poer Trench
      (Viscount Dunlo), 10 July 1889
      Four children: Richard Frederick John
      Donough, the sixth Earl of Clancarty
      (1891–1971), married (1) Edith Constance
      Rawlinson (marriage dissolved 1918) and
      (2) in 1919 Cora Marie Edith Spooner
      Lady Beryl le Poer Trench (1893–?) married in
      1914 Hon. Richard Philip Stanhope
      (1885–1916)
      Hon. Roderick (1895–?)
      Hon. Greville Sydney Rochfort, the seventh
      Earl of Clancarty[2] (1902–75) married in
      1926 Beatrice Georgiana Miller
Died at Ballinasloe, County Galway,
      31 December 1906

Shaun Glenville became a much-loved Irish comedian and a leading pantomime dame. As a boy, he gained theatrical experience in plays produced by his mother, Mary Glenville Browne, at a small theatre, later to become famous as the Abbey Theatre, Dublin. After three years with the Six Brothers Luck, Glenville joined Fred Karno's company in 1910, appearing at the Paragon as a drunken purser on board the *Wontdetainia*, a satire of life on board the *Lusitania* and the *Mauretania*.

Sister acts abounded on the halls. There were the Sisters Terry ('Unapproachable Baby Mimics'); the Sisters Sprightly ('Bright, British and Bang Up-to-Date'); and the Sisters Chester ('Grace, Beauty and Banjos Sans Pareil').

Belle Bilton, one-half of a sister act, was among the prettiest women on the halls. Her marriage into the aristocracy resulted in one of the most sensational divorce cases of the 1890s.

Belle sang agreeably enough and danced quite well, but it was her beauty which marked her out: a haunting look of tragedy behind the eyes that gave her irresistible appeal, according to one admirer. Of the two sisters, Belle was always the greater attraction – in demand everywhere she went. Seymour Hicks acknowledged their fame, but damned their talent: 'The little ditties they warbled were inane and were always followed with a stereotyped class of simultaneous movement chivalrously called dancing by their hundreds of admirers. The

Biltons' most famous effort was the acme of balderdash.'[3] Hicks was referring to their song, 'Fresh, fresh as the morning' (1896), written by Fred Gilbert. He had a point. It ran:

Belle Bilton married into aristocracy. *(Richard Anthony Baker)*

We're fresh, fresh, fresh as the morning,
Sweeter than the new mown hay.
We're fresh, fresh, fresh as the morning
And just what you want today.

At the beginning of 1887, she began an affair with a confidence trickster, Alden Weston. Unknown to her, he was married; she became pregnant by him, gave birth to his child in 1888, and could have suffered the life of a Victorian unmarried mother after Weston was sentenced to 18 months' imprison-ment with hard labour for his part in conspiring to defraud a man of £30,000. With both a baby and a career to nurture, Belle was befriended by a good-hearted young man, Isidor Wertheimer, who arranged for her to stay with his sister at his house in St John's Wood.

During the spring of 1889, after a show at the Empire, Belle visited the Corinthian Club, where she was introduced to Viscount Dunlo, two years her junior, a man without private means and entirely dependent on his father, the Earl of Clancarty. Within three months, they were married at Hampstead Registry Office, with just her sister, Flo, and one other person as witnesses. When the Earl heard the news, he flew into a fury. Amazingly, he ordered his son to leave the country. Even more astonishingly, his son agreed, deserting Belle after only a few days' marriage. The Earl then hired private detectives to keep a watch on Belle and instructed his son to begin divorce proceedings, citing Wertheimer as co-respondent.

The case went to court in the summer of 1890. Watched closely by the landed gentry and the theatre world, the hearing lasted six days. At its conclusion, the jury agreed that Belle and Wertheimer had not committed adultery. The night the case ended, Belle was at the Empire. The theatre was packed, the crowd roaring its support. Bouquets were handed over the footlights, everyone wanted to shake hands with Belle and, in the end, the band played a triumphant march to try to quell the audience's cheers.

After that, Belle could have commanded any salary she wanted. Instead, displaying an incredible forgiveness towards her husband, she reverted to being a wife, but carried on working. In 1891, she was appearing in Plymouth when the fourth Earl died, allowing Dunlo to succeed to the title. She joined her husband at once, and almost immediately the couple took up residence at the family seat in County Galway. Belle quickly endeared herself to local villagers and gentry alike. She worked hard for charity and raised four children. About a year after the birth of her youngest son, Belle developed cancer. She had an operation in Dublin in 1904 and underwent further treatment in Paris, but she succumbed to the illness shortly after her fortieth birthday.

CHAPTER 29

TRUE INDIVIDUALS

Then, as now, no entertainers became stars unless they stood in a category of their own. They might have copied established artistes in their youth, but, if they wanted to see their names move up the bill, they had to find a voice and a character of their own. One such was 'Doctor' Walford Bodie, a master of self-publicity and a man of forbidding appearance, with staring eyes and waxed mustachios, who filled theatres in Britain and America for more than forty years. He claimed to have special powers, but spurious qualifications revealed him to be a fake.

WALFORD BODIE (Samuel Murphy Brodie)
Born Aberdeen, 11 June 1869/70 (?)
Married (1) Jeannie Henry (professionally known as
    Princess Rubie; d. 24 January 1931)
  Eldest son, Albert Edward (d. 1 April 1915,
    aged 26)
  Daughter, Jeannie (d. 1909, aged 18)
(2) Florence Joan Robertshaw (professionally known
    as Tesla), London, 15 February 1932
Died Blackpool, Lancashire, 19 October 1939

As a child, Bodie taught himself conjuring and ventriloquism and, in his teens, he showed off his skills at a town hall near his home in Aberdeen. When his sister married the manager of a music hall in Norwich in 1897, Bodie went there to work with him, but soon decided he would rather be onstage than backstage. He developed an act in which he performed experiments with electricity and made out he was a faith healer:

At the performance, a volunteer (the most effective was a crippled child) was carried down to the centre of the stage. The lights were turned down and the subject hypnotised. While the orchestra played, Bodie examined the affected extremity and fussed over the child with a lavish display of concern and attention. With his powerful hands, he broke down any adhesions that may have formed under the skin. Next, Bodie connected himself to an electric condenser and applied the current to the subject by touching him with his hand or boot. Flying sparks added to the mystery. After the application of the current, the child was told to move the limb and walk across the stage. The audience shook the hall with their approval.[1]

In 1905, *The Bodie Book* was published. Its author showed little modesty:

The work is arduous. For instance, in my own case, while fighting my detractors in the press, and combatting the ignorant doubt and unbelief of a section of the doctors as well, I am constantly engaged in a far more grim contest with the pains that afflict the masses. It is the kind of work that grows more and more arduous as year by year it succeeds. Therefore, it requires a man of strong personality, indomitable will and energy and powerful physique.[2]

The medical profession was concerned that Bodie had made himself out to be a qualified doctor. In 1905, he was prosecuted for misrepresentation. Diplomas he produced from institutions called the Barrett College and the Chicago College were found to be honorary. He was fined £5 and ordered to pay 5 guineas' expenses. His career surmounted this obstacle, as well as a far more serious one four years later.

Charles Irving, a so-called pupil of Bodie, sued him for the return of £1,000 he had paid him. Bodie had told him that, if he stayed with him for three years, he would need only to write a thesis to become a qualified doctor himself. He would also learn Bodie's special skills as a hypnotist, a 'bloodless surgeon' and a 'medical electrician'. During the case, Irving said he had learned only how the

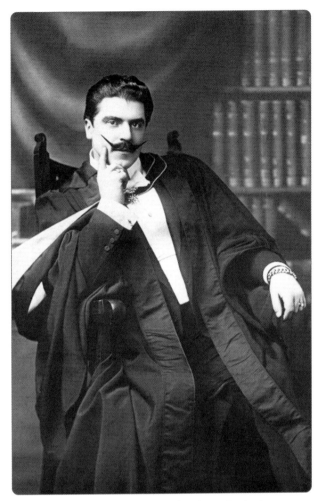

Dr Walford Bodie, Electric Wizardry. *(Tony Barker)*

tricks were done: Bodie paid a team of men to travel with him, watch his shows and volunteer to take part in them as though they were ordinary members of the audience. Irving named seven of them.

In addition, there was evidence from witnesses who had taken part in shows staged by Bodie. A man who had suffered from a withered leg since childhood had been carried onstage, although he could have walked. Bodie had broken the man's crutches across his knee, saying he would never need them again. Electric charges were applied to him and he limped offstage as well as he could. He was no better after the show than before.

On the other hand, several witnesses maintained Bodie had cured them of various disabilities: a woman who said that, since childhood, she had not had use of her legs; at Shoreditch music hall, Bodie used a magnet on her; she had not worn leg irons since and was now employed as a machinist, working a treadle with her feet; and a man who said he had had to wear splints since childhood, but, after being treated by Bodie, was now in perfect health.

Bodie lost the case and was required to pay £1,000 damages. A few nights later, he had to face angry medical students at the Coliseum in Glasgow. There were near riots; Bodie was pelted with eggs and rotten fruit; policemen who tried to restore order were injured; and the theatre itself was damaged. One of the protesters was a young James Bridie, later to become one of Scotland's major playwrights:

> Through a hole in the curtain poured the police, with batons drawn and battle in their eyes . . . Our ammunition was intact and we let them have it. They came bravely one by one and on each we registered at least a dozen hits. Peasemeal bombs, bags of maize, eggs, potatoes, herring [and] soot thickened the air and policeman after policeman leapt from the stage over the orchestra railing into the eel-pit. They were blinded and angry and they laid about [the students] with their batons. The mob hit back with ash sticks and knuckles.[3]

Bodie continued to be a music-hall attraction, although less so from then on. He carried on touring in variety, bought a houseboat on the Thames, where he threw extravagant parties, and made his last appearance in Blackpool a few weeks before his death.

Harry Champion was another true individual, who would still be popular if he were alive today. His cockney routine was extraordinary: he would belt out his songs (many of them about food) as fast as he could, often setting a quicker tempo than the introduction played by the orchestra. Wonderfully snootily, *The Times* wrote of him:

> His act . . . brimmed over with vigour and character. In very baggy and dilapidated old clothes, with hat jauntily on one side, he would shuffle rapidly to and fro, hands, feet and body all moving rhythmically to a jigging tune . . . There was nothing refined or subtle about his performance, merely a salty, irrepressible vigour which immediately put an unsophisticated audience in good humour.[4]

Harry Champion went on the halls as a boy. He learned snatches of songs and picked up a few dance steps mostly to amuse his family. Having been persuaded by his friends to try his luck as a comedian, he appeared first under the name 'Will Conray' at the Royal Victor in Bethnal Green in 1882. He was so nervous that he had to be pushed onstage, but he was popular and the hall's manager wanted him to stay on. Harry, his nerves now settled, asked for £10 a week. The two men agreed on £1 a week, but, before the end of that week, Harry was appearing at two other halls as well, Relf's in Canning Town and the Rodney in Whitechapel.

It is hard to work out what type of entertainer Harry was at the outset: he was variously described as a comic, a character vocalist and a character comic. In his autobiography, Harry Randall referred to Harry singing 'swell' songs. Harry appeared in the West End for the first time in 1883 at the Marylebone, but his progress was slow. In 1886, he introduced a new act, 'From Light to Dark', in which he appeared black-faced. At the end of 1887, he changed his name to Harry Champion, but it was another two years before he found his first successful song, 'And I'm Selling up the Happy Home', written by Harry Boden. The turning point in his career, however, came with

HARRY CHAMPION (William Henry Crump)
Born north Kensington, London, 23 March 1866
Married Sarah Potterveld, West Hackney, London,
    30 November 1889 (b. Bethnal Green, east
    London, 28 January 1869)
    Three sons, William Henry, Arthur Victor and
      Thomas Frederick
    Daughter, Florence Alice (married —— Brooker)
Died London, 14 January 1942
Left £5,861

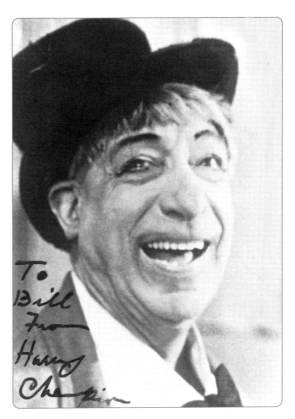

After nearly twenty years as a top-liner, Harry Champion was still the man of the moment in 1912. *(Tony Barker)*

'When the Old Dun Cow Caught Fire', by Harry Wincott. By 1894, he had so many songs that he developed his quickfire approach to try to fit as many as he could into his allotted time.

His three most successful songs were: 'Boiled beef and carrots' (1909), written by Charles Collins and Fred Murray (this song became so well known that people wanting boiled beef and carrots in London restaurants used to ask for a Harry Champion):

> Boiled beef and carrots. Boiled beef and carrots.
> That's the stuff for your Darby Kel
>   [cockney rhyming slang for 'belly'. 'Darby Kelly' is the title of an Irish folk
>   song: 'Mr grandsire beat the drum complete. His name was Darby Kelly . . .']
> Makes you fat and keeps you well.
> Don't live like vegetarians
> On food they give to parrots.
> From morn till night
> Blow out your kite [stomach]
> On boiled beef and carrots.

The other two were 'I'm Henery the Eighth I am' (1910), written by Murray and R.P. Weston; and 'Any old iron' (1911), written by Collins, E.A. Sheppard and Fred Terry:

> Any old iron, any old iron?
> Any any any old iron?
> You look neat. Talk about a treat.
> You look dapper [neat] from your napper [head] to your feet.
> Dressed in style. Brand new tile [hat] and your father's old green tie on
> But I wouldn't give you tuppence for your old watch chain.
> Old iron? Old iron?

In the Second World War, Fred Allsopp wrote a new lyric for 'Any old iron':

> I love the place where I was born.
> That's good old Bethnal Green.
> I'm what you call a Britisher.
> I love my King and Queen.
> But now we've got some trouble on with Jerry once again.
> Let's all do as we're told to uphold old England's name.
> We've got the men. We've got the pluck and courage, too.
> I'm speaking on behalf of every mother's son of you.
> Give old England all you can. Be generous and kind.
> Before you go to bed tonight, just see if you can find
> Any old iron, any old iron, any any any old iron.
> Old iron cot, old iron bicycle or anything you've got.
> An old iron plate, an old iron grate your mother used to fry on.
> And I'm going to give my country my old watch chain. Old iron, old iron.

Harry continued working until 1941 when he suffered a nervous breakdown brought on by overwork.

Paul Cinquevalli is still widely regarded as the greatest juggler ever, unsurpassed in breathtaking dexterity even seventy-five years after his death. One of his more startling feats was to use his body as a billiards table, wearing a jacket made of billiard cloth with pockets of cord and brass wire on his shoulders and back. Part of his bill matter was 'The Human Billiard Table'.

Cinquevalli juggled with everything: cannon balls, barrels, cutlery and a wide range of other domestic items, rehearsing a routine for many hours each day until he had perfected it.

PAUL CINQUEVALLI (Paul Braun-Lehmann or Emile Otto Lehmann-Braun or Emile Otto Paul Braun or Paul Braun or Paul Kestner or none of these)
Born Poland or Prussia (?), 30 June 1859
Married Adelina —— (professionally known as Adelina Price, a celebrated equestrienne in the 1880s; her act was a feature of the winter season of Charles Hengler's circus in Argyll Street before the London Palladium was built, 1887;
    d. 3 March 1908)
  Daughter
Died Brixton, south London, 14 July 1918
Left £26,218

He began to invent tricks at school. One of his favourites was to throw his pencil and slate in the air, catch the pencil, write the letter 'A' on the slate and catch the slate before it touched the ground. He was also a fine gymnast, winning five prizes for acrobatic performances at the age of 13. Cinquevalli's parents wanted him to be a priest, but, by now fascinated by gymnastics, he ran away from home when he was 14 and joined an Italian acrobatic troupe led by

Guiseppe Chiese-Cinquevalli, from whom he took his stage name. He made his first public appearance as a performer on the high wire in Odessa on the coast of the Black Sea, but, while performing in St Petersburg, he suffered an accident that changed the course of his life:

I was taking a long leap – with no friendly net beneath me – from one swinging trapeze to another. The attendant who should have wiped the moisture from the bars of the furthest trapeze had been absorbing moisture in glasses at bars more congenial and had neglected his duty. As usual, I leapt with outstretched hands, but the trapeze slid through my fingers as if it had been greased. A gasp of horror floated up from the thousands below. In the space of five seconds, I thought of father and mother, the playground, the school and pictured my own funeral. It was several days before I recovered consciousness – mashed, it seemed to me, to pieces; and for eight weary months I lay half dead in hospital. That was the end of my trapeze days and, while on the road to convales-

Paul Cinquevalli, the Human Billiard Table. *(Tony Barker)*

cence, I began afresh the tricks of my childhood; hour after hour and day after day, I spent in balancing and juggling bottles, balls, plates, anything and everything that I could lay my hands on.[5]

So, from the age of 17, Cinquevalli was a juggler. He made his first appearance in Britain in 1885 and then became a naturalised English subject. He travelled widely, astounding audiences in Australia, South Africa, India and South America. He was once asked what made a good juggler:

The first thing a juggler must do is to learn to work his limbs, especially his hands and arms, with immense rapidity. To acquire such rapidity of movement, it is necessary to go through various exercises every day and, above all, to see that each day one does the exercises a little more rapidly than the day before. Then one must train the eye to act very rapidly.[6]

Three months after the outbreak of the First World War, Cinquevalli retired, making his final appearance at the Tivoli Theatre, Melbourne.

Harry Tate, widely regarded as one of the funniest comics on the halls, worked first as a mimic and then successfully made the transition from music hall to revue and variety, becoming the foremost sketch comedian between the two world wars.

HARRY TATE (Ronald MacDonald Hutchison (*sic*))
Born Lambeth, south London, 4 July 1872
Married Julia Maud Kerslake Baker, Lambeth, south
    London, 8 July 1898
    Son, Ronald (professionally known as Harry Tate
    junior; d. 25 May 1982)
Died Northolt, Middlesex, 14 February 1940
Left £1,050

Tate was the son of a Scottish tea merchant. Although many accounts speak of him beginning his working life with the sugar firm, Henry Tate, this was not so, although it was, apparently, Marie Lloyd who suggested that he should adopt Tate as his stage name. At the outset, he impersonated Dan Leno, R.G. Knowles and Eugene Stratton. By the time he arrived in London in 1895, he had added George Beauchamp, T.E. Dunville, Gus Elen, James Fawn and George Robey to the list.

Appearing in *Aladdin* at the Theatre Royal in Leeds in 1902/3, he introduced his sketch 'Motoring' for the first time, capitalising on the growing interest in car ownership:

CHAUFFEUR. To speak expleasantly . . .
TATE. Are you aware there isn't such a word? (*To son*) Correct him, Roland.
SON. It's expleasantplosh, Papa.
TATE. It's nothing of the kind. You're worse than he is.
CHAUFFEUR. Well, sir, it's the sprockets. They are not running true with the differential gear
    and that causes the exhaust box to short circuit with the magneto ignition on the
    commutator, I don't think.

The sketch was so successful that, by the end of 1903, Tate had decided to abandon mimicry and switch entirely to sketches, most of which he wrote with Wal Pink.

Harry Tate in his best-known sketch. (*Richard Anthony Baker*)

After 'Motoring', there followed a string of sketches, in which an anarchic sense of humour predominated: 'Fishing', 'Gardening', 'Golfing', 'Wireless', 'Selling a Car', 'Billiards' and so on. In 'Running an Office', a sense of chaos is immediately purveyed:

TATE. Any letters?
CLERK. No letters, sir.
TATE. No letters?
CLERK. No, sir.
TATE. Then we must write some. Get some ink in the office. I can't keep writing with chalk.

Tate's son, Ronnie, explained that his father's company adapted the act to the town or city they were playing. There were catchphrases, such as 'I don't think', used as an ironic postscript to a thought; and 'How's Your Father?' enunciated by Tate whenever he felt the conversation was not going his way. This was not an original saying. In Feydeau's *La Dame de chez Maxim* (1899), the eponymous prostitute greeted her younger clients with ''Allo, darlin'. 'Ow's your father?' The phrase can also mean 'copulation'. Another catchphrase, 'Good-bye-ee', became so well known that it was taken up by British troops leaving to fight in the First World War, especially after a song had been wound around the word by Weston and Lee.

Tate wore a false moustache that seemed to move around his face as though it had a life of its own. W.J. MacQueen-Pope wrote:

It was difficult to believe it was false: it not only responded to every emotion and expression on Tate's mobile face, it also expressed them. It bristled, it rose, it stood on end in battle or victory, it drooped at seeming defeat. It was a living question-mark when Tate's curiosity was aroused, indeed, it asked the question for him. That moustache was a true inspiration.[7]

Without his stage make-up (and particularly his moustache), Tate was unrecognisable. James Agate once sat next to him at a Variety Artistes' Federation dinner:

I sat next to him without knowing who he was and proceeded to regale him with an account of his own performance the evening before. *Fishing* had been the sketch and I told how HT had inadvertently thrown ground-bait at the red-nosed man with the bowler hat two sizes too small, how the red-nosed man had resented this, how HT said he had mistaken him for a swan, how the aggrieved assistant said 'Do I look like a swan?' and how HT had roared 'Not now you've turned round.' Not a muscle in Harry's face moved and all he said was 'Must have been very funny'.[8]

Come the 1930s, Tate found that touring with a company of six was too expensive and so he introduced a new sketch, 'Going Round the World', which featured only him and Ronnie.[9]

The Times summarised his appeal:

Goaded into testiness now and then in spite of a natural bonhomie and arguing with a muddled logic which was delightful because so small a dash of lunacy served to separate it from the arguments of everyday life, Harry Tate was in his sketches the embodiment of the ordinary man struggling with irritations he cannot control.[10]

In John Buchan's novel *The Thirty-Nine Steps*, and in Hitchcock's free adaptation of it, there was the character Mr Memory. Then came the real-life Datas, who answered any questions put to him by his audience, often embellishing his responses with extraneous information. So that, when he was asked the name of the only American president to be elected by all the voters, he replied:

> George Washington, who was elected president in 1789. He was again elected, thus serving two terms of four years each. He was born on 11 February 1732, according to the old-style calendar, and on 22 February, according to the new. There were eleven days put onto the calendar in 1752 to make it come in line with the old Gregorian calendar of 1582 and Russia is the only country in existence which has not adopted the new style of calendar today. Am I right, sir?[11]

As a boy, Datas considered himself backward. Even so, by the time he left school at the age of 11, he had started memorising facts he thought he might find useful.

In the late 1890s, Datas worked as a boilerman with the South Metropolitan Gas Company. While there, he was taken ill with a chest complaint and spent a long time in hospital. To while away the hours, he avidly read encyclopedias and reference books, again memorising as much as he could. He used no system of mnemonics, but created what he called mind pictures that could be recalled later. Back at work, he spent his lunch hours in a local pub, answering questions put to him by his workmates and other regulars. He became something of a local celebrity with 'Am I right, sir?' tacked on as a catchphrase.

One lunchtime, the comedian Tom Bass, who was in the pub, was impressed by Datas and persuaded the owner of the Royal Standard music hall to book him. Datas was so successful that he was retained at the theatre for two months, was then booked by the Palace and went on to play nearly every music hall in Britain.

On his first trip to America in 1904, he was tested by four doctors who somehow weighed his brain and

DATAS (William John Morris Bottle)
Born Teynham, Kent, 20 July 1875
Married
    Daughter
Died (as William John Maurice Bottell),
    Croydon, Surrey,
    23 August 1956

Datas, the Living Encyclopedia. (*Tony Barker*)

found it to be the heaviest they had ever examined. There and then, they paid Datas £2,000 to leave his head to them when he died so that it could be examined more rigorously. Years later, Datas took delight in telling people that he had 'won' since he outlived all four doctors.

Offstage, Datas was a quiet, unassuming and popular man. Onstage, he brought a certain dignity to his act, which made it all the more impressive. He was once asked the age of Marie Lloyd by someone in the gallery. He took two steps forward, looked up and answered: 'Sir, a gentleman never discloses the age of a lady.' There was tremendous applause. (Marie's age was, in any case, widely known. The sports and theatre paper *The Referee* ran an Answers to Correspondents column, in which it gave Marie's age each week. It kept the answer on a print block, merely changing the age every year. Marie enjoyed the joke and in 1908 gave *The Referee* what she called a combined certificate, in which her date of birth and those of her siblings were listed.)

Herman Darewski used to tell a story about sharing digs with Datas, Houdini and the magician Carl Hertz. After a show one night, the four men sat up talking until Darewski and Hertz decided it was time for bed. As soon as they left the room, they locked the other two in. When Houdini and Datas discovered what had happened, they panicked. Houdini could not find a way to escape and Datas could not remember the name of the landlady to alert her. Good though the story is, it has an apocryphal air about it, especially when slightly differing versions are discovered. One thing Datas did forget was his name at birth. He was born 'Bottle' and died 'Bottell', undoubtedly with the accent on the second syllable.

Sam Mayo adopted a style of dress that was all his own. Decked out in a long overcoat or dressing gown and with a curious cap on his head, he accompanied himself at the piano with a vacant expression and a monotonous voice. He was billed as the Immobile One.

Sam was one of eight children born to the owner of a second-hand shop near Poverty Corner. He was introduced to the profession by one of his older brothers, Ted, who went on to be a comic singer. Sam worked in his father's shop, but, in his spare time, he collected bets and, together with Ted and another brother, Maurice, he sang in pubs and clubs.

> SAM MAYO (Samuel Cowan)
> **Born** London, 31 July 1881
> **Married** Zillah Flash (!) (professionally known
>   as Stella Stanley), Brighton, east Sussex,
>   13 August 1904 (d. 21 December 1966)
> **Died** London, 31 March 1938

Ted Cowan was the first in the family to go professional. While appearing in Sandgate, Kent, he suggested to the manager of the Alhambra that Sam would be a suitable replacement for an entertainer who had fallen ill. As the manager was known to oppose giving jobs to relatives, Ted invented the surname Mayo for Sam and it stuck.

Mayo wrote many of his own songs, including his most famous, 'The Old Tin Can' (1905), and he held the record for appearing at the greatest number of music halls in a single night: nine performances at London halls during the evening of 21 January 1905 (Bedford 6.30 p.m.; Euston 6.50 p.m.; Holborn 7.25 p.m.; Tivoli 8 p.m.; Gatti's 8.45 p.m.; Euston 9.25 p.m.; Standard 10 p.m.; Holborn 10.25 p.m.; and back at the Bedford at 10.50 p.m.).

Mayo also provided other comedians with his work. In 1919, he and Frank Leo presented the rotund comic Ernie Mayne with a popular novelty song, 'Where Do Flies Go in the Winter Time?', and came up with a sequel the following year, 'I Know Where the Flies Go', which he wrote with John P. Harrington.

Sam Mayo, the Immobile One. *(British Music Hall Society)*

GEORGE FORMBY (James Henry Booth)
Born Ashton-under-Lyne, Greater Manchester,
    4 October 1875
Married Eliza Ann Hoy, Wigan, Lancashire,
    11 August 1899 (d. 1981, aged 102)
    Thirteen children, seven of whom survived
Died Stockton Heath, near Warrington, Cheshire,
    8 February 1921
Left £26,707

A heavy gambler, Mayo was declared bankrupt three times.

By the age of 12, George Formby, through sleeping rough and not eating properly, had developed a serious chest complaint that was to plague him for the rest of his days. For years, he battled against consumption, making light of the fits of coughing he suffered on stage by muttering such asides as 'Coughing better tonight, coughing summat champion'. Billed as the Wigan Nightingale, a comic reference to his croaky voice, he was one of the first Lancashire dialect comedians to win acclaim in the south of England.

Formby had a miserable childhood. His mother, Sarah, a prostitute and a drunk, had a long criminal record. Within ten years, she committed 140 offences, including theft and vagrancy, but, most frequently, drunkenness. (On George's birth certificate, his mother marked her name with an 'x', indicating that she was illiterate. No mention of his father is made; so, strictly, Formby was illegitimate. Six months after his birth, Sarah married Frank Lawler. George was also known as George Lawler Booth.)

George often had to sing for his supper on the streets. In 1897, Dennis Clarke, the owner of the Argyle music hall at Birkenhead, heard Formby when he was appearing at a singing room in Manchester and booked him for a week at a salary of £2. Clarke felt that James Booth, Formby's real name, was not a good stage name and so 'George' was chosen in honour of George Robey and 'Formby' after the Lancashire town, whose name was seen on the side of coal wagons.

Formby's breakthrough came when he was appearing in Dublin. An agent of Oswald Stoll saw him and offered him work at £5 a week. 'I thought my fortune was made . . . That was the first lift I ever had. I

George Formby, a favourite in Sunderland and all over Britain. *(Richard Anthony Baker)*

have been through the mill single-handed . . . Many a week I have lived on bread and dripping – and been glad to have that.'[12]

Dressed in a badly fitting jacket and trousers, with enormous boots and a bowler hat that was too small, he was one of Marie Lloyd's favourite comics. She chose to watch only two comedians from the wings: Formby and Dan Leno.

His son, also George Formby, was the ukelele-playing star of a series of successful British comedy films made in the 1930s and 1940s.

In a lengthy and varied career, George Robey, who billed himself as the Prime Minister of Mirth, became a star in music hall before moving on to similar success in revue and finally playing Shakespeare. As a singer, he adopted a number of comic guises, although he was most recognisable in a small bowler hat, heavily accentuated eyebrows and what looked like clerical garb. He presented himself as a pompous man using

GEORGE ROBEY (George Wade)
Born Kennington, London, 20 September 1869
Married (1) Ethel Haydon, central London, 29 April 1898 (dissolved 1938; d. Bosham, near Chichester, January 1953)
　Son, Edward (1900–83)
(2) Blanche Littler, 30 November 1938 (d. 1981)
Died London, 29 November 1954

George Robey, the Prime Minister of Mirth. *(Richard Anthony Baker)*

strings of long words that even he did not understand. In the classic tradition, he allowed his audience to presume a risqué conclusion to a situation and then admonish them for having dirty minds.

George did well at school, particularly enjoying painting and music, especially Wagner. His father, a civil engineer, wanted him to become one too and George moved to Birmingham as clerk of works on the building of a new tramway, but found the work dull. He took up painting again, joined Handsworth football club, where he became a leading player, and learned the mandolin, which he played in duets with a guitarist friend in a charity concert at a church hall.

At a concert in 1890, he decided to sing as well (four songs then made up his entire repertoire) and, before long, he established for himself a reputation as a comic singer in the Birmingham area. Wanting a stage name, he chose 'Roby' after a firm in Birmingham. When this was misprinted as 'Robey', he adopted the new spelling.

When one of his friends organised a smoking concert in Fleet Street, George appeared, wearing a shabby black cassock, a wig that gave him a domed forehead, blackened eyebrows and carrying a rusty umbrella and a worn top hat. He sang the American song 'Where did you get that hat?' (1888). After another smoking concert at Kennington in 1891, he worked for several weeks as a stooge for a bogus hypnotist at the Royal Westminster Aquarium. The hypnotist appeared to put him into a trance and then turn him into a comic singer. The manager of the Aquarium was so impressed that he offered George the chance to sing there.

In June 1891, he was asked to be an extra turn at a Saturday matinée at the Oxford. As a result, he was invited back for the Saturday night, when he sang 'The Simple Pimple' (1891), written by E.W. Rogers. The manager of the Oxford then offered him a year-long engagement and, although he suffered a setback at the Star in Bermondsey, where he was booed, his rise to stardom was quite quick. He was soon playing four or five halls a night.

George developed his own way of making an entrance. He liked to run on stage, face the audience, apparently surprised to see them, wait for a laugh and then reprimand them with 'Out. Out. Desist!' In this way, Robey managed to get his audience to laugh before he had even started. By now, he had replaced the top hat with a flat bowler hat and the umbrella with a small cane. He still wore his wig and painted in heavy eyebrows. His admonitions grew more verbose: 'Let there be merriment by all means. Let there be merriment, but let it be tempered with dignity and the reserve which is compatible with the obvious refinement of our environment.'

Robey's songs developed into sketches with different characters materialising: the Prehistoric Man; Henry the Eighth; a theatrical landlady; Daisy Dillwater, a district nurse; and, most famous of all, the muddled and self-important Mayor of Mudcumdyke. Before the end of the 1890s, Robey's earnings rose to £100 a week.

During the First World War, he raised huge sums for charity. In 1916, he appeared in his first revue, *The Bing Boys are Here*, at the Alhambra. It was a smash hit, running for more than nine months and seen by more than 6,000 people. Its enduring song was 'If you were the only girl in the world', which Robey sang with Violet Loraine. It was written by Nat D. Ayer and Clifford Grey, who also contributed 'Another little drink' (wouldn't do us any harm), sung by Robey, Loraine and Alfred Lester.

It was during the run of a Palladium revue, *Sky High* (1925), that Robey began an affair with his leading lady, Marie Blanche, the latest in a long series of mistresses. By then, he and his wife, an Australian actress, Ethel Haydon, were living separate lives. His son, Edward, commented: 'Women were his one weakness: almost, one might say, an obsession.' At one point, he toured south Africa with Marie Blanche, the liner docking for a time at Madeira. There, face to face, he ran into his wife, who was visiting the island with two friends. After that, he did not return home and never spoke to his wife again. He starred Marie Blanche in two of his own productions, *Sky High* and *Bits and Pieces* (Princes, 1927). In December 1928, he put on another show of his devising, *In Other Words*, which, like *Bits and Pieces*, he took to South Africa.

When he returned to England, he gave up management and returned to performing solo spots, playing theatres all over the country. They included the Royal Artillery Theatre, Woolwich, which was run by Agnes Littler, whose three children, Emile, Prince and Blanche all followed theatrical careers too. During the Woolwich run, Blanche got to know Robey well and soon discovered that his financial affairs were in a hopeless mess. Within a few weeks, she was arranging his bookings, answering his letters, compiling his tax returns and even supervising his band calls. Although Robey was then 60 and Blanche 30, a romance sprang up between them. They set up home together, although another nine years elapsed before Robey obtained a divorce from his wife.

Robey's movie career began in 1900 and ended in 1952. (Notable appearances were *Chu Chin Chow* (1934) and *Henry the Fifth* (1945), in which he played Falstaff.) He starred opposite Evelyn Laye in an English version of Offenbach's *La Belle Hélène* (Adelphi, 1932), staged by C.B. Cochran. He played cabaret at the Trocadero, earning over £350 (£12,000) a week, at that time more than any cabaret performer had ever received. Robey made his last public appearance at a charity performance at Bertram Mills' Circus at Christmas 1953. In the New Year's Honours List of 1954, he was knighted.

Of his music-hall days, he had an admirable attitude:

> Give me a joke that is a joke, not a Sunday school translation of one. Give me humour that will make any man laugh, but of which no man need be ashamed. I want no furtive, shame-faced allusions to things unmention-able. The vulgarity I like must be honest – such as can be presented openly. Veiled hints and suggestions are not humour – neither are they vulgar. As a rule, they're just filthy and therefore unmanly.[13]

A younger, handsome Harry Tate before he donned his erratic moustache.
(Richard Anthony Baker)

CHAPTER 30

THE DEATH OF MUSIC HALL (NEARLY)

Music hall died from a four-pronged assault from cinema, ragtime, revue and radio. People who lived through the First World War said nothing was the same afterwards. It was certainly true of popular entertainment.

Ironically, a music hall provided one of the earliest homes for moving pictures or the Cinematograph, as it was termed by the men regarded as the inventors of cinema, Auguste and Louis Lumière. The Empire, Leicester Square, paid £150 a week for the privilege. *The Entr'acte* saw a future for it: 'Two of the pictures – the railway station and the sea-bathing – were encored . . . Visitors were acutely interested in them . . . The feature is special and will be the talk of London.'[1]

Once cinema had established itself, cine-variety bills became popular, combining films with live variety acts. Some even saw this as the future variety. Amplification in cinemas was always a problem. So, patter comedians did not fare well, but close harmony groups, pianists, ventriloquists and impressionists did. The agent Joe Collins gave a good description of the mix: 'Cinemas were winning the audience battle against music halls. Yet this was still a transition period in entertainment tastes. Though the public were now flocking to "the pictures", they still liked to see a few "live turns" on stage . . . Just for the price of a seat, you got two major films, a "short", a newsreel, some variety acts and an organ recital.'[2]

Before he teamed up with his cousin, Ben Warriss, as a double act, Jimmy Jewel worked in cine-variety. On one occasion, he played two cinemas – one in Manchester, the other in Preston – each of them showing two films. Jimmy appeared in the intervals at both as the only act on the bill. The audiences were good, he said. People were quite pleased to see a live act in between all that celluloid.

The craze for ragtime, the basis of all jazz, swept in from the United States during 1912. For more than 200 years, America's dances had been imported from Europe. Youngsters now decided they wanted something newer. Overcoming their reluctance to try dances associated with black people, bars and brothels, they strode onto the ballroom floor to do the One-Step, the Turkey Trot, the Bunny Hug and many others. Irving Berlin, whose 'Alexander's Ragtime Band' had been the smash hit of 1911, came to London to find reporters following his every move: 'Go where you will, you cannot escape from the mazes of music he has spun . . . Ragtime has swept like a whirlwind over the earth and set civilisation humming.'[3]

The latest fad was gleefully adopted by a new theatrical phenomenon, the revue, a pot-pourri of sketches and songs. The Empire, Leicester Square, staged *Everybody's Doing It* with Berlin's song of (nearly) the same name as the grand finale. It ran for 354 performances and even earned grudging approval by a representative of the Lord Chamberlain, the official censor of all theatrical productions until 1968: 'impudent, but innocuous'. At the Hippodrome, it was *Hullo, Ragtime!* which ran for 451 performances and was succeeded by *Hullo, Tango* with its hit song 'Get out and get under'.

Of the four influences that threatened music hall most, radio (or, more accurately, the wireless) was feared worst. If people 'listening-in' to the programmes of the British Broadcasting Company (it became a Corporation in 1927), could enjoy your act at home, so the argument went, why should they bother to go to a theatre? Albert Voyce, of the Variety Artistes' Federation, summed up the performers' fears: 'The artiste, who is in demand and who is identified with material of an original and distinctive character, would be most unwise to broadcast such material, since, by doing so, he would not only shorten the life of his material, but also lessen the value of his act as a going concern.'[4]

Oswald Stoll was more apocalyptic: 'When broadcasting reaches a high state of perfection, the best singers, actors, lecturers and orators will be listened to by ten million people at a time. But all the lesser fry in artistry will be wiped out. No-one will have any use for them.'[5] It was not until 1925 that an agreement was reached by the BBC and the Society of West End Theatre Managers, but the Variety Artistes' Federation refused to sign it: 'The music hall had lost its pre-1914 vitality and much of its power to attract; radio was to come to its rescue during the 1930s and might have rescued it earlier had it been given the chance.'[6] In time, such radio shows as *Music Hall* (1932–52), *Workers' Playtime* (1941–64), and *Variety Bandbox* (1942–52) all proved to be good employers of music hall and variety performers.

The first attempt to show audiences that music hall was still alive was made by the Veterans of Variety. They appeared at the London Palladium in January 1923 and made their radio debut only two months after the BBC had begun daily transmissions. Eight of them, including Charles Bignell, Lily Burnand, Marie Collins (one of Lottie's sisters), Tom Costello and Sable Fern, sped by taxi to the studios at Savoy Hill between the Palladium's first and second houses without changing or removing their make-up. They were back on stage in 1924 with a slightly different line-up. Leo Dryden, Frank Leo and Arthur Roberts had been added to the troupe.

The drama critic Archibald Haddon believed the Veterans demonstrated what was missing in contemporary entertainment: 'In everything those veterans do or say or sing there is the human touch . . . Personality, which finds its expression most effectively in the solo turn, has been discouraged on the halls by the preference given to sketches, scenas, concert numbers and spectacular attractions and the result is that the halls are being dehumanised.'[7]

The songwriter J.P. Harrington felt likewise: 'The triumphant success of the Veterans of Variety at the Palladium to my mind proves beyond the shadow of a peradventure that there is still an immense public enthusiastically appreciative of good wholesome songs of sentiment and comedy, even in blasé days of Yankee jingle and bang.'[8]

Lew Lake, who had been in turn proprietor, agent and performer, decided he would try to revive music hall in the 1930s. Variety shows, he argued, were too refined for an audience that had grown up with the 'vulgar but honest' music hall. He reckoned that, if he could re-create a bill of twenty-five years earlier, he would mount a tour of large provincial theatres and fill them. He persuaded some first-rate entertainers to join him in the venture: Vesta Victoria, Harry Champion, Fred Barnes and Fred Russell. Lew himself was to appear in one of the comedy sketches he had presented on the halls, 'The Bloomsbury Burglars'. The show had a working title of *Variety 1906–1931*. Soon, a much clumsier name emerged, *Stars who Have Never Failed to Shine*, but the neater *Stars who Never Fail to Shine* was used just as frequently.

> LEW LAKE (Lewis Lake)
> **Born** 1875 (?)
> **Married** Jessie Florence ——— (d. April 1965, aged 90)
> Two sons, Lew (Lewis Arthur Henry, d. March 1958, aged 56) and Leonard
> Three daughters, Jessie, Lydia and Rosie
> **Died** 5 November 1939

The tour (or experimental run, as Lew called it) began at the Palace in Reading. His hunch paid off. On the first night, the theatre was packed. During the first house, there were so many calls for encores that the second house was delayed by half an hour. Fred Russell, for one, was delighted: 'This new venture appears to have clicked, which goes to show there is a public for the "old stuff", when presented by experienced performers.'[9]

The show moved on to the East Ham Palace and the Wolverhampton, Liverpool and Southend Hippodromes. Everywhere, there were rave notices. The stars came and went, but there was always a strong line-up.

Fifteen years went by before Don Ross launched another attempt to revive music hall. His *Thanks for the Memory* show, also featuring a company of veterans who toured Britain, proved the surprise success of the 1948 Royal Variety Show.

Don, known to his friends as Billy, began his professional career as a journalist and apprentice stockbroker, but his sights were always set on the stage. In 1926, he auditioned in Sheffield for the male lead in a show called *Dear Louise*, which was to star one of his childhood idols, Gertie Gitana. He got the part.

Above: Southend Hippodrome: before. *(Richard Anthony Baker)*

Right: Southend Hippodrome: during. *(Lynn Tait)*

DON ROSS (Donald Ross)
Born 20 September 1902
Married Gertrude Mary Astbury
    (professionally known as Gertie
    Gitana), 24 June 1928
    (d. 5 January 1957)
Died Hove, east Sussex, 6 February
    1980
Left £47,880

Southend Hippodrome: after. *(Richard Anthony Baker)*

Don was gay and, over the years, had a number of unhappy liaisons with, among others, a soldier who committed suicide, a man hanged for matricide and a young singer who died of a brain haemorrhage. But, during the run of *Dear Louise*, Don and Gertie became engaged and, six months after the show closed in Edinburgh in December 1927, they married.

Originally a child entertainer, Gertie had scored her greatest success with an American song, 'Nellie Dean' (1905). Her quiet, rather coy performance of the song contrasts with the raucous, drunken way in which it is sung now:

There's an old mill by the stream, Nellie Dean.
Where we used to sit and dream, Nellie Dean.
And the waters as they flow
Seem to murmur sweet and low.
You're my heart's desire.
I love you, Nellie Dean.

Gertie enjoyed more than forty years' success with the song. Her brother had heard it in America and thought it might suit her. She sang it for the first time at the Palace Theatre, Plymouth, in 1907.

Gertie was born in Shropshire, her father a pottery worker, her mother, the manager of a general store. As a child, she used to line up her dolls on the outside window sill of the shop and sing and dance to them, amusing passers-by. At the age of 4, she joined an outfit called Tomkinson's Royal Gypsy Children's Troupe, which was popular at halls in the Potteries towns; at 6, she was topping the bill as Little Gitana, *gitana* being the Italian word for gypsy girl; and at 8, she joined another

Don Ross, music hall's last impresario. *(British Music Hall Society)*

GERTIE GITANA (Gertrude Mary Astbury)
Born Longport, Shropshire, 28 December
    1887
Married Donald Ross (professionally known
    as Don Ross), 24 June 1928
Died Hampstead, north London,
    5 January 1957
Left £23,585

troupe at a starting salary of £3 a week. She made her first solo appearance at the Tivoli in Barrow-in-Furness and arrived in London in 1900. By the time she was 15, Gertie was earning over £100 (by today's standards £5,500) a week, more than her father earned in a year. She first topped a bill in London at the Holborn Empire, extending her range of talents to include tap-dancing, yodelling and playing the saxophone.

Don drifted into management. Gertie's agent, George Barclay, suggested that he should see a new entertainer appearing at the Camberwell Palace, Nedlo, the Gypsy Violinist, the stage name of Charlie Olden, who eventually adopted another name, Ted Ray, and became a top-line radio comic. Ted, Gertie and Don became close friends.

Don set up an agency with Barclay's manager, Bob Wade, and, at Gertie's suggestion, they put together a revue, *Gertie, George and Ted*, in which Gertie and Ted teamed up with G.H. Elliott. Don tried to persuade Elliott to sing 'Lily of Laguna', but he refused, saying it was Eugene Stratton's song. He eventually relented.

By 1935, the agency was doing well and Don and Gertie travelled to America to see, among other things, Minksy's Burlesque Show in New York, in which a stripper, Kenza Vinton, appeared. Don booked her to appear in a show in Britain called *Don't Blush, Girls*, the first time a stripper had been seen in Britain.

Don's next venture was a circus, another success for him. In 1947, he dreamed up *Thanks for the Memory*, in which he wanted to feature Gertie, Nellie Wallace, Hetty King, Lily Morris and Talbot O'Farrell, an immaculately dressed man, who made a big name for himself as an Irish entertainer. Don cabled G.H. Elliott in Switzerland, inviting him to take part too, but he cannot have foreseen the troubles he would have putting a bill together.

Nellie and Lily, who had quarrelled in the past, refused to appear on the same stage together, although Lily had decided, in any case, that she did not

Gertie Gitana, the Star who Never Fails to Shine. *(Richard Anthony Baker)*

LILY MORRIS (Lilles Mary Crosby)
Born London, 30 September 1882
Married Archibald McDougall, Newcastle, Tyne
and Wear, 15 February 1907 (d. London,
17 August 1952)
Died London, 3 October 1952
Left £1,804

TALBOT O'FARRELL (William Henry Parrott)
Born Hull, East Riding of Yorkshire, 30 August 1875
Married Lily Winifred Brown (professionally known
as Minnie Talbot), Hull, 7 April 1898 (The Water
Rats' Queen Ratling in 1930, 1932 and 1944;
d. St Pancras, London, 23 August 1949)
Son, Richard
Died north London, 2 September 1952

want to tour again. The Moss Empires booker, Cissie Williams, warned Don that Talbot O'Farrell and Nellie Wallace were two of the most difficult people in the business: 'If you can control them for longer than three months, you are a better man than I give you credit for.' O'Farrell insisted on top billing, £175 a week, the number one dressing-room, his choice of place on the programme and the right to work only with those he chose. Don refused. He then went to see Hetty King, who was similarly demanding: 'Her attitude changed as soon you talked business. Her face went hatchet-shaped. [She said] I must be top of the bill. I must get £175 a week. I must be able to say where I will be on the bill and who I will follow on the programme and I will not work on a bill with Randolph Sutton [who she reckoned stole her material].'[10]

Don bade her goodnight, adding: 'It's my show, sweetheart, not yours.' Afterwards, Hetty told friends she regretted her behaviour. She did join *Thanks for the Memory*, but only after Ella Shields had left. And neither she nor O'Farrell was top of the bill.

Don cabled Ella Shields via the Bank of Australia in Brisbane, offering her £100 a week. Her acceptance marked her homecoming to Britain. Randolph Sutton and Wee Georgie Wood also asked to join the line-up. Don accepted Sutton, but, wisely, not Wood. It was agreed that the show should open at the Empress at Brixton in south London in February 1948.

G.H. Elliott then tried to withdraw. Don persuaded him to change his mind, but Elliott agreed only on the understanding that *he* had top billing and the number one dressing-room. In the end, all six featured artistes (Elliott, Gitana, King, O'Farrell, Sutton and Wallace) signed their contracts. Then, a row ensued after Don visited the Empress five weeks before the show opened and saw a poster advertising O'Farrell there in a Max Miller show. Don gave O'Farrell a dressing-down, told him that he would be replaced for the first week by the red-nosed comic Billy Danvers, and that he would not join the company until the second week in Liverpool.

In spite of all the problems, *Thanks for the Memory* proved a huge success. Val Parnell offered Don a two-week run at the London Palladium in July 1948 to be followed by the Royal Variety Show. Tragically, Nellie died shortly after the show, but Lily Morris then agreed to take her place, making her first appearance at the Shepherd's Bush Empire in January 1949. The show moved to Blackpool for the summer and, although it was going well, Don and Gertie decided it should close at the theatre at which it had opened, the Empress, Brixton, in December 1950. 'It was as if the cream that remained were bidding the nation "goodbye" on behalf of the British music hall they had known and loved.'[11]

Mercifully, BBC Radio recorded the show, which was transcribed onto CD in 2004. This was the line-up in order of appearance:

'My Girl's Mother'; 'On Mother Kelly's doorstep': Randolph Sutton

'My Mother's Pie Crust': Nellie Wallace

'Does your Mother Know you're Out, Cecilia?'; 'I'm not All There'; 'Burlington Bertie from
    Bow': Ella Shields

'Paddy McCarthy's Party'; 'How Ireland was Made'; 'Mother of Mine': Talbot O'Farrell

'Silver Bell'; 'You were Comin' thro the Corn, Molly Dear'; 'Why Didn't you Tell me? Never
    Mind'; 'Nellie Dean': Gertie Gitana

'We Went Gathering Nuts in May'; 'Cheerio, Keep your Chin up': Billy Danvers

'I'm Going back again to Old Nebraska'; 'Lily of Laguna': G.H. Elliott.

After Don's involvement with the show had finished, it continued throughout the 1950s
with G.H. Elliott, Hetty King and others, one of them, Dick Henderson, a stout comic, whose
signature tune was the unlikely 'Tiptoe through the Tulips'.

His son Dickie Henderson, best
remembered for playing a drunken
crooner, had his own television
programme, *The Dickie Henderson
Show*, which ran for 116 editions on
ITV between 1960 and 1968. Early
in his career, Dickie played the
Glasgow Empire with his father:

> DICK HENDERSON (Richard Henderson)
> **Born** Hull, east Riding of Yorkshire, 20 March 1891
> **Married** Winifred Dunn, Chorlton-cum-Hardy, Greater
>   Manchester, 12 September 1918
> One son, Richard Matthew (professionally known as
>   Dickie Henderson; 1920–85)
> Two daughters, Winnie and Triss (Theresa), who worked
>   as the Henderson Twins (Triss married Captain Dennis
>   Lilleyman)
> **Died** Paddington, London, 15 October 1958

I was dressed in a black dinner suit
with a ridiculous-looking black
trilby hat . . . When nothing I said or did seemed to get a laugh, I turned to the bandleader in
the pit and said out loud: 'It's like trying to get blood from a stone working for this lot.' After
that, the audience's indifference turned to hostility . . . [After I walked off] my father [was]
apoplectic with rage. So much so, in fact, that he hit me . . . Not because I failed to make the
audience laugh, but because I insulted them and blamed them for my failure. It was a lesson I
never forgot.[12]

Two further campaigns to keep music hall alive resulted from the demolition of the
Metropolitan, Edgware Road. Daniel Farson covered the hall's closure for *This Week*, a current
affairs programme transmitted by the independent television company, Associated
Rediffusion. Before the theatre was reduced to rubble, he hired it for one afternoon to make a
long-playing record on the Fontana label, featuring Elliott, Hetty, Ida Barr and others. Farson
had a particular fondness for Ida.

> IDA BARR (Maud Barlow)
> **Born** London, 17 January 1882
> **Married** (1) Gus Harris
>   (separated)
>   (2) C.W. Marriott, of American
>   Navy, April 1919
> **Died** London, 17 December 1967

The daughter of a soldier, she was born at Regent's Park
barracks in London. Her father regarded the theatre as
wicked, but Ida was stage-struck from childhood. At the
age of 15, she ran away from home, making her theatrical
debut as a chorus girl at the Theatre Royal in Belfast in
1898. For a time, she called herself Maud Laverne because
she thought it sounded 'posh', but appeared for the first
time as Ida Barr at the Bedford ten years later.

Ida Barr, Britain's Premier Singer of Ragtime Melodies.
(*British Music Hall Society*)

A redhead, she weighed 14 pounds at birth; by the time she was an adult, she was 13½ stone. She once heard a sailor point her out to his mate: 'That's Ida Barr.' 'Which one?' asked the other. 'The big fat one with red hair.' 'Ida Barr!' came the response. 'She could 'ide a bleeding pub.' During the Second World War, her bill matter was: Ida Barr – no chicken, but game.

She married Gus Harris, a comedian billed as the only Yiddisher Scotsman in the Irish Fusiliers, who topped bills during the 1920s and 1930s. His bill matter came from one of his most popular songs, 'Sergeant Solomon Isaacstein' (1916), written by R.P. Weston and Bert Lee:

> Sergeant Solomon Isaacstein.
> He's the pet of the fighting line.
> Yoi! Yoi! Yoi! Give three hearty cheers
> For the only Yiddisher Scotsman in the
>   Irish Fusiliers.

Ida left him in 1910 and sailed to New York. She enjoyed some success in America and returned to London to capitalise on the ragtime craze. Billed as England's premier singer of ragtime melodies, she helped to popularise 'Oh, You Beautiful Doll' (1910), written by Nat D. Ayer and A. Seymour Brown, and Irving Berlin's 'Everybody's Doin' It Now' (1911). She toured widely, visiting Australia, New Zealand, South Africa, Canada and the United States.

She earned good money, but, like so many music-hall people, she was over-generous and never saved. By 1960, she was living off state benefits in a two-room flat off Charing Cross Road in central London. Had it not been for Farson, she would have ended her days in obscurity. On the album, she sang the two songs with which she was most associated, the first and only record she ever made. She also appeared on television and so impressed Danny La Rue that he told Farson how good he thought she was. Farson mentioned that she was living in straitened circumstances. Characteristically, La Rue arranged a benefit concert which raised £800 for her.

With money he inherited from his parents, Farson then decided he wanted to run a music-hall pub. He leased the Waterman's Arms on the then unfashionable Isle of Dogs and, from there, he mounted a one-off, hour-long TV special, *Time, Gentlemen, Please!* in which he looked at the pub entertainment scene in London.

A new era for Collins': girlie shows. *(Richard Anthony Baker)*

This led to an Associated Rediffusion series, *Stars and Garters*, and suddenly the Waterman's Arms became one of the places central to the Swinging London of the 1960s. Among the visitors: Claudette Colbert, Groucho Marx, Clint Eastwood, Jacques Tati, Francis Bacon, William Burroughs, Frankie Howerd, Lady Diana Cooper, Tony Bennett, Sarah Vaughan and Judy Garland. That last evening ended magically with Garland singing 'Come Rain or Come Shine' to the accompaniment of the pub piano, but the Waterman's Arms did not make money. Farson was soon £3,000 in the red and he was forced out by the brewery owners.

The British Music Hall Society (with its long-winded motto 'Cherishing the Jewels of the Past and actively Supporting the Interests of the Future') also rose from the ashes of the Metropolitan. It was founded by two friends, a Lloyd's insurance underwriter, Ray Mackender, and Gerry Glover, who worked in public relations. Walking back to their home from the Met's last show in 1962, they began discussing the need for a music-hall museum in Britain. The original idea was that a small group of collectors would hold regular meetings, but they soon changed their minds and decided they would start an organisation for music-hall enthusiasts.

Don Ross, writing in the autumn 1973 edition of the Society's magazine, the *Call Boy*, recalled that, shortly after Mackender and Glover had put an advertisement in *The Stage*, announcing the formation of the Society, he helped to officiate at an auction at which photographs from the walls of Collins' music hall were to be sold. The proceeds were to be donated to the Variety Artistes' Federation. Tommy Trinder was the auctioneer and Ross was his assistant. Again and again, Mackender proved to be the successful bidder, at one point paying £45 (by today's standards £625) for a small autographed photograph of Belle Elmore.

Not long afterwards, Ross attended a meeting at Glover's and Mackender's flat at which the launching of the Society was discussed. Many names were discussed: Masks and Faces, the Stage Door, Gags and Grease Paint. It was Ross who suggested the simplest and most straightforward title, the British Music Hall Society, and he became its first president.

The Society staged a music-hall exhibition attended by more than 1,700 people at Hoxton Hall in November 1964. After that, 500 people applied for membership. Within ten years, it stood at 1,000. From then on, the Society has gone from strength to strength. The current hard-working president is Roy Hudd; the *Call Boy*, superbly edited by Patrick Newley, has appeared regularly since December 1963; the Society's omniscient historian, Max Tyler, answers queries from all over the world; and Terry Lomas leads an excellent study group, engaged on original research.

The most exciting development in the revival of music hall has been the steady reissuing of 78rpm records and cylinders, digitally remastered on compact disc. Even to be able to play such a crumbly artefact as a cylinder sounds remarkable enough. To transfer its sound to CD and make it properly audible for the first time seems nothing short of miraculous. Nonetheless, a small group of men is doing just that and introducing music-hall aficionados to the real voices of former stars. They are doing the same with early 78s, whose grooves have been severely ploughed by heavy needles for ninety years or so and the effects are equally astounding.

Only a few years ago, the transcription of cylinder and 78 rpm recordings to long-playing records (LPs) elicited only low groans from listeners. The lyric was indiscernible and the accompaniment seemed to be going on in a bathroom at the other end of a corridor. Now, with expert remastering, Marie Lloyd and Dan Leno can be made to sound almost as though they were in the studio last week.

The leader of this cottage industry is Tony Barker. In 1978, he launched an enthusiasts' magazine called *Music Hall Records*, later abbreviated to just *Music Hall*. The run was abruptly halted in 1984 and it took fourteen years of persistent nagging by well-meaning friends before Barker picked up his editor's pen again. Even in the early days, he had a cunning plan. The large part of the magazine was an intensely researched biography – one month, perhaps, the hugely popular Harry Champion and, a few months later, Ernest Shand. Some embarrassed music-hall fans were heard to mutter that they had never heard of Shand.

Barker was purposefully correcting a misconception that began with those LP reissues. Only famous songs recorded by the likes of Vesta Victoria and Harry Lauder appeared then, leading people to think there was just a tiny coterie of stars, who spent their careers singing only their well-loved hits. The truth was that there were dozens of first-rate entertainers, Shand included, singing scores of well-crafted songs. After Barker had firmly made his point in his magazine, he eventually did the same on his record label, Cylidisc, assisted by the technical brilliance of Julian Myerscough, Dominic Combe and John R.T. Davies (1927–2004), formerly of the Temperance Seven. Myerscough has his own label, Music Hall Masters, and there is a one-man band, William Clark, who largely favours single-artist albums on his label, Windyridge.

The Cylidisc website is at http://mysite.wanadoo-members.co.uk/musichall/index.jhtml; Music Hall Masters is at http://mysite.wanadoo-members.co.uk/musichallmasters/index.jhtml; and Windyridge at the more compact www.musichallcds.com.

Tony Barker can be contacted at 68 Hawkes Road, Mitcham, Surrey CR4 3JG; Julian Myerscough at 7 Alexandra Road, Lowestoft, Suffolk NR32 1PH; and William Clark at Windyridge, Kettleburgh, Woodbridge, Suffolk IP13 7JR.

So, how have these three record labels revitalised music hall? Basically, sound no longer needs to be contained on recording tape. It can move across a computer screen, rather like a heartbeat can be monitored on an electro-cardiogram. Any clicks on the recording show up like minor explosions and can be erased. The process gets much more technical than that, but the first preparation a 78 needs before its digital makeover is wonderfully untechnical – a good clean with a brush and washing-up liquid.

Some artistes were suspicious of the embryonic recording industry just as they were about radio twenty or so years later: will I get an audience in a theatre if people can listen to me at home? Others wanted to be trailblazers with the new technology, like the coster comedians, Gus Elen and Albert Chevalier, both of whom had recording contracts from 1899. Private recordings, not issued commercially, were being made even earlier. A study of the Charles Coborn papers in the British Music Hall Society's archive showed that, when Coborn was in Edison's studio in 1890, he could not at first recall the Greek translation of the chorus of 'Two lovely black eyes'. (Remember, Coborn liked to play the polyglot and sing one of his two hits in as many languages as he could.) One of Edison's staff then produced a cylinder of the song he had made some time previously and he was back on track.

Some entertainers were unaware of what was expected of them in the recording studio. In the first years of the twentieth century, the comic George Mozart made a number of records with the Gramophone Company, where his pianist was Fred Gaisberg:

I remember George Mozart . . . arriving in a four-wheeler and unloading a heavy theatrical wicker trunk. This was dragged into the studio and I asked George to rehearse while I continued my preparations. After what I thought was rather a long lapse of time, I looked into the studio to find him standing before the trumpet in full make-up, complete with red nose, whiskers and costume. Dear, simple George had anticipated television by thirty-five years. With difficulty, I explained to him that to record his songs he need not have troubled to put on his make-up.[13]

One hundred years later, the latest chart stars, singing about love, may not know it, but they had their music-hall counterparts; the comedian, who parades himself in the guise of several different comic characters, is doing no more than music hall's first funny men; and so it is with conjurers, ventriloquists, drag artists and the rest. Music hall was the basis of all modern popular entertainment. Now, thanks to the latest technology, we are hearing it properly for the first time and understanding it better than ever before.

Final Curtain

What killed music-hall? I can tell you. You're in a depressing suburban street, where there is a decaying building alleged to be a theatre. Either side of the entrance are dirt-streaked photographic frames and behind the grime are artistes' pictures full of pin holes from previous use. The commissionaire is wearing a suit handed down for ten years and it doesn't fit. At the box office, a black-dressed biddy, who has put a teapot on the seating plan, wearily tears off a ticket. The bar is 80 yards long and, at the far end on a wooden seat, is the barmaid. She's going to get up for nobody. Eventually, you get a light ale, but it has been next to the radiator all night.

Before you complain, it's Show Time and you walk in to find all of 25 people there. If you fired a cannon, you wouldn't hit anybody. Two girls come out and sing *Happy Days Are Here Again*. Into the dance and off. Next a young novice comedian. He's pinched everybody's material, but, being inexperienced, he walks off in carpet slippers. A juggling act follows. The props are dropped maybe three times, but he gets away with it. Finally, a star act you've never heard of closes the first half. With 25 people in the bar you've got no chance of being served. The two girls open the second half with *Slow Boat to China* – same act, but a different song – and the young comic returns and is even worse, having done all his best material earlier. The juggler returns and does foot juggling for a change – and then a voice says 'Ladies and gentlemen, will you please welcome a star of variety, TV and radio, the one and only Jimmy Wheeler.' And I walk out pissed – and that's what killed music-hall. (Jimmy Wheeler, quoted in the *Call Boy*, Summer 2003)

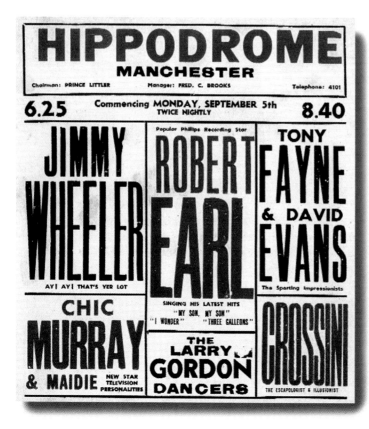

NOTES

1. In the Beginning

1. *The Town*, 3 June 1837.
2. The Chairman, who was to become a major figure in the music halls of the future, announced the turns and, if necessary, kept order in the audience.
3. W.F. Frame, *W.F. Frame Tells His Own Story*, n.p., William Holmes, n.d., pp. 30–1.
4. *The Era* was the main paper covering music hall. It first appeared largely as a sporting paper on 30 September 1838. In *All The Year Round*, Dickens wrote: 'This journal is the chronicle of the theatrical, musical and literary world: it contains synopses of all theatrical performances in this country and America; it gives profuse and erudite criticisms . . . and supports in vigorous language all dramatic institutions; it attacks in fiery terms any short-sighted, stiff-necked bigotry; in a word, it is the actor's hebdomadal [weekly] monitor and friend.' The last edition of *The Era* appeared on 21 September 1939, nearly three weeks after the outbreak of the Second World War.
5. *The Entr'acte*, 26 November 1892.
6. M. Willson Disher, *The Cowells in America*, London, Oxford University Press, 1934, p. xxxii.
7. Edmund Yates, *His Recollections and Experiences*, London, Richard Bentley, 1884, p. 172.
8. J. Ewing Ritchie, *The Night Side of London*, London, William Tweedie, 1857, p. 80.
9. *The Era*, 22 May 1859.
10. W.J. MacQueen-Pope, *The Melodies Linger On*, London, W.H. Allen, 1950, pp. 48–9.
11. *The Era*, 14 December 1856.
12. 'Appear fashionable'.
13. Ritchie, *The Night Side of London*, pp. 60–1.
14. In a varied and illustrious career, Sydney Fairbrother (1872–1941) appeared in sketches with Fred Emney.

15. Disher, *The Cowells in America*, p. 192.
16. *Ibid.*, p. 289.
17. *Ibid.*, p. 128.

2. First Generation

1. H.B. Baker, *History of the London Stage*, London, Routledge, 1904, p. 27.
2. The Kathleen Barker Archive at the University of Bristol contains a bibliography of Harry Clifton's work held by the Chappell Archive, South Woodford; the Harvard Collection; the British Music Library; Boston Public Library; parish record references; chronological references (1850–72) to performances from *The Era*, the *Theatrical Journal*, *Freeman's Journal* and other regional journals; and essays on Clifton by Miss Barker herself.
3. *The Era*, 21 July 1872.
4. *The Era*, 5 July 1863.
5. *The Era*, 21 July 1872.
6. *The Era*, 26 June 1870.
7. There were three Princess's Theatres. The first opened in 1828, the second in 1869 and the third in 1880. This last theatre was demolished in 1931 and a Woolworth's store built on its site. (Big stores liked taking over theatres. Access at the back for moving in scenery was often ideal for accepting merchandise.) The offices above the store, which have access from Eastcastle Street, are called Princess House.
8. The Vauxhall Gardens in Lambeth, the most famous of all of London's pleasure gardens, occupied 12 acres just off Kennington Lane. Known first as the New Spring Garden in Vauxhall, they opened in about 1660, although Jonathan Tyers is regarded as the Vauxhall's true founder. He greatly altered and improved the gardens and reopened them in 1732. From 1842, there were galas, masquerades and a great

variety of entertainments, but the gardens were now in decline. When an application was made for the renewal of the licence in 1853, there were many complaints about the nuisance caused by *bals masqués*, which lasted from 11 p.m. until 5 a.m. or 6 a.m. The Vauxhall closed in 1859 and builders soon went to work covering the site with streets full of small houses. Tyers Street is practically the Gardens' only surviving reminder.

9. Balaclava, a town near Sebastopol in the Ukraine, was the scene of a battle in the Crimean War on 25 October 1854. It included the Charge of the Light Brigade, in which British cavalry attacked Russian artillery.

10. The Battle of Inkerman, in which the Russians were pushed back by the British, came ten days after the Battle of Balaclava.

11. *The Era*, 28 July 1872.

3. Pioneers

1. *The Era*, 3 February 1861.

2. *The Era*, 18 September 1864.

3. Mr E. left a few clues about his identity: that he was working at Thornton's in Leeds when Mafeking was relieved (18 May 1900) and that he retired in 1916 after a career of thirty-five years. It was his disclosure that he wrote a song with G.W. Hunter called 'Hezekiah Brown' (1892) that unmasked him as John S. Evalo, who had once been one-half of a double act with Griff (Henry Haddon Griffiths), the clown: Evalo and Rossi, the Clown and the Turk. Mr E. was a mine of quirky information: that Wigan, for instance, once had a music hall without a dressing-room and that the Alhambra, Bootle, was owned by a man known locally as the One-Eyed Bishop. Evalo died in 1932.

4. *The Performer*, 17 December 1930.

5. *The Entr'acte*, 5 January 1889.

6. Archibald Haddon, *The Story of Music Hall*, London, Fleetway, 1930, p. 36.

7. *The Entr'acte*, 5 January 1889.

8. In 1866, Orton, a butcher from New South Wales, came to England, claiming to be Sir Roger Tichborne, an heir to large estates. See Chapter 4 n. 10.

9. *The Figaro*, 6 June 1874.

10. *Pall Mall Gazette*, 16 June 1886.

11. *The Era*, 23 September 1893.

12. The word 'jingo' was first used in the seventeenth century as a piece of magicians' jargon: 'hey presto' or 'hey jingo'. Its music-hall meaning was derived from an article entitled 'Jingoes in the Park' written by the secularist, George Holyoake, in the *Daily News*. It referred to a Sunday afternoon rally in Hyde Park in support of Gladstone's policy on the so-called Eastern question. In *Sixty Years of an Agitator's Life* (1892), Holyoake wrote: 'I had certainly intended to mark by a convenient name a new species of patriot who . . . had begun to infest public meetings . . . Their characteristic was a war-urging pretentiousness which discredited the silent, resolute self-defensiveness of the British people . . . The Jingoes are mainly the habitués of the turf, the tap-room and the low music halls, whose inspiration is beer, whose politics are swagger and whose policy is an insult to foreign nations' (pp. 217–18).

13. *Pall Mall Gazette*, 16 June 1886.

14. There is an excellent web site devoted to Arthur Lloyd: www.arthurlloyd.co.uk.

15. *The Era*, 24 March 1894.

16. *The Entr'acte*, 5 August 1893.

17. *The Entr'acte*, 27 September 1884.

4. Troika

1. T.S. Eliot, *Collected Essays*, London, Faber, 1932, p. 405.

2. Gyles Brandreth, *The Funniest Man on Earth*, London, Hamish Hamilton, 1977, p. 46.

3. Sam Lane, who travelled from Devon to London to seek his fortune, opened this famous East End theatre in 1841. As well as employing a repertory company, he kept a team of dramatists, who ensured a constant flow of new plays. In 1858, Lane built a new theatre with a stage almost the size of that at Drury Lane. There was seating for 3,200 people and, with standing room, the new theatre could hold as many as 4,790. When Sam died in 1871, his widow, Sara, who had been an actress at the Brit, assumed control. She was so successful that, on her death in 1899, she left a fortune of £126,000. The Britannia became a cinema in 1923 and was destroyed by enemy action in 1940.

4. *Leicester Examiner*, 1906.

5. H.C. Newton, *Cues and Curtain Calls*, London, John Lane, 1927, p. 54.
6. Brandreth, *The Funniest Man on Earth*, p. 64.
7. *Ibid.*, p. 65.
8. Seymour Hicks, *Me and My Missus*, London, Cassell, 1939, p. 185.
9. *Saturday Review*, 5 November 1904.
10. Roger Charles Doughty Tichborne (1829–54) set sail from Rio de Janeiro to New York on board a British-registered cargo vessel, which foundered four days later. An inquest concluded that there were no survivors. However, Roger's mother, Lady Tichborne, refused to believe he had died and, as part of her search for him, placed advertisements in several Australian newspapers. Orton (aka Thomas Castro) (1834–98), then bankrupt in Wagga Wagga, New South Wales, managed to convince Lady Tichborne that, in spite of much evidence to the contrary, he was her son. In 1866, he travelled to London, where Lady Tichborne granted him an allowance of £1,000 a year. On her death in 1868, the payments abruptly ended. Other members of the Tichborne family had never believed Orton's claim and, after carrying out their own researches, there began what was to become one of the longest trials in British history (188 days), at the end of which Orton was sentenced to fourteen years' imprisonment. On his release in 1884, he appeared on the halls as the Tichborne Claimant. He also ran a cigar shop near Collins' music hall. Little Tich's use of part of the Tichborne name introduced a new word into the English language: 'tichy' or 'titchy', meaning 'very small'.
11. The estate of Jeremiah Rosher at Gravesend in Kent was turned into one of the most popular Victorian pleasure gardens and flourished from 1830, when it was a place of elegance, until 1936, when it had become a rundown funfair.
12. The word was acceptable then.
13. *The Era*, 29 November 1884.
14. Before Isadora Duncan, Loie Fuller was the best known of modern American dancers. After her Serpentine Dance, she introduced a Ballet of Light, featuring seven girls in flimsy costumes. She was, briefly, a barefoot dancer. She died in 1928.
15. www.bigginhill.co.uk/littletich.htm.
16. J.B. Priestley, *Particular Pleasures*, New York, Stein and Day, 1973, pp. 189–90.

5. Dens of Antiquity

1. Guy Thorne, *The Great Acceptance*, London, Hodder & Stoughton, 1913, p. 111.
2. Frederick Charrington, *The Battle of the Music Halls*, London, Dyer Brothers, 1885, p. 7.
3. W.J. MacQueen-Pope, *Carriages at Eleven*, London, Hutchinson, 1947, p. 213.
4. *Radio Times*, 10 October 1930.
5. L.O. Chant, *Why We Attacked the Empire*, London, Marshall & Son, 1895.
6. Winston Churchill, *My Early Life*, London, Macmillan, 1930, p. 66.
7. Harry Greenwall, *The Strange Life of Willy Clarkson*, London, Long, 1936, p. 271.
8. *The Times*, 4 October 1898.
9. *Pall Mall Gazette*, 10 July 1885.
10. 'Impressions of the Theatre XXII; (45) My First Music-Hall: The Pavilion', *Review of Reviews* (September 1906).
11. As I write, Eamon tops the British charts with 'Fuck It (I Don't Want you Back)'.
12. *The Era*, 28 January 1872.
13. *The Figaro*, 6 June 1874.
14. *The Referee*, 29 January 1882.
15. *The Era*, 5 November 1924.
16. H.C. Newton, *Idols of the Halls*, London, Heath Cranton, 1928, p. 93.
17. *Sunday Times*, 16 November 1924.
18. *The Entr'acte*, 18 May 1889.
19. R. Poole, *Popular Leisure and the Music Hall in 19th Century Bolton*, Lancaster, Centre for North-West Regional Studies, University of Lancaster, 1982, p. 56.
20. Minutes of Evidence Taken before the Select Committee on Public Houses etc., 24 June 1853
21. *Revelations of Life in Nottingham* by Asmodeus (1860), quoted by Richard Iliffe and Wilfred Baguley in *Victorian Nottingham*, vol. 12, Nottingham Historical Film Unit, 1974, p. 8.
22. *The Era*, 18 November 1877.
23. F.G. Bettany, *Stewart Headlam: A Biography*, London, John Murray, 1926, p. 58.
24. *The Era*, 29 October 1913.
25. Wieland had been married previously. His first wife, Elizabeth, died in Lambeth, south London, on 15 November 1890, aged 44. They had two children, Clara, who made a career in variety and vaudeville and who married William Henry Perrette Thring (professionally known as

William Perrette) in Marylebone, London, 8 February 1899, and Lizzie, born 4 May 1887. Wieland jealously guarded Zaeo's identity. In a court case in 1892, he refused to disclose her real name.

26. *Daily Graphic*, 13 February 1892.
27. *Daily Telegraph*, 7 October 1878.
28. *The Era*, 18 January 1880.
29. *The Vigilante*, 16 April 1918.

6. *Our Foes in the North*

1. *North British Daily Mail*, 25 February 1875.
2. *North British Daily Mail*, 2 March 1875.
3. *Ibid.*
4. *Glasgow Evening Star*, 2 March 1875.
5. *Sunday Times*, 4 May 1924.
6. George Foster, *The Spice of Life*, London, Hurst & Brackett, 1939, p. 109.
7. *Sunday Times*, 14 February 1926.
8. W.H. Boardman, *Vaudeville Days*, London, Jarrolds, 1935, p. 279.
9. Gordon Irving, *Great Scot*, London, Leslie Frewin, 1968, p. 76.

7. *Empire Building*

1. Arthur Roberts, *Fifty Years of Spoof*, London, Bodley Head, 1927, p. 21.
2. Lady de Frece, *Recollections of Vesta Tilley*, London, Hutchinson, 1934, p. 29.
3. J.B. Booth, *The Old Music Hall*, London, Thornton Butterworth, 1932, pp. 78–9.
4. *The Performer*, 2 May 1912.

8. *Matchless Matcham*

1. Edwin C. Sachs and Ernest A.E. Woodrow, *Modern Opera Houses and Theatres*, London, B.T. Batsford, 1896.
2. *Sunday Times*, 1 February 2004.
3. William Lusby's first venture was the conversion of a property opposite the Vine House in the Mile End Road into a place of entertainment. It was not successful. He lost all his money, sailed to Australia and, with money he made there, returned to Britain ready to undertake a second venture, a hall called the Sugar Loaf at the back of the Pavilion Theatre, Mile End. He bought the Eagle with the money he made when he sold it. He retired in 1878, although, ten years later, he bought the Foresters, altered and improved it and, in 1893, reopened it. William Lusby died at Ilford, Greater London, on 14 October 1907.
4. The Palace's salaries book between 1911 and 1924, which is held by the British Music Hall Society, shows what the following artistes were paid each week: David Devant and Co. £300; Chung Ling Soo £225; Vesta Tilley £225; Little Tich £225; G.H. Elliott £200; George Formby £200; Gertie Gitana £200; Clarice Mayne and That £200; Arthur Prince £200; Albert Chevalier £180; Marie Lloyd £150; Harry Tate £125; Hetty King £100; R.G. Knowles £90; Nellie Wallace £80; Harry Weldon £47 10s (£47.50).
5. John Gielgud, *An Actor and His Time*, London, Sidgwick & Jackson, 1978, pp. 64–6.

9. *Mixing with Toffs*

1. *All the Year Round*, 13 May 1865.
2. *The Era*, 22 October 1904.
3. Tom Thumb, named after the ploughman's son knighted by King Arthur, was in real life Charles Sherwood Stratton. Having exhibited him in every major city and town in America, Barnum brought him to London in 1844. Barnum wanted Queen Victoria to see him before he went on public show, but the royal family were in mourning for Prince Albert's father. In time, the Queen met Tom Thumb on three occasions, giving Barnum the publicity he wanted. 'Not to have seen General Tom Thumb', he noted, 'was . . . decidedly unfashionable.'
4. *The Performer*, 12 November 1930.
5. Jolly John Nash, *The Merriest Man Alive*, London, General Publishing, 1891
6. Hicks, *Me and My Missus*, p. 183.
7. *The Era*, 22 June 1912.
8. Albert Chevalier, *Albert Chevalier, a Record by Himself*, London, John MacQueen, 1895, p. 152.
9. Stuart Dodgson Collingwood, *The Life and Letters of Lewis Carroll*, London, T. Fisher Unwin, 1898, p. 316.
10. Yvette Guilbert, *The Song of My Life*, London, Harrap, 1929, p. 198.
11. *Saturday Review*, 23 June 1906.
12. *The Performer*, 16 January 1941.
13. *The Era*, 22 June 1912.
14. Unpublished memoirs of Don Ross, privately held.
15. *Western Daily Press*, 2 July 1912.

16. Dolly Harmer, whose real name was Sarah Elizabeth Scott, died in Hampstead, north-west London, on 15 March 1956 aged 89.
17. *Sounds Familiar*, BBC Radio Four, 22 June 1970.
18. Wee Georgie Wood, *I Had to be 'Wee'*, London, Hutchinson, 1947, p. 81.
19. Wee Georgie Wood, *Royalty, Religion and Rats!*, Burnley, Central Printing Co., n.d., p. 243.
20. Daniel Farson, *Marie Lloyd and Music Hall*, London, Tom Stacey, 1972, p. 144.
21. *Ibid.*, p. 146.
22. Booth, *London Town*, pp. 107–8.

10. Across the Pond

1. *The Performer*, 7 April 1938.
2. *The Era*, 12 October 1889.
3. Peggy emigrated to Australia. Charles Cochran, writing in *Showman Looks On* (1945), recalled chatting to the chauffeur of a hired car as they drove through St James's Park in London: '"You said some nice things about my grandmother in your last book." "Who was your grandmother?" I asked. "Jenny Hill" was the reply. "Then you are related to Peggy Pryde, her daughter, who was also a very clever comedienne," I continued. He told me that Peggy Pryde was his mother and that she was then well over 80 [*sic*] and living in Australia, where she had become very popular and had settled.'
4. *The Era*, 4 July 1896.
5. Grace Horsley Darling (1815–42) and her father, William, the keeper of the Longstone lighthouse on Brownsman Island off the coast of Northumberland, rescued nine survivors of the shipwrecked SS *Forfarshire* en route from Hull to Dundee in 1838. She died of tuberculosis.
6. 'The Romantic Life Story of Marie Lloyd' by Alice Lloyd, *Lloyd's Sunday News*, 15 October 1922.
7. *The Entr'acte*, 21 April 1888.
8. Richard Anthony Baker, *Marie Lloyd, Queen of the Music Halls*, London, Robert Hale, 1990.
9. *The Era*, 5 September 1908.

12. More London Halls . . .

1. Charles Blondin, born Jean François Gravelet in France in 1824, made several crossings by tightrope of the Niagara Falls in 1859, once shackled by the ankles, once on stilts and once carrying his somewhat larger manager on his back. After several appearances at the Crystal Palace, during which he pushed a lion in a wheelbarrow across a rope and even carried his 5-year-old daughter on his shoulders, he settled at Ealing in west London and died there in 1897.
2. John Wilton died in London on 25 August 1881 at the age of 60.
3. *The Era*, 16 February 1862.

13. . . . And Others across Britain

1. F.V. St Clair, writing in *The Performer*, 29 August 1912 .
2. *The Performer*, 30 November 1922.

14. Wizard of Oz

1. *The Performer*, 1 October 1930.
2. Frank Van Straten, *Tivoli*, Melbourne, Lothian, 2003, p. 7.
3. *The Performer*, 21 July 1938.
4. *The Performer*, 25 April 1940.
5. C.W. Murphy writing in *Strand Magazine* in January 1911.
6. A.E. Wilson, *The Lyceum*, London, Dennia Yates, 1952, p. 184.
7. *Sydney Morning Herald*, May 1910.
8. Dainty Doris came from a show business family. Both her parents were music-hall entertainers. As a solo act, she first appeared on stage at the age of 4; when she was 12, she was known as Little Doris; but changed her name to Dainty Doris shortly afterwards. The highlight of her career was playing Cinderella at the Lyceum. After marrying Albert Whelan, she accompanied him on a trip to America. She retired from the stage in 1929.
9. *The Performer*, 7 April 1938.
10. Farson, *Marie Lloyd and Music Hall*, p. 133.

15. Behind the Laughter

1. *The Era*, 26 August 1866.
2. The Cremorne Gardens, 12 acres to the west of Battersea Bridge between King's Road and the river, opened in 1831. Later, they comprised a circus, theatres and side shows. After protests by the Chelsea vestry, they closed in 1877.
3. Sir William Walton appropriated the melody of 'I do like to be beside the seaside' for the Tango-

Pasodoble in his entertainment, *Façade*, which
was given its first public performance at the
Aeolian Hall, London, in June 1923.

4. Clarkson Rose, *Beside the Seaside*, London,
   Museum Press, p. 49.

5. *The Era*, 23 January 1918.

6. George Bryan Brummell set the style of male
   fashion for the first fifteen years of the
   nineteenth century. He eventually fled to France
   to avoid his creditors and died a pauper in a
   French lunatic asylum.

7. Harry Daley, *This Small Cloud*, London,
   Weidenfeld & Nicolson, 1986, p. 98.

8. *The Encore*, 8 January 1925.

9. Harry Randall, *Harry Randall, Old Time
   Comedian*, London, Samson, Low, Marston,
   1930, p. 199.

10. William C. Carter, *Marcel Proust: A Life*,
    London, Yale University Press, 2000, p. 386.

16. Sung Heroes

1. Herman Finck, *My Melodious Memories*, London,
   Hutchinson, 1937, p. 42.

2. Charles Coborn, *The Man who Broke the Bank*,
   London, Hutchinson, 1928, p. 203.

3. H. Montgomery Hyde (ed.), *Trials of Oscar
   Wilde*, London, William Hodge, 1948, p. 148.

4. *The Era*, 2 March 1889.

5. *The Era*, 9 March 1889.

6. *Encore*, 10 May 1895.

7. *The Era*, 9 October 1901.

8. *The Era*, 5 October 1922.

9. *The Era*, 12 October 1922.

10. *Ibid*.

11. *The Era*, 28 October 1893.

12. *The Entr'acte*, 13 January 1906.

13. *The Era*, 25 January 1923.

14. *The Era*, 10 March 1894.

15. George Robey, *Looking Back on Life*, London,
    Constable, 1933, p. 27.

16. De Frece, *Recollections of Vesta Tilley*, p. 129.

17. *The Era*, 10 February 1894.

18. Some of Tabrar's family were also on the halls:
    his sister, Lizzie, married another songwriter,
    Gus Levaine. They appeared as Laughing
    Levaine and Lizzie Tabra (*sic*), Vocal, Saltatorial,
    Farcical, Comical, Instrumental, Musical
    Monstrosities. The Only Lady Jester and
    Musical Grotesque in the Profession. Tabrar's
    brother, Tom, was also an entertainer, as were
    three of Joe's children: Lily, who married the

radio entertainer, Syd Walker; Joe Lord; and, the
most famous of all, Fred Earle, a tall, thin,
quiet-spoken man, who became popular at the
Oxford and other leading halls, singing songs he
had written himself, chiefly 'Seaweed' (1905).

19. Coborn, *The Man who Broke the Bank*, p. 120.

20. *Titbits*, 29 August 1931.

21. *Titbits*, 5 September 1931.

22. *The Era*, 10 February 1894.

23. *The Era*, 29 March 1916.

24. *The Era*, 10 February 1894.

17. . . . And More

1. *Daily Chronicle*, 1 November 1900.

2. *The Era*, 10 November 1900.

3. *The Era*, 1 October 1910.

4. *The Era*, 13 December 1916.

5. *The Times*, 29 July 1938.

18. Here's to the Ladies who Were . . .

1. *The Era*, 1 April 1914.

2. *The Idler*, March 1892.

3. *Daily Telegraph*, 26 September 1896.

4. *Ibid*.

5. *The Era*, 22 July 1893.

6. *Amusing Journal*, 13 January 1894.

7. Early in his career, the comedian Ted Ray
   recalled being summoned to see Barclay at his
   mansion in Brixton: 'The room in which visitors
   awaited his summons was, in fact, a huge
   drawing-room, filled with heavy furniture and
   adorned by handsome silver candelabra . . . I
   had been there biting my finger nails . . . when
   suddenly a door opened. In came a little man,
   five foot nothing high. He was wearing a cloth
   cap and a cigarette was dangling from his
   mouth. I was in for another shock – for this was
   the great George Barclay himself. I was to learn
   that indoors and out he affected his check cap.
   The cigarette was always in his mouth – and it
   was invariably a Woodbine' (Ted Ray, *Raising the
   Laughs*, London, Werner Laurie, 1952,
   pp. 73–4).

8. *Call Boy*, Spring 1982.

9. *Top of the Bill*, BBC Radio Two, 27 January
   1980.

10. *The Era*, 1 October 1924.

11. Ada Reeve, *Take it for a Fact*, London,
    Heinemann, 1954, p. 47.

12. *News of the World*, 22 January 1911.

13. Alec Guinness, *Blessings in Disguise*, London, Hamish Hamilton, 1985, pp. 9–10.
14. Betty Driver with Daran Little, *Betty, the Autobiography*, London, Granada Media, 2000, p. 67.

19. Here's to the Ladies who Weren't . . . and the Men who Were

1. Hetty King in an interview in *Call Boy* (June 1968).
2. *Variety*, 26 October 1907.
3. *Nottingham Football News*, 23 March 1907.
4. Don Ross, speaking on *Top of the Bill* on BBC Radio Two, 2 March 1980.
5. *The Era*, 4 July 1923.
6. Hargreaves's father, John, ran the Roscommon music hall in Liverpool. His mother was a serio-comic, Rosie Girton. His three brothers worked in music hall too: Robert, who wrote songs for Gracie Fields, George Formby, Hetty King and Albert Whelan (d. 1934); Tony, who partnered Dorothy Dodd in an act known as Hargreaves and Dodd (d. 1969); and Jimmy, also known as Magini, the tramp violinist.
7. *New York Dramatic Mirror*, 15 January 1920.
8. *The Entr'acte*, 30 March 1878.
9. *The Era*, 31 March 1878.
10. *The Era*, 9 June 1920.
11. *The Era*, 10 October 1908.
12. *The Era*, 19 May 1906.
13. *Variety*, 21 September 1907.
14. Wood, *Royalty, Religion and Rats!*, p. 83.
15. *The Performer*, Christmas edition 1940.
16. *Thomson's Weekly News*, 27 February 1932.

20. Wal the Ripper?

1. Osbert Sitwell, *A Free House*, London, Macmillan, 1947, p. xxx.
2. *The Times*, 1 February 1927.
3. *The Last Secret of Dr Crippen*, Channel Four, 17 July 2004.

21. The Quickness of the Hand

1. Boardman, *Vaudeville Days*, p. 160.
2. John Fisher, *Paul Daniels and the History of Magic*, London, Jonathan Cape, 1987, pp. 123–4.
3. W. Buchanan-Taylor, *Shake the Bottle*, London, Heath Cranton, 1942, p. 130.

22. I Can See your Lips Move

1. *The Performer*, 22 April 1948.

23. Burnt Cork

1. *The Times*, 13 September 1836.
2. *The Era*, 25 June 1843.
3. *The Entr'acte*, 3 October 1891.
4. British Library, Documents Room, item 53639D.
5. *The Era*, 5 May 1920.
6. G.H. and June Elliott, *Chocolate and Cream and Sawdust to Stardust*, privately published, n.d.
7. *The Era*, 28 September 1912.
8. Harry Secombe, *Strawberries and Cheam*, London, Robson Books, 1996, pp. 37–8.
9. 'My Bohemian Life-Story' by Leslie Stuart (1927), published in fourteen instalments by *Empire News* (Manchester).
10. 'I had sung this some years before at Daly's and had acquired the rights. However, George Edwardes did not consider it suited musical comedy, but, as there was great life in the song, I gave the rights back to Stuart (the gift much appreciated) and Albert Christian sang it on the halls for the first time. It had a great vogue, proving that it was more suitable in variety than in musical comedy. It is now, of course, *Soldiers of the King*' (Hayden Coffin, *Hayden Coffin's Book*, London, Alston Rivers, 1930, p. 207).
11. *The Era*, 13 January 1906.
12. An octoroon was someone who had one-eighth black blood.
13. *Sunday Times*, 15 July 1923.

24. Your Own, your Very Own . . .

1. Booth, *London Town*, p. 96.
2. *The Era*, 2 November 1901.
3. Foster, *The Spice of Life*, p. 35.
4. *The Era*, 4 August 1906.

25. Agents: Bullies and Despots

1. *The Entr'acte*, 7 September 1872.
2. Coborn, *The Man who Broke the Bank*, pp. 227–8.
3. Bullough married secondly Elsie Cotton (1886–1962) (professionally known as Lily Elsie, the musical comedy actress) at Knightsbridge, London, 7 November 1911 (divorced 1930) and thirdly, in 1930, Irene Gertrude Salter.

4. Mozart, *Limelight*, London, Hurst and Blackett, 1938, pp. 81–2.

26. *Midnight – and Still no Dick*

1. George Bernard Shaw, *Our Theatres in the Nineties*, vol. III, London, Constable, 1932, pp. 24–5.
2. *Ibid.*, p. 281.

27. *One-Hit Wonders*

1. Lizzie died 12 August 1938, aged 68. For many years, she toured with her husband, Albert Athas, as Athas and Collins. Marie died in 1950, aged 80.
2. Reeve, *Take it for a Fact*, p. 8.
3. Jose Collins, *The Maid of the Mountains: Her Story*, London, Hutchinson, 1932, p. 19.
4. *The Performer*, 30 November 1922.
5. *The Performer*, 27 August 1939.
6. *The Times*, 6 May 1944.
7. *The Era*, 26 February 1881.
8. Coborn, *The Man who Broke the Bank*, p. 176.
9. *Sporting Times*, 24 October 1908.
10. Ray, *Raising the Laughs*, pp. 133–4.

28. *Two's Company*

1. Harry (or, more formally, Henry de Frece) died on 28 January 1931 at the age of 94. Another of his sons was the actor Lauri de Frece (1880–1921), the second husband of the actress Fay Compton.
2. The 7th Earl of Clancarty was succeeded by his half-brother, William Francis Brinsley (1911–95), the founder of the *Flying Saucer Review* and the International Unidentified Object Observer Corps.
3. Seymour Hicks, *Between Ourselves*, London, Cassell, 1930, p. 94.

29. *True Individuals*

1. Ricky Jay, *Learned Pigs and Fireproof Women*, London, Robert Hale, 1986, p. 134.

2. *The Entr'acte*, 26 August 1905.
3. James Bridie, *One Way of Living*, London, Constable, 1939, p. 173.
4. *The Times*, 15 January 1942.
5. *The Playgoer*, October 1901.
6. *Cassell's Magazine*, 47/4, March 1909.
7. MacQueen-Pope, *The Melodies Linger On*, pp. 363–4.
8. James Agate, *Ego 4: Yet More of the Autobiography of James Agate*, London, George G. Harrap, 1942, p. 178.
9. The Department of Drama at Bristol University holds a Harry Tate archive, comprised of a large quantity of printed and handwritten scripts (many with corrections and notes), autographed letters from Harry Tate junior to his wife and others, often discussing the show and business negotiations; some correspondence from other entertainers, including Sir Norman Wisdom; and a number of props from the act.
10. *The Times*, 15 February 1940.
11. Jay, *Learned Pigs and Fireproof Women*, pp. 99–101.
12. *Nottingham Football News*, 27 October 1906.
13. Robey, *Looking Back on Life*, p. 178.

30. *The Death of Music Hall (Nearly)*

1. *Entr'acte*, 14 March 1896.
2. Joe Collins with Judith Simons, *A Touch of Collins*, London, Columbus Books, 1986, p. 51.
3. *Daily Express*, 20 June 1913.
4. *The Performer*, 11 April 1923.
5. The London *Evening News*, May 1923.
6. Asa Briggs, *The Birth of Broadcasting*, vol. I, London, Oxford University Press, 1961, p. 253.
7. *The Performer*, 7 August 1924.
8. *The Era*, 8 February 1923.
9. *The Performer*, 29 April 1931.
10. Don Ross, speaking on *Top of the Bill* on BBC Radio Two, 2 March 1980.
11. *The Stage*, 31 January 1980.
12. *Ibid*.
13. Fred W. Gaisberg, *Music on Record*, London, Robert Hale, 1946, p. 46.

BIBLIOGRAPHY

Abbott, John. *The Story of Francis, Day and Hunter* (London, Francis, Day and Hunter, 1952)

Ackroyd, Harold. *The Liverpool Stage* (Erdington, Amber Valley Print Centre, 1996)

Adland, David. *Brighton's Music Halls* (n.p. Baron Birch, 1994)

Agate, James. *Ego 4: Yet More of the Autobiography of James Agate* (London, George G. Harrap, 1942)

——. *Immoment Toys* (London, Jonathan Cape, 1945)

Alvarez, Francisco. *Juggling – its History and Greatest Performers* (Albuquerque, NM, privately printed, 1984)

Anderson, Terri. *Giving Music its Due* (London, MCPS-PRS Alliance, 2004)

Andrews, Frank, and Bayly, Ernie. *Billy Williams' Records* (Bournemouth, Talking Machine Review, 1982)

Annear, Robyn. *The Man who Lost Himself: the Unbelievable Story of the Tichborne Claimant* (Melbourne, Text Publishing, 2002)

Archer, R.J. *Our Only Arthur* [Roberts] (Amersham, Stocker Hocknell, 1995)

Bailey, Paul. *Three Queer Lives* (London, Hamish Hamilton, 2001)

Baird, George. *Edinburgh Theatres, Cinemas and Circuses 1820–1963* (n.p. privately printed, 1964)

Baker, Henry Barton. *History of the London Stage – Its Famous Players 1576–1903* (London, Routledge, 1904)

Baker, Richard Anthony. *Marie Lloyd, Queen of the Music-Halls* (London, Robert Hale, 1990)

Barker, Felix. *The House that Stoll Built* (London, Frederick Muller, 1957)

Barker, Kathleen. *Early Music Hall in Bristol* (Bristol, Bristol Branch of the Historical Association, 1979)

——. *Bristol's Lost Empires* (Bristol, Bristol Branch of the Historical Association, 1990)

Beerbohm, Max. *Letters to Reggie Turner* (London, Rupert Hart-Davis, 1964)

Begg, Paul, Fido, Martin, and Skinner, Keith. *The Jack the Ripper A–Z* (London, Headline Book Publishing, 1991)

Bentley, Nicolas, Slater, Michael, and Burgis, Nina. *The Dickens Index* (Oxford, Oxford University Press, 1988)

Bergreen, Laurence. *As Thousands Cheer {The Life of Irving Berlin}* (London, Hodder & Stoughton, 1990)

Bettany, Frederick George. *Stewart Headlam: A Biography* (London, John Murray, 1926)

Bevan, Ian. *Top of the Bill: The Story of the London Palladium* (London, Frederick Muller, 1952)

Bird, Peter. *The First Food Empire: A History of J. Lyons and Co.* (Chichester, Phillimore, 2000)

Boardman, W.H. *Vaudeville Days* (London, Jarrolds, 1935)

Booth, J.B. *London Town* (London, T. Werner Laurie, 1929)

——. *The Old Music Hall*, part of *Fifty Years: Memories and Contrasts* (London, Thornton Butterworth, 1932)

Brandreth, Gyles. *The Funniest Man on Earth* (London, Hamish Hamilton, 1977)

Bratton, J.S. *Music Hall: Performance and Style* (Milton Keynes, Open University Press, 1986)

Bret, David. *George Formby: A Troubled Genius* (London, Robson, 1999)

Bridie, James. *One Way of Living* (London, Constable, 1939)

Briggs, Asa. *The Birth of Broadcasting*, vol. I (London, Oxford University Press, 1961)

Buchanan-Taylor, W. *Shake the Bottle* (London, Heath Cranton, 1942)

——. *Shake it Again* (London, Heath Cranton, 1943)

Busby, Roy. *British Music Hall* (London, Paul Elek, 1976)

Carter, William C. *Marcel Proust: A Life* (London, Yale University Press, 2000)

Chant, Laura Ormiston. *Why We Attacked the Empire* (London, Marshall and Son, 1895)

Chapman, David L. *Sandow the Magnificent* (Urbana, Ill., University of Illinois Press, 1994)

Charrington, Frederick. *The Battle of the Music Halls* (London, Dyer Brothers, 1885)

Chester, Charlie. *The Grand Order of Water Rats* (London, W.H. Allen, 1984)

Chevalier, Albert. *Albert Chevalier, a Record by Himself* (London, John MacQueen, 1895)

Churchill, Winston. *My Early Life* (London, MacMillan, 1930)

Coborn, Charles. *The Man who Broke the Bank* (London, Hutchinson, 1928)

Cochran, Charles B. *Showman Looks on* (London, J.M. Dent, 1945)

Coffin, Hayden. *Hayden Coffin's Book* (London, Alston Rivers, 1930)

Collingwood, Stuart Dodgson. *The Life and Letters of Lewis Carroll* (London, T. Fisher Unwin, 1898)

Collins, Joe with Judith Simons. *A Touch of Collins* (London, Columbus Books, 1986)

Collins, Jose. *The Maid of the Mountains: Her Story* (London, Hutchinson, 1932)

Connor, Steven. *Dumbstruck: A Cultural History of Ventriloquism* (Oxford, Oxford University Press, 2000)

Cornwell, Patricia. *Portrait of a Killer* (New York, Putnam, 2002)

Cotes, Peter. *George Robey* (London, Cassell, 1959)

Crisp, Quentin. *The Naked Civil Servant* (London, Jonathan Cape, 1968)

Cullen, Tom. *Crippen, the Mild Murderer* (London, Bodley Head, 1977)

Daley, Harry. *This Small Cloud* (London, Weidenfeld & Nicolson, 1986)

Darewski, Herman. *Musical Memories* (London, Jarrolds, 1937)

De Courville, Albert. *I Tell You* (London, Chapman & Hall, 1928)

De Frece, Lady. *Recollections of Vesta Tilley* (London, Hutchinson, 1934)

Delfont, Lord. *Curtain Up!* (London, Robson, 1989)

Devant, David. *My Magic Life* (London, Hutchinson, 1913)

Dexter, Will. *The Riddle of Chung Ling Soo* (London, Avco, 1955)

Disher, M. Willson. *The Cowells in America* (London, Oxford University Press, 1934)

——. *Winkles and Champagne* (London, B.T. Batsford, 1938)

Driver, Betty with Daran Little. *Betty, the Autobiography* (London, Granada Media, 2000)

Earl, John. *The Music Hall at the Grapes Tavern 1846–1882* (London, Society for Theatre Research, Theatre Notebook, 1999)

—— and Sell, Michael. *Guide to British Theatres 1750–1950* (London, A. & C. Black, 2000)

East, John M. *'Neath the Mask* (London, Allen & Unwin, 1967)

Eliot, T.S. *Collected Essays* (London, Faber, 1932)

Elliott, G.H. *Chocolate and Cream and Sawdust to Stardust* (n.p. privately printed, n.d.)

Farson, Daniel. *Marie Lloyd and Music Hall* (London, Tom Stacey, 1972)

Fawkes, Richard. *Fighting for a Laugh* (London, MacDonald and Jane's, 1978)

Felstead, S. Theodore. *Stars who Made the Halls* (London, T. Werner Laurie, 1946)

Finck, Herman. *My Melodious Memories* (London, Hutchinson, 1937)

Fisher, John. *Funny Way to be a Hero* (London, Frederick Muller, 1973)

——. *Paul Daniels and the History of Magic* (London, Jonathan Cape, 1987)

Fitzsimons, Raymund. *Barnum in London* (London, Geoffrey Bles, 1969)

Flanagan, Bud. *My Crazy Life* (London, Frederick Muller, 1961)

Foster, George. *The Spice of Life* (London, Hurst & Brackett, 1939)

Frame, W.F. *W.F. Frame Tells His Own Story* (n.p.,William Holmes, n.d.)

Frost, Leslie. *Seats in All Parts* (n.p., Magick Enterprises,1986)

Gaisberg, Fred W. *Music on Record* (London, Robert Hale, 1946)

Gallagher, J.P. *Fred Karno, Master of Mirth* (London, Robert Hale, 1971)

Gammond, Peter. *The Oxford Companion to Popular Music* (Oxford, Oxford University Press, 1991)

Ganzl, Kurt. *The British Musical Theatre* (London, MacMillan Press, 1986)

Gielgud, John. *An Actor and His Time* (London, Sidgwick & Jackson, 1979)

Gifford, Denis. *Entertainers in British Films* (Trowbridge, Flicks Books, 1998)

Gillies, Midge. *Marie Lloyd, the One and Only* (London, Gollancz, 1999)

Glindon, Robert. *Diprose's Comic Song Book* (n.p., J. Diprose, 1845)

Glover, Jimmy. *Jimmy Glover His Book* (London, Methuen, 1911)

——. *Jimmy Glover and his Friends* (London, Chatto & Windus, 1913)

——. *Hims Ancient and Modern* (London, Fisher Unwin, 1926)

Golden, Eve, and Kendall, Kim. *The Brief, Madcap Life of Kay Kendall* (Kentucky, University Press of Kentucky, 2002)

Green, Benny (ed.). *The Last Empires* (London, Pavilion Books, 1986)

Greenwall, Harry. *The Strange Life of Willy Clarkson* (London, Long, 1936)

Guilbert, Yvette. *The Song of My Life* (London, Harrap, 1929)

Guinness, Alec. *Blessings in Disguise* (London, Hamish Hamilton, 1985)

Haddon, Archibald. *Green Room Gossip* (London, Stanley Paul, 1922)

——. *The Story of the Music Hall* (London, Fleetway, 1930)

Hallett, Terry. *Bristol's Forgotten Empire* (Westbury, Badger Press, 2000)

Harding, James. *George Robey and the Music-Hall* (London, Hodder & Stoughton, 1990)

Hartman, Ginny. *Celebrating Nellie* (n.p., privately printed, 1992)

Hatch, Anthony B. *Tinder Box: the Iroquois Theater Disaster* (Chicago, Academy, 2003)

Hibbert, H.G. *A Playgoer's Memories* (London, Grant Richards, 1920)

Hicks, Seymour. *Between Ourselves* (London, Cassell, 1930)

——. *Me and My Missus* (London, Cassell, 1939)

Hillerby, Bryen D. *The Lost Theatres of Sheffield* (Barnsley, Wharncliffe Publishing, 1999)

Hoare, Philip. *Wilde's Last Stand* (London, Duckworth, 1997)

Holdsworth, Peter. *Domes of Delight* (Bradford, Bradford Libraries and Information Service, 1989)

Holland, Charlie. *Strange Feats and Clever Turns* (London, Holland & Palmer, 1998)

Holyoake, George. *Sixty Years of an Agitator's Life* (London, T. Fisher Unwin, 1892)

House, Jack. *Music Hall Memories* (Glasgow, Richard Drew Publishing, 1986)

Howard, Diana. *London Theatres and Music-Halls 1850–1950* (London, Library Association, 1970)

Hudd, Roy, and Hindin, Philip. *Roy Hudd's Cavalcade of Variety Acts* (London, Robson, 1997)

Hulton, Edward. *When I Was a Child* (London, Cresset Press, 1952)

Hyde, H. Montgomery (ed.). *Trials of Oscar Wilde* (London, William Hodge, 1948)

Irving, Gordon. *Great Scot* (London, Leslie Frewin, 1968)

Jacob, Naomi. *Our Marie* (London, Hutchinson, 1936)

Jay, Ricky. *Learned Pigs and Fireproof Women* (London, Robert Hale, 1986)

Jewel, Jimmy. *Three Times Lucky* (London, Enigma, 1982)

Joyce, Brian. *Dumb Show and Noise: Theatre, Music Hall and Cinema in the Medway Towns* (Rochester, Pocock Press, 2003)

Kilgarriff, Michael. *Sing Us One of the Old Songs* (Oxford, Oxford University Press, 1998)

——. *Grace, Beauty and Banjos* (London, Oberon Books, 1998)

Lamb, Andrew. *Leslie Stuart, the Man who Composed Florodora* (London, Routledge, 2002)

—— and Myerscough, Julian. *Fragson, the Triumphs and the Tragedy* (Croydon, Fullers Wood Press, 2004)

Lamb, Geoffrey. *Victorian Magic* (London, Routledge & Kegan Paul, 1976)

Lauder, Harry. *Roamin' in the Gloamin'* (London, Hutchinson, 1978)

Littlejohn, J.H. *The Scottish Music Hall 1880–1990* (Wigtown, G.C. Book Publishers, 1990)

MacNeice, Louis. *Collected Poems* (London, Faber and Faber, 1966)

MacQueen-Pope, W.J. *The Melodies Linger On* (London, W.H. Allen, 1950)

——. *Carriages at Eleven* (London, Hutchinson, 1947)

——. *Marie Lloyd: Queen of the Music Halls* (London, Oldbourne, n.d.)

Maloney, Paul. *Scotland and the Music Hall 1850–1914* (Manchester, Manchester University Press, 2003)

Mander, Raymond, and Mitchenson, Joe. *British Music Hall* (London, Gentry Books, 1965)

——. *The Lost Theatres of London* (London, Rupert Hart-Davis, 1968)

——. *Pantomime* (London, Peter Davies, 1973)

——. *The Theatres of London* (London, Rupert Hart-Davis, 1975)

Manley, Bill. *Islington Entertained* (London, Islington Libraries, 1990)

Marshall, Ken. *Middlesbrough's Good Old Days* (Cleveland, C. Book, 1988)

Mellor, G.J. *The Northern Music Hall* (Newcastle, Frank Graham, 1970)

——. *They Made Us Laugh* (Littleborough, George Kelsall, 1982)

Merson, Billy. *Fixing the Stoof Oop* (London, Hutchinson, 1926)

Metcalfe, Cranstoun. *Peeresses of the Stage* (London, Andrew Melrose, 1913)

Moore, Jerrold Northrop. *Sound Revolutions* (London, Sanctuary Publishing, 1999)

Morton, W.H., and Newton, H. Chance. *Sixty Years' Service, Being a Record of the Life of Charles Morton* (London, Gale & Polden, 1905)

Mozart, George. *Limelight* (London, Hurst & Blackett, 1938)

Nash, Jolly John. *The Merriest Man Alive: Stories, Anecdotes, Adventures etc.* (London, General Publishing, 1891)

Newton, H. Chance. *Cues and Curtain Calls* (London, John Lane, 1927)

——. *Idols of the Halls* (London, Heath Cranton, 1928)

Nicholson, Renton. *An Autobiography* (London, Vickers, *c.* 1860)

Oughton, Ann. *Thanks for the Memory* (Bishop Auckland, Pentland Press, 1995)

Owen, Maureen. *The Crazy Gang* (London, Weidenfeld & Nicolson, 1986)

Parsons, Philip (ed.). *Companion to Theatre in Australia* (Sydney, Currency Press, 1995)

Partridge, Eric. *Dictionary of Historical Slang* (London, Penguin Books, 1972)

Pertwee, Bill. *Stars in Battledress* (London, Hodder & Stoughton, 1992)

Pilton, Patrick. *Every Night at the Palladium* (London, Robson Books, 1976)

Poole, Robert. *Popular Leisure and the Music-Hall in 19th Century Bolton* (Lancaster, The Centre for North-West Regional Studies, University of Lancaster, 1982)

Price, David. *Magic: a Pictorial History of Conjurers in the Theater* (New York, Cornwall Books, 1985)

Price, Victor J. *Birmingham Theatres, Concert and Music Halls* (Studley, Brewin Books, 1988)

Priestley, J.B. *Particular Pleasures* (New York, Stein and Day, 1973)

Prince, Arthur. *The Whole Art of Ventriloquism* (London, Will Goldstone, 1921)

Pulling, Christopher. *They Were Singing* (London, George G. Harrap, 1952)

Randall, Harry. *Harry Randall, Old Time Comedian by Himself* (London, Samson, Low, Marston, 1930)

Ray, Ted. *Raising the Laughs* (London, Werner Laurie, 1952)

Read, Jack. *Empires, Hippodromes and Palaces* (London, Alderman Press, 1985)

Reeve, Ada. *Take it for a Fact* (London, Heinemann, 1954)

Reynolds, Harry. *Minstrel Memories* (London, Alston Rivers, 1928)

Ritchie, J. Ewing. *The Night Side of London* (London, William Tweedie, 1857)

Roberts, Arthur. *Fifty Years of Spoof* (London, Bodley Head, 1927)

Robey, Edward. *The Jester and the Court* (London, Kimber, 1976)

Robey, George. *Looking Back on Life* (London, Constable, 1933)

Robinson, David. *Chaplin, His Life and Art* (London, Collins, 1985)

Rogers, Eddie. *Tin Pan Alley* (London, Robert Hale, 1964)

Rose, Clarkson. *With a Twinkle in My Eye* (London, J. and J. Gray, 1951)

——. *Beside the Seaside* (London, Museum Press, 1960)

Rust, Brian. *British Music Hall on Record* (Harrow, Middlesex, General Gramophone Publications, 1979)

Sachs, Edwin O., and Woodrow, Ernest A.E. *Modern Opera Houses and Theatres* (London, B.T. Batsford, 1896)

Sands, Mollie. *Robson of the Olympic* (London, Society for Theatre Research, 1979)

Saxon, A.H. *P.T. Barnum: The Legend and the Man* (New York, Columbia University Press, 1989)

Scott, Harold. *The Early Doors* (London, Nicholson & Watson, 1946)

Scott, Margaret. *Old Days in Bohemian London* (London, Hutchinson, 1918)

Secombe, Harry. *Strawberries and Cheam* (London, Robson Books, 1996)

Seeley, Robert, and Bunnett, Rex. *London Musical Shows on Record 1889–1989* (Harrow, General Gramophone Publications, 1989)

Senelick, Laurence, Cheshire, David F., and Schneider, Ulrich. *British Music-Hall 1840–1923* (Hamden, Conn., Archon Books, 1981)

Setterington, Arthur. *The Life and Times of the Great Lafayette* (n.p., Abraxas Publications, 1991)

Shaw, George Bernard. *Our Theatres in the Nineties*, vol. III (London, Constable, 1932)

Short, Ernest. *Fifty Years of Vaudeville* (London, Eyre & Spottiswoode, 1946)

Silverman, Kenneth. *Houdini!!!* (New York, Harper Collins, 1996)

Sitwell, Osbert. *A Free House* (London, Macmillan, 1947)

Slide, Anthony. *The Encyclopedia of Vaudeville* (Westport, Conn., Greenwood Press, 1994)

Stark, Seymour. *Men in Blackface* (n.p., XLibris Corporation, 2000)

Stuart, Charles Douglas, and Park, A.J. *The Variety Stage* (London, T. Fisher Unwin, 1895)

Sturgis, Matthew. *Walter Sickert: A Life* (London, Harper Collins, 2005)

Swaffer, Hannen. *Hannen Swaffer's Who's Who* (London, Hutchinson, n.d.)

Sweet, Matthew. *Inventing the Victorians* (New York, St Martin's Press, 2001)

Thorne, Guy. *The Great Acceptance* (London, Hodder & Stoughton, 1913)

Tich, Mary, and Findlater, Richard. *Little Tich* (London, Elm Tree Books, 1979)

Van Straten, Frank. *Tivoli* (Melbourne, Lothian, 2003)

Vox, Valentine. *I Can See Your Lips Moving* (Los Angeles, Plato Publishing, 1993)

Walker, Brian (ed.). *Frank Matcham, Theatre Architect* (Belfast, Blackstaff Press, 1980)

Walvin, James. *Victorian Values* (London, Deutsch, 1987)

Watters, Eugene, and Murtagh, Matthew. *Infinite Variety* (Dublin, Gill and MacMillan, 1975)

Wheeler, Terry. *High Street Entertainment Ramsgate* (n.p., privately printed, 2000)

Wilmut, Roger. *Kindly Leave the Stage* (London, Methuen, 1985)

Wilson, A.E. *The Lyceum* (London, Dennis Yates, 1952)

——. *East End Entertainment* (London, Arthur Barker Ltd, 1954)

——. *Prime Minister of Mirth* (London, Oldham, 1959)

——. *Pantomime Pageant* (London, Stanley Paul, n.d.)

Wood, J. Hickory. *Dan Leno* (London, Methuen, 1905)

Wood, Wee Georgie. *I Had To Be 'Wee'* (London, Hutchinson, 1947)

——. *Royalty, Religion and Rats!* (Burnley, Lancashire, Central Printing Co, n.d.)

Wroth, Warwick. *The London Pleasure Gardens of the Eighteenth Century* (London, Macmillan, 1896)

Wyke, Terry, and Rudyard, Nigel. *Manchester Theatres* (Manchester, Bibliography of North-West England, 1994)

Yates, Edmund. *His Recollections and Experiences* (London, Richard Bentley, 1884)

Young, Filson. *Trial of H.H. Crippen* (Edinburgh, William Hodge, 1920)

Zellers, Parker. *Tony Pastor: Dean of the Vaudeville Stage* (Ypsilanti, Michigan, Eastern University Press, 1971)

Ziethen, Karl-Heinz, and Allen, Andrew. *Juggling: The Art and its Artists* (Berlin, 1985)

INDEX